A publication sponsored by
the Society for Industrial and Organizational Psychology, Inc.,
a division of the American Psychological Association

Other Books in This Series

Career Development in Organizations
by Douglas T. Hall and Associates

Productivity
in Organizations

John P. Campbell
Richard J. Campbell
and Associates

Foreword by Raymond A. Katzell

Productivity in Organizations

*New Perspectives
from Industrial
and Organizational Psychology*

 Jossey-Bass Publishers

San Francisco • London • 1988

100917

PRODUCTIVITY IN ORGANIZATIONS
New Perspectives from Industrial and Organizational Psychology
by John P. Campbell, Richard J. Campbell, and Associates

Copyright © 1988 by: Jossey-Bass Inc., Publishers
350 Sansome Street
San Francisco, California 94104

&

Jossey-Bass Limited
28 Banner Street
London EC1Y 8QE

Library of Congress Cataloging-in-Publication Data

Productivity in organizations : new perspectives from industrial and
   organizational psychology/[contributions by] John P. Campbell,
   Richard J. Campbell, and associates; foreword by Raymond A.
   Katzell.—1st ed.

        p.   cm.—(The Jossey-Bass management series) (The Jossey-
Bass social and behavioral science series)
   Includes bibliographies and index.
   ISBN 1-55542-100-8 (alk. paper)
   1. Labor productivity.   2. Psychology, Industrial.
3. Organizational effectiveness.   I. Campbell, John Paul.
II. Campbell, Richard J.   III. Series.   IV. Series: The Jossey-Bass
social and behavioral science series.
HD57.P6987   1988
658.3'14—dc19   88-42780
                                                            CIP

JACKET DESIGN BY WILLI BAUM

FIRST EDITION

Code 8825

A *joint publication in*
The Jossey-Bass Management Series
and
The Jossey-Bass
Social and Behavioral Science Series

Frontiers of Industrial and Organizational Psychology

Contents

Foreword

One of the principal objectives of the Society for Industrial and Organizational Psychology is, according to its bylaws, to "advance the scientific status of the field." In 1982, Richard J. Campbell, then the president of the society, asked me to assume the chair of the Committee on Scientific Affairs, with the express charge of intensifying the society's pursuit of that objective. It was a charge that I, and the rest of the committee, embraced wholeheartedly.

Several new initiatives were undertaken during that year. The one that generated the greatest enthusiasm, not only in the committee but widely in the society, consisted of a plan to publish a series of volumes, each dealing with a single topic considered to be of major contemporary significance in industrial and organizational psychology. Each volume was to present cutting-edge theory, research, and practice in chapters contributed by about ten individuals doing pioneering work on the topic.

The proposal was unanimously adopted by the society's executive committee in 1983, and its implementation was entrusted to an editorial board, which I agreed to chair. It is further testimony to the vitality of the idea that every one of the distinguished and busy psychologists who was asked to join the board accepted the invitation.

Why has that plan been so favorably received? I think mainly because it is seen as filling a significant void in the media through which industrial and organizational psychologists advance their understanding of their field. Such volumes can be less kaleidoscopic than our journals and more focused than review chapters and yearbooks that scan developments in broad sectors of the field. By aiming to identify significant recent developments that may not yet have jelled into articulated patterns, these books can be more current than texts and professional works that seek to present integrated pictures of their subjects. It is that special and important niche among the publications in industrial and organizational psychology that this series is designed to occupy. The success of that endeavor should, it is hoped, facilitate progress in theory and research on the topics presented while also abetting the transition from science to practice.

The editorial board has further specified the plan in the following particulars:

- The subject matter of the volumes is to be aimed at the membership of the society, with the hope and expectation that scholars, professionals, and advanced students in cognate fields will also find it of value.
- Each volume is to be prepared under the editorship of a leading contributor to the topic it covers, who will also prepare integrating commentary, placing the chapters in a broader context.
- The choice of topics and editors will be made by the editorial board, which will also consult with the volume editors in planning each book. The chairman of the editorial board is to serve as series editor and coordinate the relationships and responsibilities of the volume editors, the editorial board, the series publisher, and the executive committee of the society.
- Volumes are to be issued when timely rather than on a fixed schedule, but at a projected rate of approximately one a year.
- The series is to be called *Frontiers of Industrial and Organizational Psychology*.

Among the first decisions that had to be made by the editorial board was the choice of a publisher. After careful consideration of several proposals, Jossey-Bass was chosen on the basis of criteria that included editorial support, production quality, marketing capability, and pricing.

The first volume in the series, Career Development in Organizations, edited by Douglas T. Hall, has amply achieved our objectives, judging by the number of sales, the laudatory book reviews, and the requests for rights for translation into other languages. Demand for that book is still strong, reflecting its cutting-edge emphasis. It is our expectation that, given such careful attention, each of our books will remain up-to-date for years.

As with the first volume, the topic of this book was chosen because of its practical and scientific significance. To edit this important work, we were successful in recruiting a leading expert, John P. Campbell; he in turn was able to line up a distinguished group of chapter contributors. We also were fortunate to enlist

Richard J. Campbell to serve as coeditor during the onerous latter stages of the volume's preparation. We now are pleased to make available to you, the reader, the product of all that talent.

In the near future, you may expect the publication of two more volumes that we have commissioned for the series: one on training and development in organizations, to be edited by Irwin L. Goldstein, and another on organizational climate and culture, to be edited by Benjamin Schneider. Additional works are under consideration for publication down the road.

This entire undertaking has required the cooperation and efforts of many able and dedicated people, most of whom must remain unnamed because of space limitations. I hope they know who they are and that they have our deep thanks. But I cannot refrain from acknowledging my colleagues on the editorial board, whose contributions have amply fulfilled our high expectations. The assistance and cooperation of the staff at Jossey-Bass also require grateful mention.

March 1988   Raymond A. Katzell
                                                 New York University
                                                 Series Editor

Preface

Declining growth in productivity has become an issue of great concern in the United States, and the individual job holder is one of the frequently cited causes of our dwindling competitiveness. Prominent in popular thinking are doubts about individuals' motivation, skills, and performance as compared with times past and workers in other nations. This book examines what industrial and organizational psychology has to say about the contributions of individuals, working alone and in groups, to productivity. It gives particular emphasis to promising future directions for research, theory, and practice that will enhance productivity. Although the focus is on the role of psychological phenomena in the productivity of *organizations,* it is our intent to consider the influence of productivity efforts on individual outcomes as well, since individual and institutional conflict might have important implications for productivity.

This is the second volume in the Frontiers of Industrial and Organizational Psychology series. It is very different from the first volume and from the subsequent volumes that are planned to follow. We should admit at the outset that there was a certain amount of internal debate about whether a volume on productivity should be part of this series. Productivity means different things to different people, and it was not perfectly clear what a volume on productivity would be about. To paraphrase Inspector Clouseau, industrial-organizational psychology could have everything to do with productivity—or it could have nothing to do with productivity. Also, the term has been heavily used in the academic literature, the popular press, corporate board rooms, and the halls of government for many years. So where is the frontier in such a hoary topic?

In spite of the age of this topic and the widespread expressions of the urgent need for improvement, productivity is not clearly understood. The frontier we explore in this volume is the contribution of human resources to productivity, an area generally acknowledged as important but where the causal links are not always clear.

Our goal in this volume is to say what we (industrial and organizational psychology) can about the problems of predicting, explaining, and improving "productivity." What's new? What's old? Where should research go? What products or procedures can human resource management use now? Responding to these questions is difficult because of the many and sometimes poorly articulated meanings of productivity. At some level it might be reasonable to argue that the study of individual behavior has very little to do with productivity. On another, if productivity is simply a word that stands in for any and all measures of individual performance, then everything is relevant and we would simply produce another textbook. We do not want to write another textbook but neither do we wish to stand mute. Our goal is to bring clarity to the concept of productivity, summarize what industrial-organizational psychology has contributed to productivity improvement, and identify the promising frontiers of theory, research, and practice. The unique aspect of this volume is the concentration on psychological variables and the search for the most promising frontiers—a broad area of focus.

Indeed, the entire book has a very broad focus. In one sense, this breadth violates an original tenet of the Frontiers series, which was to look at specific new areas in some detail. However, the editorial board felt that in this instance the departure from the original design was justified. Productivity is too important an issue to pass by. The focus of the volume was narrowed somewhat by concentrating on what seemed to be the most promising, new, or innovative topics and by limiting the discussion of independent variables, or interventions, to those things within the domain of industrial-organizational psychology. Consequently, although things like human factors and individual counseling have important implications for productivity, they are the province of engineering psychology and counseling psychology respectively, and are not included in this particular book.

This volume is intended for teachers, researchers, practitioners, and graduate students in industrial-organizational psychology, organizational behavior, management, industrial relations, and allied disciplines. We hope it will be helpful to those involved in research, innovation, and implementation of productivity enhancement efforts.

Serving as the editors for the volume was an interesting, informative, and rewarding experience. We thank the Society of Industrial and Organizational Psychology for the opportunity. In particular, Raymond A. Katzell, the editor of the Frontiers in

Industrial and Organizational Psychology series, was an excellent adviser, facilitator, and role model. His high level of scholarship was invaluable. In addition, his carrots were timely and his stick was so deftly used no one will ever see the bruises. We would also like to thank Barbara Hamilton, who lives in Minneapolis but prefers to wander the earth in search of local art, for her patience and competence in translating editorial notes into editorial changes. Finally, a very special thank you to all our contributing authors for their grace, good humor, excellent work, and high productivity.

June 1988   John P. Campbell
                                               Minneapolis

                                               Richard J. Campbell
                                               New York City

ΣΣΣΣΣΣΣΣΣΣΣ

The Authors

John P. Campbell is professor of psychology and industrial relations at the University of Minnesota. He received his B.S. (1959) and M.S. (1960) degrees from Iowa State University and his Ph.D. degree (1964) from the University of Minnesota, all in psychology. From 1964 to 1966 he was on the faculty of the Department of Psychology, University of California, Berkeley, and has been at the University of Minnesota from 1967 to the present. In 1971 he authored the first *Annual Review of Psychology* chapter on organizational training and development, and he is the author of *Managerial Behavior, Performance, and Effectiveness* (with M. Dunnette, E. Lawler, and K. Weick, 1970). Other books include *Measurement Theory for the Behavioral Sciences* (with E. Ghiselli and S. Zedeck, 1978) and *What to Study: Generating and Developing Research Questions* (with R. Daft and C. Hulin, 1984). Professor Campbell was elected president of the Division of Industrial and Organizational Psychology of the American Psychological Association in 1978. From 1974 to 1982 he served as associate editor and then editor of the *Journal of Applied Psychology*. He currently serves as the principal scientist for the *Army Selection and Classification Project* (Project A).

Richard J. Campbell is professor of psychology at New York University. He received his B.A. degree (1954) from Temple University in psychology, his M.A. degree (1958) from Ohio State University in psychology, and his Ph.D. degree (1960) in industrial psychology, also from Ohio State University. He worked more than twenty-five years in industry, primarily with the American Telephone and Telegraph Company (AT&T), prior to taking his current academic position. At AT&T he was director of management development, education, and work relationships. Campbell is coauthor of the book *Formative Years in Business* (with D. W. Bray and D. L. Grant, 1974), a member of the editorial board of *Personnel Psychology*, and a former contributing editor to *Professional Psychology*. He is a fellow of the American Psychological Association.

Paul A. Banas is manager of Corporate Employee Development Strategy and Planning at the Ford Motor Company, where he is responsible for expanding human capacities and upgrading business processes through the application of behavioral science knowledge, concepts, and techniques. He received his B.A. degree (1951) from the University of Connecticut in chemistry and his M.A. (1959) and Ph.D. (1964) degrees from the University of Minnesota in psychology and industrial-organizational psychology, respectively. He is well known for his contribution to the development and implementation of the joint UAW-Ford employee involvement process.

Lisa R. Berlinger is a doctoral student and assistant instructor of management at the University of Texas at Austin. She received her A.B. degree (1979) from Georgetown University in political theory. Her publications include a coauthored book chapter in *The Handbook of Career Theory* entitled "Career Improvisation in Self-Designing Organizations." Her research interests are in the areas of work design and organizational design.

Michael J. Burke is assistant professor of management in the Graduate School of Business Administration at New York University. He received his B.A. degree (1977) from the University of Notre Dame, his M.S. degree (1980) from Purdue University at Indianapolis, and his Ph.D. degree (1982) from the Illinois Institute of Technology. His primary research interests are in prediction models, selection and classification, and utility analysis.

Rukmini Devadas is a doctoral student in organizational psychology and theory at the Graduate School of Industrial Administration, Carnegie-Mellon University. She received her B.S. degree (1983) from Ethiraj College, Madras, India, in mathematics; her M.B.A. degree (1985) from the University of Georgia; and her M.S. degree (1987) from Carnegie-Mellon University in organizational psychology and theory. Her research interests include group decision making and group performance.

William H. Glick is associate professor of management at the University of Texas at Austin. He received his A.B. degree (1975) from the University of Michigan in psychology and his Ph.D. degree (1981) from the University of California, Berkeley, in business administration. Glick's main research has been in the areas of job and organizational design and organizational climate. In 1983 he received the Best Paper Award from the Organizational Behavior Division of the Academy of Management for a coauthored paper on common methods variance in job design research.

Paul S. Goodman is professor of industrial administration and psychology in the Graduate School of Industrial Administration at Carnegie-Mellon University, where he is also the director of the Center for the Management of Technology and Information. He received his B.A. degree (1959) from Trinity College in economics, his M.B.A. degree (1961) from Amos Tuck School at Dartmouth College, and his Ph.D. degree (1966) from Cornell University in organizational psychology. His primary interests are in the effects of technology and social systems on organizational structure and effectiveness.

Terri L. Griffith Hughson is a doctoral student in organizational psychology and theory at the Graduate School of Industrial Administration, Carnegie-Mellon University. She received her B.A. degree (1983) from the University of California, Berkeley, in psychology and her M.S. degree (1986) from Carnegie-Mellon University in organizational psychology and theory. Her research interests include the impact of technology on individual workers and small work groups.

Richard A. Guzzo is associate professor of psychology at New York University. He received his B.S. degree (1974) from the Ohio State University in psychology and his M.A. (1976) and Ph.D. (1979) degrees from Yale University in administrative sciences. His professional interests include the application of psychological principles to improve productivity, effective performance by groups at work, and the dynamics of idealist organizations.

Tove Helland Hammer is associate professor of organizational behavior in the New York State School of Industrial and Labor Relations at Cornell University. She received her B.A. degree (1969) from Cornell University in psychology and her M.A. (1972) and Ph.D. (1973) degrees from the University of Maryland in industrial and organizational psychology. Her research concentration is on the evaluation of worker participation programs and forms of employee ownership.

Daniel R. Ilgen is John A. Hannah Professor of Psychology and Management at Michigan State University. He received his B.S. degree (1965) from Iowa State University in psychology and his M.A. (1968) and Ph.D. (1969) degrees from the University of Illinois, Urbana-Champaign, in psychology and industrial and organizational psychology, respectively. He is coauthor of two books, *A Theory of Behavior in Organizations* (with J. C. Naylor and R. D. Pritchard, 1980) and *Industrial and Organizational Psychology* (with E. J. McCormick, 1985) and is also associate editor for *Organizational Behavior and Human Decision Processes.*

Howard J. Klein is assistant professor of management and human resources at the Ohio State University. He received his B.A. degree (1983) from the University of Minnesota in psychology, his M.B.A. degree (1985) from Michigan State University in human resource management, and his Ph.D. degree (1987) from Michigan State University in organizational behavior and human resource management. Klein's main research interests are in motivation and performance and his work has been published in the *Journal of Applied Psychology* and *Industrial Relations.*

Edward E. Lawler III is professor of management and organization in the Graduate School of Business Administration, University of Southern California. In 1979 he founded and became the director of the Center for Effective Organizations at the University of Southern California. He received his B.A. degree (1960) from Brown University and his Ph.D. degree (1964) from the University of California, Berkeley, both in psychology. He was formerly a member of the faculty at Yale University and at the University of Michigan, and he served as program director of the Survey Research Center at the Institute for Social Research. He is the author or coauthor of more than one hundred articles and twelve books. His most recent books include *Organizational Assessment* (1980), *Pay and Organizational Development* (1981), and *Managing Creativity* (1983).

Gerald E. Ledford, Jr., is a research scientist at the Center for Effective Organizations, Graduate School of Business Administration, University of Southern California. He received his B.A. degree (1973) from George Washington University, and his M.A. (1979) and Ph.D. (1984) degrees from the University of Michigan, all in psychology. Ledford has researched a variety of strategies for improving employee well-being and organizational effectiveness, including union-management cooperation, organization redesign, innovative reward systems, employee participation in decision making, and job redesign.

Thomas A. Mahoney is Frances Hampton Currey Professor of Organization Studies in the Owen Graduate School of Management at Vanderbilt University. He received his A.B. degree (1950) from Wabash College and his M.A. (1951) and Ph.D. (1956) degrees from the University of Minnesota, all in economics. Mahoney taught for many years in the Industrial Relations Center at the University of Minnesota. Additionally, he has held visiting appointments at other major universities. From 1981 to 1984 he served as editor of the *Academy of Management Journal*.

Patricia A. McLagan is chief executive of McLagan International, a management consulting firm specializing in human resource strategies and systems. She received her B.A. degree, Phi Beta Kappa, in English from the College of Liberal Arts and her M.A. degree in adult education from the University of Minnesota. She has worked with many major corporations to implement performance, development, staffing, career, and job design practices. She has received the Gordon M. Bliss Memorial Award, the highest recognition for professional contribution offered by the American Society for Training and Development, and is the author of many books and articles, including *Models for Excellence: The Results of ASTD's Training and Development Competency Study* (1983).

Susan M. Mohrman is a senior research scientist at the Center for Effective Organizations, Graduate School of Business Administration, University of Southern California. She received her A.B. degree (1967) from Stanford University in psychology and her Ph.D. degree (1978) from Northwestern University in organizational behavior. Her research has focused on organizational design, innovative organizational systems, and quality-of-worklife projects. She is currently conducting comparative studies of cooperation between labor and management and working closely with several high-technology firms to develop models of sociotechnical design.

Kenneth Pearlman is district manager for selection and testing in the AT&T Corporate Human Resources Department. He received his B.A. degree (1973) from Catholic University of America in psychology and his Ph.D. (1982) degree from George Washington University in industrial and organizational psychology. His main research activities have been in employment test validation, validity generalization, utility analysis, and job analysis/job family development for personnel selection. In 1982, he received the S. Rains Wallace Dissertation Award from the Society for Industrial and Organizational Psychology of the American Psychological Association. He is the editor of *Contemporary Problems in Personnel* (with others, 1983).

Robert C. Rodgers is associate professor of public administration with the James W. Martin School of Public Administration at the University of Kentucky. He received his B.A. degree (1968) from Vanderbilt University in economics, his M.P.A. degree (1974) from Cornell University, and his Ph.D. degree (1981) from Michigan State University in labor relations. He is interested in the identification of administrative policies that enhance organizational and individual productivity. These research interests have recently inspired the development and testing of theories that explain the occurrence of human error in high-risk, high-reliability systems.

Koji Taira is professor of economics in the Department of Economics and the Institute of Labor and Industrial Relations of the University of Illinois at Urbana-Champaign. He received his B.A. degree (1953) from the University of New Mexico, his M.A. degree (1954) from the University of Wisconsin, and his Ph.D. degree (1961) from Stanford University, all in economics. His main research activities have been in economic development, labor markets, industrial relations, and employment policies, and he is the author of *Economic Development and the Labor Market in Japan* (1970) and *An Outline of Japanese Economic History* (with Mikio Sumiya, 1979).

Productivity
in Organizations

1

Introduction:
What Industrial-Organizational
Psychology Has to Say
About Productivity

John P. Campbell
Richard J. Campbell

Productivity is a concept that has captured the imagination and energy of managers and behavioral scientists for decades. It has been the subject of intensive scrutiny by various strains of scholars, managers, workers, unions, and social commentators. In like manner, innovation and experimentation in the pursuit of productivity improvement are time-honored activities and can be found in almost any setting where people are working on products or delivering services. Given this long history and the ubiquitous nature of study and experimentation, can any new frontiers remain? Can they be found? Will psychological phenomena be a key feature of productivity frontiers? Are they worth looking for? We are convinced of the following: that frontiers likely remain, because of the great complexity of the concept; that the enormous practical import of productivity demands and justifies the pursuit of better understanding of the construct; and that the perspective of industrial and organizational psychology should have much to say about productivity enhancement. How much can be said can be better answered at the conclusion of this volume. For now, we use this chapter to state the case for the importance and complexity of the concept and to present the rationale for the content and structure of the book.

In spite of the long history and ambiguity of productivity, discussions concerning it have an increasing sense of urgency about them. This sense of urgency is captured quite well by Kopelman (1986), who summarizes the views of many in arguing that productivity has a direct effect on real income, on competitiveness with foreign competitors, and on ability to finance improvements in the infrastructure, not to mention national defense. Since the end of the Vietnam War, the energy crisis of the 1970s, and the rise of foreign competition, things have not been the same, and the nation seems genuinely worried about its competitive edge. In terms of national income accounting, our rate of economic growth has fallen behind that of several other countries, most notably Japan (Denison, 1984), and the manufacturing sector of the economy continues to decrease in relative magnitude. We are also now the world's largest debtor nation and have had a sizable negative balance of payments for some time. Where will things end? Will foreign investors continue to lend us money for the privilege of having us as their largest market? Can we stabilize our trade balance at a level that maintains our standard of living in the style to which we've become accustomed? Will our pie grow larger or smaller?

Many remedies have been suggested to help meet the problems of foreign competition, the trade imbalance, and other facets of the economy. Among them are assertions that the U.S. economy must become more efficient and more productive and raise the quality of its goods and services. However, this is not a book about product research and development, product engineering, production management, finance, marketing, or public policy, even though all of these have an effect on the quantity and quality of goods and services and the proficiency with which they are produced. But a finger also points at human resource utilization as a factor that influences efficiency, productivity, and quality, and industrial-organizational psychology is concerned with problems and issues affecting the optimal use of human resources.

We are left with the following situation. As a dependent variable of great interest, productivity is a frequently used concept and is seen as an important factor in a number of national economic problems. However, productivity has been given a variety of meanings, either by intent or by default. It has been used in the context of individual behavior, group achievement, the output of the firm, and the performance of the economy as a whole. Human resources are seen as an important contributor to productivity, although the causal links are not always clear. Because industrial and organizational psychology sees itself as a domain of research and practice that deals with virtually any issue pertaining to the behavior of individuals at work, it should have something to contribute to the understanding and improvement of productivity. It was such a line of reasoning that led to the decision to undertake this volume. Maybe productivity enhancement is a frontier after all, if only because interest in it has become so intense at the same time that productivity is not very clearly understood. What is it that industrial-organizational psychology has to contribute?

The many, and frequently ambiguous, meanings ascribed to productivity complicate the response. Some might reason that productivity is just a descriptive label for all manner of individual performance measures; whereas others might argue that the study of individual behavior is a rather minor, perhaps trivial, factor in the multifaceted productivity concept. Another complication is that industrial-organizational psychology itself operates at several different levels. Part of the field is concerned with quite basic research in motivation, leadership, ability assessment, and so on. Another part is concerned with a variety of applied research issues, such as training evaluation, reducing the error in performance assessment, and the validation of selection procedures. Yet another part is hell-bent to practice, practice, practice, as in doing management development, doing survey-feedback, and doing behavior modification. Are there contributions to productivity to be found at all these levels? Of course, but how should they be characterized and where is the leading edge?

Objectives for This Volume

Given the above account of how we got into this and the complications that immediately arise, the objectives of this volume in the series are the following:

1. The contributors attempt to bring some definitional clarity to the concept of productivity as it pertains to the work of industrial and organizational psychology. What are the major meanings of productivity as a variable? Where do the dependent variables, or criterion measures, addressed by industrial-organizational psychology fit into the definitional framework? Where is our leverage, if any?
2. Given the dependent variables of particular relevance for productivity, this volume attempts to summarize what the field has already contributed to productivity improvement. Useful contributions take the form of theory that can guide future action, research findings that support the use of particular actions, and the development of methods and techniques that are in fact used in practice.
3. In some measure, the contributors also try to identify the leading edge of theory, research, and practice as they pertain to produc-

tivity improvement. Where should our future investments be made?

The above objectives clearly imply an institutional rather than an individual point of view for this particular volume in the Frontiers series. That is, we are not concerned with the value placed by the individual on the dependent variables discussed in the following chapters. For example, a particular training program may be of great value to an individual because she really wants to "know electronics." However, if the particular brand of electronics being taught has no relevance for the goals of the organization, its institutional value will be minimal. The basic problem addressed in this volume is how to enhance the productivity of organizations. For the time being, we are going to act as servants of our national employment system relative to its contributions to national economic well-being.

Before the reader draws the wrong conclusions, be advised that theory, research, and practice in industrial-organizational psychology also serve the individual. The first volume in this series, *Career Development in Organizations* (Hall and Associates, 1986), was generated very much for the individual point of view. Others will be also. Furthermore, it should be clear that individuals have a stake in productivity. It can be a path not only to financial gain and extrinsic rewards but also to feelings of accomplishment, satisfaction, and self-esteem.

In the best of all possible worlds, the goals of the individual and the goals of the employment system are the same. What serves one serves the other. Obviously, this is not always the case, and the resulting conflict must be addressed. Several chapters in the volume try to do that.

It is also apparent from the above objectives that this volume is more of a "survey" than the first volume, or the other volumes that have been proposed. We make only a small apology for that. The format was dictated by the decision to consider the productivity issue. However, we tried not to make these chapters just surveys of the literature. Certainly, a lot of literature is covered, but the intent is to use that literature to highlight the critical issues, the most promising research themes, and the most valuable methods.

This book can be contrasted with two other recent volumes that have related titles and some degree of overlap. One is a volume of individual contributions edited by Arthur Brief (1984), entitled *Productivity Research in the Behavioral and Social Sciences*. The other is *Managing Productivity in Organizations: A Practical, People-Oriented Perspective,* by Richard Kopelman (1986). The nature of these two books differs from ours. The volume edited by Brief is designed to be broadly multidisciplinary, and only one chapter (by Benjamin Schneider) is devoted entirely to industrial-organizational psychology topics. It should be read to get a view of how people in sociology, management science, political science, and related fields think about productivity issues. Kopelman, on the other hand, focuses quite intensely on what we can say to management, and would-be managers, about how the products of human resource research and development can directly and operationally affect productivity. Consequently, it is meant to be a nuts-and-bolts rendition of what we can now do and a strong argument for why that has value.

Both of these books are very valuable sources. We accept the basic premises of each: that research on productivity can benefit from multiple views, and that we already know a lot about how to better manage human resources to enhance organizational productivity. Kopelman in particular makes a strong case for the urgency of addressing productivity problems and for the ability of human resource management to influence them.

The current volume is not meant to mimic either of the other two. It focuses on a particular discipline, one that is concerned with psychological phenomena. It looks at the individual person, as well as the person behaving in groups, and this is its unique niche in the study of productivity. This book differs also in that it goes beyond application and strives to root individual contributions to productivity in firm theory and research. Finally, it attempts to highlight new approaches and emphases that might benefit research on productivity issues and enhance professional practice. It is not intended to be a codification of what we already know, which is considerable. If the volume adds some clarity to the issues of how the research and development work of psychologists can affect productivity and identifies some promising directions for research or practice, then it will be a success.

Plan of the Book

The contents of this book are organized into four major sections, which are flanked by this introductory chapter and the editors' concluding chapter. The major content areas move progressively from definitional issues (Part One), to critical knowledge gained from three key areas of research (Part Two), to important findings yielded by a variety of change strategies and techniques (Part Three), to a sampling of important implementation issues illustrated by two rather distinct approaches to productivity enhancement (Part Four).

The closing chapter is the editors' view of where the book points the field in terms of promising directions and new frontiers.

Part One devotes an unusual amount of space to issues of meaning and measurement. This underscores the degree to which we perceive definitional issues and clarification of the construct as critical to progress in the understanding and enhancement of productivity. Perspectives are offered from three different vantage points. Because much of what is written or spoken about productivity comes from economists, they have their say in Chapters Two and Three. Mahoney (Chapter Two) presents frameworks used by economists in the measurement of productivity and shows how approaches used by psychologists fit into this broader scheme. He describes the basic conception of productivity as an efficiency measure and discusses the position of psychological interventions in the output/input ratio. The value of the growth accounting model is highlighted, along with its treatment of productivity as unexplained variance. The admonition that productivity measurement depends on purpose and other elements in his discussion have an eerie similarity to discussions of the "criterion problem" in the assessment of individual performance. Taira, in Chapter Three, describes Japan's approach to productivity and how it came to be what it is. The purpose of the measurement system forms a centerpiece of the chapter and illustrates the use of productivity measures for goal setting and motivational purposes. His analysis of sector productivity is important for an understanding of Japan-U.S. productivity comparisons, and he presents his view of the major antecedents of growth that have contributed to Japan's more rapid growth in certain sectors. Finally, he describes how the Japanese personnel system is designed to be compatible with and supportive of the economic system and speculates on the role of a superordinate goal as the primary driving force in the Japanese approach to productivity improvement.

As a survey of literature surveys of industrial-organizational psychology research on productivity, Chapter Four by Guzzo may not seem as if it fits here, but it does. While Guzzo's chapter provides a very useful overview of major psychological findings regarding productivity, more important for the purposes of Part One it is actually a policy-capturing study of what we in the field mean by productivity. The meaning is captured by the dependent variables that have occupied investigators, which then can be compared with the explication of Mahoney and Taira.

Chapter Five, by the editors, closes Part One by moving beyond a summary of definitional issues to present a conceptual scheme that tries to clarify the fit of industrial-organizational psychology within the productivity field, facilitate the identification of the frontiers, and provide a perspective for the parts that follow. In this sense, Part One is the actual introduction to this book and, in the view of the editors, is critical to the success of the book and efforts to better understand the construct of productivity.

In his review of the independent variables used in the psychological study of productivity, Guzzo delineates two major classes of activity: human resource management and workplace innovations. Part Two is concerned primarily with human resource management; Parts Three and Four focus on workplace innovations. Each of the chapters in Part Two deals with a great theme in the study of the behavior of individuals in organizations. It begins with what Burke and Pearlman describe as the least interventionist approach—what we know about individual characteristics and their value for recruitment, selection, and placement functions. Their Chapter Six examines the linkages between person and job characteristics and methods for estimating the effects of person-job matching systems on outputs or other outcomes. Their discussion of frontiers includes the potential role of taxonomies, validity generalization and meta-analytical methods, computer-based testing, utility analysis, abilities emerging from the domain of cognitive psychology, and recent developments in personality research.

In Chapter Seven, Ilgen and Klein review a number of major theories of effort and choice, including expectancy theory, equity theory, goal-setting theory, and social learning theory. They give examples of applications of several theories that underscore the complexity of practical interventions and the overlap among theories, and they propose a set of integrating concepts that emphasize the complementary nature of the theories. In addition, Ilgen and Klein offer a set of guidelines for productivity enhancement, with special attention directed at the difficulty of maintaining change over time.

In Chapter Eight, John Campbell critically evaluates paradigms, methods, and research findings regarding efforts to teach knowledge, skill, and task understanding in the pursuit of performance improvement. The review encompasses instructional psychology as well as the training and development literature. He offers a training design model and discusses its major parameters in terms of their implications for training design, what current research findings suggest regarding the issues it identifies, and promising avenues for future research.

The discussions in Chapters Seven and Eight constitute an apt prelude to Part Three, which deals with a variety of organizational interventions. Many of the independent variables covered by Guzzo—

for example, participation, work redesign, financial incentives, and goal setting—appear here, but the choice of treatments is necessarily selective. They are, in our opinion, closest to the frontier and are not really a part of selection, training, or motivational techniques. The mechanisms by which they seem to work are usually some combination of a better ability-job match, the learning of new knowledge or skills, and motivation enhancement.

Berlinger, Glick, and Rodgers take on job redesign in Chapter Nine, entitled "Job Enrichment and Performance Improvement." They present a critical evaluation of theoretical expectations and examine the conditions under which improved performance should be observed, including methodological and design issues that might affect the research findings. After a review of studies reporting quantitative results of the job enrichment–performance link and an analysis of potential moderators, the authors present the results of their meta-analysis. The theme of participation permeates Chapter Ten, "The Quality Circle and Its Variations." Ledford, Lawler, and Mohrman review the design of the quality circle, the history of the approach, performance and attitudinal outcomes, and the life cycle of the quality circle. They move on to present design options and environmental contingencies that influence effectiveness and success and present ways in which quality circles can move toward other forms of participative management. Their suggestions for future directions include prescriptions for future research reports that should enable sound analysis across studies. Chapter Eleven deepens the participation theme, with Goodman, Devadas, and Hughson presenting an analysis of self-managing teams. They review three major early studies, critically evaluate design limitations, and offer conclusions on the effectiveness of self-managing teams. Considerable attention is given to the interaction of human, organizational, and technological variables. They conclude with commentary on the simplicity of our conceptual models as contrasted with the complexity of actual treatments or interventions. Hammer's concluding chapter in Part Three deals with financial incentives. The conceptual anchor for her treatment of "New Developments in Profit Sharing, Gainsharing, and Employee Ownership" is the labor exchange, the trade between employer and worker of pay for effort. She compares and contrasts the three approaches, comments on the current state of their theoretical underpinnings, and evaluates the research findings. She offers a model to guide research and her expectations for future developments of each of the systems.

The two chapers in Part Four come from different traditions, although there is a fundamental similarity in that they both rely heavily on participation. The reason that they are together in a class by themselves is that their work deals with system-wide intervention and illustrates what must be done in an organization to turn research findings and theory into practical interventions. It would be a sad story indeed if *none* of what we did ever made any difference. Chapter Thirteen by McLagan, on flexible job modeling, describes the technology and its uses, which include performance measurement, training and development, and career management. In describing a large case example, she shows how the technique places strong emphasis on what is to be produced, what must be mastered, and the need to design jobs for future conditions. The chapter by Banas (Fourteen) recounts Ford Motor Company's efforts to increase employee involvement and participation and presents in some detail Ford's process for implementing employee involvement. Considerable attention is given to the role of the union and the pattern of relations between management and the union. Banas concludes with an assessment of the relationship between the program and improvements in product quality.

The final chapter presents the editors' view of where industrial-organizational psychology should be investing its energy and resources in the quest for a better understanding of productivity and its enhancement. There is no attempt to summarize or recap the broad range of content in the earlier chapters. Rather, we try to cull out and synthesize the concepts, issues, and directions that appear most promising and exciting from the robust offerings of our contributing authors. We shall say no more now except to invite you to read on into these explorations into the interplay of industrial-organizational psychology and productivity.

References

Brief, A. P. (ed.). *Productivity Research in the Behavioral and Social Sciences.* New York: Praeger, 1984.

Denison, E. F. "Productivity Analysis Through Growth Accounting." In A. P. Brief (ed.), *Productivity Research in the Behavioral and Social Sciences.* New York: Praeger, 1984.

Hall, D. T., and Associates. *Career Development in Organizations.* San Francisco: Jossey-Bass, 1986.

Kopelman, R. E. *Managing Productivity in Organizations: A Practical, People-Oriented Perspective.* New York: McGraw-Hill, 1986.

PART ONE

Productivity Concepts and Issues

Because productivity is such an important and widely used concept, the four chapters in this first part attempt to explicate the definitional and conceptual issues in a relatively thorough manner. The first two chapters were written by labor economists who also have broad experience in other behavioral sciences. Given the role that Japanese versus U.S. productivity plays in current policy discussions, we are especially fortunate that one of the two has a special familiarity with the Japanese experience. Chapter Four illustrates the contrast between what psychologists in organizations do and what productivity is. There seemed no better way to illustrate this contrast than to present a very concise summary of the research that industrial-organizational psychologists do in the name of productivity. What dependent variables do we label *productivity,* and what interventions do we use to change it? Chapter Five (by the editors) takes these studies in contrast and attempts to describe a useful way of looking at them for purposes of interpreting past results and planning future research.

2

Productivity Defined: The Relativity of Efficiency, Effectiveness, and Change

Thomas A. Mahoney

Every age has its slogans and energizing concepts. Among other concepts, concern for productivity has characterized much of the current decade. Long a concern primarily of national income economists, productivity has become a concern of business managers, politicians, and behavioral scientists. One finds references to productivity in publications ranging from *Review of Economics and Statistics* (Kuh, 1965) to *Harvard Business Review* (McConnell, 1979), *Science* (Walsh, 1979), and *Training* ("Special Report . . . ," 1979). Clearly, issues relating to productivity have captured the attention of many in our society. However, the productivity concerns, concepts, and definitions vary considerably from one analysis to another. One purpose of this essay is to provide an overview of productivity concepts and concerns, particularly as they relate to the interests of behavioral scientists.

Background

Because productivity is a historical concern of economists, it is appropriate to begin our examination within that discipline. At base, the science of economics addresses the production, distribution, and consumption of goods and services to satisfy human needs and desires. An implicit objective of an economic system is an improved standard of living for members of a society—an improved standard of living

Preparation of this chapter was supported by the Dean's Fund for Research, Owen Graduate School of Management, Vanderbilt University.

made possible by increases in total production that exceed increases in population.

Increased production is accomplished through either or both of two methods: (1) increased employment of production inputs, such as land, labor, capital, and natural resources, and/or (2) increased efficiency in the transformation of production inputs into consumable outputs. The concept of productivity is associated with the latter of these two methods, the efficiency of transformation of inputs into outputs. Increases in productivity—output achieved per unit of input—permit increased production without an accompanying increase in production inputs.

Given these two alternative routes to increased production, the relevance of productivity varies directly with the scarcity of production inputs. Concern for productivity or efficiency in the utilization of petroleum, for example, varies directly with the relative cost (and scarcity) of petroleum. Similarly, the productivity of labor is of more concern in an economy with relatively full employment than is the case in a society with abundant unemployed labor resources. Productivity concerns vary over time and tend to focus upon those input resources that are scarce and thus relatively costly.

Productivity, as a measure of efficiency, has meaning only in relative terms. There is no ideal level of productivity, and judgments are limited to "more" or "less" comparisons. Productivity in one firm may be more or less than last year or than in a comparison firm, but characterizations of "highly productive" are meaningless except in comparative terms. Two forms of comparison are relevant. Consider, first, productivity comparisons between competing economic units (societies, firms, technologies, resources). Given a choice between competing units, the more productive unit is favored, other things being equal. Thus the more productive process or technology is selected over the less productive one, assuming no other difference. A second comparison is temporal: an increase in productivity is more beneficial than a decrease or no change in productivity. Other things assumed equal, greater productivity or efficiency is always favored over less productivity. It is obvious that rate of change in productivity over time also affects productivity comparisons between economic units. A favorable productivity comparison for an economic unit at one point in time can be eroded over time by greater increases in productivity by the comparison unit. Thus while a productivity advantage relative to competitors is sought, it is a consequence of relative changes in productivity over time by the competitors.

Further understanding of reasons for concern over productivity requires that we introduce considerations of prices, assumed to be equal above. Production inputs are purchased and compensated in the form of wages, interest, and other payments; indeed, it is these compensation payments that in turn finance the purchase of outputs for consumption. Resource employment decisions reflect both productivity and cost considerations, and competing resources can command compensation differentials to the extent that they are balanced by productivity differentials. Productivity differentials permit the payment of differential input prices financed through reduced input requirements. Differences in productivity permit differences in resource compensation and thus in achieved standard of living of the recipients.

Differences in resource compensation—wages, for example—can be maintained in a competitive economy only when accompanied by compensating productivity differences. Production, sales, and employment shift over time from one producer to another as differences in productivity and resource costs change. Thus, for example, textile production in the United States moved from New England to the South as regional productivity differences failed to compensate for regional wage differences.

In summary, productivity is a measure of efficiency of production and lacks intrinsic meaning or relevance. It achieves relevance in a comparative context and, particularly, in a competitive context. The production output available for distribution to resource owners varies with achieved productivity and, in general, standards of living vary with productivity. Competition among economic units favors those producing at lowest cost either because of relatively high productivity, lower resource costs, or both. Because of the close linkage between resource compensation and standard of living, favorable productivity comparisons among competitors are necessary to maintain realized standard of living comparisons. Productivity increases exceeding those of competing units are sought as a means of increasing one's relative standard of living.

This examination of productivity concerns, while cast in terms of competing societies, can be generalized to competing firms, technologies, and resources (such as labor). The general framework applies in all instances, while specifics vary with the context.

The Data People Worry About

Productivity in the U.S. economy has been of concern since the end of World War II, for two related but different reasons. The major interest in productivity in the U.S. economy during the period 1945–1970 stemmed from commitment to public policy objectives of full employment, stable (noninflationary) prices, and free collective bargaining. Collectively bargained wages were increasing annually and, unless balanced by proportional increases in productivity, would occasion either increases in general price levels or unemployment. A major concern at that time was to maintain proportionally equal annual changes in wage levels and productivity within the U.S. economy.

The concern for productivity broadened following 1970 to address foreign comparisons as foreign economies recovered from war and became increasingly competitive with U.S. producers in world markets. U.S. producers, particularly of manufactured goods that are easily exported, encountered increasing competition from foreign producers, and the United States, which traditionally had enjoyed a foreign trade surplus, saw that surplus decline and, at times, become a deficit. Productivity and wage-rate comparisons with foreign producers became increasingly important, and, for example, textile and other manufacturing moved increasingly to foreign countries. Analyses of productivity in the media in recent years have focused upon international comparisons indicating the comparative disadvantage of U.S. producers as a consequence of lagging growth in productivity.

International comparisons of productivity are difficult to interpret, because of differences of measures among countries, different mixes of industries, and differences in prices. Nevertheless, the comparisons presented in Table 2.1 are illustrative of the comparisons occasioning concern. Table 2.1 presents comparative data for the manufacturing industries of the United States, Japan, France, Germany, Italy, and the United Kingdom. During the period 1977–1984, manufacturing productivity in the United States increased less than in other comparative countries—18.5 percent in the United States compared to 52.2 percent in Japan, for example. Change in hourly compensation over this period also varied among the countries, increasing 206.9 percent in Italy and only 44.8 percent in Japan. Accordingly, unit labor costs in local currencies actually declined in Japan (4.9 percent) while increasing 42.8 percent in the United States. Despite lagging growth in productivity in the United States, unit labor costs in this country increased less than in three of the comparison countries, because of differences in the rate of increase in compensation. Making still another adjustment for varying exchange rates, changes in unit labor costs expressed in terms of U.S. dollars are presented in column 5. Unit labor costs calculated in U.S. dollars were almost constant over 1977–1984 in Japan, France, and Germany, while they increased 42.8 percent in the United States. Changes in labor

Table 2.1. International Comparisons—Productivity and Costs 1984
(1977 = 100).

Country	Manufacturing Productivity	Hourly Compensation	Unit Labor Cost (Local)	Unit Labor Cost (U.S. $)
U.S.	118.5	169.1	142.8	142.8
Japan	152.2	144.8	95.1	107.2
France	135.9	244.0	179.5	101.0
Germany	124.8	155.0	124.2	101.3
Italy	134.7	306.9	227.2	114.5
U.K.	124.3	233.6	187.9	143.9

Source: Data extracted from "Annual Indexes . . . ," 1986, p. 101.

productivity, hourly compensation, and exchange rates combined to increase unit labor costs in U.S. manufacturing more over the period 1977–1984 than in competing countries. The implication of these comparisons is that U.S. manufacturing is relatively less competitive than foreign manufacturing and that trade as well as employment will shift from U.S. producers to foreign producers.

The evidence presented in Table 2.1 supports the conclusion that U.S. manufacturing has become relatively less competitive with foreign manufacturing. It says nothing, however, about absolute levels of productivity achieved in the different countries. While rates of change in productivity in Japan and Germany exceed those of the United States, is Japanese manufacturing today more or less productive than U.S. manufacturing? Comparison of relative productivity among countries is difficult because of different combinations of industries and products. Probably the most common comparison among countries is in terms of gross national domestic product (GNDP) per employee (see Table 2.2). This measure of overall economic activity per employee indicates that the U.S. economy in 1981 was still more productive than the comparison countries, despite a leveling in productivity since 1960. Gross domestic product per employee in Japan, for example, has increased from 26.9 percent of U.S. productivity in 1960 to 71.5 percent in 1981. Based upon this measure, the United States has lost relative advantage since 1960 but is still relatively more productive than competing countries. The comparisons presented in Tables 2.1 and 2.2 suggest that the United States has been losing its productivity advantage, although it is still more productive than foreign competitors. However, these data mask a number of more specific comparisons. Productivity levels and rates of change vary considerably among industries and among firms within an industry. Annual change in productivity in air transportation in

Table 2.2. Relative Levels in Gross National Domestic Product per Employed
Person, Selected Countries and Years, 1960–1981 (U.S. = 100).

Year	Canada	Japan	France	Germany	Italy	United Kingdom
1960	89.8	26.9	55.8	59.7	38.5	53.7
1965	88.8	35.0	62.1	63.4	44.6	51.8
1966	87.1	36.8	62.9	65.7	46.9	51.2
1967	87.3	39.8	65.4	65.0	49.5	52.9
1968	88.4	43.0	66.0	67.4	51.7	54.1
1969	89.9	47.6	69.4	71.3	55.1	54.6
1970	92.0	52.1	73.6	75.2	58.4	56.5
1971	93.6	52.6	75.1	75.3	57.8	57.4
1972	93.8	55.7	77.1	76.3	59.3	56.9
1973	94.2	57.8	78.6	78.2	61.6	58.7
1974	96.1	58.9	82.6	82.2	64.6	59.5
1975	95.3	60.4	83.4	83.3	61.7	59.2
1976	97.0	61.8	85.5	86.8	63.7	60.7
1977	95.8	63.1	85.9	88.0	63.5	60.1
1978	95.9	65.1	88.3	89.7	64.6	61.5
1979	95.5	67.8	91.6	92.7	67.2	62.4
1980	93.7	70.7	93.3	94.3	69.4	63.3
1981[a]	93.3	71.5	93.2	94.0	68.4	64.3

Note: Output based on international price weights.
[a]Data are based on preliminary estimates.
Source: Bureau of Labor Statistics, 1983, p. 69.

the United States was almost 8 percent during the period 1947–1973,
as compared with only 2 percent in steel manufacturing; and annual
change in productivity in air transportation from 1973 to 1981
dropped to less than 4 percent and in steel to less than 1 percent
(Bureau of Labor Statistics, 1983). Note further that competitive
advantage is based upon comparative labor costs that reflect both
productivity and compensation. Much textile manufacturing has
moved to foreign locations, because productivity advantages in the
United States are no longer adequate to compensate for U.S. wage
differentials. Foreign producers are not always more productive, but
they typically offer lower wage rates. The lagging rate of productivity
increase in the United States threatens the maintenance of more
favorable wage rates and living standards in the United States.

Basic Definitions

Productivity is an efficiency concept generally cast as a ratio of
output relative to input into some productive process. Operationali-

zation of the concept varies considerably, however, and discussions of productivity evidence disagreement and confusion over its meaning. Some of this confusion is evidenced in Table 2.3, which presents measures of productivity often employed by managers. All of the measures in Table 2.3 represent performance measures of one sort or another, but clear differences can be noted. Certain of the measures relate to *outcomes* of performance (for example, sales, customer satisfaction, profits), while others relate to *efficiency* of performance (for example, return on investment, cost per unit, output per employee). Only the latter efficiency measures conform to the traditional concept of productivity.

Productivity is also a performance variable and is perhaps best illustrated in comparison with other performance variables. Often any performance variable is presumed synonymous with productivity; in fact, only a subset of performance variables can be equated with productivity. The concepts of *effectiveness* and *efficiency* of performance, often associated with organizational performance, also relate to the distinction between measures of economic performance (Tuttle, 1983). Performance effectiveness relates to level of performance (production, sales, output) relative to aspirational performance goals.

Table 2.3. Measures of Productivity Used by Managers.

Measures	Profit
	Customer satisfaction
	Sales, revenues
	Market share
	Costs
	Quality, defects
	Response time
	Units produced
Indices	Sales 1981/sales 1980
	Labor costs 1981/labor costs 1980
	Activities 1981/activities 1980
Ratios	Return on investment
	Net earnings per share
	Labor cost per unit produced
	Profit per sales dollar
	Actual output/planned output
	Production cost/standard cost
	Labor hours/standard hours
	Output per employee

Source: Adapted from Sink, 1985, Tables 2.3, 2.4, and 2.5.

Gross national product (GNP) of the economy and production output of a plant are measures of output performance that measure performance effectiveness. Performance efficiency relates to the output achieved relative to inputs, regardless of level of output performance. Productivity relates to performance efficiency, not to outcome performance or effectiveness.

Ignoring measurement problems for the moment, we can distinguish between what is termed *total-factor productivity* and *partial-factor productivity*. Total-factor productivity refers to the efficiency of transformation of all inputs in combination into outputs—the efficiency of a total process. Partial-factor productivity, on the other hand, relates to the output attributable to a single input factor (for example, labor). Perhaps the most common measure of productivity is output per labor hour, a partial-factor productivity variable. In theory, partial-factor productivity is critical to making choices among competing resources for production; assuming equal per-input unit cost, the more productive inputs will be substituted for less productive inputs. Thus, for example, providing skills training to employees might be rationalized as a way of transforming inputs to increase productivity; more skilled employees are substituted for less skilled employees. As noted later, however, partial-factor productivity is difficult to operationalize as a meaningful measure, and attributions of partial-factor productivity to measures are often misleading. It is tempting to measure productivity of different production systems in terms of a common base (for example, output per labor hour), when in fact the differences in output are the result of differences in technology or product design. For example, an intervention of job redesign might be evaluated using a measure of output per labor hour. An increase in output per labor hour suggests that labor has become more productive, while in fact it might well be that the sequence of tasks is more productive. Partial-factor measures of productivity provide a basis for comparison, but associated attributions of causality are often in error.

Measuring Productivity

Conceptual productivity variables are relevant in a variety of contexts, and various productivity measures are applied. We examine several purposes of measurement before addressing the difficult considerations of measure construction.

Applications of productivity analysis essentially derive from this simple relationship:

INPUT × PRODUCTIVITY = OUTPUT

Productivity assessments become critical parameters in the projection of output targets and/or the projection of input requirements to achieve output targets. Thus, for example, output targets for the GNP can be projected on the assumption of full employment and utilized in planning monetary and fiscal policies for full employment. Alternatively, sales forecasts for a firm can be projected backward to employment forecasts based upon productivity parameters (Kendrick, 1984). Both applications require reasonably accurate projections of productivity; however, projections are usually based upon past behavior of productivity measures.

Productivity can also be treated as a policy variable to be manipulated in the achievement of output targets, particularly in a competitive context (National Center for Productivity and Quality of Working Life, 1976). Given, for example, limited inputs and a target for outputs, the required level of productivity (and proportional change) can be derived and specified as a performance goal. In a competitive context, per-unit cost is reduced by increasing productivity and thus employing fewer inputs, or by reducing the cost or compensation per unit of input; targets for productivity levels and rate of change can be derived from competitive analysis of price and cost comparisons.

Productivity measures, like all performance measures, serve to provide direction and motivation, particularly when targets and objectives are specified. As evidenced by the attention given to productivity measures for the U.S. economy in recent years, the measurement of productivity at any level of analysis, when treated as a policy variable, serves to guide performance.

If productivity is to be viewed as a policy variable, it is important to know the determinants of productivity of the system of concern in order to guide efforts to affect productivity. Many assumptions are made about the determinants of productivity, but considerable research and experimentation are still required. One approach to the analysis of productivity at the national level has been developed and applied increasingly in recent years. This approach, called *growth accounting*, is examined later in the chapter (Denison, 1974). Analyses at the level of the enterprise, work group, or technological process are more often cast in the form of experimental intervention and assessment (Sink, 1985). Growth accounting attempts to apportion changes in total-factor productivity of the economy to various influences, while assessments of smaller economic units typically attempt to measure partial-factor productivity through manipulation of a single factor.

Productivity measures can serve the same general purposes whether applied at the level of society, industry, firm, or work unit. As noted before, comparative level and rate of change are the key aspects of productivity measurement.

Level of Measurement and Analysis. Productivity measures vary, as do other measures of system characteristics, with the level of analysis. Productivity is a performance measure of a production system—a system of various components, each of which can be characterized in terms of performance. While performance of any complex system is, in part, a function of performance of its different components, measures appropriate to each level of analysis must be designed; component measures cannot be simply aggregated for a system measure. Measures for some units, such as industry, are more likely to be aggregations across firms in the industry because firms are relatively independent, while measures for a firm are not aggregations across departments because of the process links among departments. Design of a measure appropriate to a given level of analysis requires knowledge of the production linkages within the unit of concern. For example, the labor input for final product assembly might be reduced (productivity increased) by increasing the amount of assembly in earlier operations. What appears as an increase in productivity at one stage may be balanced by an apparent decline in productivity at another stage in the overall system. What appears as increased productivity in auto assembly may be accompanied by apparently reduced productivity in parts manufacturing. Outputs from and inputs to the system are the appropriate elements of a measure of productivity, not outputs from and inputs to different stages of production within the system.

Interpretation and understanding of the behavior of productivity measures also vary with the level of analysis. For example, the influence of work organization, job design, and worker motivation might be observed in measures of work-group productivity, while the influence of production level, technology, and research and development might be observed at the firm and industry levels. Only those influences that vary across units within a level of analysis are meaningful. Analyses at any level of analysis should be undertaken, however, only with awareness of influences at other levels of analysis and the potential effects of change at different levels. While influences such as industry utilization of capacity and the effects of new technology can be analyzed meaningfully in industry studies only over time, these influences should be considered and controlled in analyses of work-unit productivity. Otherwise, change in work-unit productivity occasioned by "just in time" scheduling, improved raw materials, and industry experience can be wrongfully attributed to a specific organizational intervention.

Probably more productivity data are available for the U.S. economy and for manufacturing industries than for individual organizations. Consequently, more research has addressed productivity performance at the macro levels of analysis (Nelson, 1981). Productivity concerns at the enterprise level in recent years have encouraged measurement efforts, however, and there appear to be growing efforts of measurement and analysis at the micro level (Kendrick, 1984). Measures of productivity differ significantly depending upon level of analysis, thus limiting cross-level inferences and enhancing the value of complementary macro/micro analyses of productivity.

Output Measurement. Conceptually, output is some good or service being produced—tons of coal, automobiles, artificial heart implants, or hamburgers. It is rare, however, except for very specific production processes, that a single output is produced. We might, for example, distinguish between a single primary product and a by-product that are produced by a process. By-products are rarely without value, and measures of by-products as well as desired output must be combined in some manner to measure total output. More commonly, desired output consists of several desired products requiring combined measures of output. While a physical measure of output might be possible for a single product unit, the common measure for multiple product units is some measure of monetary value, sales revenue, or value added. Output measures for assessing productivity of the U.S. economy, for example, typically employ GNDP estimates in dollar terms.

Measurement of output in dollar terms obviously requires price adjustment to estimate real output without inflated dollar estimates, because productivity measures are relevant only in relative terms. Thus the GNDP is adjusted for price inflation and commonly expressed in terms of constant dollars (National Research Council, 1979).

Constant-dollar estimates of output enable construction of a numeraire consistent in measurement over time, but they pose difficulties for substantive interpretation. While conceptually feasible, it is operationally difficult to produce constant-dollar estimates of output when the characteristics of the output are changing. For example, automobiles produced and sold for $10,000 in constant dollars are considered as equivalent, although one model may incorporate many features absent in the other—features such as airbag safety protection, cruise control, and computerized monitoring of performance. Similarly, $1 billion of hand calculators in constant dollars in different years are considered as equivalent, although the number and speed of operations possible vary considerably.

Another difficulty posed by dollar or value assessment of output relates to the valuation of outputs that are not exchanged in a market. Some arbitrary valuation of these outputs is required. Some series of measures exclude government services and the activity of nonprofit enterprises for this reason; others value such services on the basis of cost. In effect, the productivity of governmental and nonprofit production is presumed to be a constant ratio of 1.00. Shifts of economic activity from the profit sector (with annual increases in productivity) into not-for-profit sectors (government, schools, non-profit hospitals) would have the effect of reducing overall measures of productivity increases in consequence. Lagging rates of increase in national productivity may be due in part to this measurement bias and increasing relative employment in the not-for-profit sectors of the economy.

A distinction is made in analyses of national productivity between a *rate effect* and a *level effect* (Upjohn Institute, 1982). Rate effects occur when economic activity shifts from one industry to another industry with a different rate of productivity. Thus, for example, a shift of production from manufacturing industries with relatively high productivity to service industries with lower productivity would occasion lower overall measures of productivity without any change in specific industry rates. Similar changes might occur within an enterprise with multiple products and production processes; a change in product mix that increases the proportion of products requiring less input raises overall productivity of the enterprise merely because of the shift in production. An example of the rate effect for a word processor would include an analogous change in work assignment from statistical tables to text processing; the output of characters, pages, and documents increases merely because of the shift in production.

Level effects refer to actual changes in productivity within individual industries, production processes, or work assignments, assuming no change in product mix. Thus, for example, level effects would include increased yields of soybeans from the same acreage, increased tonnage of coal produced per miner, and larger numbers of letters produced per word processor. Weights can be devised to estimate the rate effect of shifting production among industries and to isolate these influences in analyses of productivity. It is not always as simple to distinguish measures of rate and level effects for individual tasks, however. Consider, for example, a multiple-line insurance agent with output measured as earned premium. A shift in sales from automobile liability insurance to life insurance would tend to increase earned premiums as a rate effect, yet increased ability of the agent to sell life insurance would illustrate a level effect. The distinction between rate and level effects is nevertheless important in trying to understand contributing causes of overall change in productivity and in identifying alternative methods for increasing productivity.

Output measurement for productivity assessment is at base arbitrary and depends critically upon the purpose of measurement. Measurement for comparability over time requires consistency of measurement and often results in sacrifice of substantive concerns. Measurement for comparability of production units at a point in time may better address substantive concerns but likely sacrifices temporal comparability. Productivity estimates for individual enterprises and work units tend to have more short-run application than societal estimates, and temporal consistency can be more easily sacrificed. The more specific the unit of analysis, the greater the ease of output definition for substantive concerns. Output measures can be quite arbitrary and specific to a given purpose when comparability demands are relaxed.

Performance ratings of individual employees provide an interesting example of the difficulties of output measurement. Measures of objective achievements under an MBO (management by objectives) or similar program can be very specific output measures but tend to lack comparability over time or among individual positions. Alternatively, generalized performance ratings provide for comparability but are more subjective and tend to lack substantive content. Performance ratings also tend to reflect both rate and level effects, and it is difficult to isolate these effects. Finally, some personnel ratings, particularly behavioral ratings, are more properly viewed as measures of input, which are considered in the next section. Performance ratings can be useful as criterion measures, but interpretation of them as measures of productivity is often in error.

Input Measurement. The definition and measurement of production inputs are more difficult both conceptually and operationally than definition and measurement of outputs. The same issues are involved, but input dimensions are more varied. At the aggregate level, for example, land, labor, and capital are identified as basic economic input resources. Yet none of these is unitary in concept or fact. Land varies in mineral deposits, fertility, and accessibility; labor varies in skill, aptitude, and potential effort; and capital varies in form and adaptability. Further, the mix of inputs constantly changes as the relative cost of different inputs changes and one resource is substituted for another. While a monetary value might be assigned to inputs as in the case of outputs, the resulting productivity ratio would merely assess relative profitability of a production unit without providing any insight into the reasons for profitability variation.

As noted earlier, total-factor productivity is some estimate of total output relative to total input; it varies with the productivity of individual inputs as well as the particular mix of inputs. Measures of partial-factor productivity are more commonly employed in order to avoid monetary valuation and to focus upon identifiable inputs. Output per labor hour, for example, is a common measure of partial-factor productivity, in part because of public policy links between labor productivity, wages, and unemployment, and in part because labor costs constitute a significant proportion of total costs.

Measures of partial-factor productivity can be misleading to the extent that they appear to attribute productivity to a single input factor. Changes in output per labor hour, for example, may be interpreted wrongly as indicative of change in the quality or inherent efficiency of labor inputs, all other factors remaining constant. In fact, change in labor productivity is often due to change in the mix of inputs and substitution of capital for labor. Labor productivity may appear to increase, while total-factor productivity remains constant.

National measures of output per labor hour have been faulted because of difficulty in measuring labor inputs, illustrating certain difficulties of input measurement (National Research Council, 1979). Labor-hour inputs in the United States are estimated from independent measures of employment and of hours; employment measures are inclusive, but hour measures are available only for direct production. A shift from direct production hours to greater use of indirect labor, such as production engineering, has the effect of increasing *measured* productivity more than *real* productivity. Further, hours paid, rather than hours worked, are measured; increases in hours paid but not worked (for example, vacations) appear to decrease productivity, while productivity per hour worked may have increased.

Measures of productivity at the industry and firm level are particularly sensitive to change in inputs. For example, the purchase of intermediate products rather than raw resources would appear to increase labor productivity, because significantly less labor is required for the same level of output of finished products; value added per labor hour may remain constant, while total output per labor hour increases. The effect on total-factor productivity and on costs of production is more relevant in such a case than the effect on productivity of labor.

A difficulty encountered in input measurement that is shared with output measurement lies in the treatment of qualitative dimensions of inputs. Labor hours, for example, vary in terms of skill and effort, yet these variations are rarely measured as change in inputs. It has been observed that labor productivity tends to decline with massive entrance of new workers into the work force, presumably because of lack of training (Kendrick, 1980). Measured productivity per labor hour declines because of change in the qualitative dimensions of labor inputs associated with change in quantity. Similarly, labor hours of input may well vary in terms of intensity of effort and attention, with consequent differences in output. Most observers would interpret this change in output only as changed productivity, while in fact it was accompanied by a change in input. Much of what we measure as change in productivity is probably due to change of input attributable to change in skill, education, motivation, attention, and even behavior, yet we classify the change as change in efficiency because of inability to measure these changes of input. This issue is considered again later in the chapter, when I discuss growth accounting as an approach to measurement and analysis of productivity.

One aspect of input measurement that is generally ignored relates to what might be termed *social cost*. Air pollution due to inefficient technology, work injuries due to fatigue or improper equipment, and other forms of social cost have traditionally been ignored in productivity measures. Some analyses of economic growth attempt to assess the impact of government regulations upon measured productivity, and the costs of compliance appear to reduce productivity (Denison, 1974). However, the apparent reduction in productivity is due in part, at least, to earlier exclusion of social costs in productivity measures.

While output definition and measurement are easier for more specific units of analysis, this is not always the case for input definition and measurement. Total-factor productivity is more relevant for budgeting and resource allocation in a single organization than is partial-factor productivity, and it is not always possible to allocate system-wide inputs to subsidiary components of a system. Staff and administrative inputs—research and development or information systems, for example—are not easily allocated as inputs to a single production process. Consequently, selected inputs such as direct labor are measured for partial-factor assessments, and other factors are not controlled. Particular care must be taken in defining and either measuring or controlling inputs of subsidiary systems in designing partial-factor productivity measures.

Purpose of Measurement. It should be obvious that measures of productivity are arbitrary and must be tailored to fit the intended purpose. Alternatively, readily available measures of productivity are limited in relevance because of manner of construction of the measures. Debates in the media over the interpretation of assessments of U.S. productivity in recent years evidence the limitations in application of these measures.

One general purpose for measuring industry and national productivity is to provide a historical series of measures to track and monitor economic performance for the purpose of developing policy recommendations to enhance economic growth. This general purpose underlies the measures maintained by the Departments of Labor and Commerce (Bureau of Labor Statistics, 1976). While the interpretation of these series is constrained by the definitions of output and input, their major advantage is relative consistency of definition over time. Observed differences in productivity measures can be accepted as indicative of change and justify research into the reasons for and correlates of change. Numerous research efforts have identified patterns of behavior in these indices that are helpful for policy analysis.

Assuming a purpose of understanding change in economic growth, what is called *growth accounting* provides a model for analysis of productivity in a broader context and also illustrates certain of the problems in assessing productivity (Denison, 1974). This approach is illustrated in Table 2.4, which presents analyses of economic growth for the periods 1948-1966, 1966-1973, and 1973-1978. These analyses attribute increases in gross product to increased inputs and to increased efficiency of production; 28 percent, 54 percent, and 67 percent of the increases in gross product in the three periods analyzed are attributed to increased inputs. The basic analytical model underlying growth accounting involves the analysis of change. Proportional change in gross product is attributed to proportional changes in inputs and efficiency, and proportional changes in efficiency are inferred as the residual change not accounted for by change in inputs. This model explicitly attributes unexplained growth to productivity: input and output can be measured, but productivity cannot be measured directly; it can only be inferred. Such a measurement model is foreign to behavioral scientists, who typically view any unexplained residual as indicative of error variance in the measurement of the dependent variable. The growth accounting approach assumes perfect measurement of growth and of identifiable inputs; because change in productivity cannot be measured directly, it is equated with the unexplained residual. The approach also illustrates problems in the conceptualization of productivity, partic-

Table 2.4. Sources of Growth in Real Gross Product in the U.S. Domestic Business Economy, 1948–1978.

	1948–1966	1966–1973	1973–1978[a]
Average annual percentage rates of change			
Real gross product	3.9	3.5	2.4
Total-factor input	1.1	1.9	1.6
Labor	0.4	1.4	1.3
Capital	2.8	3.3	2.3
Real product per unit of labor	3.5	2.1	1.1
Capital/labor substitution	0.7	0.5	0.3
Total-factor productivity	2.8	1.6	0.8
Sources of total-factor productivity growth: percentage point contribution			
Advances in knowledge	1.4	1.1	0.8
Changes in labor quality	0.6	0.4	0.7
Education and training	0.6	0.7	0.8
Health	0.1	0.1	0.1
Age/sex composition	-0.1	-0.4	-0.2
Changes in quality of land	—	-0.1	-0.2
Resource reallocations	0.8	0.7	0.3
Labor	0.4	0.2	0.1
Capital	0.4	0.5	0.2
Volume changes	0.4	0.2	-0.1
Economies of scale	0.4	0.3	0.2
Intensity of demand	—	-0.1	-0.3
Net government impact	—	-0.1	-0.3
Services to business	0.1	0.1	0.1
Regulations	-0.1	-0.2	-0.4
Actual/potential efficiency and n.e.c.[b]	-0.4	-0.6	-0.4

Note: Dash (—): Zero or negligible.
[a] Preliminary.
[b] Not elsewhere classified.
Source: Kendrick, 1980, p. 3.

ularly the specification of change in inputs. Only certain changes in inputs are identified, and other changes, such as intensity of effort, that are not identifiable are interpreted as changes in productivity. In theory, although not in practice, the model would permit attribution of all change in economic growth to change in dimensions of inputs. In this context, productivity is truly the unexplained residual of economic growth.

Incidentally, the analyses in Table 2.4 provide evidence for recent U.S. concerns about growth in productivity; increases in productivity have lagged in recent years and have contributed less to growth than in previous years. The lag in productivity change, not achieved level of productivity, provides the occasion for alarm.

Table 2.4 also notes the distinction between total-factor productivity and labor productivity. While both have declined over the periods analyzed, measures of labor productivity overstate total-factor productivity because they ignore relative increases in capital as substitutes for labor.

The remainder of Table 2.4 presents a conceptual model employed in growth accounting that attempts to apportion change in total-factor productivity to change in causal elements. The causal elements presented reflect both hypotheses and findings of earlier analyses of productivity measures. Change in certain of these elements (age/sex composition of the work force, for example) can be measured directly while others (such as advances in knowledge) can only be inferred. The single largest factor, advances in knowledge, is estimated in Table 2.4 as the residual change after accounting for change in measurable factors. However, this factor is more than advances in knowledge; it encompasses all change in effort, intensity, behavior, and methods of production that are not measurable directly. Treatment of this factor also demonstrates our limited ability to measure and assess aspects of productivity.

Whether through experimental design or statistical analysis, it is difficult to control the many factors influencing productivity and to correctly attribute causation. Advances in knowledge, the unexplained residual, is the single largest source of total-factor productivity growth in the analyses of Table 2.4. So-called advances in knowledge that influence productivity can take many forms: improved design of a tool or production process, improved scheduling and coordination, altered work shifts, or changed reward systems. While certain of these influences can be manipulated in an experimental setting, it is difficult in any sort of field experimentation to prevent concurrent change in related influences. Job redesign, for example, incorporates both change in work processing and change in motivational aspects, which cannot be isolated.

The growth accounting approach to productivity analysis does illustrate one purpose for productivity assessment: understanding the influences of change in productivity for the purpose of policy change. The analysis begins with a conceptual model of causes of growth, attributes growth not accounted for in measured production inputs to change in productivity, and then attributes this change to measured change in quality dimensions of inputs as well as changes in the application of inputs. While growth accounting is applied at the societal level, some analogous model might be appropriate at the industry, plant, and work-unit level. In contrast to common before-after assessments of productivity-enhancing manipulations, growth accounting cautions against attributing all change in productivity to an experimental manipulation. Implicitly, it cautions against generalizing change in productivity observed in an experimental manipulation from one setting to another, because it highlights the relatively large unexplained residual increase in productivity not attributable to a single cause.

The alternative approaches of growth accounting and experimental manipulation are quite different, apply to different levels of analysis, and complement each other. Growth accounting addresses change in total production, and experimental manipulation typically addresses change in productivity only. Growth accounting employs a correlational attribution analysis, while experimental analysis employs classical experimental comparisons. Growth accounting employs a model of explicit variables, but experimental manipulation typically makes explicit only the experimental variable(s). And growth accounting is particularly relevant for societal analysis, while experimental manipulation is relevant in evaluation of specific alternatives in a production process. In this sense, the two approaches are more properly viewed as complementary than as alternative.

A second possible purpose for measuring productivity is quite different. It relates to productivity measures as numeraires, or scores. Productivity measures, like profit measures, are arbitrary and can be altered with changes in methods of accounting. Like profit measures, they can be useful in focusing attention upon particular outcomes, particularly when linked with evaluation and rewards. As numeraires, productivity measures can be changed at will to reflect changed objectives, just as the scoring of basketball games is changed from time to time to affect change in performance of the game. Productivity measures in this context are not unlike other measures for performance assessment and are subject to the same considerations.

Productivity Influences

Despite the critical importance of productivity for economic growth, relatively little is known about the factors influencing productivity. Probably most available research into productivity addresses issues of national trends, although industry studies are available and company analyses are increasing. Readers are referred to more inclusive reports for details of this research (Nelson, 1981).

Many analyses of productivity are based upon partial-factor

measures of productivity—for example, output per labor hour. As such, they do not distinguish between changes in productivity resulting from changed inputs or outputs and changed efficiency in usage of inputs. Much of the change in commonly reported measures of productivity of labor is in fact attributable to change in inputs and/ or shifts in production, as illustrated in Table 2.4. Other changes are likely due to general influences, such as technological developments, industry organization, and economies of scale.

A commonly identified source of productivity of labor is the ratio of capital employed per unit of labor, increasing capital intensity being positively associated with increasing productivity. Socioeconomic factors doubtless related to intensity of capital/labor ratios would include savings patterns of society and willingness to invest in capital improvement. Various analyses attribute lagging rates of growth in U.S. productivity to lagging investment in capital and in research and development (R & D) (Malkiel, 1979). Changing national tax policies to promote investment and savings illustrate public policy attempts to influence productivity. Certainly, increases in capital investment appear to be directly related to more common measures of output per labor hour.

Note that while increasing capital investment per employee may increase measured output per employee, this need not represent any change in the partial-factor productivity of labor, because resource inputs, particularly capital, have increased. In the context of growth accounting, a proportional increase in output that is larger than the proportional increase in capital would signify that the resulting capital-labor combination is more productive than the previous combination. This can be, and often is, described as an increase in the productivity of labor, although the attribution to labor is not always clear. All that can be said with certainty is that the capital-labor combination is more productive.

Probably more critical than mere amount of capital, however, is the form and/or obsolescence of capital (Baily, 1981; Bowen, 1979). Innovations in technology and production processes contribute directly to improved productivity, and R & D expenditures have been identified as contributors to productivity in various industry studies (Nelson and Winter, 1977). The impact of much R & D investment is accomplished, however, through change in the inputs to and in the outputs of production—change that we are unable to measure adequately. The "advances in knowledge" component of growth in Table 2.4 doubtless includes a number of changes of inputs as well as new methods of production. R & D, for example, can result in development of improved tools for production and improved intermediate products, reducing the unit costs of final outputs. It is quite likely that both amount and form of capital investment have a significant impact upon both economic growth and productivity in the usual context—more of an impact than has been measured directly.

It is also believed that there are economies of scale that contribute to total-factor productivity. Some factors of production are relatively invariant with amount of production, and unit costs of production are reduced as these factors are allocated to larger volumes of production. Evidence of economies of scale is difficult to demonstrate; but productivity has been found to vary with degree of utilization of industry capacity, and a learning curve effect has been observed with the introduction of new products and processes (Joskow and Rozanski, 1977).

National productivity has been observed to vary with stage of the business cycle, declining with the onset of recession and increasing with recovery. Attributed causes of these observations include degree of capacity utilization and labor utilization: managers are slow to adjust employment to change in production, and the efficiency of labor utilization thus varies with level of production.

Table 2.4 also isolates change in labor quality as a factor in economic growth. Conceptually, change in labor quality would not be a factor in productivity change, just as change in form of capital would not be a factor. However, both are related to national productivity statistics, because change in quality and form are not measured directly. Thus, for example, productivity statistics decline with rapid expansion of the work force and with the infusion of new entrants to the work force. These declines are attributed to decline in the average skill level, which will improve as workers gain experience.

This brief review of observations regarding productivity statistics should demonstrate the difficulties in isolating true change in productivity. Most available statistics do not control for change in form of inputs or outputs and confuse change in efficiency and changed resources. A change in efficiency at one level of analysis (for example, greater output per labor hour in an industry) can be viewed as a change in input resources at a more micro level of analysis (for example, increased skill level of employees after training). The relevance of this distinction depends upon the intended application of the statistics, and it is in this context that growth accounting has emerged as a form of national economic analysis. Growth accounting addresses change in real national product and attempts to attribute change to various factors. True change in productivity remains as the unexplained residual, and attention is directed toward identifying factors subject to control and manipulation.

Implications for Research and Managerial Practice

Productivity assessment at the level of the enterprise has increased in recent years and takes many forms. Enterprise-level productivity measurement and analysis is undertaken for purposes of managerial planning and control and is related only tangentially to national productivity analysis. While industry and national productivity are related to enterprise productivity, the linkages are complex and uncertain. Enterprise productivity can often be related to specific changes in managerial practice—for example, changes that are not measured in national analyses except as the growth residual of advances in knowledge (in growth accounting).

Productivity assessment at the enterprise level serves a number of managerial purposes. The principle of comparative advantage would argue that producing units should concentrate on those activities with which they enjoy relative advantage in productivity; productivity comparisons among different plants and product lines provide guidelines to the enterprise for resource allocation. Productivity criteria are tempered, however, by consideration of costs and revenues; measures of physical productivity are of less relevance than measures of value added and profitability. Productivity assessments are also useful in the projection of input requirements and for cost estimation, given some production objective. In addition, productivity assessments for different production technologies are important in making investment decisions concerning plant and equipment; again, however, monetary returns are not always proportional to physical productivity. Finally, productivity assessment can be useful for monitoring, controlling, and motivating performance. It is this last contribution that probably holds most interest for industrial and organizational psychology.

During the last thirty years, particularly, company or enterprise productivity assessment and accounting have become more common. Various institutions, such as the American Productivity Center, have developed methods and manuals for measuring company productivity and have conducted seminars focusing upon company applications (Kendrick, 1984). It appears that these intended applications are primarily for purposes of monitoring and control. It is also likely that introduction of a productivity accounting system has a positive effect on measured productivity, and it would be worthwhile to assess the impact of productivity accounting alone upon measured productivity of an organization.

Behavioral scientists are likely to approach the concept of productivity with two different concerns. A first concern derives from a desire to influence productivity positively through behavioral interventions. Relatively little is known about the magnitude of behavioral influences upon productivity, and considerable research is warranted. One review of research evaluating psychologically based interventions concludes that worker performance is raised by one-half standard deviation by these interventions (Guzzo, Jette, and Katzell, 1985). However, it is likely that the effects vary considerably with product and technology characteristics, and with other contingency variables yet to be identified. Such research should be designed with knowledge of major societal and industrial influences on productivity and of the difficulties of partial-factor productivity assessment. Otherwise, productivity research is likely to overstate the actual impact of behavioral influences.

A second concern for productivity relates to the constant search for a "perfect criterion" for evaluative research into behavioral science interventions. So-called utility analysis in recent years has been proposed as a method of evaluating and justifying applications of behavioral science in industry (for example, selection testing and employee training) (Cascio, 1982). Productivity concepts appear as an ideal criterion for this purpose. Certainly, the concept of productivity can guide criterion development, but, as evidenced in this review, there exists no single operationalization of the concept ready for application in all instances. Productivity measures are as arbitrary as any criterion measure, and their relevance depends critically upon the intended application.

Consistent with much of motivation theory and practice, productivity management activities are designed around a framework of goal specification, planning and analysis, monitoring and assessment, and feedback concerning performance. Just as growth accounting focuses upon economic growth instead of productivity, so productivity management focuses upon some arbitrary enterprise performance objective(s). Productivity enhancement may be an element of performance achievement, but it need not be the only factor attended to.

Productivity, defined narrowly as efficiency of transforming inputs into outputs, is not the primary aim of producing organizations. Rather, producing organizations have effectiveness objectives as well as efficiency objectives, and the effectiveness objectives are likely stated in profit or value-added terms. Substitutions among inputs and outputs are as acceptable as productivity enhancement as means of accomplishing these objectives. Efficiency in the broad sense of value added is more relevant than the narrow concept of efficiency of physical transformation.

Productivity management and analysis are intended to complement financial management and to overcome certain of its limitations. Profitability of an organization or product line is viewed as a function of productivity and of price recovery (the relationship between unit price and unit cost). Profitability measures alone do not distinguish between these two factors, and improving price recovery due to inflationary trends or ability to pass along increased costs may mask declining productivity. The American Productivity Council has published a Performance Measurement System for application within companies, which provides for tracking of both productivity and price recovery (Kendrick, 1984). This measurement system is clearly related to profit measures of effectiveness and is quite appropriate for private enterprises.

Alternative approaches to productivity management, although perhaps less sophisticated, are often employed where profit performance is inappropriate because of lack of market transactions or multiple nonfinancial objectives. Although called *productivity management,* many of these approaches relate more to *performance management.* Performance objectives, such as number of clients served in a welfare agency, speed of response in a computer center, or number of patentable discoveries in R & D, are specified and monitored over time (Sink, 1985; Hage, 1983). Often these are defined in the form of partial-factor performance measures, such as clients served per counselor or patentable discoveries per professional. As with all partial-factor measures, change may be due to change in productivity or merely substitution among input factors. Interpretation of the measures is thus severely limited, but the measurement process itself is doubtless important in directing attention and effort.

Conclusion

Many of us are inclined to make what we term *productivity judgments and comparisons* when we speak of the productivity implications of work and organizational interventions. Thus, for example, we compare the relative productivity of different workers, technologies, and work processes. Commonly, these are comparisons of production capabilities and not of cost efficiency; one worker may be 20 percent more productive than another and yet require a wage 50 percent higher. As with any criterion for judgment and decision making, it is critical that we define precisely what is intended by the term *productivity* and determine the relevance of that definition to the situation at hand. The relevance of productivity measures and performance measures varies with the situation.

Many of us are also inclined to attribute productivity to the work force and to assume that change in productivity occurs through change in the work force. Thus we embark upon programs of management by objectives, work design, and teamwork to accomplish change in the work force and productivity. Many of these programs also involve change in raw materials, the combination of inputs, and even nature of outputs—changes that may have more impact upon production and productivity levels than the work force changes. Changed Medicare provisions, for example, had more impact upon reducing hospital days per patient than any improvements in work-force efficiency. Partial-factor measures of productivity can be misleading and should be viewed with suspicion unless there is strict control over all other factors.

Enhanced productivity can be a significant source of economic growth and competitive advantage. Yet productivity, defined narrowly, may be insignificant relative to improvements in the input factors and their allocation among alternative uses. Industrial and organizational psychology may well have more to offer to enhancement of work-force inputs than to the efficiency of production processing.

Finally, a word of caution is advanced to those inclined to view productivity as the ultimate criterion for validation and justification of concepts and practices based in industrial and organizational psychology. Productivity concepts, definitions, and measures are arbitrary and vary with the situation. The specification of output and input variables and measures will reflect, as always, judgments of relevance to the concerned parties. Gross national domestic product per employee, value added per labor hour, profit return on investment, and hours worked relative to standard hours will all be relevant measures of productivity in one context or another. Whether called *performance* or *productivity,* the task of criterion construction remains a situation-specific task.

What is productivity? Productivity is an efficiency concept, and its specification and measurement depend upon the intended use and application of the measure. It is a performance concept, but not the only performance concept. Performance effectiveness is often a more relevant concept and measure than performance efficiency. Performance effectiveness variables depend upon the aspirations and subjective judgments of the concerned parties. Measures of efficiency in achieving effectiveness thus must also vary with those judgments.

References

"Annual Indexes of Productivity and Related Measures, Twelve Countries." *Monthly Labor Review*, May 1986, p. 101.

Baily, M. N. "Productivity in a Changing World." *The Brookings Bulletin*, 1981, *18* (1), 1-4.

Bowen, W. "Better Prospects for Our Ailing Productivity." *Fortune*, Dec. 3, 1979, pp. 68-86.

Bureau of Labor Statistics. *BLS Handbook of Methods*. BLS Bulletin 1910. Washington, D.C.: U.S. Department of Labor, 1976.

Bureau of Labor Statistics. *Productivity and the Economy: A Chartbook*. Washington, D.C.: U.S. Department of Labor, 1983.

Cascio, W. F. *Costing Human Resources: The Financial Impact of Behavior in Organizations*. Boston: Kent, 1982.

Denison, E. F. *Accounting for United States Economic Growth, 1948-1969*. Washington, D.C.: Brookings Institution, 1974.

Guzzo, R. A., Jette, R. D., and Katzell, R. A. "The Effects of Psychologically Based Intervention Programs on Worker Productivity: A Meta-Analysis." *Personnel Psychology*, 1985, *38* (2), 275-291.

Hage, J. "Organizational Theory and the Concept of Productivity." In A. P. Brief (ed.), *Productivity Research in the Behavioral and Social Sciences*. New York: Praeger, 1983, pp. 91-126.

Joskow, P. L., and Rozanski, G. A. "The Effects of Learning by Doing on Nuclear Plant Operating Reliability." *The Review of Economics and Statistics*, 1977, *61*, 161-169.

Kendrick, J. W. "Productivity and Economic Growth." *The AEI Economist*, Nov. 1980, pp. 1-12.

Kendrick, J. W. *Improving Company Productivity*. Baltimore, Md.: Johns Hopkins University Press, 1984.

Kuh, E. "Cyclical and Secular Labor Productivity in U.S. Manufacturing." *Review of Economics and Statistics*, 1965, *47*, 1-12.

McConnell, C. R. "Why Is U.S. Productivity Slowing Down?" *Harvard Business Review*, Mar.-Apr. 1979, pp. 36-58.

Malkiel, B. G. "Productivity: The Problem Behind the Headlines." *Harvard Business Review*, May-June 1979, pp. 81-91.

National Center for Productivity and Quality of Working Life. *Improving Productivity Through Industry and Company Measurement*. Washington, D.C.: National Center for Productivity and Quality of Working Life, 1976.

National Research Council. *Measurement and Interpretation of Productivity*. Washington, D.C.: National Academy of Sciences, 1979.

Nelson, R. R. "Research on Productivity Growth and Productivity Differences: Dead Ends and New Departures." *Journal of Economic Literature,* 1981, *19,* 1029–1064.

Nelson, R. R., and Winter, S. "In Search of Useful Theory of Innovation," *Research Policy,* 1977, *6* (Summer), 36–76.

Sink, D. S. *Productivity Management: Planning, Measurement and Evaluation, Control and Improvement.* New York: Wiley, 1985.

"Special Report: Training's Crucial Role in Boosting Productivity." *Training,* Jan. 1979, pp. 17–49.

Tuttle, T. C. "Organizational Productivity: A Challenge for Psychologists." *American Psychologist,* 1983, *38,* 479–486.

Upjohn Institute. *What's Happening to American Labor Force and Productivity Measurement?* Kalamazoo, Mich.: Upjohn Institute, 1982.

Walsh, J. "Productivity Problems Trouble Economy." *Science,* 1979, *206* (19), 310–311.

3

≋≋≋≋≋≋≋≋≋

Productivity Assessment: Japanese Perceptions and Practices

Koji Taira

In Japan, productivity (*seisansei*) invaded public consciousness in 1955 and has since been perceived almost exclusively as the physical productivity of "direct" labor in manufacturing and its auxiliary industries, such as mining and utilities, which produce inputs for manufacturing. Not much attention has been paid to such indirect labor as the office work force or sectors other than industry. Neither capital productivity nor total-factor productivity has been in the active vocabulary of policy makers, business people, workers, or the general public. This attitude toward productivity reflects Japan's broader strategy for economic development, in which manufacturing is viewed as a key or leading sector and which supposes that other sectors will take care of themselves so long as manufacturing keeps growing.

Since the middle of the 1950s, there has been a national productivity movement to improve labor productivity under the aegis of the Japan Productivity Center in Tokyo and several regional productivity centers. It may seem odd that when the labor supply was practically unlimited, as it was during the 1950s, labor productivity, not capital productivity, was the objective of a national movement. In hindsight, however, the labor productivity movement was timely, because enormous economic growth was about to begin at home and abroad that, in due course, would absorb all available labor. Economic growth, measured by the growth of gross national product (GNP), was at a "miraculous" rate, exceeding 10 percent per annum on the average during the period 1955–1970. Labor shortages became a serious concern for Japan by the middle of the 1960s. The concern became more acute every year until the oil shock of 1973, which brought economic growth to a screeching halt and halved the growth rate in subsequent years. But the habit of thought and action organized around labor productivity continued.

The growth of Japan's industrial labor productivity since 1955 is quite remarkable. In that year, the Ministry of Labor (MOL) and the Japan Productivity Center (JPC) devised indices of physical labor productivity for a large number of specific industries and have subsequently followed them. However, the Ministry of Labor discontinued its measurement in 1983. The measurement of physical productivity is the ratio of output measured in physical units to the number of production workers or their hours of work. The industry indices, weighted by value added, are averaged to yield the manufacturing index. Another average index includes mining and utilities. (See Ministry of Labor, 1984; Japan Productivity Center, 1985.)

With 1955 as 100, the JPC index for 1984 stands at 983, an almost tenfold increase over the thirty-year period. Productivity growth in subperiods suggests that the growth of aggregate demand (GNP) influences productivity growth. For the period of "miracle growth," 1955 through 1973, the JPC index of manufacturing labor productivity increased at an average annual rate of 9.8 percent. For the period of growth recession, 1973 through 1984, the index shows a growth rate of 5.1 percent per annum. This chapter considers the reasons for and ramifications of the Japanese emphasis on the measurement of labor productivity and examines how the increase in productivity, as measured, has been brought about.

A National Slogan: Catch Up to and Surpass America

The whole purpose of economic policy and the productivity movement in Japan was to close the productivity gap between Japan and America as quickly as possible. In view of the seemingly unbridgeable gap between America's and Japan's productivities in the early 1950s, no productivity growth, however high, would ever have appeared high enough to the Japanese. Economic growth, already under way, snowballed into the tremendous growth of the 1960s. Along the way, Japanese asked how close they were coming to the United States. A special technique of productivity comparison was required to index Japanese productivity on the base of American, or American productivity on the base of Japanese.

Indices for Productivity Comparisons

Some Japanese economists actually tried estimating relative productivity before economists in other countries began to show interest in it. The pioneering work was Shinohara's, on the basis of the 1956 data (Shinohara, 1962). Since data problems made the comparison for this year rather tenuous, Shinohara then undertook comparisons for 1958, 1963, and 1967 (Shinohara, 1970). Shinohara identified fifty-three industrial products common to the United States and Japan in twelve manufacturing industries. He measured output of each product in physical units, expressed Japanese output as a percentage of U.S., and averaged over all the products, by a weighted-average method, to show how the Japanese industry on the whole compared with the U.S. industry. He also adjusted the Japanese-American output ratio for the relative population size and obtained a measure of Japan's standing relative to the United States on a per-capita basis. Although the use of total population rather than manufacturing employment may have overstated Japan's impressive rate of catching up, Shinohara's results (1970) are suggestive. Japan's industrial output on a per-capita basis rose from about 30 percent of America's in 1958 to 65 percent in 1967. It appeared that Japan was catching up to the United States rather quickly.

Yukizawa (1973) goes over much the same terrain as Shinohara did, though with a more focused productivity model and improved methods. Yukizawa's index covers sixty industries and obtains physical labor productivity in each of them by dividing output in physical units by the number of employees in the industry concerned. He then arrives at a bilateral physical labor productivity index by taking a weighted average of the industry-specific productivity indices. For 1958 and 1963, the overall index puts Japan at 36.1 percent and 41.0 percent of the United States, respectively. Some twenty-five years ago, then, Japan's industrial labor productivity was much less than half as high as America's. In the ensuing years, however, Japan's industrial labor productivity has increased considerably and almost caught up to America's.

Yukizawa's 1967 bilateral productivity index was picked up by the Bureau of Labor Statistics (BLS), U.S. Department of Labor, and extrapolated for additional years with the use of the productivity growth trends estimated by the BLS itself. Table 3.1 shows the results of such extrapolations for the 1970s. The weights based on American prices and those based on Japanese prices yield different averages in Table 3.1. A single index of relative productivity, if desired, can be constructed by taking an average. In view of how the Yukizawa-BLS

Table 3.1. Productivity, Relative Productivity, and Relative Income for Japan, 1970–1980.

Year	Japanese Labor Productivity: JPC Index (1970 = 100)[a]	Japanese Manufacturing Output per Hour as a Percentage of U.S. Output (U.S. = 100)		Japanese GDP Productivity as a Percentage of U.S. Productivity (U.S. = 100)	
		Using Japanese Price Weights	Using U.S. Price Weights	Manufacturing	Aggregate
1970	100.0	57.5	67.5	64.3	48.1
1971	104.5	56.4	66.2	62.9	48.9
1972	116.0	58.0	68.0	64.7	51.9
1973	139.0	63.4	74.3	68.7	54.0
1974	140.0	67.1	78.7	72.6	55.3
1975	133.2	64.9	76.2	72.0	56.4
1976	150.9	n.a.	n.a.	75.7	57.4
1977	156.6	n.a.	n.a.	80.2	58.9
1978	169.0	n.a.	n.a.	86.3	61.0
1979	189.0	n.a.	n.a.	93.5	63.7
1980	205.9	90.7[b]	106.3[b]	n.a.	n.a.

[a]The index base year is changed every five years in JPC annual publications. However, I converted the index numbers of the late 1970s to the 1970-based numbers.

[b]Estimated by applying the BLS time series of annual percentage changes in manufacturing productivity, 1974–1981.

Sources: Data extracted from Japan Productivity Center, 1982, pp. 101–104; Bureau of Labor Statistics, 1977, p. 18; Bureau of Labor Statistics, 1983, pp. 133–142.

indices change from year to year in Table 3.1, it appears unlikely that U.S.-Japanese parity in manufacturing labor productivity would have been reached before 1980.

A note of caution is desirable for a proper interpretation of bilateral productivity comparisons. This has to do with the limited availability of directly comparable industries. There are many industries that exist in one country but not in another. The dissimilar industries left out of the comparison may be more or less important in one country than another. For example, the matched industries in the Yukizawa estimates for 1967 cover 25 percent of U.S. gross value added and 32 percent of Japanese net value added, as well as 21 percent of U.S. employment and 24 percent of Japanese employment in manufacturing (Bureau of Labor Statistics, 1977, p. 17). Thus labor productivity in the matched industries relative to that in the rest of manufacturing is higher in Japan than in the United States, so the matched-industry method results in a better showing for Japan relative to the United States than would be obtained if entire manufacturing sectors were compared. The following example offers the opportunity to test this conjecture.

Japan's Ministry of Labor has also estimated Japan's manufacturing physical labor productivity relative to that of the United States for 1977 (Ministry of Labor, 1981). The results show that Japanese productivity *per worker* is 110.7 percent of U.S., while that *per hour* is 98.9 percent of U.S. According to our check on the basis of the source materials used, the matched industries cover a small part of the entire manufacturing sector: in terms of employment, 15.1 percent for the United States and 16.2 percent for Japan. Further, the value-added productivity in the matched industries is roughly equal to that of all manufacturing in the United States, but 22 percent higher in Japan. It appears, therefore, that the MOL estimates are comparing productivity in better-than-average industries of Japan with the manufacturing average of the United States. When the employment weights of matched and unmatched industries of Japan are applied to the labor productivities of these industries, the average Japanese manufacturing productivity comes down to 90.8 percent of its American counterpart. This manipulation of ratios and weights, a mere arithmetical exercise, gives a figure closer to, though still higher than, the JPC estimates shown in Table 3.1.

Value Added as a Measure of Productivity. One way to overcome the incomplete coverage of manufacturing that is unavoidable in the comparison of physical labor productivity is to use value-added data. However, then a new problem arises. Values of output in different countries are expressed in units of their respective currencies.

The question of comparability then becomes the question of appropriate exchange rate to be used for conversion of the value of a country's output to a value in units of another country's currency. It is well known that the usual foreign exchange rate will not do for the purpose. What should be used for this purpose is purchasing-power parity.

The Japan Productivity Center sponsored an international comparative study of value-added productivity of labor for the period 1970–1979. Value added in a sector is identical with gross domestic product (GDP) originating in that sector. Purchasing-power parities (United Nations estimates) are used to convert foreign currency values to those in yen. The results of this study are shown in Table 3.1. On the basis of these figures, one would say that by 1980 the value-added productivity of labor in Japanese manufacturing had come very close to parity with that in American manufacturing. A weakness of this study, admitted and defended by the JPC, is that the same purchasing-power parity is used for that of sectoral products. Ideally, the latter should have been compared on the basis of sectoral purchasing-power parities.

Aggregate Versus Sector Productivity. The JPC study also raised curiosity about international differences in aggregate GDP labor productivity. As Table 3.1 shows, although Japan's manufacturing labor productivity almost caught up to America's by 1980, Japan's aggregate labor productivity was still about two-thirds of that for the United States. This means that there are low-productivity sectors in the Japanese economy (agriculture, trade, services, and so on) and that their weight is substantial enough to pull down the national average to a level thirty percentage points below the manufacturing average. Further, during the period shown in Table 3.1, aggregate labor productivity lagged more and more behind manufacturing labor productivity over time. In 1978, employment in high-productivity sectors (manufacturing, mining, and utilities) was about one-third of total employment (Japan Productivity Center, 1982, p. 99). This ratio has been falling since the early 1970s. Since the oil shock of 1973, the productivity movement in manufacturing has been emphasizing the use of less energy and less labor. Regular employment in manufacturing fell by 10 percent between 1973 and 1979. It recovered the previous losses somewhat after 1979 but even in 1985 was still below the 1973 level. In the meantime, nonmanufacturing employment has been rising rapidly.

The relationship between labor productivity and employment in manufacturing since 1973 is different than it was before that date. During the period of growth up to 1973, aggregate demand increased at an outstanding rate, stimulating even faster growth of manufacturing output. This increased manufacturing employment, but given the developing labor shortage and the productivity movement, output per unit of labor had to increase. As a result, during this period all three—output, employment, and labor productivity—increased rapidly. After 1973, the growth of aggregate demand slowed down. The growth of manufacturing output also slowed down, and the productivity movement became more intense under the cost-cutting pressures imposed by the energy price revolution. Consequently, employment was cut back in the interest of maintaining or increasing labor productivity. From Table 3.1, one can easily calculate that during 1974–1979, the period of employment decline, manufacturing labor productivity according to the JPC index increased approximately 6 percent per annum.

But if high-productivity sectors such as manufacturing reduce their share of employment in the interest of higher labor productivity, those sectors' contribution to the growth of aggregate labor productivity must fall. Under these conditions, the faster manufacturing increases labor productivity by reducing employment, the more slowly aggregate labor productivity grows. (Indeed, with microelectronics and robots, for which the Japanese appear to be more enthusiastic than people in other countries, the conceivable ultimate of manufacturing labor productivity is at infinity, because of the disappearance of labor under full automation [unstaffed factories are *happily* looked forward to by many Japanese].) The displaced workers must find their way into low-productivity sectors, where productivity growth is then further held back. The economy ends up with enormously productive manufacturing coupled with general productivity stagnation. Although this is a technically conceivable outcome of the Japanese-style productivity consciousness (Taira, 1983b), it is unlikely that Japan's aggregate economic performance can become as erratic in the short run and stagnant in the long run as that of the United States.

What happened to the relative levels of aggregate productivity for Japan and the United States between 1979 and 1985 may be explained on the basis of respective national data (Council of Economic Advisors, 1986; Ministry of Labor, 1986). Between 1979 and 1985, real GNP increased by 26.3 percent in Japan and 11.9 percent in the United States, while total employment increased by 6 percent in Japan and 8.4 percent in the United States. As a result, aggregate output per worker increased by 19.2 percent in Japan and 3.2 percent in the United States. When these growth rates are applied to the 1979 relative level of Japan, roughly 65 percent that of the United States, the 1985 relative level of Japan rises to 75 percent that of the United

States. That is, in six years, Japan gained on the United States by a full ten percentage points! At this rate, by the turn of the next century Japan's aggregate labor productivity would fully catch up to America's: the dream come true! (For a few more experiments with catch-up arithmetic, see Taira [1983b].)

Labor Productivity Differentials by Size of Firm. Reference was made above to considerable intersectoral labor productivity differentials. There are also interindustry differentials within the manufacturing sector. According to the MOL comparison of Japan and the United States, Japan's labor productivity is higher than America's in iron and steel, machinery, ceramics, transportation equipment, and electric and electronic appliances. The products of these industries make up the bulk of Japan's exports. Japan does less well than America in food processing, apparel, chemicals, and nonferrous metals. These industries are weak in export performance, although this does not automatically imply that these industries in the United States are strong exporters to Japan. The U.S. business person's lack of motivation to sell abroad and Japan's well-known trade barriers seem to hamper trade flows according to comparative advantage with respect to the products of which Japan is a less efficient producer.

Far more fascinating is another kind of labor productivity differential: that by size of firm. In any country, there is a tendency for labor productivity to increase as the size of firm increases, at least due to the possibilities of economies of scale. What is peculiar about Japan's productivity differentials by size of firm is their sheer magnitude; they are larger than one should observe in any advanced market economy. Statistics are available on the basis of plants or establishments, but because the size of firm is correlated with the size of plant, large firms tend to have large plants. We will make do with the available statistics and speak of plant and firm interchangeably. Table 3.2 shows that in 1977 labor productivity in plants with 1,000 workers was more than 60 percent above the manufacturing average, while that in plants with fewer than 10 workers was more than 40 percent below the average. The U.S. data in Table 3.2 show far more compressed, and somewhat erratic, productivity differentials by size of plant.

Even if the average manufacturing labor productivities of Japan and the United States converge, the contrasting and persistent interplant productivity differentials in Japan (as shown in Table 3.2) suggest that larger plants are far more productive in Japan than in the United States, but that smaller plants do better in the United States than in Japan. When this is taken together with the interindustry productivity differentials mentioned earlier, the nature of U.S.-

Table 3.2. Value-Added Productivity Differential by Size of Establishment:
Japan and the United States, 1977
(by Percentage; Manufacturing Average = 100).

Japan		United States	
Size by Number of Workers	Value-Added Differential	Size by Number of Workers	Value-Added Differential
1–3	35.4	1–4	81.5
4–9	58.3	5–9	79.9
10–19	58.3	10–19	77.6
20–29	77.6	20–49	80.7
30–49	81.2	50–99	82.1
50–99	88.6	100–249	87.5
100–199	104.6	250–499	94.1
200–299	117.3	500–999	109.5
300–499	131.9	1,000–2,499	122.1
500–999	151.3	2,500 and over	126.4
1,000 and over	164.0	*Median plant size, 356 workers*	
Median plant size, 93 workers			

Sources: Ministry of International Trade and Industry, 1977; Bureau of the Census, 1977.

Japanese economic competition becomes clear. The industries in which Japan excels in productivity are the ones associated with significant economies of scale and dynamic technological changes. They are therefore dominated by large firms and large plants. These are the industries and firms of Japan that have been taking U.S. markets away from their U.S. counterparts. It is no wonder that large firms in America's key industries are under considerable strain due to international competitive pressure. But smaller firms are not doing too badly in the United States; steel mills go under, "minimills" get by or even prosper.

Antecedents of Growth

If the above data characterize the state of Japan's productivity growth, what factors seem to have caused it? The following factors stand out as being the most important antecedents of the inter- and intranation differences.

Japanese Industrial Organization. Interplant productivity differentials of the kind discussed above reflect in part a special type of industrial organization peculiar to Japan. Due to the lack of an American equivalent, we have to refer to it by its Japanese name: *keiretsu,* which denotes a hierarchical group of firms rank-ordered according to size, bound together by strings of subcontracting relationships between larger and smaller firms, and directed or managed by the largest firm in the group. (See Sato [1980, 1985] for a number of articles on industrial organization in Japan.) The Japanese use a family metaphor to describe the vertical relationships. The leading firm is parent; the first-line subcontractors dealing directly with the parent are children; the second-line subsubcontractors dealing with the first-line subcontractors are grandchildren; and so on to the nth grandchildren. All the while the size of firm decreases from the first to the nth grandchild.

This system of vertical integration is also a chain of monopsonistic control. The parent forces its terms of purchase on the children, who force their terms of purchase on the grandchildren, and so on. In this system, the parent is the assembler or processor of the final product for the market, and the other *keiretsu* firms are producers of various stages of inputs, parts, or components. If the competitive pressure forces the parent to cut costs, that firm forces lower input prices on the subcontractors, and so on. By accident of history, the parent firm is unionized, but subcontractors are not. (The unions are also large-firm phenomena in Japan [Taira, 1970].) The parent's answer to the cost pressure is higher productivity, which in part means more capital per unit of labor. The Japanese credit system is biased in favor of large firms, so that a large parent firm can avail itself of cheap credit for greater mechanization and automation. This is also encouraged by the productivity movement. Smaller firms are short of capital, and the credit system discriminates against them. Under the circumstances, in addition to efforts to improve productivity, smaller firms must do what the parent cannot do: cut wages or keep them from rising. The cost squeeze and the pressure on wages increase as the size of firm decreases along the chain of subcontracting. *Keiretsu*, then, is a system that generates wage differentials by size of firm, commensurate with productivity differentials. (How smaller firms can get away with substantially lower wages is a complex issue [Taira, 1970].) Thus one would say that the considerable international competitiveness of large Japanese firms is supported by numerous low-cost small producers, although this is not the same as the classic "cheap labor" situation.

The distribution of manufacturing employment by size of plant is highly skewed; the 1977 Japanese *Census of Manufactures* shows that large plants employing 1,000 or more workers account for only 15 percent of manufacturing employment, while plants employing fewer than 100 workers account for 56 percent (Ministry of International Trade and Industry, 1977). This makes Japan's typical plant extremely small by international standards. For example, when the median size is defined as "that above (or below) which half the number of employees in an industry are engaged," it is 440 for Britain (1973), 410 for Germany (1970), and 380 for the United States (1972) (Prais, 1981, pp. 9-10). By this definition, our calculation from the data for Table 3.2 puts the 1977 median plant size for the United States at 356, while Japan's median plant employed only 93 persons in 1977. Subsequently, the median Japanese plant shrank further as large firms continued to cut back employment for some years. In Japan, labor productivity in the median plant is less than 54 percent of that in plants with 1,000 or more workers, as may be seen from Table 3.2. Thus it appears that low-priced parts and components produced by low-productivity labor in numerous smaller firms are collected by a small number of large firms and assembled into final products. Many of these products find their way to the U.S. consumer or final user markets.

Capital Intensity. High labor productivity in large Japanese firms and the extensive out-sourcing of their intermediate inputs are associated with other differences between Japanese firms and their American counterparts. Higher labor productivity results from higher capital intensity (more capital per worker). Extensive out-sourcing of inputs and concentration on final assembly reduce the value added by a firm as a percentage of the gross value of output. The interaction of the two tendencies may result in a lower rate of return on capital than would be the case if capital intensity were lower or more inputs were produced internally. A comparison of the financial conditions of large Japanese and American firms bears out these speculations (Itami, 1978).

Itami studied pairs of Japanese and American firms based on similarities of their products: Hitachi and GE, Komatsu and Caterpillar, and Toray and E. I. Du Pont de Nemours. (As an extra reference, he also studied Matsushita of Japan.) In 1975, none of the Japanese firms had caught up to its American counterpart in labor productivity (measured by value added per worker). GE's value-added productivity of labor was 20 percent higher than Hitachi's; Caterpillar's, 50 percent higher than Komatsu's; and Du Pont's, 70 percent higher than Toray's (Itami, 1978, p. 29). But GE's capital intensity was only 60 percent of Hitachi's; Caterpillar's, equal to Komatsu's; and Du Pont's, 90 percent of Toray's (p. 30). The ratio of value added to sales (value of output) is most telling: Hitachi's 28 percent against GE's 54 percent; Komatsu's 22 percent against Caterpillar's 51 percent; and Toray's 26 percent against Du Pont's 59 percent (p. 20). (Thus if labor productivity is measured by sales per worker, not by value added per worker,

Japan's labor productivity would be higher than America's.) The rate of return on assets also shows a predictable pattern: Hitachi's 7.1 percent against GE's 11 percent; Komatsu's 6 percent against Caterpillar's 19 percent; and Toray's 5 percent against Du Pont's 15 percent (p. 10). Itami concludes that capital is rather poorly used in Japanese firms. He considers this to be due to the inefficiency of management—a surprising evaluation contrary to popular beliefs about Japanese management.

Itami's findings are entirely consistent with what one would expect from the Japanese-style productivity movement—that is, emphasis on physical labor productivity. If we take "sales" as equal to the quantity of output times price, then labor productivity measured by sales per unit of labor is higher in the Japanese firms than in the American. This means that, assuming the same product prices, the physical labor productivity (volume of output per worker) is higher in Japan than in America. This bias in favor of physical volume may well be the result of the drive for physical labor productivity; that is, the priority for the Japanese firms has been to catch up to American productivity by this measure, and they have succeeded in attaining this objective. Along the way, however, the Japanese firms have used capital almost wastefully to raise the degree of capital intensity as a means of improving physical labor productivity. This may seem odd in a supposedly capital-scarce country. But the truth is that early on Japan found an unbeatable way of overcoming the constraint of capital shortage: the Japanese propensity to save rose to the world's highest level. A most ruthless command economy could not have squeezed more savings from its populace than Japan did almost effortlessly and without coercion. Japan's industrial policy and the productivity movement have since channeled the fast-growing savings of the nation into major firms in key industries for fastest possible capital formation and labor productivity growth.

Role of Labor-Management Relations. Market opportunities remain unexploited unless appropriate products are produced and put on the market. Likewise, best technologies remain unused unless workers are able and willing to use them. Smooth worker adaptation to new and changing technologies is a minimum requisite for the growth of labor productivity. Worker resistance to new technologies and different work rules dampens productivity growth. To management, then, the most urgent question is how to obtain a climate of labor-management relations least resistant to technological changes and a work force capable of working with changing technology.

Japanese labor in the early 1950s was not hospitable to management. Any management initiative was taken by workers as only another trick to harass them. *Productivity* was understood by workers and unions as a management code word for mass layoffs to bring about a "rationalization" of production. Consequently, worker ability and ingenuity were vastly underutilized. Although Japanese labor-management relations soon became a paragon of harmony, at which point many students of Japan naively assumed that harmony was natural for the Japanese, we do well to remember that distrust and hostility between management and labor were common in Japanese workplaces during the first ten years after the war (Shimada, 1983).

Under the circumstances, the leaders of the Japanese productivity movement were extremely careful about the industrial-relations aspects of management efforts to improve productivity. To win the support and cooperation of workers and unions, they offered safeguards against methods and results of productivity improvement that might be harmful to workers. Thus in 1955 arose the "three principles of productivity," which might be considered a sort of social contract between labor and management. These are, in condensed form, as follows:

1. . . . In order to minimize temporary frictions which may disturb the national economy, the government and the people must cooperate on suitable measures. . . .
2. In developing concrete measures to increase productivity, labor and management . . . must cooperate in discussing, studying and deliberating such measures.
3. The fruits of improved productivity must . . . be distributed fairly among management, labor and the consumer [Japan Productivity Center, 1983, p. 7].

Note that nothing is mentioned about shareholders in the third principle. In Japan, shareholders generally do not count as a party to the distribution of the firm's output. They are believed to earn far more by capital gains, which are tax-free in Japan. Labor unions were initially rather hostile to the productivity movement, but ideologically moderate unions were gradually won over to its cause. Thirty years later, in 1985, the board of directors of the Japan Productivity Center was represented by businesses, unions, JPC staff, and others as follows:

Businesses	25
Unions	14

JPC headquarters	4
Regional JPC	9
Others (largely academic)	11
TOTAL	63

Among the businesses represented on the JPC board are some of the companies and business groups of Japan that are already household words in the United States: for example, Mitsui, Mitsubishi, Sumitomo, Hitachi, Komatsu, and Nippon Steel. The unions are mostly those affiliated with the ideologically moderate Domei (Japan Confederation of Labor), entrenched largely in the private sector. Public-sector unions affiliated with Sohyo (General Council of Trade Unions) are conspicuously absent. According to the well-known pattern of union distribution by firm size, unions in Japan are principally large-firm phenomena. Thus the JPC board of directors may in effect be a mechanism for joint consultation of managers and union leaders from large firms of Japan. It is clear that the JPC is committed to the ideal of tripartism.

National Policy. The idea of a national productivity movement was proposed in 1954 by two highly respected academic leaders: Professor Kazuo Okochi of the University of Tokyo, who later became president of the university, and Professor Ichiro Nakayama of Hitotsubashi University, then president of the Central (National) Labor Relations Board and later head of a new labor-oriented educational and research organization, the Japan Institute of Labor. Okochi and Nakayama, widely respected throughout Japan (including the labor movement), were instrumental in reformulating the idea of productivity in a manner acceptable to labor.

The Japan Productivity Center formally came into being in 1955. Under a technical assistance program, the United States financially supported the fledgling JPC for several years. Hundreds of American productivity experts visited Japan to teach seminars and to lecture at symposiums. Tens of thousands of Japanese visited the United States in the 1950s to observe productivity in practice. (How the Japanese reacted to American productivity on these visits is much like the earlier experiences of European productivity teams who visited the United States under similar technical assistance programs. The European views are epitomized in Hutton [1953].) Americans taught and Japanese learned modern management techniques for management development, marketing, industrial engineering, materials handling, and so on, as well as goals and processes of collective bargaining and "business unionism."

Prior to the rise of the productivity movement at the top national level, another movement began that later reinforced Japan's drive for productivity. A Japanese Union of Scientists and Engineers (JUSE) was organized in 1946. One of its major activities was to stimulate public interest in quality control. Americans were also involved in educating the Japanese on the importance of quality control during the Occupation years, 1945–1952. During these years, thousands of young new managers were suddenly thrust into business leadership as a result of General MacArthur's "trust busting" (dissolution of giant dynastic houses of business, such as Mitsui, Mitsubishi, and so on) and the forced retirement of numerous prewar and wartime business leaders because of collaboration with the Japanese military. These new managers were at a loss as to the ways of business in the totally new postwar environment (for their apparent incompetence and lack of experience, they were then often jeered as "third-rate managers"—*santo juyaku*) and naturally receptive to any idea that might help them perform better.

Importing American Management. In 1949 and 1950, engineers from the Civilian Communications Section of the Occupation Administration helped rebuild Japan's battered communications industry (Tsurumi, 1982). These engineers, claiming that Japan needed some basic principles of modern industrial management for top management, offered the Japanese a series of seminars on these principles, covering "the policy, organization, controls, and operations of what they considered to be a model American company" (Tsurumi, 1982, p. 14). "Model" was not "actual," of course. American engineers taught the Japanese what they thought possible in an ideal company of their dreams. They also taught practical techniques, including those of statistical quality control. Soon after, Dr. W. E. Deming was invited to Japan, and the Deming Prize was established to be awarded on a competitive basis to the company with the best quality performance record. In 1954, another quality expert of America, Dr. J. M. Juran, visited Japan (Crocker, Charney, and Chiu, 1985). The Japanese government also stimulated quality consciousness: in 1949, it passed the Industrial Standards Law, under which companies meeting the quality requirements prescribed by the Ministry of International Trade and Industry (commonly known as MITI) could display a special label on their products. The Korean War, which broke out in 1950, added a further stimulus to the importance of industrial standards, because America's military procurement orders to Japanese producers required quality standards defined by the U.S. Department of Defense (Cole, 1979, p. 136).

The Quality Control Circle. As if by a magic wand, the

statistical concepts of quality control were transformed into thousands of workplace movements called *quality control (QC) circles.* Cole characterizes a QC circle as follows (1979, p. 135): "A QC circle is a relatively autonomous unit composed of a small group of workers, usually led by a foreman or senior worker, and organized in each work unit. It is in principle a 'spontaneously' formed study group, which concentrates on solving job-related quality problems, broadly conceived as improving methods of production as part of company-wide efforts. At the same time it focuses on the self-development of workers. This includes: development of leadership abilities of foremen and workers, skill development among workers, identification of natural leaders with supervisory potential, improvement of worker morale and motivation, and the stimulation of teamwork within work groups."

"Spontaneity" of the QC circle is nuanced in this description, but it is apparent that the group has acquired a kind of self-management, which power-hungry managers would resent, and a right to detect and repair deficiencies in the production process, which turf-conscious engineers would not welcome. In this form, the quality movement implies a devolution of managerial power to ordinary workers. It can become a movement for job power and shop autonomy, a rather dangerous idea that eventually might undermine managerial authority over the workplace. How to ensure that small groups active as quality circles do not become workers' tools for insubordination or sabotage but continue to concentrate on problem solving and efficiency improvement becomes a critical management problem.

The Japanese Personnel System. The Japanese knew that a balance-of-power problem existed and worked out a solution: the so-called Japanese employment system. This system offers a synthesis of two contradictions: top-down the productivity movement (which may be seen in the earlier discussion of the history of the Japanese productivity movement) and the pressure from shop-level small groups, which claim workers' power over jobs (at least in a potential sense) in proportion to their spontaneous problem-solving contributions. The objective of the Japanese employment system is to reduce the role of power, to break power down into many dimensions to be shared widely by different people. Formal strata, such as executives, managers, engineers, office staff, supervisors, skilled workers, unskilled workers, and so on, are prevented from becoming a hierarchy of power by the use of bottom-up management. In the *ringi* system, for example, power to initiate and innovate rests with the lower level of employees, while the honor of legitimizing a decision belongs to the higher level. Where quality circles are strong and effective, engineers and managers become de facto assistants to workers.

In the hierarchy of the Japanese employment system, as one rises higher one's power becomes more like the privilege to serve. Likewise, the power to rule becomes more substantive as one descends in the hierarchy, the ultimate being the self-rule of ordinary employees. In order not to let this situation degenerate into counterproductive egoism or factionalism, the Japanese company generates and maintains a company culture with an accent on consensus and cooperation. The company culture encourages individual employees to think of the company as a community, as something more than a mere aggregate of individuals. Acculturation or indoctrination is consciously applied to all company personnel. As a consequence, all employees, as members of the company community, generally think alike concerning the general interest of the company. Consensus among them easily arises, without coercion, about ways to maximize the good of the company; given the available mechanisms for fair sharing, that company benefit eventually also maximizes the individual's gains.

In this system, the overriding managerial problem is how to ensure the homogeneity of the members regarding their personal attributes and social backgrounds, so that they can think alike and perform equally well. The solution is found in careful recruitment, training, and indoctrination of the employees. The amount of care Japanese companies take in hiring new employees is legendary (Bronfenbrenner, 1985). A well-run company has a long-term personnel plan and recruits once a year, limiting hiring to the fresh graduates of a small number of select schools and colleges. The company makes efforts to attain a maximum degree of homogeneity of the new recruits regarding all conceivable personal data, such as family background, school records, native intelligence, ideological tendencies, health, aptitude, interests, taste, appearance, height, weight, and so on.

The consistent practice over many years of recruiting fresh graduates of homogeneous qualities from the same set of schools or colleges ensures the rationality of using age or length of service as a principal device to rank the employees. In addition, the permanent membership in the company is limited to male employees. A separate management system, with lower expectations for performance, applies to females. Male employees are regarded as permanent until retirement at a uniformly fixed age. Thus, between entry and exit, promotions from within according to seniority attain predictable regularity and generate a sense of equal opportunity and fair play. Because all the employees, old and young, share common educational backgrounds, promotions within the company by seniority work like promotions from lower to higher grades in schools and colleges, on the basis of credit hours earned.

In addition to recruitment, Japanese companies emphasize training and indoctrination. Fresh recruits are most carefully cared for. In Japan, every company unabashedly strives to generate and promote its own culture distinct from every other company's. Some recruits drop out at the initial stage of training and indoctrination, failing to cope with the discipline of life in the "boot camp," but the company has allowed for such attrition in its personnel plan. The recruits who survive the rigors of training and indoctrination and decide to stay are the members the company is looking for.

Training on and off the job continues throughout the company career. Permanent employees share a common pay scale and a common set of opportunities for promotions. Everyone is salaried and entitled to twice-yearly bonuses.

Because all permanent employees are members of the firm, the company makes further efforts to ensure social equality among them by various tangible devices, symbols, rituals, and customs. The well-known uniform, worn by everyone in a Japanese company, from president down to janitor, is one of them. The democratization of the parking lot on the basis of first come, first served, with no reserved space for anyone, is another. Eating in the shared canteen, socialization after hours, intense emotional expressions of gifts and concern on all humanly important occasions (birthdays, marriages, childbirths, illnesses, deaths, and so on) are also ubiquitous. These practices ensure a combination of social democracy and communal solidarity.

An observer can readily infer that in the Japanese employment system, labor unions have realized practically everything that they earlier struggled for: job security, promotion from within and by seniority, status equalization, clear rules of work and career, and so on. From an American perspective, it might appear that the company has totally capitulated. In addition, the company accepts (or perhaps co-opts) the union as a partner for decision making over a wide range of issues. A specific device for such close relationships is labor-management joint consultation, which is a machinery for joint governance with respect to all matters of interest to the employees, ranging from investment decisions to work assignments and transfers.

After labor and management have done what they can through consultation, there still remains one divisive matter: adjustment of salaries to changing (mostly increasing) fortunes of the firm. This distributional issue is the proper domain of collective bargaining, with all its implications for game play and contests of strength. This issue, more than anything else, keeps the unions alive. Workers must feel that they have won the pay increases that they deserve through tough bargaining. At least once a year, in the spring, workers and unions stage waves of offensives to win pay increases. This practice is called *shunto* (spring offensive). However, disagreements over one or two percentage points in the rate of pay increase do not wreck the basically sound relationships of trust between labor and management.

Superordinate Goal. Although one can offer all kinds of rational explanations for the Japanese employment system and the industrial peace it seems to bring about, one still wonders whether there are other forces at work. It is well known that when two adversaries suddenly bury their conflict and begin to cooperate, it is usually because a more dangerous common enemy looms on the horizon: the Hobbesian Leviathan. Faced with Leviathan, even strong adversaries agree to live with one another in an orderly society. Perhaps the United States, the target every Japanese knew Japan had to catch up to and surpass, was Japan's Leviathan. Since the catch-up mentality was everywhere throughout Japan, it is possible that the climate of industrial relations was influenced by it. Thus Japanese nationalism finally bound Japanese labor and management together. (The matter was probably not as straightforward as this remark sounds, inasmuch as the Japanese owed their democracy and union-ism to the postwar reforms promoted by the American Occupation government. The international help that revived Japanese unionism might have made Japanese unions more internationalist than nationalist. This awaits further study and analysis.)

Conclusion

The above description of the Japanese employment system is a description of a model. In the real world, varying degrees of deviations from it are expected. Even at the level of the model, one can readily see that the company policy to obtain and perpetuate employee homogeneity involves questionable principles and practices from a broader social perspective: the model is discriminatory on grounds of age, sex, ethnicity, social origin, education, and so on, and it also vastly interferes with the private lives of the employees. (These problems are discussed elsewhere [Taira, 1983a, 1985].) What is important to note is that the system is the solution that the Japanese companies and unions worked out in the wake of their earlier mutually destructive relationships.

The system works well in a context of dynamic growth of the firm, where distributional issues do not divide labor and management because the firm can afford to give what the union asks for. Under such favorable conditions, all company personnel can display a great team spirit and a positive, welcoming attitude toward new technological opportunities. The industrial-relations system then works in perfect accord with the requirements of productivity improvement. However, any system fluctuates in effectiveness over time. Indeed, the Japanese employment system worked at its best during the period of "miracle growth." Since the oil shock of 1973 drastically reduced the growth potential of the Japanese economy, the employment system has been under considerable strain (Taira and Levine, 1985).

Japan has come a long way since the "humiliation" of defeat in the last war, which was terminated by Japan's unconditional surrender to the allied powers in August 1945. Today a vocal right wing in Japanese politics claims that the war is not over; it has only changed its form from military to economic. Japan earlier disguised that war as "catching up" to advanced countries. In recent years, many public figures and intellectual leaders have discarded the disguise and begun openly to redefine Japan's international economic relations in terms of war. (Drucker [1986] apparently caught this unfortunate strain of Japanese sentiment and called Japan's trade with the United States neither free nor fair trade, but "adversarial trade," whose objective was to "beggar thy neighbor.") In this context, the productivity movement appears to have been an extension of the wartime mobilization policy.

In Europe, the productivity movement did not capture as much national enthusiasm as it did in Japan, nor did it persist as relentlessly as in Japan. One suspects that the Japanese must have attached a much larger meaning to productivity than its usual economic, instrumental one relating output to input. In Japan, it may have been a minor religious movement headquartered at the temple of the Japan Productivity Center. The gospel of this religion was national salvation, or at least restoration of Japanese pride and dignity in the eyes of the world public.

Economists may not stray far into these noneconomic analyses of productivity. But even they should not assume that Japan's sustained productivity growth over forty years has been due to what they all too facilely want to assume as causal: the market forces. It is unlikely that the productivity movement, with exclusive emphasis on labor productivity as it happened in Japan, could have sprung principally from the profit motive of business people. Nor were workers and unions drawn into it by a calculation of gains. When the productivity movement arose in the mid fifties, economists would have rejected the idea on grounds of inauspicious relative factor endowments: dire shortage of capital and overflowing labor.

Fortunately, the supply of capital needed for productivity improvement quickly expanded, thanks to an unusual upward shift in the propensity to save even when, by international standards, incomes appeared insufficient to enable anyone to save—another enigma of the Japanese economy that economists to this day have been hard put to explain by economic logic alone. Perhaps we should leave this excursion into the recent history of Japanese productivity at that level: enigma. Enigma or not, the basic fact is clear: in Japan, labor productivity has increased at an astonishing rate in the last thirty years.

References

Bronfenbrenner, M. "An Essay on Negative Screening." In T. Shishido and R. Sato (eds.), *Economic Policy and Development: New Perspectives*. London and Sydney: Croom Helm, 1985.

Bureau of Labor Statistics. *Comparative Growth in Manufacturing Productivity and Labor Costs in Selected Industrialized Countries* (BLS Bulletin #1958). Washington, D.C.: U.S. Department of Labor, 1977.

Bureau of Labor Statistics. *A BLS Reader on Productivity*. BLS Bulletin 2171. Washington, D.C.: U.S. Department of Labor, 1983.

Bureau of the Census. *Census of Manufactures*. Washington, D.C.: U.S. Department of Commerce, 1977.

Cole, R. E. *Work, Mobility, and Participation*. Berkeley: University of California Press, 1979.

Council of Economic Advisors. *Economic Report of the President*. Washington, D.C.: U.S. Government Printing Office, 1986.

Crocker, O. L., Charney, C., and Chiu, J. S. L. *Quality Circles*. New York: Methuen, 1985.

Drucker, P. "Japan and Adversarial Trade." *The Wall Street Journal*, Apr. 1, 1986.

Hutton, G. *We Too Can Prosper: The Promise of Productivity*. London: Allen & Unwin, 1953.

Itami, H. "A Japanese-American Comparison of Management Productivity." *Japanese Economic Studies*, 1978, 7 (1), 3-41.

Japan Productivity Center. *Rōdō Seisansei No Kokusai Hikaku Ni Kansuru Kenkyū* [Studies in the international comparison of labor productivity]. Tokyo: Japan Productivity Center, 1982.

Japan Productivity Center. *The Productivity Movement in Japan.* Tokyo: Japan Productivity Center, 1983.

Japan Productivity Center. *Practical Handbook of Productivity and Labor Statistics.* Tokyo: Japan Productivity Center, 1985.

Ministry of International Trade and Industry. *Kōgyō Tōkeihyō* [Manufacturing statistics (popularly called Census of manufactures)]. Tokyo: Japanese Government, annual, especially 1977.

Ministry of Labor. *Rōdō Hakusho* [White paper on labor]. Tokyo: Japanese Government, 1981–1986.

Ministry of Labor. *Rōdō Seisanei No Jittai* [The condition of labor productivity]. Tokyo: Japanese Government, annual.

Prais, S. J., and others. *Productivity and Industrial Structure.* London: Cambridge University Press, 1981.

Sato, K. (ed.). *Industry and Business in Japan.* New York: M. E. Sharpe, 1980.

Sato, K. (ed.) *"Keiretsu* and Subcontracting in Japan's Automobile Industry." *Japanese Economic Studies,* 1985, *13* (entire issue 4).

Shimada, H. "Japan's Postwar Industrial Growth and Labor-Management Relations." In *Industrial Relations Research Association, Proceedings of the Thirty-Fifth Annual Meeting.* Madison, Wis.: Industrial Relations Research Association, 1983.

Shinohara, M. *Growth and Cycles in the Japanese Economy.* Tokyo: Kinokuniya, 1962.

Shinohara, M. *Structural Changes in Japan's Economic Development.* Tokyo: Kinokuniya, 1970.

Taira, K. *Economic Development and the Labor Market in Japan.* New York: Columbia University Press, 1970.

Taira, K. "Labor Productivity and Industrial Relations in the United States and Japan." In *Industrial Relations Research Association, Proceedings of the Thirty-Fifth Annual Meeting.* Madison, Wis.: Industrial Relations Research Association, 1983a.

Taira, K. "Nichibei Seisansei Kyōsō To Nippon No Shinro" [Japanese-American productivity competition and Japan's direction]. *Ekonomisuto,* 1983b, *51* (19), 18–23.

Taira, K. "Japan's Lifetime Employment Revisited." Unpublished faculty working paper (no. 1197), College of Commerce and Business Administration, University of Illinois at Urbana-Champaign, 1985.

Taira, K., and Levine, S. B. "Japan's Industrial Relations: A Social Compact Emerges." In H. Juris, M. Thompson, and W. Daniels (eds.), *Industrial Relations in a Decade of Economic Change.* Madison, Wis.: Industrial Relations Research Association, 1985.

Tsurumi, R. "American Origins of Japanese Productivity: The

Hawthorne Experiment Rejected." *Pacific Basin Quarterly,* 1982, 7 (Spring/Summer), 14–15.

Yukizawa, K. "Changes in Japanese-United States Productivity Differentials and the Yen-Dollar Problem." *Japanese Economic Studies,* 1973, *1* (4), 33–62.

4

CECECECECECECE

Productivity Research:
Reviewing Psychological
and Economic Perspectives

Richard A. Guzzo

Concern with productivity runs deep in American society, taking up much ink and air time. Productivity causes, consequences, and statistics are debated regularly. Organizations have responded to the productivity concern in many ways, such as by creating a position of manager of productivity to initiate and oversee efforts to improve productivity. Anyone who has a stake in the economic well-being of the society has a legitimate claim to a concern with productivity.

As Mahoney points out in Chapter Two, *productivity* may mean different things to different people. We use the term with reference to things as diverse as machinery, humans, corporations, and nations. Although the exact definition of productivity differs when we apply the term to each of these entities, the definitions share a common core.

This common core is a ratio of outputs to inputs, a ratio that reflects the efficiency with which resources are transformed into outputs (for example, see Chapter Two and Kopelman, 1986a). The inputs to a productive process include costs of raw materials, quantity of human labor, and other factors. Outputs can be expressed in terms of the number of items produced, their quality, or their market value. Thus no single formula exists to assess productivity for all entities. But the logic is the same for all formulas: productive entities—whether a machine, person, or nation—yield the greatest output per input consumed.

Differing Views of Productivity: Economics and Psychology

Two disciplines—though not the only two—that have much to say about productivity in the workplace are economics and psychology.

They study productivity in different ways and at different levels of analysis. In Mahoney's terms in Chapter Two, research in economics more often concerns total-factor productivity (that is, how all inputs are transformed into outputs), while research in psychology more often concerns partial-factor productivity (how select inputs relate to outputs). Mahoney suggests that this latter focus might be best thought of as a concern with performance rather than with productivity per se. Further, economics adopts a broader level of analysis than does psychology in examining productivity. Economists' analyses of productivity are replete with measures of productivity calculated for the nation or for industrial sectors (for example, transportation, mining, farming). Psychology, especially industrial-organizational psychology, deals less with measures of national productivity and more with measures of local productivity (of individuals, work groups, and organizational units).

Complementary Connections. Psychological and economic studies of productivity complement each other. Each discipline breeds its own knowledge of determinants of productivity and, from that knowledge, makes recommendations for improving productivity. There is often surprising convergence of recommendations emanating from the two disciplines. Two examples show this.

One comprehensive, broad-brush analysis of productivity growth and improvement in the United States is the report of the White House Conference on Productivity (1984). Data from economics almost exclusively provide the basis for the report. It cites four factors determining productivity and recommends ways of acting on them to enhance productivity. The factors are capital formation, government policies, private-sector management initiatives, and the use of human resources. "Private-sector management initiatives" refers to attempts made by corporations to adopt innovative work practices (for example, increased participation, job redesign), new ways of increasing product quality, new technologies, and information management systems. "The use of human resources" refers to the securing and development of skilled, motivated workers. These two factors, workplace innovations and human resource management, are also central to the psychological study of productivity and its improvement. Research evidence pertaining to how these factors relate to productivity is summarized in this chapter.

Another example of the complementarity of economic and psychological perspectives on productivity improvement is the work of the economist Denison (1984). Denison presents a total-factor analysis of determinants of the rate of productivity growth in the United States and their relative impact. From the analysis, he recommends partial-factor changes (and projects their likely contribution to productivity improvement). These changes include increasing the amount of private investment, drawing into the labor force unemployed but able workers, removing productivity—minimizing labor agreements, reducing work days lost to labor-management disputes or sickness and accidents, and increasing use of incentives and rewards for productivity gains. Many of these changes (for example, use of incentives, minimizing absence and disruptions) are consistent with psychology's prescriptions for productivity improvement.

Characteristics of Productivity Research in Psychology

In psychological studies of productivity, there is no single theme, no anchor to which all investigations are tied. Existing psychological research on productivity is characterized by many methods, measures, perspectives, and objectives. While in many studies productivity is a primary concern, in other research productivity is a secondary concern. A study of labor-management cooperation, for example, might primarily address (1) how such cooperation is secured and (2) its effects on productivity or enjoyment of work. Consequently, more studies exist in the literature that concern productivity than just those labeled "productivity studies."

Further, studies of productivity differ greatly in their method. Some studies rely on quantitative analyses, often coupled with rigorous research designs. Others are more qualitative in nature, often involving a study of a single case. Some studies take place in contrived or simulated work settings, while others take place in existing places of work.

The range of theoretical starting points for studies of productivity is also diverse. For example, several theories of motivation exist that could provide the conceptual foundation for designing and interpreting research.

A major contribution of the psychology perspective is in the measurement of work performance and the recognition that individual output is but one component of productivity (Schneider, 1984). Categories of productivity measures common to research in industrial-organizational psychology are spelled out by Katzell, Bienstock, and Faerstein (1977). These are measures of (1) output (including quantity, quality, and value), (2) withdrawal from work (chiefly through absenteeism and turnover), and (3) disruptions (such as accidents, strikes, and grievances). This categorization is consistent with the notion of productivity as a ratio of outputs to inputs.

Measures of output, withdrawal, and disruptions are "partial"

measures of productivity. For example, output measures in psychological research usually deal with only one variable or aspect of output,
such as the quantity produced by an individual or team. Rarely is the
net value of such outputs determined. Similarly, measures of output
quality are usually recorded as changes in attributes of quality, such
as percent of products that are defective or time spent reworking
defective products. The monetary value of such changes is rarely
calculated, and even more rarely is a calculation made of the change
in the overall productivity ratio as a function of measured changes in
any one aspect of output.

The situation is similar for withdrawal measures. Absenteeism
and turnover are two forms of withdrawal generally regarded as costly
to an organization. The costs of paying absent employees and their
substitutes, and of filling vacancies made by those who left, reside in
the input side of the productivity equation. That is, the efficiency of
transforming inputs into outputs declines as these particular types of
labor-related input costs rise. Psychological research on productivity
that uses withdrawal as a criterion usually assesses neither the actual
costs of withdrawal nor the overall change in the productivity
equation related to changes in withdrawal.

Psychological research on withdrawal makes use of only partial
measures of productivity, as does research on output. The same is true
for research investigating disruptions at work. In most cases, only a
few factors in the productivity equation are assessed, but the
assumption is made that a favorable change in these factors will result
in a detectable change in overall productivity. While it is reasonable
to expect that a drop in the costs of absenteeism, for example, will
result in a change in overall productivity, there is little empirical
evidence for this assumption.

In summary, psychological research on productivity is very
diverse in terms of methods and perspectives. A conspicuous characteristic of this research is a reliance on partial measures of productivity
taken at the level of individual or unit performance. Though the
existing corpus of research is diverse, it gains some unity—perhaps
forced—by reviews of the literature. The next section reviews the recent
reviews and presents a summary account of what we know from
research about productivity and its improvement.

Conquered Frontiers: What We Know

The evidence first discussed concerns the effects on productivity
of recruitment and selection. Considered next is the impact of training
programs, followed by appraisal and feedback, goal setting, financial

incentives, participation, work redesign, work rescheduling, and large-scale organizational change efforts. These latter practices define the conditions and management style under which people work.

Recruitment. Recent research on the relationship between methods of recruitment and worker productivity has mainly concerned the contrast between the productivity of workers recruited with realistic previews of jobs versus those recruited without such previews. A realistic job preview (Wanous, 1980) is a means by which prospective employees gain accurate, authentic information about a job. Often while being recruited, applicants learn only the "bright side" (for example, highest possible salary). Such a one-sided message may ultimately lead to dissatisfaction or low performance when the reality of the job sets in.

Several reviews exist of the effects of realistic job previews on subsequent productivity. These are summarized by Premack and Wanous (1985), who provide a comprehensive, quantified review that superannuates earlier works. Premack and Wanous found a modest effect of realistic previews on job performance that depended on the method of preview: audio-visual presentations influenced performance; written presentations did not. Turnover, however, which declined as a result of realistic previews, was affected more consistently by such previews. It is noteworthy that multiple measures have been used to study the effects of realistic job previews, rather than a single component of productivity.

Kopelman (1986a) concurs with Premack and Wanous's (1985) conclusions regarding the effects of realistic previews on turnover and performance. Other reviewers (Guzzo, Jette, and Katzell, 1985; McEvoy and Cascio, 1985) reach different conclusions, having found realistic previews to have negligible effects on turnover. However, the Premack and Wanous (1985) review provides the strongest data, because it assessed the largest population of experimental studies.

Selection. Estimates of the contribution of selection and placement to productivity vary from small to huge. Estimates of the productivity payoffs can be highly conjectural, for several reasons. One is the difficulty of measuring productivity gains in a productivity-type metric. A second is the lack of systematic study of the *actual* productivity differences of people selected via a test or other instrument versus those selected on some other basis. That is, most studies are *pro*spective rather than *retro*spective. Prospective studies concern what the value of a selection device could be; retrospective studies concern the value realized through the use of a selection device.

Schmidt, Hunter, Outerbridge, and Trattner (1986) provide a retrospective study of differences in performance of white-collar employees selected years earlier by cognitive ability tests versus those selected by other means. They found that test-selected employees outperformed non-test-selected employees by just under 10 percent. This difference could translate into productivity gains worth from about $1,700 to nearly $16,000 per year per worker, depending on the job level and salary. Given the number of white-collar employees hired by the federal government each year, the gains in productivity attributable to the use of valid tests could cumulate astronomically. There are few demonstrations of selection-based productivity gains comparable to the work of Schmidt, Hunter, Outerbridge, and Trattner.

Schmidt, Hunter, McKenzie, and Muldrow (1979) provide an example of a prospective study estimating the anticipated productivity gain due to the use of an aptitude test to select computer programmers for the federal government. They calculated that a productivity gain valued at $65,000 per year per selected applicant could accrue through the use of the test. Further, if each of the hundreds of programmers hired annually by the government were selected on the basis of the aptitude test, the productivity gain in the programmer work force could be in the tens of millions annually. These estimates of the dollar value of worker productivity gains make use of new techniques for valuing employee contributions (for example, Cascio, 1982).

Overall, it appears that selection practices can contribute significantly to increased productivity (for example, Kopelman, 1986a). In most cases, this conclusion is based on a measure of some aspect of output, such as the quantity of work produced by employees. The contribution of selection practices to the enhancement of other components of productivity is less well understood.

Training. A widely used human resource practice for improving productivity is training (Katzell and Guzzo, 1983; Kopelman, 1986a). Training takes many forms. Managers might undergo training to help them become proficient in dealing with difficult subordinates, for example, or to increase their decision-making skills. People at any level in an organization might be trained to learn a new technical skill, such as how to operate a computer. Methods of training vary greatly too. Some methods involve careful modeling and practicing of specific behaviors, while other methods involve general study. Common to all training is the intent to change employees' skills, behaviors, or attitudes in a way that will enhance job performance, either immediately or in the long run.

In their meta-analysis comparing the effects of various productivity improvement programs, Guzzo, Jette, and Katzell (1985) found training to be, on average, the most powerful means of increasing productivity. The effect of training was strongest on output measures of productivity. Further, the positive effects of training were consistent across types of employees (Guzzo, Jette, and Katzell, 1985).

Burke and Day (1986) examined the effects of training on managerial employees. They examined a wide variety of methods (for example, lecture, behavioral modeling, and sensitivity training) and topics (for example, decision making, general management skills) of managerial training. Burke and Day found that, on average, managerial training improved not only knowledge but job performance. Job performance measures included cost reductions and quality and quantity of work. Overall, training thus appears to be an effective practice for improving the productivity of managerial and nonmanagerial employees.

Appraisal and Feedback. In this context, feedback is information gained about one's actions at work. Feedback can come from many sources, including the job itself, co-workers, customers, one's boss, and performance appraisal practices. Not only are the sources of feedback numerous, but so also are its media. Publicly posted data, informal remarks, and formal, structured performance review meetings with a superior are all different routes of feedback.

It has long been known that feedback is essential to the rapid and efficient learning of a new task. It is now known that feedback at work also plays a role in maintaining or raising performance in well-learned tasks.

L. L. Cummings (1982) reviewed many studies of feedback and concluded that it can improve employee productivity. Others examining the feedback literature concur. Guzzo, Jette, and Katzell (1985) found that changes in organizational practices to provide increased feedback to employees were associated with notable gains in productivity, especially in terms of the quality and quantity of output. Pavett, Broedling, and Huff (1986), updating the review of Guzzo and Bondy (1983) and Katzell and Guzzo (1983), continued to find evidence that feedback is an effective means of raising the quality and quantity of performance, as well as reducing accidents or the potential for accidents. Pavett, Broedling, and Huff note that many recent studies of feedback's effects reflect the perspective of organizational behavior modification (for example, Luthans and Kreitner, 1985). Kopelman (1986a) distinguishes between subjective and objective performance feedback—the former refers to feedback from appraisals predicated on ratings or judgments; the latter refers to appraisals that are relatively indisputable—and focuses on objective feedback. After reviewing forty-two studies of its effects, Kopelman reached the conclusion that "objective feedback is a productivity improvement technique that does not *usually* work, it virtually *always* works" (p. 185, emphasis in original). Kopelman (1986b) also reports that the results of laboratory and field research on effects of feedback on performance are quite similar, although the effects of feedback have been stronger in field research.

Goal Setting. Goal setting is an often-investigated technique applied to improve productivity at work. Although much early research on goal setting was done in laboratory settings, sundry field studies have since appeared. The results of the research—laboratory and field—are quite consistent: goal setting is a motivational technique with demonstrable productivity payoffs when output aspects of productivity are assessed, especially quantity of output (Latham and Lee, 1986; Tubbs, 1986). Output quality also seems responsive to goal-setting techniques, as do safety-oriented and accident-prevention behaviors of employees. In particular, goals that are specific, challenging, and accepted have the greatest impact on performance.

There are, however, several unsettled issues about the use of goal setting to improve performance. These include the durability of goals' effects (L. L. Cummings [1982] and Katzell and Guzzo [1983] discuss evidence that effects may fade over time) and the factors leading to goal acceptance (Latham and Lee, 1986).

Management by objectives (MBO) is a technique meant to improve productivity among managers and their units. It typically involves the establishment of agreed-upon goals or objectives to be fulfilled in a bounded period of time. It also calls for the formulation of plans for meeting the goals, monitoring of managerial performance in terms of progress toward and attainment of the goals, and appraisal and reward of managers in terms of goal attainment. Thus more in the organizational environment changes with MBO interventions than with simpler goal-setting interventions.

The success of MBO as a strategy for raising productivity, though, is less pronounced than that of goal setting. L. L. Cummings (1982), Guzzo, Jette, and Katzell (1985), and Kopelman (1986a) all cite either weaker or less frequent productivity gains from MBO than goal-setting programs. Because MBO brings about many changes in an organization, there are many possible reasons why it often fails to increase productivity.

Financial Incentives. Economists and psychologists freely prescribe financial incentives for increased productivity. But psychologists, if they rely on their literature, are likely to be fussy about how incentive programs get designed and implemented.

There is ample evidence that the use of financial incentives can lead to increased productivity (for example, see L. L. Cummings, 1982; Hatry, Greiner, and Gollub, 1981; Jenkins, 1986; Kopelman, 1986a; Locke and others, 1980; Preiwisch, 1981). However, the effects of financial incentives on worker productivity are quite variable. For example, Guzzo, Jette, and Katzell (1985) found that of eleven productivity improvement practices examined, none had greater variability in its effects than the use of financial incentives. Their conclusion was that the effects of financial incentives appear to depend heavily on the circumstances in which they are applied, a conclusion like that reached by others (for example, Hatry, Greiner, and Gollub, 1981; Heneman, 1984; Whyte, 1955).

Money can stimulate increases in quality and quantity of work as well as decreases in accidents, absenteeism, and other labor-related costs. Most frequently, financial rewards are contingent on individual performance. Sometimes, however, rewards are based on the performance of a small group or unit in an organization. Financial rewards can also be contingent on overall organizational performance. These three forms of incentive pay plans—individual, group, and organizational—all share the characteristic that the specifics of their design must fit with the organizational conditions in which they are implemented, if they are to be successful in raising productivity. Lawler (1971, 1981) provides extensive discussion of the complexities of fitting pay plans to organizational conditions.

In conclusion, financial incentives can stimulate improved productivity, if used properly. Several aspects of productivity can be affected by incentives, including the quality and quantity of output as well as withdrawal (for example, absenteeism) costs. The effects of incentives, however, are highly sensitive to situational influences.

Participation. Many organizations have instituted participative management practices as a means of enhancing both the quality of the work life and productivity of employees. Participation can take many forms—among them, worker-management councils, employee representation on important committees or other decision-making bodies, one-on-one consultation with subordinates by a manager, and suggestion systems. What does the research evidence tell us about the effects of participation on productivity?

Conclusions are mixed. Reviews by Locke and Schweiger (1979) and Schweiger and Leana (1986), for example, conclude that participative management practices are not consistently associated with productivity gains. Both reviews find, however, that participation raises employee satisfaction at work, suggesting that quality of worklife ends may be attained through participation.

Other reviewers of the literature reach different conclusions.

Sashkin (1984) and Lawler (1986), for example, conclude from the literature that participation is indeed a route to improved organizational effectiveness and strongly advocate participative management practices. The review of Guzzo, Jette, and Katzell (1985) does not focus exclusively on participation's effects on productivity. However, that review asserts that productivity gains are significantly associated with changes in supervisory practices; and frequent change in supervisory style involves a shift toward more participative management practices.

How is it that divergent conclusions exist about the effects of participation? One reason has to do with values. How one reads an ambiguous literature may reflect one's basic beliefs and attitudes about how organizations "ought" to be. A second reason has to do with the absence of a shared definition of participation. The lack of a shared definition has real consequences for how one reviews the literature. Schweiger and Leana (1986), for example, excluded from analysis "multivariate studies" (p. 150) involving, presumably, participation in which more than one aspect of managerial practice changed. For Lawler (1986), on the other hand, participation is necessarily multivariate. That is, adopting participative management practices means changing the distribution of power and information and changing reward practices, among other things. With such unreconciled views of participation, it is little wonder that divergent conclusions exist about the effects of participation on productivity.

Work Redesign. Work redesign, also referred to as *job enrichment,* is a change toward providing workers more control over the way they perform their job, increased responsibility and feedback, more activities in the job, and duties of greater significance and completeness. Several recent reviews of research on the effects of work redesign reach the conclusion that work redesign is a viable means of enhancing productivity.

Guzzo, Jette, and Katzell (1985) found that work redesign had slightly stronger effects on output aspects of productivity (for example, quality of products) and a lesser (though positive) effect on withdrawal (turnover, absenteeism) from work. Stone (1986) found that field studies revealed a moderate positive relationship between the scope (or level of enrichment) of one's job and performance on that job. However, Stone's review of the results of comparable laboratory studies was not completely in accord with those of field studies. In another review, McEvoy and Cascio (1985) conclude that job enrichment is effective in reducing turnover. The data of McEvoy and Cascio and Guzzo, Jette, and Katzell (1985) converge in showing that job enrichment is more powerful in reducing withdrawal from work than are realistic job previews. Lawler's (1986) narrative review of evidence also concludes that job enrichment enhances productivity. Kopelman (1986a), however, demurs. Nonetheless, the bulk of the evidence indicates that work redesign can be a source of improved productivity.

Work Rescheduling. Alternative schedules usually take the form of compressed work weeks or flexible daily work hours. The benefits of such practices can be substantial in terms of off-the-job considerations. Employees may be better able to manage their commuting, home, or child-care obligations with such practices than without. But do alternative work schedules affect employee productivity at work?

After reviewing many studies, Kopelman (1986a) found virtually no change in employee output attributable to the use of alternative work schedules. This was true for both compressed work weeks and flexible working hours. However, flexible working hours were found to reduce absenteeism a small amount. Guzzo, Jette, and Katzell (1985) reviewed a smaller set of studies and found that alternative work schedules had a small but positive impact on both output and absenteeism. Ralston, Anthony, and Gustafson (1985) suggest that previous research cannot provide a definitive statement about whether alternative work schedules enhance productivity. Their own study found that productivity gains could result from flexible working hours when workers had to share limited physical resources (for example, a computer). Apparently, use of flexible hours reduces wasted time during the use of shared resources.

As regards affective responses to jobs, alternative work schedules, especially arrangements permitting flexible daily work hours, clearly relate to employee satisfaction and the quality of work life (Guzzo, 1983; Kopelman, 1986a).

In summary, while alternative work schedules may have substantial off-the-job benefits, their on-the-job productivity benefits are modest at best. Evidence suggests that absenteeism can be reduced through such work arrangements. Their effect on output, however, is small and may depend on situational factors.

Organization Development. The term *organization development* here denotes large-scale behavioral science–based efforts to change organizations. Such efforts may be predicated on any of several theoretical frameworks (for example, socio-technical systems theory: Trist, 1981). Organization development often involves the application of several of the productivity programs discussed above (for example, training, work redesign, participation) and may take a long time to carry out and assess.

Evidence concerning the impact of organization development efforts is not conclusive. Guzzo, Jette, and Katzell (1985), reviewing primarily complex socio-technical interventions in organizations, found that such large-scale change efforts often paid off with significant gains in productivity. These interventions appeared much more powerful in influencing the quality or quantity of work than in reducing the costs of turnover or withdrawal.

Other evidence, though, makes for less optimistic conclusions about the effects of such change efforts. Terpstra (1981), for example, argues that how we investigate organization development interventions shapes our conclusions about their effects. Specifically, Terpstra argues that methodologically weak studies (in terms of the capacity to draw causal inferences from them) are likely to lead to the conclusion that organization development raises productivity, while methodologically stronger studies of organization development do not lead to such a conclusion. The relationship between research rigor and research conclusions has received much attention in the organization development literature. De Meuse and Liebowitz (1981) and Woodman and Sherwood (1980) discuss how conclusions about the effectiveness of team development interventions may depend on the rigor of research. Eden (1985) reports a study demonstrating that the more rigorous the research design, the less likely one is to conclude that team development enhances productivity.

In summary, evidence exists that organization development interventions can raise productivity, although this evidence often comes from weaker rather than stronger methods of research.

Summary. The available evidence indicates, beyond doubt, that individual performance/productivity improvements occur with psychologically based programs for managing human resources. Several of the programs (feedback, training, selection, goal setting, work redesign) seem quite robust in their impact on productivity. The productivity effects of other programs (realistic previews, financial incentives, work rescheduling) appear to depend on how and where they are implemented. The effects of still other programs appear negligible (MBO) or uncertain (participation, organization development).

Implications. How does the evidence just reviewed relate to national concerns about declining rates of productivity growth? The answer seems quite clear. Psychological research has identified several practices that, when implemented, improve individual performance in organizations. The more widely used these practices, the greater their cumulative contribution to productivity growth in the United States. Thus one part of the cure for ailing rates of U.S. productivity growth is the use of productivity-enhancing, psychologically based management practices.

However, I believe that the contributions of these practices to productivity improvement are often overlooked. More often than not, popular prescriptions for productivity improvement focus on national economic policies and international issues rather than day-to-day management practices. The practices reviewed here offer some options, some alternative methods of managing the workplace to improve productivity. As such, they should be available in the repertoire of each enterprise's management practices.

The practices just reviewed represent partial-factor cures to a complex problem of sustained productivity growth. The practices are by no means the only prescriptions available to enhance productivity, nor is productivity determined primarily by the things that goal setting, work redesign, training, and the like attempt to change. Productivity growth depends on several other factors, such as taxation policies, foreign trade regulations, and technological advances. The adoption of other methods of productivity improvement in no way excludes the use of the management practices described here, just as their adoption in no way excludes the adoption of those other methods.

Moving On

Where do we go from here? Having demonstrated that a variety of psychologically based management practices can raise productivity, how can we best move on to learn more? This section considers these questions, beginning by briefly commenting on the limitations of present knowledge.

Limitations to What We Know. As was already mentioned, data about productivity improvement practices are often equivocal. The equivocalness arises from two major types of deficiencies, theoretical and methodological. For example, it was noted that no widely held theory of the meaning and effects of participation exists. The absence of coherent theory is a characteristic common to other techniques for productivity improvement, such as organization development interventions. Continued research, especially research that examines contingencies between a technique's effects and situational factors at work, is essential to the development of crystallized theories of productivity and its improvement.

Methodological inadequacies also limit our knowledge. These inadequacies have many sources, such as a lack of programmatic pursuit of a topic (goal setting is an exception), poor measurement, and confounded causal variables. There is a dilemma, however, in conducting rigorous research on productivity improvement practices:

being rigorous sometimes interferes with what we try to study. Blumberg and Pringle (1983), for example, assert that the attempt to be rigorous (that is, to measure with precision, to create experimental and control groups) actually resulted in the cessation of a quality-of-worklife/participation intervention in a coal mine. Others (for example, Lawler, 1977; Lawler and Associates, 1985) also make the case that rigorous research in organizations can be unrealistic and even counterproductive. The dilemma of rigorous research in organizations is inherently unsolvable. Awareness of the dilemma, however, is no excuse for abandoning programmatic, sophisticated research on productivity improvement issues. The dilemma rather suggests that we must be flexible in our approach to conducting research in field settings.

Another limitation to knowledge comes from what is ignored in the research literature. Several practices that may contribute to improved productivity are not yet well researched. For example, the productivity impact of behavioral decision aids in organizations has not received much research attention, nor has the effect on productivity of career management practices. There are many other management practices that have psychological roots yet to be investigated for their effects on productivity.

What Is Needed to Move On? The continual cumulation of research findings is necessary to expand our knowledge of productivity and its improvement. It is essential to summarize and integrate existing data on the effects of psychologically based programs for productivity improvement. By doing so, we can experience greater certainty and more precision in our conclusions, avoid redundancy in future research, sharpen our theories, be more explicit about the comparative effects of various programs, and understand better the influence of situational factors on the impact of productivity improvement programs. This cumulation of evidence should go on at all levels of analysis and within each disciplinary perspective on productivity.

In the realm of productivity, research is needed that advances theory and practice simultaneously. Too often the primary—or only—goal of a research project is either to induce some change in productivity one way or another or to test theoretical notions about an existing intervention program. The topic of productivity improvement will not be well served by research that is either apractical or atheoretical. Needed are studies with the dual aims of helping an organization improve its productivity and helping advance our theoretical understanding of productivity.

Organizations also need to adopt more freely an experimenting attitude toward productivity research. An experimenting organization (Waters, Salipante, and Notz, 1978) is one that is systematic in its implementation and monitoring of behavioral science–based change efforts. Further, the experimenting organization gives the behavioral science researcher a part-managerial role, with responsibilities for producing beneficial consequences for the organization. Researchers must prepare to accept such a role. Simply put, a stronger joining of forces of science and practice will help advance our knowledge of productivity and its improvement.

Lastly, the need to anticipate changes in management practices is great. Innovations in managing often occur with little available theoretical or research basis—as examples, the use of skill-based pay (Lawler and Associates, 1985), job sharing, and work-at-home arrangements. Researchers should become better prepared to antici-pate future innovations that might affect productivity and investigate them as, or before, they get implemented.

The above is a short list of things needed for advancing our understanding of productivity and its determinants. What is a short list of things we should *not* spend our time doing in the pursuit of understanding productivity? This short list has only two items on it: integrating levels of analysis and defining constructs specifically.

Thomas and Brief (1984) state that research on productivity is segmented according to academic discipline (such as psychology or economics) and that each discipline pursues its own level of analysis. Measures of productivity differ greatly according to level of analysis (for example, individual versus national productivity). Further, factors that determine a firm's productivity are probably different from those that determine international differences in productivity growth rates. What damage results from segmentation according to discipline? According to Thomas and Brief, the damage is minimal in most cases. That is, each discipline has unique contributions to make to understanding productivity and its improvement. Forcing an integra-tion of the two is therefore unnecessary and probably impossible. There will be neither a grand interdisciplinary theory of productivity nor a completely circumscribed set of methods for its improvement. When it comes to productivity research and theory, let a hundred flowers bloom.

The second item on the short list of things *not* to do concerns the vagueness often inherent in psychological terms and constructs. *Participation,* for example, is a term that enjoys little agreement about its meaning. *Feedback, job enrichment,* and *organization development* are also relatively vaguely defined terms. Yet in spite of the vagueness, we know a lot about the relationships between these terms and productivity.

Kaplan (1964) argues that no terms in the behavioral sciences are without vagueness. And this is not bad, he argues. Terms need be defined only as much as is necessary to provide a usable empirical meaning. Concepts such as *feedback, job enrichment,* and *participation* do provide usable meanings. Many organizations have acted on those terms, and many researchers have investigated the consequences of those actions. Unambiguous definitions are not the starting points for inquiry, but the end points (Kaplan, 1964). As regards the study of productivity, then, we can continue to progress with vague terms; and engaging in critical definitional struggles would unnecessarily distract us from that progress.

References

Blumberg, M., and Pringle, C. D. "How Control Groups Can Cause Loss of Control in Action Research: The Case of Rushton Coal Mine." *Journal of Applied Behavioral Science,* 1983, *19,* 409–425.

Burke, M. J., and Day, R. R. "A Cumulative Study of the Effectiveness of Managerial Training." *Journal of Applied Psychology,* 1986, *71,* 232–245.

Cascio, W. F. *Costing Human Resources: The Financial Impact of Behavior in Organizations.* Boston: Kent, 1982.

Cummings, L. L. *Improving Human Resource Effectiveness.* Berea, Ohio: ASPA Foundation, 1982.

De Meuse, K. P., and Liebowitz, S. J. "An Empirical Analysis of Team-Building Research." *Group and Organization Studies,* 1981, *6,* 357–378.

Denison, E. F. "Productivity Analysis Through Growth Accounting." In A. P. Brief (ed.), *Productivity Research in the Behavioral and Social Sciences.* New York: Praeger, 1984.

Eden, D. "Team Development: A True Field Experiment at Three Levels of Rigor." *Journal of Applied Psychology,* 1985, *70,* 94–100.

Guzzo, R. A. *Programs for Productivity and Quality of Working Life.* Work in America Institute Studies in Productivity, no. 32. Elmsford, N.Y.: Pergamon Press, 1983.

Guzzo, R. A., and Bondy, J. S. *A Guide to Worker Productivity Experiments in the United States, 1976–81.* Elmsford, N.Y.: Pergamon Press, 1983.

Guzzo, R. A., Jette, R. D., and Katzell, R. A. "The Effects of Psychologically Based Intervention Programs on Worker Productivity: A Meta-Analysis." *Personnel Psychology,* 1985, *38,* 275–291.

Hatry, H. P., Greiner, J. M., and Gollub, R. J. *An Assessment of Local Government Motivational Programs.* Washington, D.C.: Urban Institute, 1981.

Heneman, R. L. *Pay for Performance.* Work in America Institute Studies in Productivity, no. 38. Elmsford, N.Y.: Pergamon Press, 1984.

Jenkins, G. D. "Financial Incentives." In E. A. Locke (ed.), *Generalizing from Laboratory to Field Settings.* Lexington, Mass.: Lexington Books, 1986.

Kaplan, A. *The Conduct of Inquiry.* Scranton, Pa.: Chandler, 1964.

Katzell, R. A., Bienstock, P., and Faerstein, P. H. *A Guide to Worker Productivity Experiments in the United States, 1971-75.* New York: New York University Press, 1977.

Katzell, R. A., and Guzzo, R. A. "Psychological Approaches to Productivity Improvement." *American Psychologist,* 1983, *38,* 468-472.

Kopelman, R. E. *Managing Productivity in Organizations.* New York: McGraw-Hill, 1986a.

Kopelman, R. E. "Objective Feedback." In E. A. Locke (ed.), *Generalizing from Laboratory to Field Settings.* Lexington, Mass.: Lexington Books, 1986b.

Latham, G. P., and Lee, T. W. "Goal Setting." In E. A. Locke (ed.), *Generalizing from Laboratory to Field Settings.* Lexington, Mass.: Lexington Books, 1986.

Lawler, E. E., III. *Pay and Organizational Effectiveness: A Psychological View.* New York: McGraw-Hill, 1971.

Lawler, E. E., III. "Adaptive Experiments: An Approach to Organizational Behavior Research." *Academy of Management Review,* 1977, *2,* 576-585.

Lawler, E. E., III. *Pay and Organization Development.* Reading, Mass.: Addison-Wesley, 1981.

Lawler, E. E., III. *High-Involvement Management: Participative Strategies for Improving Organizational Performance.* San Francisco: Jossey-Bass, 1986.

Lawler, E. E., III, and Associates. *Doing Research That Is Useful for Theory and Practice.* San Francisco: Jossey-Bass, 1985.

Locke, E. A., and Schweiger, D. M. "Participation in Decision Making: One More Look." In B. M. Staw and L. L. Cummings (eds.), *Research in Organizational Behavior.* Vol. 1. Greenwich, Conn.: JAI Press, 1979.

Locke, E. A., and others. "The Relative Effectiveness of Four Methods of Motivating Employee Performance." In K. D. Duncan, M. M.

Gruneberg, and D. Wallis (eds.), *Changes in Working Life.* New York: Wiley, 1980.

Luthans, F., and Kreitner, R. *Organizational Behavior Modification and Beyond.* Glenview, Ill.: Scott, Foresman, 1985.

McEvoy, G. M., and Cascio, W. F. "Strategies for Reducing Turnover: A Meta-Analysis." *Journal of Applied Psychology,* 1985, *70,* 342–353.

Pavett, C. M., Broedling, L. A., and Huff, K. H. "Productivity in Organizations." In J. Zeidner (ed.), *Human Productivity Enhancement.* New York: Praeger, 1986.

Preiwisch, C. F. "GAO Study on Productivity-Sharing Programs." In V. M. Buehler and Y. K. Shetty (eds.), *Productivity Improvement.* New York: AMACOM, 1981.

Premack, S. L., and Wanous, J. P. "A Meta-Analysis of Realistic Job Preview Experiments." *Journal of Applied Psychology,* 1985, *70,* 706–719.

Ralston, D. A., Anthony, W. P., and Gustafson, D. J. "Employees May Love Flextime, but What Does It Do to the Organization's Productivity?" *Journal of Applied Psychology,* 1985, *70,* 272–279.

Sashkin, M. "Participative Management Is an Ethical Imperative." *Organization Dynamics,* 1984, Spring, pp. 5–22.

Schmidt, F. L., Hunter, J. E., McKenzie, R., and Muldrow, T. "The Impact of Valid Selection Procedures on Workforce Productivity." *Journal of Applied Psychology,* 1979, *64,* 609–626.

Schmidt, F. L., Hunter, J. E., Outerbridge, A. N., and Trattner, M. H. "The Economic Impact of Job Selection Methods on Size, Productivity, and Payroll Costs of the Federal Work Force: An Empirically Based Demonstration." *Personnel Psychology,* 1986, *39,* 1–29.

Schneider, B. "Industrial and Organizational Perspective." In A. P. Brief (ed.), *Productivity Research in the Behavioral and Social Sciences.* New York: Praeger, 1984.

Schweiger, D. M., and Leana, C. R. "Participation in Decision Making." In E. A. Locke (ed.), *Generalizing from Laboratory to Field Settings.* Lexington, Mass.: Lexington Books, 1986.

Stone, E. F. "Job Scope–Job Satisfaction and Job Scope–Job Performance Relationships." In E. A. Locke (ed.), *Generalizing from Laboratory to Field Settings.* Lexington, Mass.: Lexington Books, 1986.

Terpstra, D. E. "Relationship Between Methodological Rigor and Reported Outcomes in Organization Development Evaluation Research." *Journal of Applied Psychology,* 1981, *66,* 541–543.

Thomas, A., and Brief, A. P. "Unexplored Issues in Productivity

Research." In A. P. Brief (ed.), *Productivity Research in the Behavioral and Social Sciences.* New York: Praeger, 1984.

Trist, E. L. *The Evaluation of Socio-Technical Systems.* Toronto: Ontario Quality of Working Life Centre, 1981.

Tubbs, M. E. "Goal Setting: A Meta-Analytic Examination of the Empirical Evidence." *Journal of Applied Psychology,* 1986, *71,* 474–483.

Wanous, J. P. *Organizational Entry.* Reading, Mass.: Addison-Wesley, 1980.

Waters, J. A., Salipante, P. F., and Notz, W. W. "The Experimenting Organization: Using the Results of Behavioral Science Research." *Academy of Management Review,* 1978, *3,* 483–492.

White House Conference on Productivity. *Productivity Growth.* Springfield, Va.: National Technical Information Service, 1984.

Whyte, W. F. *Money and Motivation.* New York: Harper & Row, 1955.

Woodman, R. W., and Sherwood, J. J. "The Role of Team Development in Organizational Effectiveness: A Critical Review." *Psychological Bulletin,* 1980, *88,* 166–186.

5

Industrial-Organizational
Psychology and Productivity:
The Goodness of Fit

John P. Campbell
Richard J. Campbell

The previous three chapters have provided a rather detailed look at the
meaning and measurement of productivity. The examination has been
from two different disciplines (economics and psychology), from two
different nations (Japan and the United States), and from several
different lines of reasoning. Mahoney explicates the variable from an
almost deductive perspective; Taira creates a historical account of
management-government practice relative to productivity measurement; and Guzzo infers meaning from the behavior of researchers. In
spite of these differing perspectives and the variation in methods of
explication, what emerges is not a series of qualifications to every
generalization or conclusion that might be offered. There is a
considerable amount of conceptual order and similarity, particularly
if the entire problem is "modeled" in a reasonable way. Therefore,
what we would like to do in this chapter is to look back at the previous
three chapters, work through their similarities and differences, and
then suggest a general framework for looking at productivity issues.

True to our discipline, or as good chauvinists, we would like
to characterize these issues from the perspective of psychological
measurement as it applies to *the* criterion problem in the assessment
of job performance (Dunnette, 1963; Wallace, 1965; Campbell, 1986).
We submit that the *form* of the criterion problem is the same for
economists as it is for psychologists. Likewise, it is the same for
national policy makers as it is for managers of the firm, as it is for
supervisors of a work group, as it is for chairs of academic depart-

ments. Some of the misleading conventional wisdoms are even the same. This does not imply that the *content* of the variables at the various levels of analysis is the same or that their true score correlations with other variables are the same. However, if the measurement problems are of a common form, then dealing with the specific content differences can be approached more clearly.

Some Relevant Distinctions

Before describing a common model, we would like to summarize the relevant definitional issues. First, there is a clear consensus that it is useful to reserve the term *productivity* for efficiency indices. That is, the indicator in question is a ratio of outcomes, measured in some way, to inputs, also measured in some way. Note that no supreme "authority" or definitive data base has dictated that certain ratio indicators of productivity are "valid." The judgment that they are a useful way to look at things is just that, a value judgment. The consensus has emerged from years of experience with such indicators and frequent debate about their pros and cons as aids to decision making.

Definitionally speaking, it is not necessary that measurement be in dollar terms; however, both numerator and denominator must be aggregated over the same unit of analysis. Thus a ratio of the total value of goods and services produced to the labor costs involved in producing them could be calculated for the entire economy, a particular industry, a specific organization, a work group, or even an individual. Useful comparisons across economies, industries, organizations, groups, or individuals are a function of measurement comparability across observations, which may be easier to establish for some units of analysis than others. For example, comparing the ratio of the value of total output to total labor hours for two different steel producers in the United States may be an easier measurement problem than comparing steel industries across nations or comparing the performance efficiencies of two individuals from different kinds of firms. In the former case, the two countries may have very different measurement methods for assessing industrial output. In the latter instance, it may be virtually impossible to put the performance of individuals from different organizations on a comparable metric.

Mahoney (in Chapter Two) argues that productivity ratios, as they are currently used, are legitimate for many comparative purposes, but the absolute value of the ratio is of limited meaning. That is, we have no way of determining whether a particular value for a productivity index is good or bad. When these concerns are translated into psychologists' terms, the issues become the construct validity of the productivity index and the criterion-referenced properties of the metric itself. An index would be a construct-valid measure of productivity if multiple lines of evidence, such as correlations with other variables or patterns of results over time, are in accordance with the way it is defined. Does the index measure what people want it to measure? To the extent that *expected* empirical relationships are confirmed—and to the extent that confirmed expectations are frequent, nonredundant (that is, the same prediction is not confirmed over and over again), and potentially capable of being negated by data—the more valid is a particular index as a manifestation of productivity. This is saying nothing more than that productivity is a construct and can be examined via tenets of construct validation (Cronbach and Meehl, 1955).

The criterion-referenced issue concerns how high is high or how low is low. That is, what does a particular value of a productivity ratio imply about the level of functioning of an individual, organization, industry, or economy? The answer cannot be given by comparisons to a normative distribution. The scale value must give the degree of accomplishment directly, such as when the score on a job sample measure for auto mechanic performance indicates directly the level of expertise in terms of what the mechanic is able to do. Similarly, a criterion-referenced measure of productivity would indicate directly whether a specific value for the ratio was in an optimal range, or was too high or too low. Mahoney is asserting that we do not have criterion-referenced measurement for productivity variables. So far, meaning can be inferred only from normative comparisons. It is our observation that the same is true for individual criterion measures used by industrial-organizational psychology. As much as some people long for criterion-referenced measurement for the purpose of setting standards of performance (Wigdor and Green, 1986), we are hard pressed to think of very many examples. The periodic flight checks required of incumbent airline pilots may come close, but only for ensuring minimal qualifications.

Productivity as a ratio can be contrasted with several other related variables. (Campbell, Dunnette, Lawler, and Weick (1970) explore some of these distinctions.) In the context of the individual as a unit of analysis, we can distinguish among *behavior, performance,* and *effectiveness*. Individuals exhibit lots of "behaviors" at work. They might read newspapers, trade publications, or help-wanted ads. They might trouble-shoot malfunctions in office equipment or try to fix their personal stereo sets. They might discuss work procedures with colleagues, curse and swear at their boss, or arrange social engagements for much later in the day. Behaviors are the observable things people do while at work. To avoid becoming mired in a definitional swamp, the term *observable* is used very broadly. Copying manuscripts and solving design problems are different in that the latter most likely requires considerably more silent cognitive behavior before an observable solution is produced. Nevertheless, they are both "behaviors," and their presence or absence can be recorded in some fashion. The content of performance is defined as the aggregate of those behaviors that are relevant for the organization's goals and that can be scaled (measured) in terms of the level of the individual's contribution to the goal(s) of interest. The critical incident procedure as manifested in Behaviorally Anchored Rating Scales (Smith and Kendall, 1963) is directed at performance measurement defined in this manner. That is, individual episodes of behavior judged to be critical for the organization's goals are described and aggregated into homogeneous categories of incidents henceforth labeled *dimensions of performance,* and then scaled in terms of the level of expertise the incident represents on its dimension. The term *effectiveness* is reserved for the outcomes of performance. For example, as the result of "communicating well with production supervisors" and "trouble-shooting production problems," a production manager will have an influence on the amount of production turned out by his or her unit. The amount of production is one outcome of that manager's performance, or an index of effectiveness. Again, performance is the level of expertise with which an individual executes behaviors that have relevance for one or more goals of the organization. It is what the organization is willing to pay the individual to do. Effectiveness is some aggregate of the outcomes of performance. Effectiveness outcomes are what the organization is paid to produce. Feedback about performance should be directed at the individual. Feedback about effectiveness has a broader audience and is directed at the organization as well as the individual. Effectiveness is the bottom-line result of individual performance. However, the covariance between performance and effectiveness may itself vary as a function of the degree to which the effectiveness measure is controlled by things other than the individual's performance. For example, a production manager who exhibits high performance may have a low-producing (ineffective) unit because a vendor was struck by lightning or for any of several other reasons that are not under the manager's control, such as having to depend on other managers who are not such high performers. From the organization's point of view, the trick in all of this is to (1) keep non–performance related behaviors at a minimum, (2) scale performance fairly and accurately, and (3) develop a good understanding of how the performance of individuals is related, or not related, to effectiveness. It is *not* our purpose to argue that outcome measures should necessarily be changed to make them more responsive to individual performance. They serve different purposes and should be designed to best serve them.

Mahoney uses the term *effectiveness* in virtually the same way. It is some measure of the total output, or the results of performance, of a unit, firm, or industry. It is quite possible to think of organizational behavior and performance or national behavior and performance in the same way as well. Organizations exhibit all sorts of behaviors that have varying degrees of judged relevance for their basic goals. At the industry level, dimensions of performance might be such things as the categories of operations that its equipment performs, which can be assessed in terms of equipment proficiency, or the collective actions of its sales staff. Both of these components, as well as others, contribute to the industry's effectiveness, or value of total output. Productivity is simply the ratio of effectiveness to the cost of enhancing that level of effectiveness.

Chapters Two and Three distinguish total-factor productivity from partial-factor productivity and sector productivity. Partial-factor productivity decomposes total productivity into the productivity of labor, productivity of capital, and the like. Sector productivity refers to either total-factor or partial-factor productivity assessed within various sectors of the economy, as defined by type of industry (manufacturing, agriculture, mining) or size of the firm. This is directly analogous to thinking of overall individual performance as a composite of distinguishable performance components and worrying about whether the decomposition is the same across different subpopulations of jobs (managerial, professional, skilled). The questions that occur relative to individual criterion components, such as what their relative reliability is and how they should be "weighted" in the composite, are also relevant for the components of total productivity.

Having said all this, it is clear from the Guzzo review of reviews in Chapter Four that research on productivity in industrial-organizational psychology seldom actually uses an index of productivity as a dependent variable. Research is reviewed around three types of dependent variables: (1) output measures of quantity, quality, and value; (2) the costs of withdrawal from work due to turnover or absenteeism; and (3) disruptions to work from accidents, strikes, and grievances. While outcome measures look like the numerator of a productivity ratio, and withdrawal and disruptions make sense as components of the denominator, they are virtually never combined in the form of ratios. Also, the output measures are not always output measures (*effectiveness* in our terminology). A number of studies in that category in fact used ratings of *performance* as the criterion variable, and not a measure of effectiveness, as defined above. What the interventions are being related to, then, are measures of individual performance effectiveness, or personnel costs. In terms of understanding the link between psychologically based interventions and the productivity of units, firms, or industries, it is probably better that the ratio *not* be calculated at the individual level. As is argued below, it would only obscure rather than clarify things.

Modeling Performance and Productivity

One inference that we have tried to establish so far is that while economics and psychology may use a different unit of analysis, which leads to different ingredients for a productivity index, the basic conceptual framework and the issues that attend it are very much the same. We would like to discuss briefly a synopsis of what we believe the commonality to be. The intent is to illuminate the link between the interventions of applied behavioral science and the functioning of organizations and groups of organizations as reflected in productivity measures.

First, neither individual performance nor industry productivity is *one thing*. Each of them is multidimensional, in the structural modeling sense (James, Mulaik, and Brett, 1982). There is not one factor, one ratio, or one anything that can be pointed to and labeled as job performance or as industry productivity. Mahoney rightly points out that there are many possible indices of productivity, and the choice of index is a function of the purpose for which it will be used. *The* productivity index is as much an anachronism as *the* criterion (Dunnette, 1963). It is both proper and necessary to ask how many components of each there are and what their content is. A major assumption is that the correlations among the components do not approach their respective reliabilities and that distinctive information is provided by the scores on each component.

Saying that performance or productivity is multidimensional does not preclude using just one index to make a specific personnel or policy decision. As argued by Schmidt and Kaplan (1971) some years ago, it seems quite reasonable to *scale* the importance of each major factor relative to a particular decision that must be made and to combine the weighted component scores into a composite that is the most useful one within the context of that decision. For example, with a new or inexperienced work force, the day-to-day coaching performance of a supervisor may be the most highly valued performance component in individual supervisory performance, while national electronics manufacturing productivity may be the highest priority productivity component for purposes of meeting foreign competition. The identification of the components of performance or productivity, the scaling of their relative importance, and the rules for combining them into composites to best illuminate various personnel or policy decisions are what constitute a theory of performance or a theory of productivity. The final choices about the content of the components and the rules of combination are value-dictated by the purposes of measurement and the validity of particular measures or procedures for serving those purposes. The specifications of goals or purposes are value judgments. At the level of the firm, we can call them management decisions. At the national policy level, they are political decisions. Their form is the same. As described by Taira (Chapter Three), Japanese policy has been to emphasize labor productivity and to concentrate this priority in particular sectors of the economy—namely, large producers of manufactured goods for export. The theory under which the U.S. economy has operated is somewhat different. It seems to us that there has been less attention paid to the productivity of labor and much more to stockholder equity, or capital productivity, and that there has been relatively little national debate about what our productivity model should be.

Another way of saying all this is that there is no ultimate criterion of individual, organizational, or national productivity. We should adopt whatever model of productivity best serves organizational or national goals and is supported by the available data. In our view, that model is multidimensional and makes a distinction among performance, effectiveness, and productivity at each level of analysis, whether it be the individual or the firm. The most basic variable is performance, or what can the individual or firm *do?* As a result of what the individual or firm does, what is the outcome or result? Given a particular result, how efficiently did the individual or firm achieve that level of effectiveness?

Identifying the most relevant dimensions of performance and developing valid measures of them is a continuous process of policy-capturing research (as in using the critical incident method to describe episodes of individual performance *or* organizational performance), synthesis of expert judgments about what performance *should* be, and empirical verification of the expected relationship between the measure and other phenomena.

Assessment of performance is a separate judgment from assessment of effectiveness. Our model dictates that we should be able to portray when high performance does not correspond with high effectiveness, or vice versa. If there is a disparity, it invites an investigation of the reasons and should lead to a more accurate diagnosis of why the bottom line is not being achieved. Similarly, assessment of effectiveness is distinct from assessment of productivity. Again, if there is a disparity, it invites an investigation of the cost components.

Antecedents of Performance

If performance, as defined above, is the avenue by which individuals have an impact on productivity, it might be useful to inquire about the basic antecedents of performance—or, more properly, antecedents of individual differences on each major performance factor. That is, where are the possible points of influence for industrial-organizational psychology?

For now, we would like to think about the question in a rather simple way and say that the observed level of performance on any major component of job performance is a function of six major antecedents:

1. *Abilities* or stable characteristics of individual differences, such as general verbal ability, mathematical aptitude, eye-hand coordination, or upper-body strength, that make it possible for people to learn or execute certain cognitive, psychomotor, or physical behaviors.

2. *Knowledge and skills* that are job-specific and that can be mastered over some reasonable length of time, such as four years in engineering school.

3. *Task or goal understanding* that informs the individual as to what is to be done. High ability and high skill cannot be put to use if individuals do not know what the organization wants them to accomplish.

4. The *choice to perform* controls whether or not the individual will direct effort at the task goals. That is, a very able and highly trained individual who understands quite well the task to be done may simply choose not to do it.

5. The *level of effort* expended after the choice to perform is made may also produce variation in performance. Not everyone works as hard as everyone else.

6. Finally, the *persistence of effort* expenditure over the long term may produce individual differences in performance even if ability, skill, task understanding, choice to perform, and initial effort level are held constant.

This list is not meant to be a great revelation and is certainly not original with us. We simply want to emphasize that variation in performance can *result* from changes in any or all of these major antecedents and that the causes of performance differences may not be the same for each component or factor in a multidimensional model of performance. Interactions are also possible. For example, providing clearer goals and greater understanding of what is to be done may change the choice to perform; once people truly understand the goals of a job (or some part of the job), they may want none of it, or vice versa. Interventions to enhance productivity by increasing performance or reducing the costs of performance must work through these major antecedents. Much theory and research in industrial-organizational psychology is directed at how to influence them. Are abilities used to greater advantage by a selection or classification strategy? How should training be designed to maximize skill acquisition? Are operant or cognitive models a better explanation of why effort level varies or why certain individuals choose to perform? If quality circles work, why do they work? Do they alter the choice behavior of the participant, do they result in new knowledge or skill, do they generate a higher level of sustained effort, or do they produce a better understanding of work tasks or problems?

In the best of all possible worlds of industrial-organizational psychology research and theory, the nature and content of performance would be understood and the way in which an intervention acts to increase performance would be clearly explicated. As will be seen in the following chapters, we currently have a better understanding of how some interventions work than we do of others. Much remains to be done, and a basic assumption in this volume is that toleration of the "black box" is a thing of the past. Statements such as "If it predicts, use it," or "If it works, don't worry about why," are not compatible with the scientist-practitioner model.

The Link Between Individual Performance and Aggregate Productivity

Developing a complete description of the causal links between the interventions designed by applied psychology and the productivity of the firm or industry would be a complex task indeed and might consume most of the GNP in the process. We agree with Guzzo (Chapter Four) that we can stop far short of that and still be assured that the contributions of industrial-organizational psychology are of considerable value.

Individuals can affect productivity in two major ways: by better execution of those behaviors that directly contribute to the organization's goals, and by better controlling the costs of doing so. Using a productivity ratio as a dependent variable for individuals would obscure these two causal links. The studies reviewed by Guzzo demonstrate that when the data are organized around these two contributions to productivity, the results indicate that improvement in both the numerator and denominator can be generated from industrial-organizational psychology interventions.

From the perspective of the productivity model described above, the further enhancement of productivity via personnel programs and interventions can come from several sources, including the following.

First, we need better models of performance for jobs. Developing a better model of performance means that we generate a clearer picture of the major components of performance *and* how they fit into the goals of the organization. What is it we want managers to do well? What should supervisors be able to do? Should airline pilots be "team builders"? If we don't know what a valid description of high performance is, it is difficult to plan interventions to promote it. A better performance model for major job families would better focus intervention efforts. It is still something of a mystery why we have spent so much time on models, or theories, of abilities, personality, and interests and so little on models of job performance. Hoping to find the ultimate criterion in some "objective" archival measure of individual output is not very productive.

Second, we must induce economists, organization theorists, and other interested parties to develop a renewed interest in modeling productivity according to the specifications outlined above. For example, the components of partial-factor productivity that are part of the current literature are still at a very high level of aggregation. Would it be possible to look at the latent structure of firm or industry productivity in more hierarchical terms by decomposing labor productivity into management productivity, R & D personnel productivity, engineering productivity, machine operator productivity, staff support productivity, or some other reasonable job family approach? The basic notion here is that different kinds of jobs contribute to total output in very different ways. New product ideas tend to come from certain job families; other jobs control the day-to-day quality of goods produced; and management spends a great amount of time setting objectives, working out schedules, controlling costs, and directing effort. The content of the numerator and denominator of the productivity ratio would seem to be a function of very different things for these different jobs. If we had valid indicators of these decomposed productivity ratios, intervention strategies could be tied directly to them. As Mahoney comments, the partial-factor productivity score itself could serve as a goal. To say it another way, the weights that industrial-organizational psychologists give to performance components could be tied directly to the content of partial-factor productivity ratios.

Third, the linkage of individual performance to organizational productivity is influenced to a considerable degree by the goal consensus that exists between the individual and the supervisor, the supervisor and the manager, and so on. Articulating a theory of performance and a model of productivity should reveal whatever conflict exists. If reasonable methods can be used to deal with these conflicts constructively, performance goals of the individual should be brought much closer to the productivity goals of the firm.

Fourth, job design could reorient itself toward changing job content to achieve a better match between job activities and organizational goals (except for the activities of college professors, of course). In other words, besides viewing job redesign as a means for influencing individual motivation and quality of work, let's take a very institutional point of view and try to develop a better match between the content of performance and the operating goals of the organization.

Fifth, we could do a great deal more basic research on the generic knowledge, skill, and ability requirements for basic performance dimensions. Let's try to develop some better theory about the more fundamental KSAs that determine performance in a job family. A better data base along these lines would also enhance the optimum development of intervention strategies.

Sixth, we can continue to find new and better ways of measuring and predicting relevant individual differences, matching people to jobs, teaching people new knowledge and skill, promoting more advantageous choice behavior, coordinating effort, and communicating more effectively. That is, old interventions (the independent variable) can be improved and new ones can be developed.

Seventh, the highest-payoff interventions should become an integral part of managing the business. Selection, training, goal setting, or any other intervention cannot be a "program" that is the responsibility of a consultant. Management must be induced to accept accountability for their content and their continued existence.

In all of these endeavors, there is much room for theory, for research, and for practice. Let the scientist-practitioner model bloom.

Conclusion

We hope that we have argued for a workable picture of the productivity issue, pointed to the places where industrial-organizational psychology can have an effect, and characterized what that effect might be. The following chapters will attempt to describe in more detail where the promising developments are and where we might direct our efforts in the future—whether it be in theory, research, or practice.

References

Campbell, J. P. "When the Textbook Goes Operational." Paper presented at the 94th meeting of the American Psychological Association, Washington, D.C., Aug., 1986.

Campbell, J. P., Dunnette, M. D., Lawler, E. E., III, and Weick, K. E. *Managerial Behavior, Performance, and Effectiveness.* New York: McGraw-Hill, 1970.

Cronbach, L. J., and Meehl, P. E. "Construct Validity in Psychological Tests." *Psychological Bulletin,* 1955, *52,* 281-302.

Dunnette, M. D. "A Modified Model for Selection Research." *Journal of Applied Psychology,* 1963, *47,* 317-323.

James, L. R., Mulaik, S. A., and Brett, J. M. *Causal Analysis: Assumptions, Models, and Data.* Beverly Hills, Calif.: Sage, 1982.

Schmidt, F. L., and Kaplan, L. B. "Composite vs. Multiple Criteria: A Review and Resolution of the Controversy." *Personnel Psychology,* 1971, *24,* 419-434.

Smith, P. C., and Kendall, L. M. "Retranslation of Expectations: An Approach to the Construction of Unambiguous Anchors for Rating Scales." *Journal of Applied Psychology,* 1963, *47,* 149-155.

Wallace, S. R. "Criteria for What?" *American Psychologist,* 1965, *20,* 411-418.

Wigdor, A. K., and Green, B. F. (eds.). *Assessing the Performance of Military Personnel: Evaluation of a Joint Service Research Project.* Washington, D.C.: National Academy Press, 1986.

PART TWO

Individual Differences, Motivation, Learning, and Productivity

With the conceptual and definitional work behind us, this next section attempts to examine the mechanisms of industrial-organizational psychology interventions from their most basic perspective. We have essentially three principal options: obtain people who possess the necessary qualifications (Chapter Six), induce individuals to make the right choices among alternative courses of action once they are on the job (Chapter Seven), or teach people the knowledge and skill necessary to meet the demands of the position (Chapter Eight). These three options are rooted in the three great themes of psychological research and theory: individual differences, motivation, and learning. They encompass the most basic building blocks that industrial-organizational psychology has at its disposal. They are the basis of ingredients with which more multifaceted interventions are built.

6

Recruiting, Selecting, and Matching People with Jobs

Michael J. Burke
Kenneth Pearlman

The focus of this chapter is on how the process of matching people to jobs—through personnel recruitment, selection, or classification procedures—affects individual productivity in organizations. Such procedures, which collectively can be termed *human resource allocation systems,* represent one set of methods, among many, whose purpose is to facilitate or optimize this matching process. The issue of improving the match between worker characteristics and job requirements has been described as the process common to all methods of productivity improvement in work settings (Dunnette, 1982, p. 1).

A unique aspect of approaching the issue of productivity enhancement through use of appropriate human resource allocation systems lies in the fact that such systems are fundamentally *noninterventionist* in nature. That is, they deal with the three primary elements of work systems—people, jobs, and work contexts—as they presently exist, with the goal of optimizing the fit among these elements. This strategy is premised on the assumption that the better this fit, the higher individual productivity will be.

By contrast, the perhaps more commonly recognized methods of improving productivity are essentially *interventionist* approaches. That is, they are premised on the need to change one or more elements in the work system through programs, procedures, or policies designed to improve the skill, knowledge, or motivation level of people (for example, through employee training and individual or team development programs), or to modify the requirements of jobs (for example, through redesign of equipment, work or information flow, or job content) or the contexts in which they are performed (for example, through modification of employee feedback and reward systems, reporting relationships, or work-group structures).

Thus, from a practical standpoint, a uniquely appealing feature of approaching productivity enhancement through personnel recruitment, selection, or classification strategies is that employment of such strategies typically requires little if any systemic organizational change or broad new program development. As a result, the cost and difficulty of implementing such strategies are typically substantially less than those associated with most interventionist strategies.

To give a somewhat oversimplified, but not unrealistic, example, suppose an insurance company were to replace a relatively low-validity procedure, such as an unstructured employment office interview (for example, having a validity of .14; see Hunter and Hunter, 1984, Table 9), with a relatively high-validity procedure, such as a cognitive ability test (for example, having a validity of .61; see Hunter and Hunter, 1984, Table 1), for selection of its salespeople. Also assume that the standard deviation of salesperson job performance in terms of annual dollar sales is $50,000 (Bobko, Karren, and Parkington, 1983), one out of every five job applicants is hired (in a top-down fashion based on their test scores), and the cost of both procedures is $100 per applicant (or $500 per hire).

Using formulas presented in the next section, the estimated gain in annual dollar sales per hire through use of the ability test would be $32,900. This gain would be achieved at no additional cost or processing time, and would involve no substantive change in the company's structure or operating procedures, requiring only that job applicants spend their hour in the employment office taking a test rather than being interviewed. By contrast, posthire salesperson training or development programs are likely to cost many thousands of dollars per employee in terms of salaries or fees to trainers, administrative costs, and salary and lost revenue costs of the employees being trained.

This example is not meant to imply mutual exclusivity of the two strategies, which can and should, where appropriate, be used in combination (Schmidt, Hunter, and Pearlman, 1982; Schmidt and others, 1985a, p. 769). It is merely intended to make the point that optimal recruitment, selection, and classification procedures can, *by themselves*, contribute substantially to increased individual productivity, often at comparatively little cost to the organization and typically with minimal change or disruption of existing organizational structures and processes. This fact is often not well recognized outside of the industrial-organizational psychology community; even within this community, it has not been widely appreciated prior to the publication of several empirical demonstrations (described later in this chapter) within the last ten years or so.

Discussion of the effects of personnel recruitment, selection, and classification on employee productivity involves consideration of at least four distinguishable, although related, areas of research and development: that pertaining to the measurement and description of characteristics of people (that is, research on individual differences and personnel selection procedures), the measurement and description of characteristics of jobs (the field of job analysis and job classification), methods for determining relationships or linkages between person characteristics and job characteristics (construct and criterion-related validity issues), and methods for translating the effects of formal person-job matching systems (for example, operational employee selection programs) into economic or productivity terms (the field of utility analysis).

These content areas are organized within this chapter in terms of three sections. The first section provides a brief review of the theoretical and empirical underpinnings of the person-job matching process. The second section focuses on issues confronted in operationalizing our knowledge and techniques of personal attribute–job characteristic linkages in real organizations. It consists of a review and analysis of methods for establishing the validity and utility (that is, productivity consequences) of human resource allocation systems. The third section is concerned with the limits of our current state of knowledge and practice and the types of research needed to expand these limits.

Our discussion of these subjects is cast more in terms of selection than recruitment or classification, because personnel selection historically has been the point of departure for application of most of the methodological and theoretical developments relevant to human attribute–job performance relationships that we will be considering in this chapter. Moreover, there has been little comprehensive or systematic theoretical work on recruitment until recently (Boudreau and Rynes, 1985; Rynes and Boudreau, 1986), and pure classification research and application have been mostly limited to military settings (one of the few areas where such work is both applicable and practical to conduct).

This chapter is not by any means intended to provide an exhaustive review of each of the content areas noted above. Rather, our intent is to focus on historical and recent developments that are, in our opinion, closest to the "frontiers" of the field and that have the most relevance to the issue of improving individual productivity in organizations.

Classification of People and Jobs

Fundamental to the development and application of useful recruitment, selection, and classification procedures is the need for appropriate taxonomic systems that classify and interrelate characteristics of people and jobs (Pearlman, 1980). In theory, such systems should also encompass characteristics of the work environment or context in which jobs are performed. However, with a few exceptions (for example, Wetrogan, Olson, and Sperling, 1983), there has been relatively little taxonomic research and development with respect to such characteristics (other examples and reviews of this literature are summarized by Fleishman and Quaintance, 1984, pp. 405–406). Moreover, recent meta-analytic research, discussed later in this chapter, suggests that contextual or situational variables are likely to have little impact on the relationships between many person and job characteristics. This chapter, therefore, will not explicitly address job context issues, although possible areas where they may be important will be discussed in the final section.

Historically, taxonomic research related to work performance has been carried out within the framework of either of two broad approaches, termed "the two worlds of human behavioral taxonomies" by Dunnette (1976, p. 477). One approach is concerned with the *characteristics of the worker*—that is, the underlying human attributes related to job performance. The other approach is concerned with the *characteristics of the work*—that is, the nature of the content, process, or behavioral requirements of jobs or work performance. Those adopting the former approach have attempted to define and systematize sets of human attributes (for example, abilities, skills, areas of knowledge, personality characteristics, interests, and experiences) hypothesized to be related to various types of jobs or categories of work performance. Those adopting the latter approach have attempted to define and systematize the attributes of jobs and work performance in terms either of the behaviors or processes involved or of their intrinsic properties. Extensive discussion of the conceptual and methodological issues involved in such taxonomic research is provided by Fleishman and Quaintance (1984) and by Peterson and Bownas (1982).

Each of the two taxonomic approaches noted above has produced a great deal of rigorous programmatic research. Research on human individual differences, based largely on the use of standardized paper-and-pencil measures of human attributes, has resulted in significant progress toward the definition or systematizing of a number of attribute domains. Examples include such domains as cognitive abilities (Ekstrom, French, and Harman, 1979; Guilford,

1967), physical and psychomotor abilities (Fleishman, 1964, 1972), personality characteristics (Browne and Howarth, 1977; Derman, French, and Harman, 1978), vocational interests (Holland, 1976), and life experiences (Owens and Schoenfeldt, 1979).

Similarly, job analysis and classification research has resulted in the development of a number of systematic approaches to the study of jobs and work performance (McCormick, 1979). Such research has relied heavily on the use of structured job analysis questionnaires or checklists. Examples include McCormick's Position Analysis Questionnaire methodology (McCormick, Jeanneret, and Mecham, 1972) for identifying and defining underlying behavioral dimensions of jobs; Fine's Functional Job Analysis methodology (Fine, 1955, 1986) for defining complexity of worker functions; the task characteristics approach (Farina and Wheaton, 1973) to the description of tasks in terms of a large number of variables related to the type of goals, responses, procedures, and stimuli involved in their performance; and the Ability Requirements approach (Fleishman, 1975) to the description of tasks in terms of the underlying abilities required for their performance.

Unfortunately, integrative research within each of these two taxonomic worlds has been the exception rather than the rule. For example, each domain of human individual differences has tended to be studied and treated independently, with only isolated research studies that have attempted to examine relationships among domains (for example, Costa, McCrae, and Holland, 1984; Eberhardt and Muchinsky, 1982; Neiner and Owens, 1985). Similarly, each major job analysis or job classification research program tends to reflect a particular set of underlying assumptions about the level of analysis and content or descriptive basis of the system, with few such systems integrating multiple levels of analysis or descriptive bases.

Moreover, and perhaps more critically from the perspective of this chapter, integrative research *between* these two approaches has also been the exception. That is, there have been relatively few attempts to systematically study and establish linkages between characteristics of people and jobs. Such linkages are critical, because they provide the fundamental content required for use in any human resource allocation system. That is, they specify the degree to which given human attributes contribute to effective performance and productivity on given jobs or given aspects of jobs.

An example of such a system of linkages is illustrated in Table 6.1, which shows a hypothetical matrix representing the relationship between various human attributes (columns) and various jobs or job characteristics (rows). The values in the matrix can be viewed as

Table 6.1. Hypothetical Attribute-Job
Characteristic Matrix.

	AT1	AT2	AT3	AT4
J/JC1	34	53	11	46
J/JC2	19	47	28	35
J/JC3	78	54	39	64
J/JC4	11	49	41	32

Source: Adapted from Dunnette, 1982.

representing any quantitative measure of association (for example, validities, variance percentages, covariances, expert ratings of relevance, and so on) indicative of the degree of relationship between the two.

Peterson and Bownas (1982, pp. 50-51) describe three important problems or issues encountered in developing and operationalizing an integrated attribute-job characteristic framework (like that illustrated in Table 6.1), or "job-requirements matrix," as they term it. These issues are central to our understanding of, and ability to accurately quantify, the productivity implications of personnel selection or classification systems, as will be seen in our later discussions of validity and utility.

In somewhat simplified form, these issues can be stated as follows. First, what human attribute and job characteristic categories should be included in the system? This is fundamentally a sampling issue concerning the representativeness and comprehensiveness of the system, which in turn depends on how the domain of relevant jobs or job characteristics is defined and what categories of human attributes are required to explain or predict all or most of the predictable variance in individual productivity within this domain. For example, if the job domain were defined as "supervisory," would the category of cognitive ability attributes be sufficient to account for most of the individual differences in productivity, or would inclusion of attribute categories such as temperament, interest, or knowledge enhance explanation? Such questions imply the need for information not only about the relationship between attributes and jobs or job characteristics, but about the interrelationships within and among different attribute categories and within and among different job characteristic categories.

The second issue is how general or specific these categories should be. This can be viewed as an issue of differential prediction, or the degree to which attribute-job characteristic relationships are moderated by the level of specificity with which they are defined and measured. Continuing the above example, would the relationship between a cognitive ability attribute, such as verbal ability, and different supervisory job characteristics be relatively constant (for example, like that shown for Attribute 2 across Job Characteristics 1–4 in Table 6.1) or highly variable (like that shown for Attribute 1)? If this relationship is relatively constant, it implies that the taxonomy of job characteristics is overly specific and hence less than optimal; that is, it means that the specific supervisory job characteristics included could be aggregated to a more general level of description with little loss of information (at least with respect to their relationship with verbal ability). As described in greater detail in Pearlman's (1980) discussion of taxonomic utility, the optimal resolution of this issue is the creation of a system in which person and job characteristics are defined at a level of generality or specificity such that, in a matrix such as that shown in Table 6.1, between-cell value differences are maximized and within-cell value differences (for example, representing the relationships between a given attribute and components or subcomponents of a given job or job characteristic) are minimized.

The final major issue encountered in the development of an attribute–job characteristic matrix is how the values in the matrix should be determined. This is primarily a methodological issue concerning both the process by which such values are obtained and the quantitative index by which they are specified. Broadly speaking, the methodological possibilities can be classified as being based on either direct judgment (for example, expert ratings of the degree to which individual differences in given attributes contribute to performance or productivity differences in given jobs or job characteristics) or empirical research (for example, experimental or correlational studies examining such attribute-performance relationships), with a variety of quantitative indices possible (for example, beta weights, correlation or validity coefficients, overlap estimates, probabilities, mean ratings), depending on the process used. One of the more problematic aspects of this issue, as Peterson and Bownas (1982, p. 51) discuss, stems from the previously noted fact that person-oriented and job-oriented taxonomic research have been conducted in relative isolation from one another, such that there is little in common in the methods and types of data generated from these two taxonomic worlds.

The three issues described above have been at least partially addressed in several long-term programmatic research efforts that perhaps best represent the few exceptions to the general lack of integration between person-oriented and job-oriented classification systems. These are the Ability Requirements approach developed by

Fleishman and colleagues (Fleishman and Quaintance, 1984), the research program on the Position Analysis Questionnaire (PAQ) by McCormick and colleagues (McCormick, Jeanneret, and Mecham, 1972), and the occupational classification, vocational guidance, and aptitude testing research programs of the Labor Department's U.S. Employment Service (USES: see Pearlman, 1980, for a description).

Each of these research programs has progressed and been refined over several decades. Although characterized by differences in approach, method, content, and level of analysis, they reflect the common goal of providing a unified and broadly applicable framework that interrelates characteristics of people and jobs. Other research programs sharing this goal include work by Owens and Schoenfeldt (Owens and Schoenfeldt, 1979; Schoenfeldt, 1974) on the extension of Owens's biographical data–based developmental-integrative model (Owens, 1971) of person classification (see Schoenfeldt, 1982, for a summary) and work by Cunningham and colleagues on the Occupation Analysis Inventory (Cunningham and others, 1971; Neeb, Cunningham, and Pass, 1971), an approach to person and job classification conceptually similar to the PAQ program.

The above programs vary in the manner in which they address the three major attribute–job characteristic linkage issues discussed above. For example, in terms of comprehensiveness and the generality or specificity of categories included, the Ability Requirements approach provides good coverage of human cognitive, perceptual, physical, and psychomotor abilities but excludes personality and interest domains. These attributes are linked to a very molecular level of job characteristics (that is, specific tasks), although nothing inherent in this approach precludes analysis or linkage of person attributes to more general job characteristics or even entire jobs. The PAQ attribute–job dimension linkage research (Marquardt and McCormick, 1972) was based on a fairly comprehensive set of person characteristics, but its set of job characteristics (that is, the PAQ job elements) sampled more heavily from lower-level jobs than more complex jobs. The USES approach links person characteristics (cognitive, perceptual, and psychomotor abilities, and interest factors) with jobs as a whole and job families, rather than with specific job characteristics. In terms of the issue of quantifying the relationship between person and job characteristics, all of these programs rely heavily on the use of human judgment at one or more stages of this linkage process, although empirical research data (for example, experimental and correlational laboratory studies in the Ability Requirements approach, and test validation results in the USES approach) have been used to varying degrees to supplement, refine, or confirm such judgments.

In our view, the above research programs have been more successful in addressing the problem of determining or quantifying (or developing methods to permit the determination of) attribute–job characteristic relationships (which was their primary purpose) than in addressing the issues of system representativeness or comprehensiveness and of generality/specificity of attributes and job characteristics. We view the former of these two issues as less critical than the latter, in that the representativeness and comprehensiveness of the job characteristic and attribute domains are fundamentally driven by the purpose of the system (use in human resource allocation systems, in the present context) and the scope of coverage (that is, the domain of relevant jobs) required to fulfill that purpose. That is, the attribute and job characteristic domains can be specified as broadly or narrowly as desired to suit the purpose of the system.

The issue of the optimal level of generality or specificity of attribute and job characteristic categories is more problematic and more crucial to the ultimate utility of the framework for use in human resource allocation systems. In theory, the number of cells representing potentially useful combinations of attributes and jobs or job characteristics can vary from a very few (as in the structure developed by Hunter, 1983a, which defined a matrix of three ability composites and five broad job families ordered on the basis of job complexity, for a total of fifteen cells considered sufficient to account for most of the performance variance across 12,000 jobs predictable through the use of ability measures) to an enormously large number (as in the structure proposed by Peterson and Bownas, 1982, based on a synthesis of existing attribute taxonomies and the job dimensions of the PAQ, producing a total of 2,860 cells).

It is important to recognize that this is fundamentally an issue that can be resolved only through empirical research. A significant shortcoming of most previously developed attribute–job characteristic linkage systems is that they have, by necessity, had to begin with provisional assumptions or hypotheses concerning the appropriate level of generality without a strong a priori basis for the validity of these assumptions. Yet no system developed to date has included the research necessary to test them. It is only within about the last ten years, largely through the development, application, and continued refinement of methods for cumulating research results across studies (as we discuss below and in the following sections), that research explicitly designed to address this issue (for example, Pearlman, 1982; Schmidt, Hunter, and Pearlman, 1981) has emerged.

The foregoing discussion suggests two strategies for the future that, in our view, hold the most promise for expanding the limits of previous approaches and overcoming the problems inherent in any attempts to develop an integrated attribute–job characteristic framework. The first of these strategies is what Peterson and Bownas (1982, pp. 98–99) describe as a "grand design." This essentially amounts to a massive, large-sample, predictive validation study involving all relevant attribute taxonomies, a wide range of jobs, and a number of different performance criteria. The results of such a study would, as Peterson and Bownas note, produce the fundamental attribute–job characteristic linkage data required for a human resource allocation system designed to maximize productivity within either a personnel classification context (that is, optimal assignment or matching of individuals to a set of jobs) or a personnel selection context (that is, determining which individuals are best matched to a single job).

This design has the advantages of being empirically based and permitting a high degree of methodological and statistical control of variables. Its disadvantages lie in the typically formidable practical constraints on its implementation. Despite these constraints, the major components of such a design have been operationalized in an ongoing and wide-ranging military selection and classification research program known as Project A, sponsored by the Army Research Institute (Human Resources Research Organization and others, 1984).

The second such strategy involves use of recently developed methods for the cumulative analysis of previous research results. Such methods, discussed in more detail in the following section, are known in general as *meta-analysis,* or as *validity generalization analysis* when applied to the study of attribute–job characteristic relationships. Essentially, this strategy could be used to define and quantify cells in an attribute–job characteristic matrix by cumulating the results of all available prior research on such relationships. This strategy has the advantages of being empirically based and having higher statistical power (in terms of its total sample base) than is typically attainable in any single study. Its major constraint lies primarily in the availability of relevant data for cumulation, an issue to which we return later in this chapter. The best examples of large-scale applications of this strategy are found in the recent work of Hunter on both civilian (Hunter, 1983a) and military (1983b, 1983c, 1985) occupations.

In sum, both of these strategies largely overcome the major problems inherent in previous approaches. Their methods for determining and quantifying attribute–job characteristic matrix cell values are highly controlled, rigorous, and empirically based. They are (or can be) as comprehensive in scope as allowed for by practical constraints (for the "grand design" strategy) or by the available prior research base (for the meta-analytical strategy). Perhaps most important, both strategies allow for rigorous empirical tests, and hence derivation, of the appropriate degree of generality or specificity of attribute and job characteristic categories through systematic examination of the degree to which cell values are moderated by various levels of category aggregation. Further research issues related to the application of these strategies are considered in the final section of this chapter.

Linking Personnel Selection and Productivity

The development and quantification of an integrated attribute-job characteristic matrix as suggested in Table 6.1 will provide the necessary data for optimizing personnel selection and classification decisions and, consequently, organizational productivity. In this section, we will provide an overview of validation issues related to quantifying individual attribute–job performance relationships, as well as discuss key developments and issues concerning modeling the linkage between validity estimation and utility estimation within a decision-theoretic framework. In doing so, we will emphasize empirical research (that is, correlational studies) for determining the values in the attribute–job characteristic matrix.

Validity Estimation

Within the context of the present chapter, *validation* can be viewed as the process of accumulating evidence to support the inferences from the scores on any one or a combination of personnel assessment procedures (that is, standardized paper-and-pencil tests, work samples, biographical data forms, and so on); and *validity* refers to the degree to which that evidence supports such inferences. Such inferences are typically quantified as criterion-related validity coefficients. Due to the large volume of existing criterion-related validity data on personnel selection procedures, and the need for such data in conducting decision-theoretic utility analyses (as described below), the present discussion will emphasize issues related to and results of criterion-related validation studies.

Estimating Population Validity Coefficients. Referring to Table 6.1, if we were able to assess the relationship between an attribute (predictor) and measured performance on the job characteristic (criterion) in a population of interest, with no measurement error, then we would have computed the true (population) correlation or disattenuated validity coefficient, ρ_{XY}. Because we almost never have the population available and almost always have measurement error, our observed correlation coefficients ("validity coefficients" in personnel selection) underestimate the population validity coefficients between selection procedures and job performance criteria.

In addition, it is well recognized that the statistical artifact of range restriction also lowers these estimated true relationships. Although a series of studies (Alexander, Alliger, and Hanges, 1984; Forsyth, 1971; Forsyth and Feldt, 1969; Greener and Osburn, 1979; Gross and Fleischman, 1983; Linn, Harnisch, and Dunbar, 1981a) provides a better grasp of the true (population) relationships between predictors and criteria, most of the studies examined the impact of correcting observed validity coefficients for only one factor (for example, criterion unreliability). More recently, personnel researchers have been exploring the effects of correcting correlation coefficients for both range restriction and measurement reliability (Bobko, 1983; Lee, Miller, and Graham, 1982; Raju, Burke, and Normand, 1986). Continued research in this latter area should yield valuable information concerning true predictor-criterion relationships and the sampling distribution of double- and triple-corrected correlation coefficients (that is, coefficients corrected for predictor and criterion reliability and range restriction). As will be discussed below, knowledge of such relationships will greatly enhance our determination of the practical benefits (that is, economic or productivity gains) to be realized from the use of job-related selection and placement measures.

Validity Generalization. As discussed above, personnel researchers were aware that differences between the same or similar predictor-criterion relationships were affected by statistical artifacts such as range restriction and measurement error. Only recently, however, based on the work of Schmidt and Hunter (1977), were corrections for these statistical artifacts integrated into systematic procedures for estimating the degree to which estimates of true validity for the same predictor-criterion relationship generalize across jobs and settings (Callender and Osburn, 1980; Pearlman, Schmidt, and Hunter, 1980; Raju and Burke, 1983; Schmidt, Gast-Rosenberg, and Hunter, 1980). In addition, Raju, Fralicx, and Steinhaus (1986) have proposed two validity generalization models, *covariance* and *regression slope,* which are less dependent on distributions of artifacts employed in procedures based on the correlation model. Regardless of procedure or model employed, validity generalization (VG) is the degree to which inferences from scores on measures can be generalized across different jobs or situations. The methods of assessing VG are a subset of a general class of procedures known as *meta-analysis.* Readers interested in other aspects of meta-analysis are referred to Bangert-Drowns (1986), Glass (1976), Hedges and Olkin (1985), Hunter, Schmidt, and Jackson (1982), and Slavin (1986).

A number of studies have applied the correlation-based VG procedures to selection test data for different occupations (Brown, 1981; Lilienthal and Pearlman, 1983; Pearlman, Schmidt, and Hunter, 1980; Pearlman, 1982; Schmidt, Gast-Rosenberg, and Hunter, 1980; Schmidt and Hunter, 1977; Schmidt, Hunter, and Caplan, 1981; Schmidt and others, 1979a; Schmitt and others, 1984) and for predicting first-year grades in law school (Linn, Harnisch, and Dunbar, 1981b). In addition, a number of more recent studies have presented VG results for cognitive ability tests in law enforcement occupations (Hirsh, Northrop, and Schmidt, 1986) and semiprofessional occupations (Trattner, 1985), and for alternative (that is, nontest) selection procedures (Hunter and Hunter, 1984), training and experience ratings in personnel selection (McDaniel and Schmidt, 1985), employment interviews (Whetzel, McDaniel, and Schmidt, 1985), and a paper-and-pencil clerical test used by the U.S. Postal Service to hire sorting machine operators (Schmidt and others, 1985b).

For the most part, these empirical investigations have shown that the effects of sampling error, along with between-study variation in range restriction and measurement unreliability, account for much of the observed variance in validity studies for single predictor-criterion relationships. These empirical investigations have been helpful in examining (and largely dispelling) the traditional doctrine that validities are situationally specific and, more important in the present context, in providing population validity coefficient estimates. The implications of the findings from the above empirical studies and from computer simulation studies (Callender and Osburn, 1980; Callender and Osburn, 1981; Callender and others, 1982; Dribin, 1981; Osburn and others, 1983; Raju and Burke, 1983; Raju, Fralicx, and Steinhaus, 1986) are that inferences from scores on personnel selection procedures can be generalized across situations for similar test-job combinations, as well as across jobs and broad job families, and that the results of the correlation-based VG procedures yield approximately the same results (Burke, Raju, and Pearlman, 1986; Pearlman, 1982; Raju and Burke, 1983). Researchers should be aware of continued work and critiques regarding VG/meta-analysis models and procedures (Bullock and Svyantek, 1985; Burke, 1984; Burke and Raju, 1988; Carlberg and others, 1984; James, Demaree, and Mulaik, 1986; Kemery, Mossholder, and Roth, 1987; Orwin and Cordray, 1985; Sackett, Harris, and Orr, 1986; Sackett and others, 1985; Schmidt and others,

1985a; Slavin, 1984; Spector and Levine, 1987), as well as continued applications of meta-analytical techniques to investigate the generalizability of inferences from selection procedures other than cognitive ability tests (Hough, 1987). These latter meta-analytical studies will provide useful data for further development of an integrated attribute-job characteristic matrix, as described earlier.

Utility Estimation

Translating personnel program effectiveness, typically represented by a criterion-related validity coefficient from a VG analysis or individual validation study, into economic terms has received considerable attention of late (see, for example, Boudreau and Berger, 1985; Bobko, Karren, and Kerkar, 1987; Bobko, Karren, and Parkington, 1983; Burke and Frederick, 1984; Cascio, 1982; Cascio and Ramos, 1986; Cronshaw and Alexander, 1985; Hunter and Hunter, 1984; Landy, Farr, and Jacobs, 1982; Mathieu and Leonard, 1987; Schmidt and others, 1979b; Schmidt, Hunter, and Pearlman, 1982). A substantial portion of this literature is based on applications or methodological issues related to decision-theoretic utility equations that are derived from the linear regression model. More specifically, a great deal of this work focuses on modifications to and extensions of Brogden's (1946, 1949) equations and problems of estimating components of these equations.

Following Brogden (1949), the gain in the average dollar utility of performance based on the inferences from a valid selection procedure as compared to a random selection process ($\Delta \bar{U}$) can be expressed as:

$$\Delta \bar{U} = \rho_{XY} \cdot SD_Y \cdot \bar{X} \qquad (1)$$

where ρ_{XY} is the population correlation between scores on the predictor and the dollar value of an employee's performance, SD_Y is the standard deviation of performance in dollars, and $\bar{X}$ is the mean standard score on the predictor. Equation 1 highlights the value of population (true operational) validity coefficients, discussed above, in determining the dollar implications of validated selection procedures. The basic utility equations presented by Brogden can be modified to yield gain in utility of one nonrandom selection procedure over another nonrandom selection procedure (Cronbach and Gleser, 1965; Schmidt and others, 1979b), as well as to incorporate the cost of selection (Cronbach and Gleser, 1965).

Schmidt, Hunter, and Pearlman (1982) and Landy, Farr, and

Jacobs (1982) have also modified Equation 1 in order to make it more directly applicable to organizational interventions such as training programs. In addition, decision-theoretic utility equations can be modified to incorporate the effects of discounting, variable costs, and taxation on utility estimates (Boudreau, 1983; Cronshaw and Alexander, 1985), as well as to incorporate employee movement (Boudreau and Berger, 1985; Steffy and Werling, 1985) and the effects of recruitment activities (Boudreau and Rynes, 1985). Both Schmidt, Hunter, and Pearlman (1982) and Landy, Farr, and Jacobs (1982) have also provided formulas for converting statistics such as r, t, and F to effect sizes (for use in the modified equations). As emphasized by Raju and Burke (1986), these extensions of utility analysis are significant, because they now make it possible to assess the financial contribution of many personnel strategies, in addition to personnel selection.

The Brogden-Cronbach-Gleser (BCG) model assumes that there is a linear relationship between the predictor and job performance measured in dollars. Hunter and Schmidt (1982) reviewed the available empirical evidence (Hawk, 1970; Sevier, 1957; Tupes, 1964) concerning linearity and homoscedasticity and concluded that the research findings, taken together, indicate that the linear homoscedastic model generally fits the data in the area well. According to Hunter and Schmidt (1982, p. 245), the linearity assumption, the only truly critical assumption, is particularly well satisfied. The BCG utility equations also assume that predictor scores are normally distributed. This assumption of normality is actually not needed in utility analysis research and was used by Brogden and by Cronbach and Gleser primarily for derivational convenience. In sum, the statements of Hunter and Schmidt (1982) and the relevant research findings concerning the assumptions underlying the above utility formulations are encouraging and should lead to a wider acceptance of decision-theoretic utility equations in the areas of personnel recruitment, selection, and classification.

Of the three parameters in Equation 1, $\bar{X}$ can be estimated by simply averaging the standard scores of hired (selected) applicants. For the second parameter, ρ_{XY}, it has been suggested that the corrected correlation (validity) coefficient (that is, corrected for range restriction and criterion unreliability) between the predictor and job performance typically expressed as a rating (ρ_{XR}) be used as an estimate of ρ_{XY}, the correlation between the predictor score and job performance expressed in dollars. Very little, however, is known about the assumption that $\rho_{XY} = \rho_{XR}$. The accuracy of this estimate depends upon the degree to which job performance measured in dollars (Y) is linearly related to job performance expressed as a rating (R). The tenability of the assumption of a linear relationship between R and Y has been addressed by Hunter and Schmidt (1982). They argue that departures from linearity result from rating error and are thus not a property of the underlying relationship between R and Y. That is, Hunter and Schmidt assert that ceiling effects due to leniency produce an artificial nonlinear relation between job performance ratings and the actual dollar value of performance. Also, according to Schmidt and others (1979b), the proposed estimate of ρ_{XY} based on supervisory ratings would probably underestimate the true value and therefore would lead to an underestimate of total gain in utility. This is further substantiated by Schmidt and others' (1985a) argument that correlations of mental ability tests with job sample measures tend to be larger than correlations of mental ability tests with ratings. Considering that job samples are typically more objective measures of performance than ratings, it is plausible that estimated true validity coefficients based on ratings, and hence, associated utility values, are underestimates.

The proposed estimate of the second parameter (ρ_{XY}), ρ_{XR}, as noted in the above discussion, is well understood by personnel researchers and is generally easy to obtain. That is, estimates of ρ_{XR} are generally available from the selection test validation literature. Future validity generalization analyses of selection test validation studies, for unanalyzed data bases, will add significantly to the application of decision-theoretic utility equations.

The third important parameter, SD_Y, is the most difficult to estimate in practice. In actuality, the dollar value of each applicant's job performance is needed to estimate the standard deviation. The difficulties of obtaining such an estimate are evident when one considers that some applicants are often rejected. Even when job incumbents are considered, complex cost-accounting procedures are generally believed to be needed to estimate the dollar value of each incumbent.

Recently, Schmidt and others (1979b) and Cascio (1982) have proposed practical alternatives for estimating SD_Y that do not rely on laborious and time-consuming cost-accounting procedures. The procedure proposed by Schmidt and others, which we will refer to as the *percentile estimation procedure*, estimates the dollar value to the organization of the goods and services produced by the average employee and those produced by an employee at the eighty-fifth percentile. Assuming that the dollar value of employees is normally distributed, these authors suggest that the difference between the values associated with the fiftieth and eighty-fifth percentiles be used as an estimate of SD_Y. Their procedure also calls for estimating the dollar value of an employee at the fifteenth percentile, which is then used to obtain a second estimate of SD_Y. These two estimates are averaged to produce the final estimate of SD_Y.

The Cascio-Ramos Estimate of Performance in Dollars (CREPID) (Cascio, 1982; Cascio and Ramos, 1986) proportionately distributes the annual salary for a job to each principal job activity based on a weight for each employee's job performance on each activity. These ratings are then translated into dollar values for each person's performance relative to each principal activity. The sum of the dollar values for each employee's performance on each principal activity equals the value of the employee's job performance to the organization. The standard deviation of these sums is assumed to be equal to SD_Y.

Over the last several years, there has been a great deal of empirical research concerning the measurement properties of these and modified methods for estimating SD_Y (Bobko, Karren, and Parkington, 1983; Burke and Frederick, 1984; Cascio and Ramos, 1986; Eaton, Wing, and Mitchell, 1985; Pearlman, 1985; Reilly and Smither, 1985; Schmidt and others, 1979b; Schmidt, Mack, and Hunter, 1984; Weekley and others, 1985). Although this volume of research has produced some useful insights, there have been as many new questions raised as have been answered with respect to SD_Y estimation (Bobko, Karren, and Kerkar, 1987). These new or unanswered questions are primarily related to the complexity of judgment-based SD_Y measurement issues (for example, questions concerning the dimensionality of judgment-based SD_Y estimates). Below, we will comment further on SD_Y estimation and offer suggestions for future research.

Empirical Research Related to the Estimation of SD_Y. The important development that has kindled research interest and increased the potential applicability of the BCG equations is the percentile estimation procedure proposed by Schmidt and others (1979b) for estimating the standard deviation of job performance in dollars. Using this procedure, these authors estimated the average SD_Y for computer programmers to be $10,413. Using this value for SD_Y and different combinations of selection ratio and previous selection procedure validity, they demonstrated the substantial economic impact of the decisions from a validated test on programmer productivity in the federal government and U.S. economy. In addition, Cascio and Silbey (1979) employed the percentile estimation procedure to evaluate the economic value of the assessment center as a selection device for second-level managers. Their study was instrumental in demonstrating that even decisions based on relatively costly personnel selection procedures can yield substantial economic gains.

Schmidt, Mack, and Hunter (1984) applied the percentile

estimation procedure to the job of U.S. Park Service ranger to examine the impact of differences among three selection strategies: (1) top-down selection, (2) minimum required test score equal to the mean, and (3) minimum required test score at one standard deviation below the mean. Top-down selection produced an increase in average productivity of about 13 percent. When the minimum required test score was equal to the mean, estimated economic gain was only 45 percent of that for top-down selection. Finally, the estimated dollar gain was 16 percent of the top-down result when the test cutoff score was set at one standard deviation below the mean. This study demonstrated the considerable economic implications of different personnel selection strategies.

Burke and Frederick (1986) used an interdisciplinary approach to incorporate Boudreau's (1983) utility equation modifications concerning taxation, discounting, and variable costs. They compared the total and per-selectee utility estimates for an assessment center used to select sales managers when three variations of the percentile estimation procedure, as well as 40 and 70 percent of mean salary (the range hypothesized by Hunter and Schmidt, 1982, to contain SD_Y), were used for estimating SD_Y. They concluded that for most cases, the different SD_Y estimation procedures produced similar utility estimates. The resulting estimated dollar gains from use of the assessment center to select sales managers were substantial in all cases. Furthermore, it was noted that the dollar gains from the current selection strategy were, at a maximum, only 63 percent of estimated top-down selection utility gains. These findings further established the value of decision-theoretic utility analysis for evaluating personnel programs, regardless of the type of SD_Y estimation procedure used.

In addition, Murphy (1986) has presented formulas for calculating the average ability of individuals actually selected when the proportion of initial offers accepted is less than one. Murphy demonstrated that under realistic circumstances, current utility formulas could overestimate utility gains by 30 to 80 percent. His simulated demonstrations are consistent with the work of Schmidt, Mack, and Hunter (1984) and the empirical demonstration of Burke and Frederick (1986) concerning the utility of an organization's selection strategy that departs from a top-down policy.

Much of the current research related to decision-theoretic utility equations has focused on the measurement properties of SD_Y estimation procedures and evaluations of their convergence (for example, Bobko, Karren, and Parkington, 1983; Burke and Frederick, 1984; Eaton, Wing, and Mitchell, 1985; Pearlman, 1985; Reilly and Smither, 1985; Weekley and others, 1985; see Bobko, Karren, and

Kerkar, 1987, for a review). The various SD_Y estimation procedures have produced somewhat similar results. Differences in results obtained by authors such as Burke and Frederick (1984), Reilly and Smither (1985), and Weekley and others (1985) are not surprising when one considers that for the judgment-based SD_Y estimation procedures these authors employed, the judges were often using, in addition to salary considerations (which are the valuation base for CREPID and 40 and 70 percent rules), other dimensions (Burke, Day, and Frederick, 1987). Essentially, the criterion or valuation base is defined differently for alternative SD_Y estimation procedures, and the resulting differences in SD_Y can be expected a priori for certain SD_Y estimation procedures. It is unlikely that continued efforts related to the convergence of alternative SD_Y estimation procedures will yield valuable insights. An exception to this latter statement may apply with respect to research focusing on the convergence of SD_Y estimation procedures having the same (and a clear) valuation base (for example, CREPID and 40 and 70 percent rules). We will return to the conceptual definition of the criterion below.

Where does the above decision-theoretic utility work leave us in terms of estimating the productivity implications of personnel selection programs? With respect to decision making, we are moving closer to the conclusion that the adoption of any type of personnel selection procedure having a positive validity coefficient estimate (for example, a lower bound credibility value from a VG analysis) will lead to substantial economic utility. This is considering that costs are minimal, which is the case for most cognitive ability tests. Essentially, our current utility equations and SD_Y estimation procedures are adequate for the purpose of rank-ordering the dollar impact of alternative personnel selection procedures within a specific context. The magnitude of the total estimated dollar gain, however, is going to vary depending on the type of SD_Y estimate employed, whether or not economic concepts (that is, inflation, taxation, variable costs, discounting) are incorporated in the analysis, the extent to which assumptions of the analysis (for example, top-down selection) adequately reflect the situation, and whether employee movements are considered. It is likely that further adjustments will be made as we more accurately model personnel selection contexts. For example, we have little knowledge concerning the interaction of external selection with internal selection (such as promotions or transfers) or with employee training programs (or other organizational interventions) in terms of effects on estimated utility. Similarly, research examining the impact of alternative affirmative action plans on selection utility (Hunter, Schmidt, and Rauschenberger, 1977) has been limited. Other research prospects for modeling the link between personnel selection and productivity will be discussed below.

Empirical Research on the Utility of Individual Differences in Job Performance. Both Munsterberg (1913) and Hull (1928) stressed the importance of the study of individual difference data with respect to worker output. That is, Hull was interested in the ratio of the work output of the least efficient to the most efficient worker in a variety of occupations. In essence, this ratio provided an indication of the range of job performance. For an organization with a variety of jobs, the study of such performance ratios had important implications. Most notably, jobs where the range of performance was relatively large (as indicated by a large ratio) were the most likely to benefit from personnel programs. A number of researchers have reported productivity ratios for work under nonpiecework compensation systems (Lawshe, 1948; Rothe, 1946, 1947, 1970; Rothe and Nye, 1958, 1961; Stead and Shartle, 1940; Tiffin, 1947), piecework compensation systems (Rothe, 1941, 1978; Rothe and Nye, 1959), and uncertain compensation systems (Evans, 1940; Hull, 1928; Lawshe, 1948; McCormick and Tiffin, 1974; Stead and Shartle, 1940; Wechsler, 1952).

Related to the above work on productivity ratios is the pioneering utility analysis work of Richardson (1944) and Jarrett (1948). Extending the earlier work of Richardson, Jarrett demonstrated that when performance is measured objectively, the ratio of mean production of a selected group to mean production of an unselected group can be expressed as:

$$E' = r(v \cdot \frac{z}{p}) \tag{2}$$

where E' refers to the productivity ratio, r is the validity coefficient, v represents the ratio of the standard deviation of the criterion to the mean of the criterion (the coefficient of variation), z is the ordinate of the normal curve at the point of truncation on the predictor, and p is the selection ratio. When multiplied by 100, this production ratio becomes the percentage of improvement in production. This work is noteworthy because it demonstrated that E', and consequently the percentage of improvement in production resulting from the use of a valid selection procedure, is directly proportional to the validity coefficient itself.

Recently, Schmidt and Hunter (1983) have also addressed the problem of expressing individual differences in performance output in terms of percentage increase in output. That is, they were interested in comparing the standard deviation of output (SD_p) as a percentage of mean output for a job with their predicted upper and lower bound values for SD_p. The data for their study were gathered from the studies cited above that reported performance ratios, as well as from studies that reported the mean and standard deviation of actual employee production or output. The latter included work produced under nonpiecework compensation systems (Barnes, 1958; Klemmer and Lockhead, 1962), piecework compensation systems (Barnes, 1937, 1958; Viteles, 1932), and uncertain compensation systems (Wechsler, 1952). Schmidt and Hunter's findings indicated that whenever employee output was self-paced and there was no piecework or other incentive system, the standard deviation of employee output could be estimated as 20 percent of mean output.

The practical implication of the above work is that the utility of personnel programs can now be expressed in terms of percentage increase in employee output. For example, one may be interested in expressing or projecting the utility of a personnel selection procedure in terms of percentage increase in work-force output. Substituting into Jarrett's equation for E' the following components (or alternatively substituting SD_p for SD_Y into Equation 1 above), selection utility can be expressed in terms of percentage increases in output:

$$\Delta\%\bar{U} = \rho_{XY} \cdot SD_p \cdot \bar{X} \qquad (3)$$

where $\Delta\%\bar{U}$ is the mean percentage change in utility per selectee and the other terms are as previously defined (where $\bar{X}$ is in standard score form). If one assumes a value of 20 for SD_p (the conservative figure for SD_p noted by Schmidt and Hunter, 1983), a selection ratio of .25 with top-down selection, and a validity of .4, then $\Delta\%\bar{U}$ equals 10.2. Thus one would expect approximately a 10.2 percent increase in employee output as a result of implementing the new selection procedure. Although it may be difficult to express utility gains for some jobs in terms of percentage increase in employee output, other recent developments in decision-theoretic utility analysis, discussed earlier, have increased our ability to examine the dollar productivity implications of decisions for most personnel selection programs.

The foregoing discussion raises the question of what the most appropriate metric is for utility estimation. Prior to addressing this question, it should be noted that it is SD_Y that translates the product of the validity coefficient and mean standard test score in the BCG utility paradigm (Equation 1) into the appropriate utility estimates. Thus utility estimates can be expressed in units of measured performance, percentage increases in performance, or dollars. The value of these alternative metrics is likely to depend on the type of organization (for example, service versus manufacturing), the degree to which performance can be measured objectively, and the context of the decision to be made. For example, Bobko, Karren, and Kerkar (1987), in discussing Kaplan's work (Kaplan, 1984; Kaplan and Bush, 1982), note that a more reasonable metric for expressing the impact or benefit of health programs is the number of years of life that they produce. Furthermore, they hypothesize that as the utility metric reflects organizational definitions, utility-analytical feedback to decision makers may be more accepted, more readily understood, and subject to less distortion in communication. We encourage research concerning the efficacy of alternative metrics within the same and different decision-making contexts. This suggestion is consistent with the position advanced by Rauschenberger and Schmidt (1987) that the major challenges for utility researchers lie less in the solution of remaining technical issues than in developing more appropriate and useful ways of communicating utility analysis results to organizational decision makers.

Extending What We Know

Hunter and Schmidt (1982) emphasize that the manner in which people are fitted to jobs in the economy has a significant impact on organizational and national productivity. For example, under the most conservative assumption about individual differences in job performance (that is, SD_Y as only 16 percent of mean output), they estimate that a personnel assignment strategy involving univariate selection could lead to a $13.5 billion increase in national productivity over random selection. Moreover, they stress that the estimated productivity difference between current use of univariate selection models and future use of multivariate selection models is likely to be in the range of $43 to $54 billion per year. It is thus apparent that improvements in personnel selection and classification procedures can have substantial impacts on both organizational and national productivity.

Against this backdrop, we will in this section expand our previous discussion of the validity and utility of human resource allocation systems to focus on gaps in our current state of knowledge and suggest some types of research needed to fill these gaps. In doing so, we will highlight some current trends in measurement theory and personnel selection as well as incorporate relevant advances in personality assessment.

Validity Estimation

A number of research prospects exist for raising the validity ceiling (that is, the limit on the accuracy of inferences that can be made from personnel selection procedures). Some prospects include but are not limited to the promise of computer-based testing, possible gains from additions to ability-based selection, and potential gains from development and confirmatory analyses of job performance models.

Computer-Based Testing. Over the past several decades, the use of computers in psychological assessment has steadily increased (see Burke and Normand, 1987, for a review). A particularly advantageous use of the computer in personnel selection is tailored or adaptive testing, in which a computer program adjusts the test difficulty to the ability of the examinee. A computer-adaptive test uses a multistage process to estimate a person's ability several times during the course of testing, and the selection of successive items is based on those ability estimates. Such tests are both more reliable and require fewer items than conventional paper-and-pencil tests or computerized versions of such tests. For present purposes, it is not critical to distinguish between different item-response theory models for estimating parameters in computer-adaptive testing (for example, Rasch and three-parameter logistic models; see Lord, 1980). However, the distinction between nonadaptive testing based on classical measurement theory and computer-adaptive testing based on item-response theory is important relative to the purpose of this chapter. For more technical commentaries and reviews of the adaptive testing literature, see Green and others (1984), Hulin, Drasgow, and Parsons (1983), McBride (1982), Vale (1981), Weiss (1982, 1985), and Weiss and Betz (1973).

Computer-based testing is a potentially ripe area for raising the validity ceiling via the development of new types of ability and personality tests (that is, measures of psychological constructs), as well as via the computerization of currently available conventional (paper-and-pencil) test-item banks. For example, with respect to cognitive ability tests, the computer offers unique capabilities for developing certain types of spatial and memory tests (Hunt, 1986). Improvements in the measurement of these and other important psychological constructs may push the productivity-related inferences made from various cognitive ability factors toward their threshold values for many jobs. Far too little attention has been given to applying the unique capabilities of the computer to the development of new types of items and tests. To date, little computer-adaptive testing research has been conducted in industrial settings, and, to our knowledge, only one general computer-adaptive cognitive ability test is commercially available (McBride, 1986).

Another important research issue with respect to both adaptive and nonadaptive computer-administered testing concerns cost-effectiveness. The very limited research (Budgell, 1982; Urry, 1977) indicates that this form of assessment can be cost-effective from the standpoint of standardization of adaptive testing procedures and reduced testing time. This is likely to vary as a function of an organization's size and job candidate processing flow, among other factors. However, the cost-effectiveness of adaptive or nonadaptive testing relative to conventional testing within a given organization is an empirical question to which decision-theoretic utility analysis can be usefully applied.

With respect to the computerization of conventional tests (referred to as *nonadaptive computer tests*), the limited available research on the equivalency of computer versus paper-and-pencil test results has provided partial support for the equivalence of these two modalities (Bersoff, 1983; Elwood and Griffin, 1972; White, Clements, and Fowler, 1985). It should be emphasized, however, that a high correlation (unless it is close to unity) between scores obtained through both methods is not in itself sufficient evidence for demonstrating equivalence and thus for using the norms from the conventional test. Approximately identical test-score frequency distributions in which no change in examinee rank is observed between the conventional and computerized versions would provide stronger evidence of their equivalence. This is a very important issue on which more research is clearly needed.

In sum, the potential of adaptive and nonadaptive computer-based testing for improving the cost-effectiveness of personnel selection and classification programs appears promising. Although the magnitude of possible increases in validity may not be large relative to the validity of current cognitive ability test composites (with the possible exception of validity increases resulting from the development of new types of measures, as discussed above), computer-based testing systems have the potential of being a more cost-effective and psychometrically sound means of personnel selection or classification.

Additions to Ability-Based Selection and the Development of Job Performance Models. Recently, the *Journal of Vocational Behavior*, in a special issue entitled "The g Factor in Employment," published a series of articles and commentaries on the role of general cognitive ability in employment testing. Jensen (1986) explains how the general mental ability factor, g, is derived from factor analyses of large and diverse sets of tests, and why g provides a useful operational definition of intelligence. Most relevant to the present chapter is Hunter's (1986) paper, which, based on hundreds of test validation studies (see Hunter, 1983a), concludes that general cognitive ability predicts performance ratings in all lines of work, though validity coefficients are higher for more complex jobs than for simpler jobs. Hunter also noted that only very meager gains in predictive validity are made by considering specific cognitive aptitudes above and beyond the measurement of general cognitive ability. This latter finding, as well as other evidence concerning the causal role of general cognitive ability in job performance, led Hunter to conclude that general cognitive ability is the best means for selection for all jobs where training follows hiring, which includes almost all entry-level jobs.

Hunter's conclusion is informative with respect to partially addressing (that is, at least with respect to individual ability characteristics and job performance components) the question of what the latent structure is of the true covariance matrix (as illustrated in Table 6.1) generated by the two taxonomic worlds discussed in the first section of this chapter. Hunter (1983a) demonstrates that three ability domains (general cognitive ability, perceptual ability, and psychomotor ability) are valid predictors of general job performance (proficiency) for all jobs, and that when jobs are grouped by level of complexity, differential prediction is very effective. However, even after jobs are grouped by complexity, there is some remaining within-group variation in true validity. The degree to which job characteristics other than complexity might account for additional variation remains to be systematically explored. Nevertheless, Hunter's and other meta-analysts' research provides strong evidence for the value of VG/meta-analytical methods in addressing questions related to the number of populations or subpopulations (that is, person or job characteristics) necessary to explain the nonartifactual variance in large distributions of validity coefficients.

In our view, it is unlikely that the value of the search for a relatively large number of exchangeable subpopulations (for example, large numbers of job families) to account for the nonartifactual variance in distributions of attribute-performance relationships will outweigh the costs involved. In general, the search for the best set of relevant subpopulations is often a difficult and an expensive one, and one in which the overall gain decreases rapidly as the number of variables being considered increases (Novick, 1982). For the broader purpose of maximizing the gain in personnel selection (predictive) efficiency and resultant organizational productivity, the increases are likely to be small when one considers a relatively large number (for example, greater than ten) of subpopulations. Consequently, there may be little incentive for organizations to develop complex personnel selection or classification systems. The available evidence suggests that such systems can approach optimal utility when structured in terms of fairly broad factors (that is, general rather than specific attributes and broad job families rather than individual jobs or job components).

Other potentially relevant aspects of ability-based selection have been emerging from the domain of cognitive psychology, where research on measuring the processes underlying intelligence (see Hunt, 1978; Sternberg, 1977, 1986), assessing the ability to cope with novelty (Sternberg, 1985), and assessing synthetic and insightful thinking (Gardner, 1983) has signaled a trend toward identification and measurement of a broader set of component abilities underlying intelligence. Consistent with our above comments on the development of complex selection systems, we have seen little evidence of the likelihood of such research improving predictive effectiveness (that is, beyond the level attainable through traditional general mental ability measures) in a personnel selection context. This is not to say that research on expanded conceptions of intelligence is without merit. Such work may well have important theoretical implications and lead to the development of new construct measures useful in diagnostic or educational testing.

Also relevant to the issue of magnitude of impact of individual difference variables on job performance is the issue of completeness (that is, inclusion of all relevant variables) of causal performance models. That is, our already tested causal models of performance (see Guastello, 1987; Hunter, 1986; McDaniel, 1986; Schmidt, Hunter, and Outerbridge, 1986) do not always include potentially relevant personality, interest, and situational context variables. A notable exception in this regard is the research on Project A, mentioned earlier. The question of magnitude of impact will remain open until more refined and inclusive job performance models are developed and tested. For practical purposes, the magnitude of impact of general cognitive ability on job performance will remain high and therefore can be used, based on present knowledge, for sound personnel selection or classification.

With regard to other developments that might lead to increases in predictive effectiveness within the personnel selection and classification context, recent developments in personality research would suggest exploring the central roles of the traits Negative Affectivity (NA) and Positive Affectivity (PA), as well as their corresponding mood factors (that is, positive and negative affect) (see, for example, Costa and McCrae, 1980; Emmons, 1986; Watson and

Clark, 1984; Watson and Tellegen, 1985). NA is a general and pervasive factor of subjective distress. A number of apparently diverse personality scales, including constructs variously called trait anxiety, neuroticism, ego strength, general maladjustment, repression-sensitization, and social desirability, have been shown to be measures of this stable trait (Watson and Clark, 1984). PA, a general and stable trait, reflects an individual's level of energy, excitement, and enthusiasm. The constructs of PA and NA offer promise in understanding potential interactions between personality traits and other predictors in the explication of job performance. In addition, although some research has focused on the role of NA with respect to peer ratings (Bass and Fiedler, 1961; Kaplan, 1968), improved measures of NA and PA (Tellegen, 1982) may assist in understanding the impact of NA and PA on such performance criteria as supervisory ratings in personnel selection. Consistent with Weiss and Adler's (1984) conclusions, we have barely scratched the surface of the ways in which personality constructs such as NA and PA may enter into job performance models.

In addition to incorporating personality and cognitive ability variables, causal models of job performance would likely benefit from considering the role of other individual difference variables (Hough, Kamp, and Barge, 1986), training and development experiences (Howard, 1986; McDaniel and Schmidt, 1985), organizational characteristics and reward structures (Henderson, 1985; Mobley and others, 1979), and situational opportunities and constraints (Peters and O'Connor, 1980). This suggestion is not contrary to the finding discussed earlier that situational characteristics do not significantly moderate cognitive ability–job performance relationships. It is quite plausible that individual difference variables other than cognitive ability (for example, personality), as well as other individual difference variables that might be correlated with situational context variables (for example, personal values or work attitudes), could be usefully employed in causal job performance models and prediction/selection contexts.

In addition, we note that there may be situations or jobs (for example, high-level management positions, nuclear submarine engineers) involving substantial costs (in terms of the consequence of error) and benefits of individual performance where noncognitive predictors or situational context variables have substantial relevance. Consideration of such possibilities is constrained by the scope of existing VG analyses and results (which primarily encompass ability measures used in selection for less than high-level jobs or for relatively populous occupations) and by our limited knowledge base concerning intercorrelations among diverse types of individual difference variables, as well as the relationship between situational characteristics and individual difference variables. There is thus a clear need for more VG/meta-analytical research on nonability performance predictors, primary studies of predictors on which there exist insufficient data for cumulation, and further development and confirmatory analyses of causal job performance models.

Utility Estimation

As with validity estimation, a number of research directions exist for enhancing our understanding of the economic gains of sound personnel selection and classification systems. In addition to the prospects noted above, we will briefly discuss research possibilities concerned with defining the economic value of individual performance, and developing or refining utility models and equations to overcome problems with SD_Y and to model complex recruitment/selection/classification processes and decisions.

SD_Y *Research.* Research to date has yielded some interesting findings concerning alternative SD_Y estimation procedures and greatly increased interest in and awareness of the economic value of personnel programs. However, the conceptual definition of the value of individual performance, and hence the accuracy of procedures for estimating the variability of individual performance values (and consequently personnel program utility), has remained a subject of debate (see comments of Cascio, 1986; Schmidt, 1986; Steffy and Maurer, 1986). For example, Schmidt (1986) has pointed out that certain SD_Y estimation procedures (for example, CREPID) do not conform to the conceptual definition of SD_Y (embodied in the BCG paradigm) that the value of an employee's output is its value as sold. Steffy and Maurer have also provided some insightful comments concerning the issue of economic value of performance from individual, job, institutional, and market levels of analysis. That is, they note that both labor economists and accountants suggest that economic value is principally embodied not in individuals but in the job, its value defined by wages and other labor costs (opportunity costs) required to obtain some base rate of "successful" job performance. Their work represents a noteworthy step with respect to integrating what are sometimes conflicting views of labor economics, accounting, and industrial-organizational psychology. Continued discourse with respect to the comments offered by Steffy and Maurer is likely to clarify the appropriateness of current SD_Y estimates for various purposes, as well as assist in efforts to define and measure the economic value of individual performance. Clarification of the appropriateness of alternative conceptual definitions of the economic value of individual performance will be helpful.

Another important step in utility estimation is that we move toward establishing systematic linkages between job or job family taxonomies and SD_Y values. It may be possible to construct a matrix with jobs or job families as the columns and alternative utility metrics (discussed earlier) as the rows and examine the extent to which we can group jobs for the same metric. Such a matrix may also have alternative SD_Y estimation procedures as rows, if these procedures are to be considered as conceptually distinct. A job-utility metric matrix would also highlight jobs or job families for which an alternative metric (that is, other than dollars) is more appropriate. Derivation of values for such a matrix would provide valuable information in terms of future research related to estimating system (that is, total departmental or organizational) utilities, as well as for exploring issues related to the generalization (across jobs or situations) of selection utility estimates.

Nevertheless, there is sound evidence, as noted earlier, that regardless of how we define and estimate SD_Y with current procedures, we will invariably obtain an SD_Y value that leads to correct decisions (Boudreau, 1984; Burke and Frederick, 1986). Boudreau (1984) notes that it may not always be necessary to obtain exact or even approximate SD_Y estimates in order to make accurate decisions regarding alternative personnel programs. Instead of estimating the level of expected utility for each alternative program, he suggests focusing on the identification of "break-even" values (that is, minimum SD_Y values for utility gain to meet the costs associated with a selection program) that are critical to making decisions. While we strongly agree that break-even analysis offers a useful framework for practical decision making in many situations, we also view as worthwhile continued efforts toward improving the accuracy with which we can evaluate the utility of personnel/human resource programs.

Utility Model and Equation Development/Refinement. One promising development that may circumvent estimating the most problematic component of current utility equations, SD_Y, is a utility analysis approach recently developed by Raju, Burke, and Normand (1987). These researchers propose expected utility equations for personnel selection programs, as well as for organizational interventions, that do not rely on SD_Y. Their approach is based on the assumption that the relationship between job performance expressed as an overall (weighted or unweighted) rating (R) and the dollar value of an employee's job performance (Y) is linear. Algebraically, this relationship can be expressed as:

$$Y = (A \cdot R) + B \tag{4}$$

where A and B are the multiplicative and additive constants, respectively. Prior to addressing the question of the meaning and estimation of A and B, several important features of Equation 4 will be noted. First, Equation 4 implies that Y and R measure the same construct but expressed in different units. Second, Equation 4 also implies that the correlation between the predictor score and job performance expressed as a rating and the correlation between the predictor score and the dollar value of an employee's job performance are equal; that is, $\rho_{XR} = \rho_{XY}$. This equality is assumed in Brogden's utility model, whereas here it follows directly from Equation 4. Third, the standard deviation of Y can be expressed as:

$$SD_Y = A \cdot SD_R \tag{5}$$

which has important practical implications for this proposed approach. Additional significant consequences of the assumptions embodied in Equation 5 are explored by Raju, Burke, and Normand (1987).

In contrast to the BCG equations, where one needs to know SD_Y, application of Equations 4 and 5 depends upon knowing A. Related to estimating the new component, A, of this utility approach, Raju, Burke, and Normand (1987) note that current SD_Y estimation procedures, as well as the economic and accounting literatures, offer useful ways of defining and measuring A. In particular, these authors stress that economic and accounting theory valuation concepts can be more easily incorporated within the context of their approach, because the focus is no longer on SD_Y but on measuring A, which can be more directly linked to the job's contribution to the productivity of the organization. The estimation of SD_Y focuses on measuring the variability in the dollar value of individual employee performance, whereas the proposed formulation would transform measured performance to a dollar (or other) metric by the use of the constant A, representing the job's contribution to productivity. In this regard, the product of $A\ SD_R$ (standard deviation of measured performance) is similar to the CREPID SD_Y estimate. However, in this approach A does not need to be defined as mean salary. Future research on the usefulness of accounting and economic concepts in defining and estimating A would be enlightening. This notion of an interdisciplinary approach to utility analysis is consistent with the recent arguments of Cascio and Silbey (1979), Boudreau (1984), and Burke and Frederick (1986). It should also be noted that this approach presents a common framework for studying the convergence/divergence of the results of current procedures for estimating SD_Y. In particular, it offers the promise of clarifying discrepancies in obtained results between CREPID and 40 and 70 percent salary rules for estimating SD_Y.

Extensions by Boudreau and Berger (1985) within the current decision-theoretic utility analysis framework have also added significantly to our ability to describe the consequences of employee movements into and out of an organization (that is, acquisitions and separations). The significant utility work of Schmidt, Hunter, and Pearlman (1982) and Boudreau and Berger has made it possible to model, in addition to personnel selection, the effects of other organizational interventions or human resource programs for a single job. Recently, Ledvinka and Ladd (1987) have proposed a multiple-job approach (and computer simulation) for estimating utility of departments or entire organizations. Their utility modeling is an important development in estimating utility when one is examining more than single programs for one job. As Ledvinka and Ladd (1987) conclude, "Human resource programs are interdependent; altering the utility of one affects the utility of others. A true assessment of the value of human resource programs must take those interdependencies into account" (p. 32). We look forward to forthcoming research on the above models and refinements and encourage innovations in utility analytic work to model institutional and market factors (see, for example, Bergmann and Martin, 1987) as well as system dynamics and time-related factors (see Steffy and Maurer, 1986).

Conclusion

Research in industrial-organizational psychology has contributed substantially to individual and organizational productivity enhancement through progressive development of the attribute(predictor)–performance relationship knowledge base and by providing a set of utility-analytical procedures for translating the inferences from this knowledge base into understandable metrics (that is, dollar gains, percentage improvements, and so on) useful for practical decision-making purposes. Numerous research prospects concerning the potential future contribution of selection research to productivity enhancement were discussed. Our future success as personnel researchers will be largely a function of the extent to which we can continue to translate the results of such research into improved conceptions, calculations, and communication of validity and productivity outcomes.

References

Alexander, R. A., Alliger, G. M., and Hanges, P. J. "Correcting for Range Restriction When the Population Variance Is Unknown." *Applied Psychological Measurement*, 1984, *8*, 431-437.

Bangert-Drowns, R. L. "Review of Developments in Meta-Analytic Method." *Psychological Bulletin*, 1986, *99*, 388-399.

Barnes, R. M. *Time and Motion Study*. New York: Wiley, 1937.

Barnes, R. M. *Time and Motion Study*. (2nd ed.) New York: Wiley, 1958.

Bass, A. R., and Fiedler, F. E. "Interpersonal Perception Scores and Their Components as Predictors of Personal Adjustment." *Journal of Abnormal and Social Psychology*, 1961, *62*, 442-445.

Bergmann, T. J., and Martin, G. E. "Optimal Large-Scale Manpower Recruitment Policies." *Human Resource Planning*, 1987, *10*, 93-101.

Bersoff, D. N. *A Rationale and Proposal Regarding Standards for the Administration and Interpretation of Computerized Psychological Testing*. Report prepared for Psych Systems, Inc., Baltimore, Md., 1983.

Bobko, P. "An Analysis of Correlations Corrected for Attenuation and Range Restriction." *Journal of Applied Psychology*, 1983, *68*, 584-589.

Bobko, P., Karren, R., and Kerkar, S. P. "Systematic Research Needs for Understanding Supervisory-Based Estimates of SD_Y in Utility Analysis." *Organizational Behavior and Human Decision Processes*, 1987, *40*, 69-95.

Bobko, P., Karren, R., and Parkington, J. J. "Estimation of Standard Deviations in Utility Analyses: An Empirical Test." *Journal of Applied Psychology*, 1983, *68*, 170-176.

Boudreau, J. W. "Economic Considerations in Estimating the Utility of Human Resource Productivity Improvement Programs." *Personnel Psychology*, 1983, *36*, 551-576.

Boudreau, J. W. "Decision Theory Contributions to HRM Research and Practice." *Industrial Relations*, 1984, *23*, 198-217.

Boudreau, J. W., and Berger, C. J. "Decision-Theoretic Utility Analysis Applied to Employee Separations and Acquisitions." *Journal of Applied Psychology*, 1985, *70*, 581-612.

Boudreau, J. W., and Rynes, S. L. "The Role of Recruitment in

Staffing Utility Analysis." *Journal of Applied Psychology*, 1985, *70*, 354–366.

Brogden, H. E. "On the Interpretation of the Correlation Coefficient as a Measure of Predictive Efficiency." *Journal of Educational Psychology*, 1946, *37*, 65–76.

Brogden, H. E. "When Testing Pays Off." *Personnel Psychology*, 1949, *2*, 171–183.

Brown, S. H. "Validity Generalization and Situational Moderation in the Life Insurance Industry." *Journal of Applied Psychology*, 1981, *66*, 664–670.

Browne, J. A., and Howarth, E. "A Comprehensive Factor Analysis of Personality Questionnaire Items: A Test of 20 Positive Factor Hypotheses." *Multivariate Behavioral Research*, 1977, *12*, 399–427.

Budgell, G. R. *Preliminary Analysis of the Feasibility of Computerized Adaptive Testing and Item Banking in the Public Service.* Report prepared for the Public Service Commission, Ottawa, Canada, 1982.

Bullock, R., and Svyantek, D. "Analyzing Meta-Analysis: Potential Problems, An Unsuccessful Replication, and Evaluation Criteria." *Journal of Applied Psychology*, 1985, *70*, 108–115.

Burke, M. J. "Validity Generalization: A Review and Critique of the Correlation Model." *Personnel Psychology*, 1984, *37*, 93–115.

Burke, M. J., Day, R. R., and Frederick, J. T. "Estimating Performance Standard Deviations in Dollars: An Exploratory Investigation with Four Managerial Samples." Unpublished manuscript, New York University, 1987.

Burke, M. J., and Frederick, J. T. "Two Modified Procedures for Estimating Standard Deviations in Utility Analyses." *Journal of Applied Psychology*, 1984, *69*, 482–489.

Burke, M. J., and Frederick, J. T. "A Comparison of Economic Utility Estimates for Alternative SD_Y Estimation Procedures." *Journal of Applied Psychology*, 1986, *71*, 334–339.

Burke, M. J., and Normand, J. "Computerized Psychological Testing: Overview and Critique." *Professional Psychology*, 1987, *18*, 42–51.

Burke, M. J., and Raju, N. S. "An Overview of Validity Generalization Models and Procedures." In R. Schuler, S. Youngblood, and V. Huber (eds.), *Readings in Personnel and Human Resource Management.* St. Paul, Minn.: West, 1988.

Burke, M. J., Raju, N. S., and Pearlman, K. "A Comparison of the Results of Five Validity Generalization Procedures for Tests Used in Clerical Occupations." *Journal of Applied Psychology*, 1986, *71*, 349–353.

Callender, J. C., and Osburn, H. G. "Development and Test of a New

Model for Validity Generalization." *Journal of Applied Psychology*, 1980, *65*, 543–558.

Callender, J. C., and Osburn, H. G. "Testing the Constancy of Validity with Computer Generated Sampling Distributions of the Multiplicative Model Variance Estimate: Results for Petroleum Industry Validation Research." *Journal of Applied Psychology*, 1981, *66*, 274–281.

Callender, J. C., and others. "The Multiplicative Validity Generalization Model: Accuracy of Estimates as a Function of Sample Size and Mean, Variance, and Shape of the Distribution of True Validities." *Journal of Applied Psychology*, 1982, *67*, 859–867.

Carlberg, C. G., and others. "Meta-Analysis in Education: A Reply to Slavin." *Educational Researcher*, 1984, *13*, 16–23.

Cascio, W. F. *Costing Human Resources: The Financial Impact of Behavior in Organizations.* Boston: Kent, 1982.

Cascio, W. F. "Comments on Research Needs in Utility Analysis." In J. Ledvinka (chair), *Research in Progress: Utility Analysis.* Symposium presented at the 1st annual conference of the Society for Industrial and Organizational Psychology, Chicago, Apr. 1986.

Cascio, W. F., and Ramos, R. A. "Development and Application of a New Method for Assessing Job Performance in Behavioral/ Economic Terms." *Journal of Applied Psychology*, 1986, *71*, 20–28.

Cascio, W. F., and Silbey, V. "Utility of the Assessment Center as a Selection Device." *Journal of Applied Psychology*, 1979, *64*, 107–118.

Costa, P. T., and McCrae, R. R. "Influence of Extraversion and Neuroticism on Subjective Well-Being: Happy and Unhappy People." *Journal of Personality and Social Psychology*, 1980, *38*, 668–678.

Costa, P. T., Jr., McCrae, R. R., and Holland, J. L. "Personality and Vocational Interests in an Adult Sample." *Journal of Applied Psychology*, 1984, *69*, 390–400.

Cronbach, L. J., and Gleser, G. C. *Psychological Tests and Personnel Decisions.* Champaign: University of Illinois Press, 1965.

Cronshaw, S. F., and Alexander, R. A. "One Answer to the Demand of Accountability: Selection Utility as an Investment Decision." *Organizational Behavior and Human Performance*, 1985, *35*, 102–118.

Cunningham, J. W., and others. *The Development of the Occupational Analysis Inventory: An "Ergonomic" Approach to an Educational Problem.* Center for Occupational Education Research Monographs, no. 6. Raleigh, N.C.: North Carolina State University, 1971.

Derman, D., French, J. W., and Harman, H. H. *Guide to Factor-Referenced Temperament Scales 1978.* Princeton, N.J.: Educational Testing Service, 1978.

Dribin, L. S. "A Monte Carlo Study of the Additive and Multiplicative Models of Validity Generalization." Unpublished doctoral dissertation, Illinois Institute of Technology, 1981.

Dunnette, M. D. "Aptitudes, Abilities, and Skills." In M. D. Dunnette (ed.), *Handbook of Industrial and Organizational Psychology.* Skokie, Ill.: Rand McNally, 1976.

Dunnette, M. D. "Critical Concepts in the Assessment of Human Capabilities." In M. D. Dunnette and E. A. Fleishman (eds.), *Human Performance and Productivity.* Vol. 1: *Human Capability Assessment.* Hillsdale, N.J.: Erlbaum, 1982.

Eaton, N. K., Wing, H., and Mitchell, K. "Alternate Methods of Estimating the Dollar Value of Performance." *Personnel Psychology,* 1985, *38,* 27-40.

Eberhardt, B. J., and Muchinsky, P. M. "Biodata Determinants of Vocational Typology: An Integration of Two Paradigms." *Journal of Applied Psychology,* 1982, *67,* 714-727.

Ekstrom, R. B., French, J. W., and Harman, H. H. "Cognitive Factors: Their Identification and Replication." *Multivariate Behavioral Research Monographs,* 1979, no. 79-2.

Elwood, D. L., and Griffin, R. H. "Individual Intelligence Testing Without the Examiner: Reliability of an Automated Method." *Journal of Consulting and Clinical Psychology,* 1972, *38,* 9-14.

Emmons, R. A. "Dual Nature of Happiness: Independence of Positive and Negative Moods." In L. Roberson (chair), *Recent Research on Cognition and Affect: Implications for Industrial/Organizational Psychology.* Symposium presented at the 94th annual meeting of the American Psychological Association, Washington, D.C., Aug. 1986.

Evans, D. W. "Individual Productivity Differences." *Monthly Labor Review,* 1940, *50,* 338-341.

Farina, A. J., Jr., and Wheaton, G. R. "Development of a Taxonomy of Human Performance: The Task Characteristics Approach to Performance Prediction." Ms. 323. *JSAS Catalog of Selected Documents in Psychology,* 1973, *3,* 26-27.

Fine, S. A. "A Structure of Worker Functions." *Personnel and Guidance Journal,* 1955, *34,* 66-73.

Fine, S. A. "Job Analysis." In R. A. Berk (ed.), *Performance Assessment: Methods and Applications.* Baltimore, Md.: Johns Hopkins University Press, 1986.

Fleishman, E. A. *The Structure and Measurement of Physical Fitness.* Englewood Cliffs, N.J.: Prentice-Hall, 1964.

Fleishman, E. A. "Structure and Measurement of Psychomotor Abilities." In R. N. Singer (ed.), *The Psychomotor Domain: Movement Behavior.* Philadelphia: Lea & Febiger, 1972.

Fleishman, E. A. "Toward a Taxonomy of Human Performance." *American Psychologist,* 1975, *30,* 1127-1149.

Fleishman, E. A., and Quaintance, M. K. *Taxonomies of Human Performance: The Description of Human Tasks.* Orlando, Fla.: Academic Press, 1984.

Forsyth, R. A. "An Empirical Note on Correlation Coefficients Corrected for Restriction in Range." *Educational and Psychological Measurement,* 1971, *31,* 115-123.

Forsyth, R. A., and Feldt, L. S. "An Investigation of Empirical Sampling Distributions of Correlation Coefficients Corrected for Attenuation." *Educational and Psychological Measurement,* 1969, *29,* 61-71.

Gardner, H. *Frames of Mind: The Theory of Multiple Intelligence.* New York: Basic Books, 1983.

Glass, G. V. "Primary, Secondary, and Meta-Analysis of Research." *Educational Researcher,* 1976, *5,* 3-8.

Green, B. F., and others. "Technical Guidelines for Assessing Computerized Adaptive Tests." *Journal of Educational Measurement,* 1984, *21,* 347-360.

Greener, J. M., and Osburn, H. G. "An Empirical Study of the Accuracy of Corrections for Restriction in Range Due to Explicit Selection." *Applied Psychological Measurement,* 1979, *3,* 31-41.

Greener, J. M., and Osburn, H. G. "Accuracy of Corrections for Restriction in Range Due to Explicit Selection in Heteroscedastic and Nonlinear Distributions." *Educational and Psychological Measurement,* 1980, *40,* 337-346.

Gross, A. L., and Fleischman, L. "Restriction of Range Corrections When Both Distribution and Selection Assumptions Are Violated." *Applied Psychological Measurement,* 1983, *7,* 227-237.

Guastello, S. J. "A Butterfly Catastrophe Model of Motivation in Organizations: Academic Performance." *Journal of Applied Psychology* (monograph), 1987, *72,* 165-182.

Guilford, J. P. *The Nature of Human Intelligence.* New York: McGraw-Hill, 1967.

Hawk, J. "Linearity of Criterion-GATB Aptitude Relationships." *Measurement and Evaluation in Guidance,* 1970, *2,* 249-251.

Hedges, L. V., and Olkin, I. *Statistical Methods for Meta-Analysis.* Orlando, Fla.: Academic Press, 1985.

Henderson, R. I. *Compensation Management: Rewarding Performance.* Reston, Va.: Reston, 1985.

Hirsh, H. R., Northrop, L. C., and Schmidt, F. L. "Validity Generalization Results for Law Enforcement Occupations." *Personnel Psychology,* 1986, *39,* 399–420.

Holland, J. L. "Vocational Preferences." In M. D. Dunnette (ed.), *Handbook of Industrial and Organizational Psychology.* Skokie, Ill.: Rand McNally, 1976.

Hough, L. M. "Overcoming Objections to Use of Temperament Variables in Selection." In R. C. Page (chair), *New Perspectives on Personality and Job Performance.* Symposium presented at the 95th annual meeting of the American Psychological Association, New York, Aug. 1987.

Hough, L. M., Kamp, J. D., and Barge, B. N. "Utility of Temperament, Biodata, and Interest Assessment for Predicting Job Performance: A Review and Integration of the Literature." Unpublished manuscript, Personnel and Decisions Research Institute, Minneapolis, Minn., 1986.

Howard, A. "College Experiences and Managerial Performance." *Journal of Applied Psychology* (monograph), 1986, *71,* 530–552.

Hulin, C. L., Drasgow, F., and Parsons, C. K. *Item Response Theory: Application to Psychological Measurement.* Homewood, Ill.: Dorsey Press, 1983.

Hull, C. L. *Applied Testing.* New York: Psychological Corporation, 1928.

Human Resources Research Organization and others. *Improving the Selection, Classification, and Utilization of Army Enlisted Personnel: Annual Report Synopsis, 1984 Fiscal Year.* Research Report 1393. Alexandria, Va.: U.S. Army Research Institute for the Behavioral and Social Sciences, 1984.

Hunt, E. B. "Mechanics of Verbal Ability." *Psychological Review,* 1978, *85,* 109–130.

Hunt, E. B. "Cognitive Research and Future Test Design." In *The Redesign of Testing for the 21st Century: Proceedings of the 1985 ETS Invitational Conference.* Princeton, N.J.: Educational Testing Service, 1986.

Hunter, J. E. *The Dimensionality of the General Aptitude Test Battery (GATB) and the Dominance of General Factors over Specific Factors in the Prediction of Job Performance.* Washington, D.C.: U.S. Employment Service, 1980.

Hunter, J. E. *Fairness of the General Aptitude Test Battery (GATB): Ability Differences and Their Impact on Minority Hiring Rates.* Washington, D.C.: U.S. Employment Service, 1981.

Hunter, J. E. *Test Validation for 12,000 Jobs: An Application of Job Classification and Validity Generalization Analysis to the General Aptitude Test Battery.* USES Test Research Report 45. Washington, D.C.: U.S. Department of Labor, 1983a.

Hunter, J. E. *Validity Generalization of the ASVAB: Preliminary Report.* Rockville, Md.: Research Applications, 1983b.

Hunter, J. E. *Validity Generalization of the ASVAB: Second Report.* Rockville, Md.: Research Applications, 1983c.

Hunter, J. E. "Differential Validity Across Jobs in the Military." Unpublished manuscript, Michigan State University, 1985.

Hunter, J. E. "Cognitive Ability, Cognitive Aptitudes, Job Knowledge, and Job Performance." *Journal of Vocational Behavior,* 1986, *29,* 340-362.

Hunter, J. E., and Hunter, R. F. "Validity and Utility of Alternative Predictors of Job Performance." *Psychological Bulletin,* 1984, *96,* 72-98.

Hunter, J. E., and Schmidt, F. L. "Fitting People to Jobs: The Impact of Personnel Selection on National Productivity." In M. D. Dunnette and E. A. Fleishman (eds.), *Human Performance and Productivity.* Vol. 1: *Human Capability Assessment.* Hillsdale, N.J.: Erlbaum, 1982.

Hunter, J. E., Schmidt, F. L., and Jackson, G. B. *Meta-Analysis: Cumulating Research Findings Across Studies.* Beverly Hills, Calif.: Sage, 1982.

Hunter, J. E., Schmidt, F. L., and Rauschenberger, J. M. "Fairness of Psychological Tests: Implications of Four Definitions for Selection Utility and Minority Hiring." *Journal of Applied Psychology,* 1977, *62,* 245-260.

James, L. R. "Criterion Models and Construct Validity for Criteria." *Psychological Bulletin,* 1973, *80,* 75-83.

James, L. R., Demaree, R. A., and Mulaik, S. A. "A Note on Validity Generalization Procedures." *Journal of Applied Psychology,* 1986, *71,* 440-450.

Jarrett, F. F. "Per Cent Increase in Output of Selected Personnel as an Index of Efficiency." *Journal of Applied Psychology,* 1948, *32,* 135-145.

Jensen, A. R. "*g:* Artifact or Reality?" *Journal of Vocational Behavior,* 1986, *29,* 301-331.

Kaplan, M. F. "Elicitation of Information and Response Biases of Repressors, Sensitizers, and Neutrals in Behavior Prediction." *Journal of Personality,* 1968, *36,* 84-91.

Kaplan, R. M. "The Connection Between Clinical Health Promotion and Health Status." *American Psychologist,* 1984, *39,* 755-765.

Kaplan, R. M., and Bush, J. W. "Health-Related Quality of Life Measurement for Evaluation Research and Policy Analysis." *Health Psychology*, 1982, *1*, 61–80.

Kemery, E. R., Mossholder, K. W., and Roth, L. "The Power of the Schmidt and Hunter Additive Model of Validity Generalization." *Journal of Applied Psychology*, 1987, *72*, 30–37.

Klemmer, E. T., and Lockhead, G. R. "Productivity and Errors in Two Keying Tasks: A Field Study." *Journal of Applied Psychology*, 1962, *46*, 401–408.

Landy, F. J., Farr, J. L., and Jacobs, R. R. "Utility Concepts in Performance Measurement." *Organizational Behavior and Human Performance*, 1982, *30*, 15–40.

Lawshe, C. H. *Principles of Personnel Tests*. New York: McGraw-Hill, 1948.

Ledvinka, J., and Ladd, R. T. "Computer Simulation of Multiple-Job Systems and Its Application to Utility Analysis." Unpublished manuscript, University of Georgia, 1987.

Lee, R., Miller, K., and Graham, W. "Corrections for Restriction of Range and Attenuation in Criterion-Related Validation Studies." *Journal of Applied Psychology*, 1982, *67*, 637–639.

Lilienthal, R. A., and Pearlman, K. *The Validity of Federal Selection Tests for Aides/Technicians in the Health, Science, and Engineering Fields*. OPRD Personnel Research Report 83-1. Washington, D.C.: U.S. Office of Personnel Management, 1983.

Linn, R. L., Harnisch, D. L., and Dunbar, S. B. "Corrections for Range Restriction: An Empirical Investigation of Conditions Resulting in Conservative Corrections." *Journal of Applied Psychology*, 1981a, *66*, 655–663.

Linn, R. L., Harnisch, D. L., and Dunbar, S. B. "Validity Generalization and Situational Specificity: An Analysis of the Prediction of First-Year Grades in Law School." *Applied Psychological Measurement*, 1981b, *5*, 281–289.

Lord, F. M. *Applications of Item Response Theory to Practical Testing Problems*. Hillsdale, N.J.: Erlbaum, 1980.

McBride, J. R. "Adaptive Mental Testing: The State of the Art." Ms. 2455. *JSAS Catalog of Selected Documents in Psychology*, 1982, *12*, 24.

McBride, J. R. "A Computer Adaptive Edition of the Differential Aptitude Tests." Paper presented at the 94th annual meeting of the American Psychological Association, Washington, D.C., Aug. 1986.

McCormick, E. J. *Job Analysis: Methods and Applications*. New York: AMACOM, 1979.

McCormick, E. J., Jeanneret, P. R., and Mecham, R. C. "A Study of

Job Characteristics and Job Dimensions as Based on the Position Analysis Questionnaire (PAQ)." *Journal of Applied Psychology,* 1972, *56,* 347-368.

McCormick, E. J., and Tiffin, J. *Industrial Psychology.* Englewood Cliffs, N.J.: Prentice-Hall, 1974.

McDaniel, M. A. "The Evaluation of a Causal Model of Job Performance: The Interrelationships of General Mental Ability, Job Experience, and Job Performance." Unpublished doctoral dissertation, George Washington University, 1986.

McDaniel, M. A., and Schmidt, F. L. *A Meta-Analysis of the Validity of Training and Experience Ratings in Personnel Selection.* OSP Report 85-1. Washington, D.C.: U.S. Office of Personnel Management, Office of Staffing Policy, 1985.

Marquardt, L. D., and McCormick, E. J. *Attribute Ratings and Profiles of Job Elements of the Position Analysis Questionnaire (PAQ).* Occupational Research Center Report 1. West Lafayette, Ind.: Department of Psychological Sciences, Purdue University, 1972.

Mathieu, J. E., and Leonard, R. L., Jr. "Applying Utility Concepts to a Training Program in Supervisory Skills: A Time-Based Approach." *Academy of Management Journal,* 1987, *30,* 316-335.

Mobley, W. H., and others. "Review and Conceptual Analysis of the Employee Turnover Process." *Psychological Bulletin,* 1979, *86,* 493-522.

Munsterberg, H. *Psychology and Industrial Efficiency.* Boston: Houghton Mifflin, 1913.

Murphy, K. R. "When Your Top Choice Turns You Down: Effects of Rejected Offers on the Utility of Selection Tests." *Psychological Bulletin,* 1986, *99,* 133-138.

Neeb, R. W., Cunningham, J. W., and Pass, J. J. *Human Attribute Requirements of Work Elements: Further Development of the Occupation Analysis Inventory.* Center for Occupational Education Research Monographs, no. 7. Raleigh, N.C.: University of North Carolina, 1971.

Neiner, A. G., and Owens, W. A. "Using Biodata to Predict College Choice Among College Graduates." *Journal of Applied Psychology,* 1985, *70,* 127-136.

Novick, M. R. "Educational Testing: Inferences in Relevant Subpopulations." *Educational Researcher,* 1982, *11,* 4, 6-10, 28.

Orwin, R., and Cordray, D. "Effects of Deficient Reporting on Meta-Analysis: A Conceptual Framework and Reanalysis." *Psychological Bulletin,* 1985, *97,* 134-147.

Osburn, H. G., and others. "Statistical Power of Tests of the

Situational Specificity Hypothesis in Validity Generalization Studies: A Cautionary Note." *Journal of Applied Psychology*, 1983, *68*, 115–122.

Owens, W. A. "A Quasi-Actuarial Basis for Individual Assessment." *American Psychologist*, 1971, *26*, 992–999.

Owens, W. A., and Schoenfeldt, L. F. "Toward a Classification of Persons." *Journal of Applied Psychology* (monograph), 1979, *65*, 569–607.

Pearlman, K. "Job Families: A Review and Discussion of Their Implications for Personnel Selection." *Psychological Bulletin*, 1980, *87*, 1–28.

Pearlman, K. "The Bayesian Approach to Validity Generalization: A Systematic Examination of the Robustness of Procedures and Conclusions." *Dissertation Abstracts International*, 1982, *42*, 4960B. Unpublished doctoral dissertation, George Washington University, 1982.

Pearlman, K. "Development of a Dollar Criterion for High-Level Sales Jobs." Paper presented at the 93rd annual meeting of the American Psychological Association, Los Angeles, Aug. 1985.

Pearlman, K., Schmidt, F. L., and Hunter, J. E. "Validity Generalization Results for Tests Used to Predict Job Proficiency and Training Success in Clerical Occupations." *Journal of Applied Psychology*, 1980, *65*, 373–406.

Peters, L. H., and O'Connor, E. J. "Situational Constraints and Work Outcomes: The Influences of a Frequently Overlooked Construct." *Academy of Management Review*, 1980, *5*, 391–397.

Peterson, N. G., and Bownas, D. A. "Skill, Task Structure, and Performance Acquisition." In M. D. Dunnette and E. A. Fleishman (eds.), *Human Performance and Productivity*. Vol. 1: *Human Capability Assessment*. Hillsdale, N.J.: Erlbaum, 1982.

Raju, N. S., and Burke, M. J. "Two New Procedures for Studying Validity Generalization." *Journal of Applied Psychology*, 1983, *68*, 382–395.

Raju, N. S., and Burke, M. J. "Utility Analysis." In R. A. Berk (ed.), *Performance Assessment: Methods and Applications*. Baltimore, Md.: Johns Hopkins University Press, 1986.

Raju, N. S., Burke, M. J., and Normand, J. "The Asymptotic Sampling Distribution of Correlations Corrected for Attenuation and Range Restriction." Unpublished manuscript, Illinois Institute of Technology, 1986.

Raju, N. S., Burke, M. J., and Normand, J. "A New Model for Utility Analysis." Unpublished manuscript, Illinois Institute of Technology, 1987.

Raju, N. S., Fralicx, R., and Steinhaus, S. D. "Covariance and Regression Slope Models for Studying Validity Generalization." *Applied Psychological Measurement*, 1986, *10*, 195-211.

Rauschenberger, J., and Schmidt, F. L. "Measuring the Economic Impact of Human Resource Programs." *Journal of Business and Psychology*, 1987, *2*, 50-59.

Reilly, R. R., and Smither, J. W. "An Examination of Two Alternative Techniques to Estimate the Standard Deviation of Job Performance in Dollars." *Journal of Applied Psychology*, 1985, *70*, 651-661.

Richardson, M. W. "The Interpretation of a Test Validity Coefficient in Terms of Increased Efficiency of a Selected Group of Personnel." *Psychometrika*, 1944, *9*, 245-248.

Rothe, H. F. "Output Rates Among Chocolate Dippers." *Journal of Applied Psychology*, 1941, *25*, 94-97.

Rothe, H. F. "Output Rates Among Butter Wrappers: II. Frequency Distributions and a Hypothesis Regarding the 'Restriction of Output.'" *Journal of Applied Psychology*, 1946, *30*, 320-327.

Rothe, H. F. "Output Rates Among Machine Operators: I. Distributions and Their Reliability." *Journal of Applied Psychology*, 1947, *31*, 484-489.

Rothe, H. F. "Output Rates Among Welders: Productivity and Consistency Following Removal of a Financial Incentive System." *Journal of Applied Psychology*, 1970, *54*, 549-551.

Rothe, H. F. "Output Rates Among Industrial Employees." *Journal of Applied Psychology*, 1978, *63*, 40-46.

Rothe, H. F., and Nye, C. T. "Output Rates Among Coil Winders." *Journal of Applied Psychology*, 1958, *42*, 182-186.

Rothe, H. F., and Nye, C. T. "Output Rates Among Machine Operators: II. Consistency Related to Methods of Pay." *Journal of Applied Psychology*, 1959, *43*, 417-420.

Rothe, H. F., and Nye, C. T. "Output Rates Among Machine Operators: II. A Nonincentive Situation in Two Levels of Business Activity." *Journal of Applied Psychology*, 1961, *45*, 50-54.

Rynes, S. L., and Boudreau, J. W. "College Recruiting in Large Organizations: Practice, Evaluation, and Research Implications." *Personnel Psychology*, 1986, *39*, 729-757.

Sackett, P. R., Harris, M. H., and Orr, J. M. "On Seeking Moderator Variables in the Meta-Analysis of Correlational Data: A Monte Carlo Investigation of Statistical Power and Resistance to Type I Error." *Journal of Applied Psychology*, 1986, *71*, 302-310.

Sackett, P. R., and others. "Commentary on Forty Questions About Validity Generalization and Meta-Analysis." *Personnel Psychology*, 1985, *38*, 697-798.

Schmidt, F. L. "Questions to Be Raised About Utility Analysis." In J. Ledvinka (chair), *Research in Progress: Utility Analysis*. Symposium presented at the 1st annual conference of the Society for Industrial and Organizational Psychology, Chicago, Apr. 1986.

Schmidt, F. L., Gast-Rosenberg, I., and Hunter, J. E. "Validity Generalization Results for Computer Programmers." *Journal of Applied Psychology*, 1980, *65*, 643–661.

Schmidt, F. L., and Hunter, J. E. "Development of a General Solution to the Problem of Validity Generalization." *Journal of Applied Psychology*, 1977, *62*, 529–540.

Schmidt, F. L., and Hunter, J. E. "Individual Differences in Productivity: An Empirical Test of Estimates Derived from Studies of Selection Procedure Utility." *Journal of Applied Psychology*, 1983, *68*, 407–414.

Schmidt, F. L., Hunter, J. E., and Caplan, J. R. "Validity Generalization Results for Two Groups in the Petroleum Industry." *Journal of Applied Psychology*, 1981, *66*, 261–273.

Schmidt, F. L., Hunter, J. E., and Outerbridge, A. N. "Impact of Job Experience and Ability on Job Knowledge, Work Sample Performance, and Supervisory Ratings of Job Performance." *Journal of Applied Psychology*, 1986, *71*, 432–439.

Schmidt, F. L., Hunter, J. E., and Pearlman, K. "Task Differences as Moderators of Aptitude Test Validity in Selection: A Red Herring." *Journal of Applied Psychology*, 1981, *66*, 166–185.

Schmidt, F. L., Hunter, J. E., and Pearlman, K. "Assessing the Economic Impact of Personnel Programs on Workforce Productivity." *Personnel Psychology*, 1982, *35*, 333–347.

Schmidt, F. L., Mack, M. J., and Hunter, J. E. "Selection in the Occupation of U.S. Park Ranger for Three Modes of Test Use." *Journal of Applied Psychology*, 1984, *69*, 490–497.

Schmidt, F. L., and others. "Further Tests of the Schmidt-Hunter Bayesian Validity Generalization Procedure." *Personnel Psychology*, 1979a, *32*, 257–281.

Schmidt, F. L., and others. "The Impact of Valid Selection Procedures on Work Force Productivity." *Journal of Applied Psychology*, 1979b, *64*, 609–624.

Schmidt, F. L., and others. "Forty Questions About Validity Generalization and Meta-Analysis." *Personnel Psychology*, 1985a, *38*, 697–798.

Schmidt, F. L., and others. "Further Within-Setting Empirical Tests of the Situational Specificity Hypothesis." *Personnel Psychology*, 1985b, *38*, 509–524.

Schmitt, N., and others. "Metaanalyses of Validity Studies Published

Between 1964 and 1982 and the Investigation of Study Characteristics." *Personnel Psychology,* 1984, *37,* 407–422.

Schoenfeldt, L. F. "Utilization of Manpower: Development and Evaluation of an Assessment-Classification Model for Matching Individuals with Jobs." *Journal of Applied Psychology,* 1974, *59,* 583–595.

Schoenfeldt, L. F. "Intra-Individual Variation and Human Performance." In M. D. Dunnette and E. A. Fleishman (eds.), *Human Performance and Productivity.* Vol. 1: *Human Capability Assessment.* Hillsdale, N.J.: Erlbaum, 1982.

Sevier, F. A. C. "Testing the Assumptions Underlying Multiple Regression." *Journal of Experimental Education,* 1957, *25,* 323–330.

Slavin, R. E. "Meta-Analysis in Education: How Has It Been Used?" *Educational Researcher,* 1984, *13,* 6–15.

Slavin, R. E. "Best-Evidence Synthesis: An Alternative to Meta-Analytic and Traditional Reviews." *Educational Researcher,* 1986, *15,* 5–11.

Spector, P. E., and Levine, E. L. "Meta-Analysis for Integrating Study Outcomes: A Monte Carlo Study of Its Susceptibility to Type I and Type II Errors." *Journal of Applied Psychology,* 1987, *72,* 3–9.

Stead, W. H., and Shartle, C. L. *Occupational Counseling Techniques.* New York: American Books, 1940.

Steffy, B. D., and Maurer, S. D. "The Dollar-Productivity Impact of the Human Resource Function: Conceptualization and Measurement." Unpublished manuscript, University of Minnesota, 1986.

Steffy, B. D., and Werling, S. "Incorporating Human Resource Planning Models into Utility Analysis to Determine the Long-Term Economic Impact of Selection and Training." Paper presented at the 47th annual meeting of the Academy of Management, San Diego, Calif., Aug. 1985.

Sternberg, R. J. *Intelligence, Information Processing, and Analogical Reasoning: The Componential Analysis of Human Abilities.* Hillsdale, N.J.: Erlbaum 1977.

Sternberg, R. J. *Beyond IQ: A Triarchic Theory of Human Intelligence.* New York: Cambridge University Press, 1985.

Sternberg, R. J. "The Future of Intelligence Testing." *Educational Measurement: Issues and Practice,* 1986, *5,* 19–22.

Tellegen, A. "Brief Manual for the Differential Personality Questionnaire." Unpublished manuscript, University of Minnesota, 1982.

Tiffin, J. *Industrial Psychology.* (2nd ed.) Englewood Cliffs, N.J.: Prentice-Hall, 1947.

Trattner, M. H. *Estimating the Validity of Aptitude and Ability Tests for Semi-Professional Occupations Using the Schmidt-Hunter Interactive Validity Generalization Procedure.* OSP Report 85-3. Washington, D.C.: U.S. Office of Personnel Management, Office of Staffing Policy, 1985.

Tupes, E. C. "A Note on Validity and Nonlinear Heteroscedastic Models." *Personnel Psychology,* 1964, *17,* 59-61.

Urry, V. W. "Tailored Testing: A Successful Application of Latent Trait Theory." *Journal of Educational Measurement,* 1977, *14,* 181–196.

Vale, C. D. "Design and Implementation of a Microcomputer-Based Adaptive Testing System." *Behavior Research Methods and Instrumentation,* 1981, *13,* 399-406.

Viteles, M. S. *Industrial Psychology.* New York: Norton, 1932.

Watson, D., and Clark, L. A. "Negative Affectivity: The Disposition to Experience Aversive Emotional States." *Psychological Bulletin,* 1984, *96,* 465-490.

Watson, D., and Tellegen, A. "Toward a Consensual Structure of Mood." *Psychological Bulletin,* 1985, *98,* 219-235.

Wechsler, D. *Range of Human Capacities.* (2nd ed.) Baltimore, Md.: Williams and Wilkins, 1952.

Weekley, J. A., and others. "A Comparison of the Three Methods of Estimating the Standard Deviation of Performance in Dollars." *Journal of Applied Psychology,* 1985, *70,* 122-126.

Weiss, D. J. "Improving Measurement Quality and Efficiency with Adaptive Testing." *Applied Psychological Measurement,* 1982, *6,* 473-492.

Weiss, D. J. "Adaptive Testing by Computer." *Journal of Consulting and Clinical Psychology,* 1985, *53,* 774-789.

Weiss, D. J., and Betz, N. E. *Ability Measurement: Conventional or Adaptive?* Research Report 73-1. Minneapolis: Psychometric Methods Program, University of Minnesota, 1973.

Weiss, H. M., and Adler, S. "Personality and Organizational Behavior." In B. M. Staw and L. L. Cummings (eds.), *Research in Organizational Behavior.* Greenwich, Conn.: JAI Press, 1984.

Wetrogan, L. I., Olson, D. M., and Sperling, H. M. "A Systemic Model of Work Performance." Paper presented at the 91st annual meeting of the American Psychological Association, Anaheim, Calif., Aug. 1983.

Whetzel, D. L., McDaniel, M. A., and Schmidt, F. L. "The Validity of Employment Interviews: A Review and Meta-Analysis." In H. Hirsh (chair), *Meta-Analysis of Alternative Predictors of Job*

Performance. Symposium presented at the 93rd annual meeting of the American Psychological Association, Los Angeles, Aug. 1985.

White, D. M., Clements, C. B., and Fowler, R. D. "A Comparison of Computer Administration with Standard Administration of the MMPI." *Computers in Human Behavior,* 1985, *1,* 153–162.

7

Individual Motivation
and Performance:
Cognitive Influences
on Effort and Choice

Daniel R. Ilgen
Howard J. Klein

A rarely questioned assumption is that the productivity of any unit is, in part, related to the way in which the individuals who staff that unit perform their jobs. More specifically, it is assumed that the unit's productivity is a monotonically increasing function of the effectiveness of the individuals who make up the unit (where effectiveness is defined in terms of outputs judged to be appropriate for the jobs in question). This assumption applies to units of all sizes, from the productivity of a local bakery when attributed to the performance of the kitchen staff to that of the United States when linked to the commitment of the American work force to "hard work."

It was noted in Chapter Two that productivity, as typically defined, is an index of efficiency for a firm, industry, nation, or other identifiable unit and is usually expressed as a ratio of the unit's outputs compared to inputs. Equating productivity with performance or effectiveness at the individual level fails to capture the efficiency notion of most construals of productivity (see Chapter Two; Tuttle, 1983). Individual performance is typically expressed only in measurable outputs defined in terms of quality or quantity, depending on the

Work on this chapter was supported, in part, by the Naval Training System Center, Human Factors Division, Orlando, Florida. Although the support is greatly appreciated, the ideas expressed herein are those of the authors and are not necessarily endorsed by the supporting agency.

nature of the job. In some cases, it may be both feasible and desirable to express such outputs in efficiency terms; quite often it is not.

If one is interested in productivity as a function of individual behavior, there are two options. First, efforts can be made to define all individual performance in efficiency units. There are, however, a number of drawbacks to this position. One of the most telling is the fact that individual productivity represents what Mahoney (in Chapter Two) labels *partial-factor productivity;* it is subject to influence from a number of variables exogenous to the individual subsystem. Therefore, observed variance in productivity so defined may be misleadingly attributed to individuals. Another drawback is that even though the definition can be limited to efficiency, the definition in use by society at large is much less restrictive. As a result, this restricted definition is likely to confuse rather than enlighten.

A second alternative is to focus attention on individual performance while at the same time recognizing that performance is not synonymous with productivity. Individual performance is usually one of many components of the productivity of a unit, and, other things being equal, unit productivity covaries positively with individual performance. This is the assumption underlying most interventions aimed at influencing productivity through human resource management, as these activities are frequently aimed at improving the skill levels of people and/or their motivation to work. Thus programs and practices called *productivity improvement programs* have as their goal increasing individual performance via increased work skills and/or motivation. This second option, therefore, addresses issues related to work performance, assuming that individual performance is one of the major human systems components of productivity while recognizing that performance is not and does not ensure productivity. This is the approach taken in the present chapter.

Individual Performance

In almost all organizations, individuals hold positions (roles or jobs) and are evaluated on their performance. The specific nature of these evaluations varies widely in terms of both practice and quality, but, at an abstract level, the characteristics of the evaluations are relatively universal. In particular, some means exist for (1) identifying those products believed to be important for the position, (2) measuring the products produced, (3) evaluating these products, and (4) making some judgments about the extent to which the individuals' own behaviors contributed to the products (Naylor, Pritchard, and Ilgen, 1980). The end result of this process is a judgment about individuals' performance.

Assuming that individuals' performance is, to some extent, a function of their behavior and that their performance affects productivity, it becomes important to understand why individuals choose to behave the way they do. Only through such understanding is it possible to predict behavior and thereby construct or modify conditions in the work setting so as to encourage individual behavior consistent with the overall goals of the organization. Theories of human behavior provide a basis for understanding and predicting behavior in general, as well as the subset of behaviors that contribute to performance at work.

Unfortunately, theories of human behavior are nearly as numerous as the number of theoreticians available to generate them. The theories currently in vogue in much of psychology are overwhelmingly cognitive. Cognitive theories attribute the causes of behavior to individuals' processing of information. According to these views, behavior results from *decisions* or *action choices*. Research into cognitive theories aims to model action choices. Variations of observed behavior from that predicted by the models are attributed to limitations in the models and/or to limitations in the information-processing capabilities of individuals. Cognitive theories have been described as "cold," in the sense that emotional or affective contributions to action are either ignored or downplayed (Sorrentino and Higgins, 1986).

In contrast to cognitive theories of behavior are "warm" theories (Sorrentino and Higgins, 1986), in which relatively stable individual differences represent the primary explanatory variables. Individual differences are posited to influence perceptions of social and physical environments and reactions to them. Here such constructs as needs, values, and attitudes are evoked to explain behavior.

As will be seen from the review of theories that follows, the warm and cold perspectives have frequently been combined in attempts to explain behavior. After the theories are presented, we shall describe some applications based on one or more of the theories, provide suggestions for integration across theories, and discuss the implications of an integrated view for human performance at work. Before turning to the individual theories, the limits we have imposed on our examination of the performance of individuals at work are discussed.

Effort and Choice: Limiting the Criteria

Behavior is often construed as resulting from some multiplicative function of the person's *ability* to perform the behaviors in question and his or her *motivation* to do so (Vroom, 1964). *Ability* refers to those personal characteristics that relate to the capability to perform the behaviors of interest, whereas *motivation* deals with the willingness to invest effort in those behaviors. For our purposes, we shall focus on the motivational influences on behavior. Ability-focused discussions of behavior and productivity are covered in Chapters Six and Eight of this volume.

Motivation concerns those psychological processes that cause the arousal, direction, and persistence of behavior (Mitchell, 1982). *Arousal* and *persistence* involve the investment of time and effort in a particular behavior, and *direction* refers to the specific behaviors in which the time and effort are invested (Naylor, Pritchard, and Ilgen, 1980). Naylor, Pritchard, and Ilgen argue that motivation, as defined above, can be viewed as an issue of resource allocation on the part of the individual. At the most basic level, an individual has only two resources to invest: his or her *time* and *effort*. The meaning of time as a resource is straightforward; it is simply the number of time units devoted to performing the behavior. Effort is more complex. Conceptually, effort represents some amount of energy invested in the behavior per unit of time. Anecdotally, it is easy to see the difference between low effort and high for equal time periods in examples such as reading a chapter while also watching television, versus concentrating exclusively on the chapter. Practically, measuring effort, especially measuring it in a fashion that isolates it from time alone, is extremely difficult if not impossible in most cases. As a result, we shall consider effort as a primary criterion of motivation and time invested in a behavior as one indication of effort.

Finally, the directional component of motivation refers to the choice of behaviors in which a person decides to invest effort. The set of behaviors in which effort can be invested at any given time is almost limitless. For example, a letter carrier on a postal route can sit in the mail delivery truck, drive the truck, sort mail, place mail in the mailboxes, stop for a cup of coffee, talk with a person on the route, throw rocks at a barking dog, and any number of other behaviors. Identifying the content of the total set of behaviors is impossible and, fortunately, uninteresting. Of more importance is understanding which behaviors the person will choose to display. For this reason, the second criterion of interest is behavioral choice.

In sum, it is argued that motivation is concerned with the arousal, direction, and persistence of behavior and that these conditions are reflected in individuals' choices (1) of behaviors and (2) of the amount of effort devoted to the behaviors chosen. Productivity from an individualistic motivational perspective involves these choices for that subset of behaviors affecting the productivity of the unit. Some authors have defined this set of behaviors very broadly to include absenteeism, turnover, and many other behaviors at work (Katzell and Guzzo, 1983). In our case, we shall limit the set to those behaviors relevant to performing the subtasks allocated to the job in question and resulting in the production of the goods and/or services appropriate for the job. This limitation will direct our focus to the choices in the workplace that affect beliefs and expectations that lead employees to allocate their time and effort at work into behaviors related to task accomplishment. In particular, setting goals, receiving feedback about performance, and providing information about rewards or sanctions associated with performance behavior will be seen as some of the more important conditions that impact such choices. In the next section, we look more closely at theory and practice concerned with influencing employee choices about performance-related work behaviors.

Theories of Effort and Choice

The following pages briefly review approaches to motivation that highlight cognitive processes: expectancy theory, equity theory, goal-setting theory, cognitive evaluation theory, social learning theory, attribution theory, and schema theory.

Expectancy Theory. While the basic premises of expectancy theory can be traced back to Lewin (1938) and Tolman (1932), Vroom (1964) provided the first comprehensive formulation regarding work behavior. Many authors have since proposed extensions and refinements of Vroom's models (for example, Graen, 1969; Lawler, 1971; Naylor, Pritchard, and Ilgen, 1980), but the general underlying assumptions of the theory have remained essentially unchanged.

The basic notion of expectancy theory is that people choose tasks and/or effort levels that they believe will most likely lead to valued outcomes. According to the theory, three elements influence beliefs, which in turn influence choices. The first element is the amount of effort the person believes he or she invests in the behavior. The second element is the person's performance on the task or on some other class of behaviors (for example, absences). These elements are sometimes termed "first-level outcomes" (Campbell, Dunnette, Lawler, and Weick, 1970). Finally, according to the theory, it is assumed that there exists some set of additional second-level outcomes that hold some value to individuals (for example, money, friendliness of co-workers, supervisory recognition).

Motivation derives from a combination of three beliefs involving the elements just described. The first of these, termed an *expectan-*

cy, is a belief about the degree of association between levels of effort
and levels of performance (Ilgen, Pritchard, and Nebeker, 1981).
Expectancies are high when increases in effort are believed to lead to
increases in task performance and low when no connection between
working hard and performance level is perceived. The second belief,
termed an *instrumentality,* links performance to second-level outcomes. According to the theory, instrumentalities are individual
beliefs about the covariation between levels of first-level outcomes and
levels of each second-level outcome (for example, beliefs about the
relationship between levels of performance and those of pay). The
final belief, termed a *valence,* involves a person's subjective evaluation
of second-level outcomes. With respect to pay, these evaluations are,
for example, the attractiveness or anticipated value of $10 an hour, $20
an hour, and so on.

The motivational force on an individual to put forth effort is
a function of expectancies, instrumentalities, and valences. Vroom
(1964) presented two motivational models, the first a behavioral choice
model and the second a valence model. The valence model has
typically been tested against two criteria: occupational choice and job
satisfaction. The valence model applies when no behavior is involved
(for example, with job satisfaction) or when the expectancy term is
invariant and high (that is, there is certainty), as is the case when a
person chooses among occupations or job offers. Almost every test of
the valence model has produced strong, statistically significant results
(Mitchell, 1974).

The behavioral choice model has been tested primarily as a
predictor of effort, job performance, and organizational or occupational choice. This model is typically construed as the product of an
expectancy that effort will lead to the first-level outcome of interest
times the sum of the products of the instrumentalities between the
first-level outcome and all second-level outcomes of interest times the
valences of those second-level outcomes.

Most empirical studies of the behavioral choice model provide
some but not strong support (Mitchell, 1974). In general, studies
predicting organizational or occupational choice are more strongly
supported than those predicting effort or performance (Wanous, Keon,
and Latack, 1983). There have been a number of methodological issues
raised regarding tests of expectancy theory that suggest that research
to date may underestimate the theory's predictive power (Behling and
Starke, 1973; Ilgen, Pritchard, and Nebeker, 1981; Mitchell, 1974;
Schmidt, 1973; Whaba and House, 1974).

Equity Theory. Equity theory is traceable to early work on
social comparisons (Homans, 1961) and on cognitive dissonance

(Festinger, 1957). Adams (1963) presented the theoretical model most influential in work settings. The theory rests upon three main assumptions: (1) that people develop beliefs about what constitutes a fair and equitable *return* for the *contributions* they make to their jobs, (2) that they compare their own returns and contributions to those of others, and (3) that beliefs about unfair treatment (inequity) create tension that motivates people to reduce the tension (Carrell and Dittrich, 1978). Mechanisms for reducing perceived inequities include: (1) cognitively distorting the inputs or returns/outcomes, (2) acting on the comparison other to change his/her inputs or outcomes, (3) changing one's own inputs or outcomes, (4) changing the person to whom a comparison is made, and (5) leaving the situation where inequity is felt (Campbell and Pritchard, 1976). Equity theory predicts that individuals will choose a method of inequity reduction that is personally least costly (Adams, 1963). However, predicting which mode will be seen as least costly has proved to be quite difficult.

With respect to work settings, research has addressed almost exclusively performance quantity and quality as a function of over- or underpayment. Predictions regarding the effects of underpayment have consistently been supported: when workers are paid by the hour, inequity reduction typically takes the form of lowered performance, while under piecework or bonus conditions, those who feel underpaid tend to increase the quantity of their output while decreasing quality. The underpayment hypothesis is, however, not particularly interesting, because its behavioral predictions are indistinguishable from those of more parsimonious theories.

Overpayment effects are far more interesting but have received far less support. The theory predicts that feelings of overpayment inequity, in comparison to feelings of equity, will lead to increased performance quality and quantity under hourly pay conditions but only to increased quality when pay is contingent on performance quantity. The better-designed studies seem to suggest that the predicted overpayment effects can occur, but that the effects are not very large (Campbell and Pritchard, 1976; Vecchio, 1981). As with expectancy theory, the equity theory findings are tempered by theoretical and methodological limitations (Mowday, 1979). One major limitation to date regards the determination of whether overpayment inequity is a relatively enduring state. If it is not, equity theory adds complexity but little predictive value to more parsimonious explanations of behavior.

Goal-Setting Theory. Goal-setting proponents can be found as far back as scientific management study (Taylor, 1911) and the work on aspiration level by Mace (1935), Lewin (Lewin, Dembo, Festinger, and Sears, 1944), and Ryan (1958). Recent interest in goal setting is primarily attributable to the program of research conducted by Locke and Latham and their colleagues (Latham and Yukl, 1975; Locke, 1968; Locke, Shaw, Saari, and Latham, 1981).

Goal-setting theory suggests two cognitive determinants of behavior: intentions and values. Intentions are viewed as the immediate precursors of human action. The second cognitive process manifests itself in the choice or acceptance of intentions and subsequent commitment to those goals (Locke, 1968). It is the recognition that instructions will affect behavior only if they are consciously accepted that makes goal setting a cognitive theory of motivation (Landy and Becker, 1987).

A goal is that level of performance the individual is trying to accomplish; it is the object or aim of behavior. According to Locke (1968), goals direct attention and action. Additionally, they mobilize effort in proportion to the perceived requirements of the goal or task (Locke, Shaw, Saari, and Latham, 1981). Goal theory holds that once a hard task is accepted, the only logical thing to do is to try until the goal is achieved or until a decision is reached to lower or abandon the goal (Locke, 1968).

Substantial evidence supports the conclusion that difficult goals, if accepted, result in higher levels of performance than easy ones. A recent meta-analysis by Mento, Steel, and Karren (1987) revealed a corrected average effect size (d) of .58 between goal difficulty and performance. It has also been found that specific goals lead to greater outputs than vague goals such as "do your best" (Locke, 1968; Locke, Shaw, Saari, and Latham, 1981; Mento, Steel, and Karren, 1987).

Research further suggests that both goals and feedback are necessary to improve performance and that participation, incentives, and individual differences impact performance primarily through goal setting (Locke, Shaw, Saari, and Latham, 1981). Results regarding these key variables are, however, inconsistent (Hollenbeck and Klein, 1987). While the conclusion of Locke, Shaw, Saari, and Latham (1981) that "the beneficial effect of goal setting on task performance is one of the most robust and replicable findings in the psychological literature" (p. 145) is justifiable, much remains to be learned about how and under what conditions goals affect individual performance.

Cognitive Evaluation Theory. Cognitive evaluation theory (CET) is based on the combination of White's (1959) notion of competence motivation and DeCharms's (1968) notion of personal control. The former assumes that people are motivated to perform well on a task to the extent that task performance provides a feeling of accomplishment. The latter position holds that feelings of accomplishment can be experienced only when people feel responsible for their own behavior. Combining the two positions leads to the prediction that jobs or tasks will be motivating to the extent that (1) people feel personally responsible for performance and (2) performing well leads to feelings of accomplishment.

Although feelings of personal control and accomplishment are the critical psychological states, CET focuses attention primarily on elements in the task environment that affect these states. In particular, the theory is concerned with the interaction between the types of rewards associated with task performance: intrinsic rewards—those mediated by the persons performing the task (for example, the feeling of accomplishment that results from doing a good job)—and extrinsic rewards—those mediated by agents external to the persons (for example, money, praise).

The most interesting and controversial prediction from CET is that attaching extrinsic rewards to performance decreases the extent to which the task is intrinsically motivating. Presumably, if extrinsic rewards are associated with performance, control over performance shifts from the performers to the extrinsic rewards. For work settings, the prediction is that making pay contingent on performance decreases the persons' feelings of control and sense of accomplishment.

Research by Deci (1971, 1972) and others (Pritchard, Campbell, and Campbell, 1976) in the laboratory and in the classroom (Lepper and Green, 1975) has tended to support the hypothesis of an interaction between intrinsic and extrinsic rewards. However, laboratory research simulating work settings and field research in work organizations have not been able to replicate the interaction (Guzzo, 1979; Fisher, 1978). The reasons for this are not clear. One suggestion is that the distinction between intrinsic and extrinsic rewards is less in field settings, where extrinsic rewards such as pay may serve as signs of the intrinsic condition of accomplishment (Dyer and Parker, 1975). Another possibility is that the interaction does not occur with pay when well-established norms exist for paying people for working on the task (Fisher, 1978).

Social Learning Theory. Social learning theory holds that it is the cognitive representations of future outcomes that generate the motivation for current behavior. Actions are seen as largely under anticipatory control rather than as direct functions of the consequences of past actions (Bandura, 1977a).

According to Bandura, people process, weigh, and integrate diverse sources of information concerning their capabilities and regulate their behavior choices and effort expenditures accordingly. These "efficacy expectations" determine how much effort individuals will expend and how long they will persist in the face of obstacles and aversive experiences. Bandura's notion of efficacy expectations, termed *self-efficacy,* is similar to the concept of outcome expectancies in expectancy theory, but there is a subtle difference. An outcome expectancy is an estimate of the extent to which a given behavior will lead to certain outcomes. An efficacy expectation is the conviction that one can successfully execute the behaviors required to produce those outcomes (Bandura, Adams, and Beyer, 1977).

Efficacy expectations are acquired in many ways, including performance accomplishments, vicarious experience, verbal persuasion, and emotional arousal (Bandura, 1977a). Social learning theory suggests that while past personal experiences provide the most dependable source of efficacy expectations, most human behavior is learned observationally, through modeling (Bandura, 1977a). Social learning theory also posits that efficacy expectations by themselves are not sufficient to produce desired performance. There are many things that individuals know with certainty that they can do and yet do not do because they have no incentive to do so (Bandura, 1977a, 1977b). Recent studies by Bandura and Cervone (1983, 1987), Locke, Fredrick, Lee, and Bobko (1984), and Hollenbeck and Brief (1987) suggest that self-efficacy is strongly related to future task performance. Training procedures derived from the behavior modeling principles of social learning theory have also been highly successful in numerous applications (Decker and Nathan, 1985).

Attribution Theory. Attribution theory has developed from two separate lines of research, one identified largely with the work of Rotter (1966) and the other with that of Heider (1958). It concerns the process by which individuals develop causal explanations of past behaviors—one's own or those of others. These beliefs about past performance then influence future performance. Weiner and others (1971) propose that individuals utilize four main elements for explaining and predicting outcomes of tasks: ability, effort, task difficulty, and luck. These elements represent the influence of two orthogonal dimensions: stability and control.

While Kelley (1973) suggests that "causal attributions play an important role in providing the impetus to action and decisions among alternative courses of action" (p. 127), research has, for the most part, not entirely supported this contention. Findings indicate that attributions for past behavior do not influence subsequent actions directly. Rather, attributions influence behavior through cognitively formed *expectancies* for future success (McMahan, 1973). The empirical evidence regarding causal attributions and their effects on outcome expectancies seems to indicate that a past failure, if attributed to stable causes (for example, ability or task difficulty), will lead to lower outcome expectancies. Failure attributed to lack of effort or bad luck (that is, an unstable source), on the other hand, has the effect of raising expectancies for subsequent performance. The direction of these effects is the opposite following past success (Diener and Dweck, 1978; Dweck, 1975; McMahan, 1973; Meyer, 1980; Weiner, Heckhausen, Meyer, and Cook, 1972).

Schema Theory. The motivational approach that is most explicit in exploring the actual cognitive processes underlying behavior originates from cognitive psychology and centers on the construct of the schema. Bartlett (1932), who is credited with much of the early development of the concept, defines a schema as an organized structure of past ideas and experiences that influences the present interpretation of events. Neisser (1976) emphasizes that schemata are everchanging knowledge structures that influence not only the retrieval of past cognitions but also serve as formats or "cognitive maps" for proactively searching out and assimilating information. Motivationally, a schema is thus not only a pattern *of* action but also a pattern *for* action. From a schematic viewpoint, motivation is not initiated by outside forces external to the person that bring otherwise passive systems to life. Rather, motives derive from schemata that assimilate information and direct action.

While there are relatively few studies specifically demonstrating overt behavioral effects of schemata, schemata are assumed to include plans for action (Markus and Zajonc, 1985). There is also indirect evidence from diverse areas of study for the proposition that schemata direct behavior. From work in cognitive psychology, it appears that behavioral specifications are encoded in memory in the same manner as other types of information (Rosch and Mervis, 1975; Rosch, 1978). Additional evidence from perception research suggests that, as schemata develop for the recognition of events, behavior-specifying information is included (Barker, 1968).

Applications of Effort and Choice Theories

Having presented cognitively focused theories of motivation, we now turn to some examples of how they have been or could be applied in work settings to enhance motivation and thus productivity. Applications based on three of the previously discussed theories— expectancy theory, goal-setting theory, and social learning theory—are provided below. For each of these theories, general guidelines for its application are provided, along with a more detailed description of a recent intervention.

Expectancy Theory. The basic tenets of expectancy theory, as discussed earlier, suggest that individuals will be motivated to be highly productive if and only if three conditions are met. First, the individuals must believe that their efforts will result in high performance. That is, there must be a strong perceived expectancy between effort and performance. Second, they must perceive that high productivity rather than low productivity will be rewarded and/or low productivity will be punished. Finally, those rewards must be highly valent to them.

Nadler and Lawler (1977) provide a number of more specific implications for the enhancing of motivation based upon expectancy theory. First, the organization must identify what kinds of behaviors it desires and describe them in specific and measurable terms. The desired levels of performance must be seen as obtainable by the individuals to ensure a perceived effort-to-performance expectancy. It is also necessary to determine what outcomes are valued by employees. Those outcomes desired should then be clearly and explicitly linked to standards of performance. Nadler and Lawler further stress the need to analyze the situation for conflicting expectancies and instrumentalities. Conflicts arise when investing time and effort in performance-related activities increases the probability of attaining one valued outcome but decreases the probability of receiving another outcome of value.

Nebeker and Neuberger (1985) developed and evaluated a performance-contingent reward system based on expectancy theory for small-purchase buyers and supply clerks employed in the purchase division of a supply department in a naval shipyard. In this intervention, productivity standards were developed for each job/task. These standards were expressed as the length of time in which a qualified worker could be expected to complete the task working at a normal pace. Standards were set at approximately the seventieth percentile of the preintervention rate. Individual productivity was measured objectively and quantitatively (controlling for quality), and feedback was provided at the individual level on a weekly basis via computer-generated efficiency reports. Financial bonuses above regular wages were also provided as rewards. For each hour saved, an employee earned a bonus equal to 30 percent of his or her average hourly rate.

The trial period was superior to the baseline period for both buyers and clerks on every measure of productivity and production. Production efficiency in terms of requisitions per labor hour increased 26 percent. Overtime hours were reduced by 94 percent, workload backlog for the buyers was cut 51.7 percent, and procurement average lead time in days dropped by 42.6 percent. The net savings generated during the seventeen-week trial period exceeded $14,000.

Pritchard (1986a, 1986b) and his colleagues addressed productivity enhancement directly with a very promising organizational intervention system based on the measurement of productivity and derived from the expanded expectancy theory developed by Naylor, Pritchard, and Ilgen (1980). Pritchard (1986b) argued that, at any level of aggregation in an organization (for example, individual, work group, division, and so on), there exists some underlying effectiveness construct based on how well the person/unit is accomplishing its goals and objectives. Furthermore, he assumed that effectiveness, so defined, can be assessed by a measurement system that meets the criteria listed in Table 7.1. Four steps for the development of such a system were listed: (1) identification of salient products for effectiveness, (2) identification of indicators of these products, (3) establishment of the contingencies between products and effectiveness, and (4) the combination of products and indicators in one measure at the desired level of aggregation.

The crux of Pritchard's measurement system is the development of measures, all of which result from extensive involvement of personnel working in the units under investigation. Constructing the measurement system begins with defining a *product*. (In Pritchard's system, *products, indicators,* and *contingencies* have a very specific meaning.) *Products* are the relatively tangible or observable objects or things that the unit in question is expected to produce as a result of its activities. For example, in a motor vehicle maintenance unit studied by Pritchard (1986b) and his colleagues, quality of repairs, timeliness of repairs, and maintenance of a supply of qualified repair persons through on-the-job training were three products that unit

Table 7.1. Criteria for an Effective Measure of Productivity According to Pritchard's System.

1. Is capable of yielding a single index of productivity at every meaningful unit of analysis within the organization
2. Identifies subindices of productivity
3. Addresses the existence of multiple tasks within jobs and units
4. Can be applied at any level of the organization
5. Is valid
6. Is flexible
7. Is accepted
8. Has positive motivational properties

personnel identified as central to the effectiveness of the unit. For each product, there are subproducts, termed *indicators* or *indices,* which are manifestations of products. For the maintenance example, repair return rate and percentage of quality control inspections passed were indices of quality.

Once the set of products and indicators is identified, employees are presented with a judgment task designed to map levels of indicators onto a scale of effectiveness. For Pritchard, this scale ranged from +100 for maximum effectiveness through 0 for neutral effectiveness to –100 for minimum effectiveness. The end result of this process is a series of curves that represent the way in which indicators and thus products produced by the unit are related to the unit's effectiveness. Figure 7.1 depicts sample curves for the maintenance unit example.

The development of a family of effectiveness-to-indices curves is extremely useful for several reasons. First, the slope of the curves reflects the importance of the indicator in question to the overall effectiveness of the unit. Those indicators with steeper slopes are more important than those for which the slope is less steep. For example, in the unit profiled in Figure 7.1, the return rate was more important than training. Second, the curves make clear the fact that effectiveness is often not a linear function of the level of indicators.

The value of the effectiveness measurement system is that it can be used with goal setting, feedback, incentives, and other motivational processes. Field research with the system has been very encouraging. The development of the system along with feedback in five units within a larger organization led to productivity improvements of 50 percent on the average (Pritchard, 1986a). When goal setting was added to the feedback, the average productivity increased to 74 percent over baseline.

Goal Setting. Locke and Latham (1984) outline several principles for enhancing employee motivation through goal theory. First, the general objective or tasks to be done must be determined. It must also be specified how the performance in question will be measured. Next, the standard or target to be reached must be explicitly stated. The target or goal should be specific rather than vague, and it should be challenging yet attainable. A specific time span for the attainment of the goal should also be determined. If multiple goals are set, these should be rank-ordered so that effort can be directed in proportion to the importance of each goal. Finally, coordination requirements need to be determined to ensure that the goals of different people are not conflicting.

Locke and Latham also discuss several other issues key to successful goal-setting implementations. Steps must be taken to ensure goal commitment, be it by instruction and explanation, participation in goal setting, incentives, or supportiveness. In addition, action plans, feedback, training, facilitative company policies, and resources of time, money, and assistance are all necessary. Action plans aid in the search for means of accomplishing goals and help to guide those efforts toward goal attainment. Feedback is necessary to assess goal progress and make appropriate changes in behavior. Training is important to ensure that individuals have the skills and knowledge necessary to attain the goal. Company policies and resources are needed to facilitate goal accomplishment and to eliminate performance constraints or blocks to goal accomplishment.

The effectiveness of goal-setting programs for increasing productivity has been demonstrated in a number of applications across a wide variety of jobs and industries (Locke and Latham, 1984; Latham and Lee, 1986; Latham and Yukl, 1975). Recently, Kim (1984) applied goal-setting techniques to salespeople in several branches of a large retail organization. In this intervention, the goals consisted of both specific selling activities and specific sales levels in dollar terms. Goals were participatively set, and supervisors were given training to facilitate the implementation of the program. Feedback was given every two weeks at both the group and individual level. The intervention was documented for five consecutive two-week periods.

Controlling for initial group differences in selling performance, departments in which goal setting was introduced exhibited significantly higher selling performance than departments in which goal setting was not introduced. In one department using goal setting, hourly sales per salesperson increased more than 32 percent on the average, compared to the 3 percent increase in the control group. The dollar value of the increase for this one department was estimated at $50,000 for the twenty-week period.

Social Learning Theory. The most common application of social learning theory in work organizations is behavior modeling training (Goldstein and Sorcher, 1974). Behavior modeling relies on social learning theory to facilitate behavior change by increasing the efficacy expectations of individuals. The behavior modeling process, described below, provides all four of the previously discussed mechanisms through which self-efficacy is acquired: verbal persuasion, vicarious learning, performance accomplishment, and emotional arousal.

Behavior modeling training consists of four basic elements: modeling, role playing, social reinforcement, and transfer training. In order for the training to be effective, individuals must attend to what the model is doing, be able to recall and do what the model is doing,

Figure 7.1. Examples of Effectiveness Contingency Curves

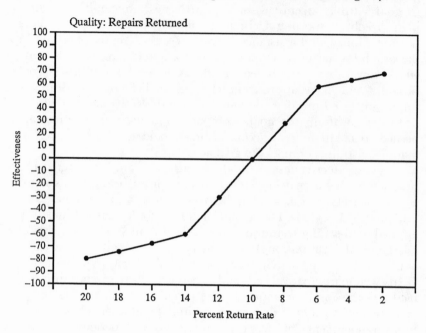

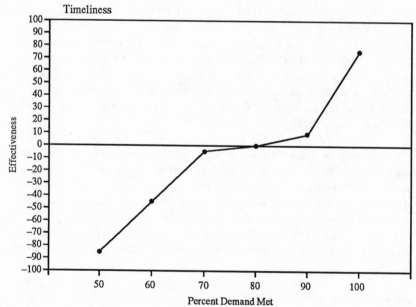

Source: Pritchard, 1986b.

for Three Indices of Maintenance Shop Productivity.

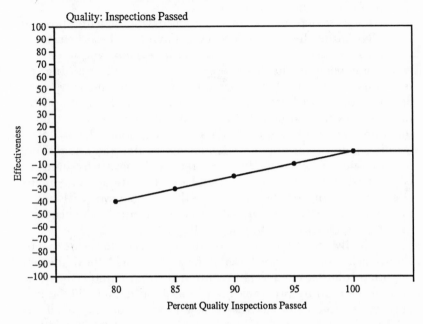

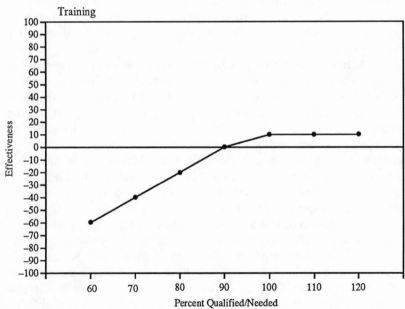

and be motivated to apply the learned behaviors once they return to their jobs (Decker and Nathan, 1985).

The first step in implementing a behavior modeling program is to determine the desired or key behaviors. These behavioral standards are then used to write the learning points and to develop ways for models to display those behaviors. In the training, the individual is presented these learning points and then the model depicting the desired behaviors. The latter is typically accomplished through presentation of videotaped materials showing actors doing the desired behaviors. The next step is overt behavioral rehearsal of the learning points, typically via role playing. During the role playing, social reinforcement in the form of praise and constructive feedback is provided. While the modeling and role playing account for the effective learning of the behaviors, those behaviors will not be maintained unless the individual perceives performing the behaviors to be rewarding (Decker and Nathan, 1985).

Finally, attention is given to issues of transfer, to ensure that the learned behaviors are carried over to the work setting. One of the most important transfer enhancers is continued social reinforcement, not only in the training program but also back on the job. The trainee must be reinforced for the use of new behavior on the job if that behavior is to be maintained (Decker and Nathan, 1985). In addition, goal setting should also be used to facilitate transfer, with the specific behavioral standards from the training serving as the goals (Wexley and Latham, 1981).

Behavior modeling has been shown to be an effective method for changing employee behaviors in a number of industrial applications (Decker and Nathan, 1985). Katzell and Guzzo (1983) reviewed 207 recent American experiments with productivity enhancement and found training to be the most frequently used productivity enhancement intervention, and behavior modeling was one of the most successful training methods. A carefully controlled behavior modeling intervention was recently evaluated by Meyer and Raich (1983). This application, like that of Kim (1984), was aimed at improving the effectiveness of salespeople in a large retail organization. Training was provided to salespeople in several departments of seven different stores. Counterparts in seven other stores in the same city served as controls.

The behavior modeling program of Meyer and Raich (1983) followed the general procedures described above. Specific standards of sales behavior were identified for each aspect of a sales interaction and were presented as learning points. Videotaped models were developed and presented to demonstrate these behavior standards. The employees then practiced these situations in role-playing rehearsals, with their performance reinforced by their supervisors, who had been trained as instructors.

Sales performance for six months prior to training was compared to performance for the six months after training for both the trained and untrained groups. The performance measure was average commission earned per hour worked. The average per-hour earnings for those trained increased 7 percent, whereas earnings of those who had not received training declined 3 percent. In addition, only 7 percent of the trained employees turned over during the six months following the training, compared to 22 percent of those who had not been trained.

Integrating Concepts

We have presented what we believe are the primary theoretical positions regarding individuals' effort and choice as they relate to employee performance and productivity. The preceding sample of applications represents research within a particular theoretical position that demonstrates a positive influence on individuals' performance. Lacking, however, are integrating principles across the theories and application strategies. With respect to the latter, most if not all productivity enhancement efforts aimed at organizational personnel (as contrasted with those that focus on the technological system) have been initiated from within one theoretical perspective and have been loath to incorporate others.

The lack of integration is unfortunate. The diversity of perspectives gives the impression that there are few general principles across positions. Yet this conclusion is unjustified, for two reasons. First, the three applications we discussed in the preceding section, although generated from within one point of view, incorporated constructs from others. Pritchard's (1986a, 1986b) expectancy theory interventions worked best when paired with goal setting, and transfer from behavior modeling training back to the job was better when performance goals were set (Wexley and Latham, 1981). For goals to be effective, it was assumed that the performer saw some connection between goal accomplishment and the receipt of some positive reinforcers; in other words, goals worked when nonzero instrumentalities existed between goal accomplishment and valued outcomes. Thus all three approaches explicitly included constructs from other theoretical positions.

A less explicit condition facilitating integration among the theories is the fact that the constructs developed within positions share a great deal in common across positions. This overlap has both negative and positive effects. On the negative side, manipulation of variables within one theoretical framework can often be construed as confounding variables from another. For example, goal-setting research often varies goal difficulty but restricts the goals to a range known to be possible given the performers' ability. From an expectancy theory perspective, this requirement ensures that, at least at the objective level, expectancies are greater than zero. The implications of this from an expectancy theory perspective are, however, virtually ignored when goals are the primary focus.

On a more positive note, the overlap and shared nature of the constructs developed within the separate theories provide a basis for integration among them. Integration is, in our opinion, necessary. It is necessary because the theoretical perspectives rarely contradict and often complement each other. In fact, in one case, data generated and interpreted from within one theoretical position could not be distinguished from those of another, in spite of very different interpretations offered for the same pattern of results. (See Locke's [1980] comparison of the goal setting of Latham with the behavior modification research of Komaki.) These conditions suggest that a summary of integrating concepts should be possible.

Constructs for Understanding Behavior

The integration that follows is based on our belief that the constructs developed from different theoretical positions share a great deal in common. With these commonalities taken into account, it is possible to reduce the set of variables that are believed to be important for influencing job performance and at the same time capture the processes influencing performance posited by each position. The remaining constructs should represent those that are most important with less overlap than is presently the case, with variables generated from within particular theories. A more limited but "purer" set of constructs may also provide better cues for guiding interventions aimed at improving performance on the job. In Table 7.2 we present an outline for an integration that will be developed and discussed.

Common Processes. We suggest that cognitive influences on individual performance, as outlined in Table 7.2, are driven by two processes. The first of these is *sense making.* Many theories assume that the actors in a performance-oriented system attempt to make sense out of their environment and their place in it. Attribution theory focuses narrowly on making sense out of performance. According to the theory, whether observing their own performance or the performance of others, people are not content simply to record a level of

Table 7.2. An Integration of Effort and Choice Theories.

Constructs	Relevant Theories
I. Understanding behavior	
A. Process	
1. Sense making	Attribution theory
	Schema theory
	Expectancy theory
	Goal-setting theory
	Equity theory
2. Limited hedonism	Expectancy theory
	Goal-setting theory
B. Beliefs	
1. Settings	All
2. Behavior	All
3. Valence or "value"	Expectancy theory
	Equity theory
	Cognitive evaluation theory
	Social learning theory
II. Learning	
1. Direct communication	Expectancy theory
	Goal-setting theory
2. Experience (including feedback)	All
3. Modeling	Social learning theory

performance in memory; they attempt to put the performance in perspective by developing a personal theory about why a particular level of performance existed. We would argue that personal performance theories result from trying to make sense of performance behavior in the behavior setting.

Sense making is more implicit in other theories. Schemata are, for the most part, continuous scenarios in which new observations are made to fit into the pattern of beliefs that already exists in the minds of the observer. This fitting and modifying process is done in a manner that maintains a certain level of logical consistency, at least from the perspective of the person who holds the particular schematic view; logical consistency is making sense. Expectancy and goal-setting theories, by their limited or quasi rationality assumption, can also be construed as heavily dependent on a sense-making mechanism. Both theories are based on the assumption that individuals make some evaluations of the subjective expected utilities associated with the investment of time and effort in working on tasks. We would argue that weighting and evaluating behavioral alternatives and then selecting some subset of actions is a process that involves attempts on the part of the actors to understand the nature of their place in that environment and to choose courses of action that make the most sense to them.

Although equity theory does not address rationality as directly as expectancy and goal-setting theories, it is no less rational. The primary difference is that the decision rule changes; that is, what "makes sense" changes. Rather than investing time and effort in behaviors that maximize returns, the individuals compare themselves to others to make sense out of the ratio of personal inputs to outcomes and then choose a course of action that is "fair" or "equitable."

The second overarching process represented in the various theories we shall call *limited hedonism*. As a process guiding behavior, hedonism posits that individuals select behaviors that will maximize their own personal return. Cognitive theories, such as expectancy and goal setting, incorporate hedonistic processes into the rationality assumption. The selection of the course of action with the highest subjective expected utility is a hedonistic response. Behavioral theories that deny or downplay the role of cognition in behavior choice are also very hedonistic in their assumption that behavior is a function of its consequences; specifically, behaviors with the most positive consequences will be repeated most frequently. Although the equity theorists would strongly argue that equity norms are fundamentally different from hedonistic ones, even equity has been construed in hedonistic terms. Lawler (1971) argued that outcomes (for example, rewards) can attain their value to the individual because of the extent to which they are fair or equitable.

Although some form of a hedonistic mechanism is common in many theories, none of the positions expects people to attempt to maximize their own returns with respect to their own personal standards every time they behave. Cognitive limitations, contextual constraints on behaviors, and many other factors modify the ability or even desire of persons to pursue strictly hedonistic responses on every occasion. Therefore, the limiting assumption is that, over time, people will tend to show patterns of behavior that follow a general hedonistic model.

Common Beliefs. Whereas sense making and hedonism represent underlying processes implied in theories of work motivation, beliefs represent the content of theories. In particular, three classes of beliefs can be identified. The first of these is *beliefs about settings* or environments in which the person is located. These beliefs can be viewed as relatively passive, in the sense that they do not impact behavior directly. For expectancy and goal setting, these beliefs are those that deal with the relationship between performance and outcomes—more specifically, instrumentalities. For equity theory, these are beliefs about the input-to-outcome ratios of comparison others. In schema theory, these are the schemata themselves.

The second set of beliefs represent *beliefs about behavior* and its antecedents or consequences. Expectancy, goal-setting, attribution, and social learning theories all assume that people hold beliefs about the extent to which investing time and effort in performance behaviors will affect performance. Expectancy and social learning theories make these beliefs central in the "expectancy" and "self-efficacy" constructs respectively. Goal-setting theory suggests that such beliefs are necessary for goals to affect behavior; Locke and his colleagues stress that the performer must believe that a goal can be accomplished if goals are to be accepted (Locke, Shaw, Saari, and Latham, 1981). In attribution theory, attention is focused on beliefs about the reasons for past performance. Yet these beliefs about the past have motivational relevance in that they affect beliefs about the efficacy of future behavior.

The final set of beliefs are more affectively oriented. They represent *beliefs about the emotional value* that individuals expect they will receive for attaining certain types of conditions. For expectancy theory, valences represent the affective value persons believe will be incurred from achieving particular levels of outcomes. For equity theory, it is the belief that a particular input-to-outcome ratio has a given value to the person. Rather than address value-oriented beliefs directly, cognitive evaluation theory assumes that the person holds such beliefs about the reward value of working on the task and then focuses on the derivation of this reward value from the interaction of intrinsic and extrinsic performance outcomes. Social learning theory would couch this type of belief in reinforcement terms.

Acquisition of Beliefs (Learning). The first two processes discussed earlier are necessary but not sufficient for addressing productivity through individual performance; it must also be possible to influence individual performance. Sense making and limited hedonism are assumed to be relatively stable operating procedures that are not, themselves, subject to influence. Beliefs, on the other hand, can be created and changed. These effects are accomplished through the process of learning. Therefore, attempts to influence productivity, from a cognitive perspective, can be viewed as attempts to establish, change, or modify the three kinds of beliefs just described.

Beliefs are learned, and they are learned through three primary methods (Bandura, 1977a; Naylor, Pritchard, and Ilgen, 1980). First, they can be learned through *direct communication* or instruction. In this case, the individual is provided with certain information that is incorporated into his or her belief system. Direct communication is very effective for learning beliefs about conditions in the work environment but is less so for learning about one's own behavior or about how outcomes will be valued.

A second mode of affecting beliefs is through *experience.* Experience that includes feedback about the effectiveness of performance also makes it possible to establish beliefs about behavior in the setting of interest.

Finally, a person can learn vicariously from watching others. This is called *modeling.* Modeling occurs if observing the behavior of others—and the consequences of that behavior to the others (that is, whether or not the others are reinforced for their behavior)—influences the observer's own behavior in a manner similar to the expected influence of the reinforcers on the person being observed. It has frequently been demonstrated that beliefs can be learned through modeling—even beliefs about the value of outcomes. For example, Weiss and Shaw (1979) found that the degree to which people liked working on an electronics assembly task was affected by overhearing conversations of others about the extent to which they enjoyed working on the task.

Guidelines for Productivity Enhancement

Based on the above review of relevant theory and research, we would like to outline where and how motivational considerations could influence productivity. We move from the general to the specific.

General Principles. To the extent that our integrating constructs (see Table 7.2) adequately capture the processes and content of individual performance, six general principles should be useful for designing systems for the purposes of enhancing productivity. First, because it is assumed that people on the job will attempt to make sense out of their situation and to behave in a manner that they will find rewarding, attempts should be made to influence the sense new employees make of the work setting. Extreme care must be taken to design environments in such a way that they are easily understood by the persons who operate in them. Furthermore, individuals' understanding of their work environment should be consistent with the productivity goals of the organization. Often, from an organizational perspective, we fail to learn how a system is perceived by the people who use it and, as a result, are surprised when the responses are different from those anticipated (Goldstein, 1986). The work described earlier by Pritchard (1986a, 1986b) is an excellent example of investing a great deal of care in understanding the users' view of productivity-relevant concepts such as effectiveness.

A second principle is related to the first and needs little elaboration. It stresses simply that care must be taken to learn the outcomes that are valued by the subgroup of people whose performance is of interest. Research on comparable worth by one of the authors (Hollenbeck, Ilgen, Ostroff, and Vancouver, 1986) suggested that a conception of worth based solely on money, like that often proposed by advocates of comparable worth, ignores the fact that when given the option to choose jobs without restriction, women prefer jobs possessing outcomes valued more than pay. Worth, in their sample, was more broadly based than simply pay. This research stresses the need to understand the value of outcomes before arbitrarily assuming standards for outcome value for populations of employees.

Establishing performance standards (goals), creating contingencies between effort, performance, and valued outcomes, and providing means for receiving performance feedback are the third, fourth, and fifth general guidelines. Feedback is critical because it affects the ability of the employees to experience the nature of the contingencies. Here again, Pritchard's work on measuring productivity is valuable. Graphs such as those presented in Figure 7.1 highlight the nature of relevant contingencies in ways that are grasped easily. In addition, they highlight the fact that the association between variables important for productivity may not be linear.

The sixth point to keep in mind is that individual performance at work is of concern over an extended period of time. Unfortunately, neither commonly used research methods nor the conceptual models of our discipline are very good at understanding the dynamics of change. At a superficial level, it is recognized that sense making is an ongoing process, likes and dislikes change, and perceptions of self-efficacy as well as situations are not constant. The precise implications of these conditions are not nearly as clear. We can only suggest that when organizations attempt to impact individual productivity, conditions that are installed be constantly monitored—and changed if the data from the monitoring indicate that such change is necessary.

Specific Practices. Our suggested mechanisms for impacting performance from a cognitive perspective are selection and placement, socialization practices (including establishment of realistic expectations about the job prior to hiring, and training for new employees), goal setting, contingency management, performance feedback, and attitude surveys. These are the same types of practices that frequently have been used in the past. The major difference is that the application of the practices is guided by a unified focus on employee beliefs. Each practice, and the implications of the cognitive emphasis, is discussed briefly below.

Selection and placement practices approach employee performance through creating a good match between employees' knowledge, skills, abilities, and values and the demands of the jobs in which these employees are placed. The utility of these techniques for affecting performance is well documented. From a cognitive perspective, the impact of selection and placement is on beliefs about the extent to which investing time and effort in the job will lead to successful job performance and on beliefs about the extent to which jobs meet the job holders' perceived needs.

Typically, selection and placement practices direct attention to relatively stable individual difference characteristics, such as abilities, and their direct effect on the employees' capability to perform the jobs to which they are assigned. From the point of view taken in this chapter, abilities are seen as also impacting performance indirectly. In particular, the employees' own beliefs about the level of performance reached and the reasons for reaching that level affect performance by affecting expectations for the future. This additional role of selection and placement, as a means of affecting beliefs, has typically been ignored.

Socialization, both on the job and before employees are hired, serves to shape employee responses at work in directions consistent with the goals of the organization. Realistic job previews (Ilgen and Seely, 1974; Wanous, 1980) have been shown to be effective for creating initial expectations about job conditions in new employees that are in line with actual job conditions. However, the literature on realistic previews provides little guidance about the types of information that should be included in the preview, nor does it focus directly on performance-related elements of productivity. From the cognitive perspective offered here, realistic previews about the likelihood that effort and time invested in the job will lead to successful job performance and about the outcomes associated with successful performance should be useful for shaping the expectancy and instrumentality beliefs of new employees.

Other socialization processes, such as initial training programs, are often used to shape the behaviors of new employees (Van Maanen and Schein, 1979). Although these practices are very commonly used, there is again little guidance as to the nature of the content of such experiences. As with realistic job previews, the beliefs that are identified as important for individual productivity provide a basis for guiding the content of formal socialization practices.

Training, in addition to shaping the behaviors of newcomers, is an effective means of changing performance potential for those who have been with the organization for some time. The emphasis of most training is on changing employee skills. Yet in the process of skill enhancement, beliefs are also changed. In particular, individuals' beliefs about the likelihood that time and effort devoted to the task affects their level of performance (performance expectancy beliefs) should change to the extent that their task skills change. From a motivational perspective, more attention should be paid to such motivational elements in training programs.

Performance *goals* provide direction to effort. Such goals may be established by the employee, as is the case with self-set goals, by supervisors or other organizational representatives, or by some combination of the two. Management by objectives (MBO) is an example of a practice involving joint supervisor-subordinate goal setting.

All of the practices mentioned thus far involve working directly with employees to affect their beliefs or to select those who hold beliefs that are consistent with the job. *Contingency management* directs attention to conditions in the work setting—a process that should impact employee beliefs. Specifically, either through supervisory practices or through the design of the work environment, a focus on contingencies attempts to associate valued outcomes with desired behaviors such that employees are rewarded for displaying those behaviors. An emphasis on the establishment of contingencies between valued outcomes and behavior is the central concern of expectancy theory and of behavior modification procedures. Directing attention to the contingencies at work should be central to creating conditions that encourage effective performance.

Along with the establishment of contingencies between desired behaviors and valued outcomes is the need to provide *feedback* to the employees about the nature of their behavior. This feedback may be indigenous to the task itself, as is the case for the house painter who can see immediately how much of the structure has been painted, or externally provided (Ilgen, Fisher, and Taylor, 1979). Regardless of its source, performance feedback is a necessary condition for effective performance (Locke, Shaw, Saari, and Latham, 1981). Efforts must be taken to structure conditions at work so that meaningful performance feedback is available.

One final practice that would seem valuable from a cognitive view of performance effectiveness is the use of *attitude surveys* to collect information about two sets of beliefs. First, surveys are useful for learning the nature of employee beliefs about contingencies. In particular, surveys should reveal the extent to which employee beliefs about expectancies and instrumentalities match those believed by managers to exist for the employees. Discrepancies between employee and management views provide a basis for exploring ways to modify employee beliefs and/or job conditions to create more desirable beliefs. Second, surveys are useful for learning the value that employees attach to a number of different outcomes, so that contingencies can be established between performance and outcomes that are valued.

Conclusion

To the extent that individual effort and choice can be expected to impact organizational productivity, cognitive theories exist that offer suggestions for impacting productivity. Several efforts have been made to enhance performance through the application of these theories, examples of which have been reported. For the most part, however, these interventions have been undertaken from within one or perhaps two of the general cognitive theories. We have suggested that this narrowness of scope is neither desirable nor necessary. In an attempt to integrate the various positions, we have suggested that there are a very small number of processes and constructs that pervade the cognitive views. Concentrating on these elements and incorporating a few general principles for addressing individual productivity may be useful for structuring future productivity interventions. Suggestions for implementing these general principles involve many common practices, with changes in focus only.

References

Adams, J. S. "Toward an Understanding of Inequity." *Journal of Abnormal and Social Psychology,* 1963, *67,* 422–436.

Bandura, A. *Social Learning Theory.* Englewood Cliffs, N.J.: Prentice-Hall, 1977a.

Bandura, A. "Self-Efficacy: Toward a Unifying Theory of Behavioral Change." *Psychological Review,* 1977b, *84,* 191–215.

Bandura, A., Adams, N. E., and Beyer, J. "Cognitive Processes Mediating Behavior Change." *Journal of Personality and Social Psychology,* 1977, *35,* 125–139.

Bandura, A., and Cervone, D. "Self-Evaluation and Self-Efficacy Mechanisms Governing the Motivational Effects of Goal Systems." *Journal of Personality and Social Psychology,* 1983, *45,* 1017–1028.

Bandura, A., and Cervone, D. "Differential Engagement of Self-Reactive Influences in Cognitive Motivation." *Organizational Behavior and Human Decision Processes,* 1987, *38,* 92–113.

Barker, R. G. *Ecological Psychology: Concepts and Methods for Studying the Environment of Human Behavior.* Stanford, Calif.: Stanford University Press, 1968.

Bartlett, F. C. *Remembering: A Study in Experimental and Social Psychology.* New York: Cambridge University Press, 1932.

Behling, O., and Starke, F. A. "The Postulates of Expectancy Theory." *Academy of Management Journal,* 1973, *16,* 373–388.

Campbell, J. P., Dunnette, M. D., Lawler, E. E., III, and Weick, K. E. *Managerial Behavior, Performance, and Effectiveness.* New York: McGraw-Hill, 1970.

Campbell, J. P., and Pritchard, R. D. "Motivational Theory in Industrial and Organizational Psychology." In M. D. Dunnette (ed.), *Handbook of Industrial and Organizational Psychology.* Skokie, Ill.: Rand McNally, 1976.

Carrell, M. R., and Dittrich, J. E. "Equity Theory: The Recent Literature, Methodological Considerations, and New Directions." *Academy of Management Journal,* 1978, *55,* 523–524.

DeCharms, R. *Personal Causation.* Orlando, Fla.: Academic Press, 1968.

Deci, E. L. "Effects of Externally Mediated Rewards on Intrinsic Motivation." *Journal of Personality and Social Personality,* 1971, *18,* 105–115.

Deci, E. L. "The Effects of Contingent and Non-Contingent Rewards and Controls on Intrinsic Motivation." *Organizational Behavior and Human Performance,* 1972, *8,* 217–229.

Decker, P. J., and Nathan, B. R. *Behavioral Modeling Training: Principles and Applications.* New York: Praeger, 1985.

Diener, E., and Dweck, C. S. "An Analysis of Learned Helplessness: Continuous Changes in Performance, Strategy, and Achievement Cognitions Following Failure." *Journal of Personality and Social Psychology,* 1978, *31,* 451–462.

Dweck, C. S. "The Role of Expectations and Attributions in the Alleviation of Learned Helplessness." *Journal of Personality and Social Psychology,* 1975, *31,* 674–685.

Dyer, L., and Parker, D. F. "Classifying Outcomes in Work Motivation Research: An Examination of the Intrinsic-Extrinsic Dichotomy." *Journal of Applied Psychology,* 1975, *60,* 455–458.

Festinger, L. A. *A Theory of Cognitive Dissonance.* New York: Harper & Row, 1957.

Fisher, C. D. "The Effects of Personal Control, Competence, and Extrinsic Reward Systems on Intrinsic Motivation." *Organizational Behavior and Human Performance,* 1978, *21,* 273–288.

Goldstein, A. P., and Sorcher, M. *Changing Supervisor Behavior.* Elmsford, N.Y.: Pergamon Press, 1974.

Goldstein, I. L. *Values and Interventions: How and Where Are We Looking?* Presidential address, meeting of the Society for Industrial and Organizational Psychology, Washington, D.C., Aug. 1986.

Graen, G. "Instrumentality Theory of Work Motivation: Some Experimental Results and Suggested Modifications." *Journal of Applied Psychology,* 1969, *53,* 1-25.

Guzzo, R. A. "Types of Rewards, Cognitions, and Work Motivation." *Academy of Management Review,* 1979, *4,* 75-86.

Heider, F. *The Psychology of Interpersonal Relations.* New York: Wiley, 1958.

Hollenbeck, J. R., and Brief, A. P. "The Effects of Individual Differences and Goal Origin on the Goal Setting Process." *Organizational Behavior and Human Decision Processes,* 1987, *40,* 292-314.

Hollenbeck, J. R., Ilgen, D. R., Ostroff, C., and Vancouver, J. B. "Sex Differences in Occupational Choice, Pay, and Worth: A Psychological Approach to Understanding the Male-Female Wage Gap." Unpublished paper, Department of Psychology, Michigan State University, 1986.

Hollenbeck, J. R., and Klein, H. J. "Goal Commitment and the Goal-Setting Process: Problems, Prospects, and Proposals for Future Research." *Journal of Applied Psychology,* 1987, *72,* 212-220.

Homans, G. C. *Social Behavior: Its Elementary Forms.* San Diego, Calif.: Harcourt Brace Jovanovich, 1961.

Ilgen, D. R., Fisher, C. D., and Taylor, M. S. "Consequences of Individual Feedback on Behavior in Organizations." *Journal of Applied Psychology,* 1979, *64,* 349-371.

Ilgen, D. R., Pritchard, R. D., and Nebeker, D. M. "Expectancy Theory Measures: An Empirical Comparison in an Experimental Simulation." *Organizational Behavior and Human Performance,* 1981, *28,* 189-223.

Ilgen, D. R., and Seely, W. "Realistic Expectations as an Aid to Coping with a Stressful Environment." *Journal of Applied Psychology,* 1974, *59,* 452-456.

Katzell, R. A., and Guzzo, R. A. "Psychological Approaches to Productivity Improvement." *American Psychologist,* 1983, *38,* 468-472.

Kelley, H. H. "The Process of Causal Attribution." *American Psychologist,* 1973, *28,* 107-128.

Kim, J. S. "Effect of Behavior Plus Outcome Goal Setting and

Feedback on Employee Satisfaction and Performance." *Academy of Management Journal*, 1984, *27*, 139–149.

Landy, F. J., and Becker, L. J. "Motivation Theory Reconsidered." In L. Cummings and B. Staw (eds.), *Research in Organizational Behavior*. Vol. 9. Greenwich, Conn.: JAI Press, 1987.

Latham, G. P., and Lee, T. W. "Goal Setting." In E. A. Locke (ed.), *Generalizing from Laboratory to Field Settings*. Lexington, Mass.: Lexington Books, 1986.

Latham, G. P., and Yukl, G. A. "A Review of Research on the Application of Goal Setting in Organizations." *Academy of Management Journal*, 1975, *18*, 824–845.

Lawler, E. E., III. *Pay and Organizational Effectiveness: A Psychological View*. New York: McGraw-Hill, 1971.

Lepper, M. R., and Green, D. "Turning Play into Work." *Journal of Personality and Social Psychology*, 1975, *31*, 479–486.

Lewin, K. *The Conceptual Representation and the Measurement of Psychological Forces*. Durham, N.C.: Duke University Press, 1938.

Lewin, K., Dembo, T., Festinger, L., and Sears, P. S. "Level of Aspiration." In J. M. Hunt (ed.), *Personality and the Behavior Disorders*. New York: Roland Press, 1944.

Locke, E. A. "Toward a Theory of Task Motivation and Incentives." *Organizational Behavior and Human Performance*, 1968, *3*, 157–189.

Locke, E. A. "Latham vs. Komaki: A Tale of Two Paradigms." *Journal of Applied Psychology*, 1980, *65*, 16–23.

Locke, E. A., Fredrick, E., Lee, C., and Bobko, P. "Effects of Self-Efficacy, Goals, and Task Strategies on Task Performance." *Journal of Applied Psychology*, 1984, *69*, 241–251.

Locke, E. A., and Latham, G. P. *Goal Setting: A Motivational Technique That Works!* Englewood Cliffs, N.J.: Prentice-Hall, 1984.

Locke, E. A., Shaw, K. N., Saari, L. M., and Latham, G. P. "Goal Setting and Task Performance: 1969–1980." *Psychological Bulletin*, 1981, *90*, 125–152.

Mace, C. A. *Incentives: Some Experimental Studies*. Report 72. London: Industrial Health Research Board, 1935.

McMahan, I. D. "Relationships Between Causal Attributions and Expectancy of Success." *Journal of Personality and Social Psychology*, 1973, *28*, 108–114.

Markus, H., and Zajonc, R. B. "The Cognitive Perspective in Social Psychology." In S. Lindsey and E. Hanson (eds.), *The Handbook of Social Psychology*. New York: Random House, 1985.

Mento, A. J., Steel, R. P., and Karren, R. J. "A Meta-Analytic Study of the Effects of Goal Setting on Task Performance: 1966-1984." *Organizational Behavior and Human Decision Processes*, 1987, *39*, 52-83.

Meyer, H. H., and Raich, M. S. "An Objective Evaluation of a Behavior Modeling Training Program." *Personnel Psychology*, 1983, *36*, 755-761.

Meyer, J. P. "Causal Attribution for Success and Failure: A Multivariate Investigation of Dimensionality, Formation, and Consequences." *Journal of Personality and Social Psychology*, 1980, *38*, 704-718.

Mitchell, T. R. "Expectancy Models of Job Satisfaction, Occupational Preference, and Effort: A Theoretical, Methodological, and Empirical Appraisal." *Psychological Bulletin*, 1974, *81*, 1053-1077.

Mitchell, T. R. "Motivation: New Directions for Theory, Research, and Practice." *Academy of Management Review*, 1982, 7, 80-88.

Mowday, R. T. "Equity Theory Predictions of Behavior in Organizations." In R. D. Steers and L. W. Porter (eds.), *Motivation and Work Behavior*. (2nd ed.) New York: McGraw-Hill, 1979.

Nadler, D. A., and Lawler, E. E., III. "Motivation: A Diagnostic Approach." In J. R. Hackman, E. E. Lawler, III, and L. W. Porter (eds.), *Perspectives on Behavior in Organizations*. New York: McGraw-Hill, 1977.

Naylor, J. D., Pritchard, R. D., and Ilgen, D. R. *A Theory of Behavior in Organizations*. Orlando, Fla.: Academic Press, 1980.

Nebeker, D. M., and Neuberger, B. M. "Productivity Improvement in a Purchasing Division: The Impact of a Performance Contingent Reward System." *Evaluation and Program Planning*, 1985, *8*, 121-134.

Neisser, U. *Cognition and Reality: Principles and Implications of Cognitive Psychology*. New York: W. H. Freeman, 1976.

Pritchard, R. D. "Enhancing Organizational Productivity." Unpublished paper, Department of Psychology, University of Houston, 1986a.

Pritchard, R. D. "The Measurement and Enhancement of Organizational Productivity." Unpublished paper, Department of Psychology, University of Houston, 1986b.

Pritchard, R. D., Campbell, K. M., and Campbell, D. J. "Effects of Extrinsic Financial Rewards on Intrinsic Motivation." *Journal of Applied Psychology*, 1976, *62*, 9-15.

Rosch, E. H. "Principles of Categorization." In E. H. Rosch and B. B. Lloyd (eds.), *Cognition and Categorization*. Hillsdale, N.J.: Erlbaum, 1978.

Rosch, E. H., and Mervis, C. B. "Family Resemblances: Studies in the

Internal Structure of Categories." *Cognitive Psychology,* 1975, *4,* 328-350.

Rotter, J. B. "Generalized Expectancies for Internal Versus External Control of Reinforcement." *Psychological Monographs,* 1966, *80* (entire issue 609).

Ryan, T. A. "Drives, Tasks, and the Initiation of Behavior." *American Journal of Psychology,* 1958, *71,* 74-93.

Schmidt, F. L. "Implications of a Measurement Problem for Expectancy Theory Research." *Organizational Behavior and Human Performance,* 1973, *10,* 243-251.

Sorrentino, R. M., and Higgins, E. T. "Motivation and Cognition: Warming Up to Synergism." In R. M. Sorentino and E. T. Higgins (eds.), *Handbook of Motivation and Cognition.* New York: Wiley, 1986.

Taylor, F. W. *The Principles of Scientific Management.* New York: Norton, 1911.

Tolman, E. C. *Purposeful Behavior in Animals and Men.* East Norwalk, Conn.: Appleton-Century-Crofts, 1932.

Tuttle, T. C. "Organizational Productivity: A Challenge for Psychologists." *American Psychologist,* 1983, *38,* 479-486.

Van Maanan, J., and Schein, E. H. "Toward a Theory of Organizational Socialization." *Research in Organizational Behavior,* 1979, *1,* 209-264.

Vecchio, R. P. "An Individual-Difference Interpretation of the Conflicting Predictions Generated by Equity Theory and Expectancy Theory." *Journal of Applied Psychology,* 1981, *66,* 470-485.

Vroom, V. H. *Work and Motivation.* New York: Wiley, 1964.

Wanous, J. P. *Organizational Entry: Recruitment, Selection, and Socialization of Newcomers.* Reading, Mass.: Addison-Wesley, 1980.

Wanous, J. P., Keon, T. L., and Latack, J. C. "Expectancy Theory and Occupational/Organizational Choice: A Review and Test." *Organizational Behavior and Human Performance,* 1983, *32,* 66-86.

Weiner, B., Heckhausen, H., Meyer, W., and Cook, R. E. "Causal Ascriptions and Achievement Behavior: A Conceptual Analysis of Effort and Reanalysis of Locus of Control." *Journal of Personality and Social Psychology,* 1972, *21,* 239-248.

Weiner, B., and others. "Perceiving the Causes of Success and Failure." In E. Jones and others (eds.), *Attribution: Perceiving the Causes of Behavior.* Morristown, N.J.: General Learning Press, 1971.

Weiss, H. M., and Shaw, J. B. "Social Influences on Judgments About Tasks." *Organizational Behavior and Human Performance,* 1979, *24,* 126-140.

Wexley, K. N., and Latham, G. P. *Developing and Training Human Resources in Organizations.* Glenview, Ill.: Scott, Foresman, 1981.

Whaba, M. A., and House, R. J. "Expectancy Theory in Work and Motivation: Some Logical and Methodological Issues." *Human Relations,* 1974, *27,* 121–147.

White, R. W. "Motivation Reconsidered: The Concept of Competence." *Psychological Review,* 1959, *66,* 297–333.

8

㲳㲳㲳㲳㲳㲳㲳㲳㲳

Training Design
for Performance Improvement

John P. Campbell

This chapter will try first to describe the linkage between training and productivity and list the questions that can be asked about this linkage. Then the current literature will be matched with the question taxonomy to consider in general terms what we already know or don't know. After identifying training design as a potentially crucial source of variance in training effects, current theory and research will be summarized around critical design parameters and organized into a set of prescriptions for maximizing the effects of training on productivity.

The Training to Productivity Linkage

As discussed in Chapter Two, the term *productivity* is most appropriately applied to the value of outputs per unit of labor (for example, per hour or person month). Consequently, it is a measure that is characteristic of a system, industry, firm, or other aggregate unit, not an individual. Change in individual performance is only one possible cause of change in a productivity index. Improved equipment design, better weather, increased sales via better advertising, deferment of salary increases, and so on all influence productivity indices. Further, during any particular period, the contribution of individual performance to productivity is probably not uniform across different jobs in the organization. If a smart manager finds a crucial piece of manufacturing equipment at a small West German engineering firm and consequently unit production in the manager's own firm is increased 30 percent, that manager's performance is a major contributor to the resulting increase in the productivity index. The converse could also be true. That is, due to other factors, the manager's performance could have very little effect on productivity. This distinction between performance (what people actually do) and effectiveness (the organizational outcomes) was made some time ago by Campbell, Dunnette, Lawler, and Weick (1970).

If individual performance is defined as the sum of all the things people *do* on a job that make some contribution to the organization's goals, then performance is most certainly multidimensional. Further, a specific training or development program most likely is not directed simultaneously at every major component of performance. For example, training in interpersonal relations, applications of company policies and practices, and equipment operation are seldom combined in one program.

Further, any major component of performance is without doubt multiply determined. People may do well on a particular part of their job because (1) they have the aptitude for it, (2) they have acquired the necessary knowledge and skill, (3) they understand what specific tasks or goals are to be addressed at particular times, (4) they choose to start working, (5) they choose to expend high effort, and (6) they choose to persist in their efforts for however long it takes. Training does not address all of these performance determinants. It seems reasonable to think of aptitude as the province of selection, and choice behavior as being under motivational control; these antecedents are discussed in other chapters. Training is a formal attempt to teach knowledge, skill, and task understanding. It is also true that the performance determinants in this list are not totally independent. For example, more complete information about a job acquired through orientation training may influence choice behavior. We will come back to these interaction issues later. For now, the important points are that productivity is an attribute of an organization or larger system, individual performance is one among many determinants of productivity, training outcomes are only one determinant of performance, and training is usually directed at specific components of performance, not total performance. Training competes with and interacts with better selection and enhanced motivation as strategies for improving productivity through higher individual performance.

Given these distinctions as background, we can now ask about the current and future contributions of industrial-organizational psychology to the productivity via training issue.

What Do We Want to Know?

There are a number of questions that can be asked about the relationship(s) implied in the chapter title. Some are useful, and some are not. A list of possibilities is as follows.

1. First, it is nonsensical to ask the general question of whether training affects productivity. Of course it does. Neither additional research nor industrial-organizational psychology is needed to convince the world at large that a strategy of pure trial and error for learning a job will not get us very far. Even the heaviest capital investment and most sophisticated equipment cannot produce goods and services without trained personnel to take advantage of them. No reasonable person would dispute the assertion that job training has a significant impact on productivity, as it has been explicated in Part One.

2. At the other end of the spectrum, it is sensical, but naive, to ask at what point the marginal costs of training equal the marginal benefits, particularly when the costs and benefits of training are only one component of a canonical variate that includes the costs and benefits of selection improvements, new incentives, changes in equipment design, improved production processes, and the like. The difficulties involved in estimating univariate, single-stage utility functions (as in Schmidt, Hunter, and Pearlman, 1982; Landy, Farr, and Jacobs, 1982) pale in comparison to the task of estimating the optimatization function that specifies how resources should be allocated across alternative "treatments," not all of which are independent of one another.

3. In between these two extremes are a number of summative evaluation questions that might be of interest. For example, does a specific training program result in increased job performance? What is the estimated utility to the organization of any performance increase resulting from a specific training program? Does training produce cost savings in the form of fewer absences, less turnover, fewer accidents, fewer grievances, and so on? While questions such as these sound reasonable, they incorporate one principal source of confusion. Increases on many of these variables can be a function of a number of things besides increases in specific skills, such as changes in work processes, motivational contingencies, or other components of performance not related to training. Conversely, the effects of real changes in a skill can be totally swamped by these other factors, such that no mean differences in a global performance measure are observed. The moral is simply that, depending on the scope and nature of the training program, the changes produced by training may not be isomorphic with the measure of performance.

4. A much more direct question to ask is whether the training program produces the specific changes it was designed to produce. For example, if an electronic maintenance training program was designed to teach methods for diagnosis of electrical equipment malfunctions,

do people make more correct diagnoses after training than before? Notice that even if trained individuals do make more correct diagnoses, the mean difference in overall supervisor performance ratings between a trained and untrained group might not be different, for a variety of reasons. Asking whether a program achieves the specific objectives it was designed to accomplish is a much more direct and relevant question than whether it produces changes in overall job performance. If the objectives of training have nothing to do with performance, the fault lies not with the training experience itself but with whoever enumerated the objectives.

5. The previous question deals with how well a specific training program achieves its specific objectives. This is a very organizationally relevant and applied concern. Additional "scientific" questions could also be asked about how more basic domains of instructional content or generic instructional methods facilitate the acquisition of basic individual capabilities. For example, will teaching people to analyze problems in terms of a specific theory of problem analysis lead to better generic problem-solving behavior? While a particular organization may not care about supporting the exploration of these more basic questions, in the long run such research may have considerable payoff for the enhancement of job performance in the total economy. Realistically, there is a strong interplay between these two kinds of question asking. Doing a number of studies on specific programs can generate useful substantive generalizations, if the independent variables (training programs) and dependent variables (criteria) are fully described in each study and the commonalities across studies are understood. However, blurring the distinction can become crucial. For example, if a meta-analysis is done on evaluation programs but a variety of independent and dependent variables are mixed together, how is the overall effect size to be interpreted?

6. Yet another class of questions has to do with how training should be designed to maximize achievement of its objectives. Here the emphasis shifts from a concern with the effects produced by a training or development program already designed and executed to a concern with how future programs should be designed and/or executed. Again, such questions can be asked from a very applied perspective that is specific to a particular training problem in a specific organization, or from a more basic perspective, where the objective is to build general principles of training design.

7. Finally, we could go even further down the road of basic research and attempt to investigate basic principles of learning,

instruction, and skill acquisition that explain the processes involved in learning new responses.

Where does the current training and development literature fall along this array of questions, and what does it say about training effects on productivity?

Training and Development Plus Instructional Psychology

As noted by Latham (1988), the way the training and development literature is characterized and the conclusions that are drawn from it are dependent upon the areas of research and practice that are designated as its appropriate content. Three principal sources seem to account for most of the content. The first two are described by Latham as the training and development "professional" literature and the training and development "scientific" literature. The *Journal of the American Society of Training and Development* and *Training* are examples of the former, while examples of the latter are *Personnel Psychology* and the *Journal of Applied Psychology*. Given that training and development is itself a multi-billion-dollar industry, it is surprising that there have been only four reviews of the training and development literature (Campbell, 1971; Goldstein, 1980; Wexley, 1984; Latham, 1988). Similarly, there have been only four general textbooks appropriate for undergraduates (McGehee and Thayer, 1961; Bass and Vaughn, 1966; Wexley and Latham, 1981; Goldstein, 1986). In spite of this rather limited archival record, useful results have been produced that can be cast against the major kinds of questions posed earlier (see, for example, Latham, 1988).

A third source has come to prominence during the past ten or fifteen years that seems to be recapitulating the phylogeny of the traditional lack of contact between the study of human learning and the design and evaluation of training. That is, the field of instructional psychology has taken shape during that period and has generated seven chapters in the *Annual Review of Psychology* (Gagné and Rohwer, 1969; Glaser and Resnick, 1972; McKeachie, 1974; Wittrock and Lumsdaine, 1977; Resnick, 1981; Gagné and Dick, 1983; Pintrick, Cross, Kozma, and McKeachie, 1986). Things progressed so far so fast that a review of the reviews was provided by Menges and Girard (1983).

The dominant themes in instructional psychology have changed somewhat since 1969. In the beginning (Gagné and Rohwer, 1969), the emphasis was on the design of the learning/training environment and specifications of the external (to the learner) conditions that facilitate learning. The domain has broadened considerably since then and now includes heavy doses of ability assessment, cognition, and developmental psychology. The latter is there because a lot of research on instruction is carried out with school children. For our purposes, the definition of Glaser and Resnick (1972) is particularly relevant. They distinguish instructional psychology from the study of learning and memory in general by portraying the former as an attempt to *design* or *specify* "the most effective way of achieving knowledge and mastering skills" (p. 207). That is, instructional psychology attempts to be prescriptive about the content to be mastered, the learner attributes that are most relevant, the optimal methods of instruction, and the outcomes that should be assessed. It responds to Bruner's (1966) criticism that traditional learning theory and research describe processes that take place but do not tell the training designer, teacher, or student what to *do*.

Theory and research in instructional psychology seem made to order as major contributors to the basic research foundation of training and development. However, the *current* literatures in training and development and instructional psychology seem to exist side by side, as described in their respective *Annual Review of Psychology* chapters, with little or no integration or cross-referencing. Wexley (1984) made a valiant attempt to bring the two together, at least in the context of training design, but he had very little integrative literature to work with. The situation is indeed reminiscent of the lack of contact between organizational training and research in learning that was lamented for so long by so many (Campbell, 1971). All this is in spite of the fact that Robert Gagné coauthored the first *Annual Review* chapter on instructional psychology and has also participated heavily in the design of skills training for the U.S. Army.

The next section briefly compares the knowledge produced to the questions that can be asked. The meta-question to keep in mind is, Where should industrial-organizational psychology direct its efforts so as to enhance the contribution of training and development to productivity improvement?

A Brief Characterization of the Empirical Literature

The research literature in training and development has matured considerably since it was first reviewed in the *Annual Review* (Campbell, 1971). Latham (1988) rightly observes that it is now more theory-based and more positive in result. It is not the purpose here to review this whole body of evidence. Instead, the major types of research will be noted and matched with the taxonomy of questions discussed earlier.

Summative Evaluation. By far the largest category of empirical research is still straightforward summative evaluation, in which the central question is whether a particular training program produces beneficial results. The comparison is either between a trained group and an untrained group or a before and after comparison, or both. There are a number of reviews that deal with this kind of research. Management development in general (Burke and Day, 1986), and behavior modeling (Decker and Nathan, 1985) and sensitivity training (Campbell and Dunnette, 1968; Smith, 1975) in particular, are examples. The studies in these sources use a variety of dependent variables, but the dominant criterion is general job performance. Consequently, the effect sizes calculated from these data are most likely a considerable underestimate of the actual treatment effect, for the reasons discussed earlier. An admirable exception is the evaluation of behavior modeling reported by Latham and Saari (1979). In that study, several different measures were tied directly to the objectives of the program.

This category of research is indicative of a number of other relevant points as well. Note that the reviews are organized around a particular method, not a particular skill or knowledge to be learned. This serves the advocates of the method but not the users of a particular outcome. That is, the user may not be so concerned with whether management development works or doesn't work but instead would like to know the best procedure for making managers better leaders of problem-solving groups. While a number of reviews do try to organize studies around types of dependent variables such as measures of "attitudes" or "performance ratings" (see Burke and Day, 1986; Smith, 1975), such organization is ad hoc; the individual studies, with few exceptions, were certainly not designed to focus on particular capabilities of generic importance.

In total, the evaluation studies of this type do show significant positive effects for training, but the information value of this kind of conclusion is limited and it may be time to lay the summative evaluation paradigm aside. Some alternative ways to expend research effort are discussed later in this chapter.

Comparative Summative Evaluation. Less research attention has been devoted to the comparative question of which of two or more training methods produces the most beneficial effects when compared on the same criterion measures. The most prominent example is the comparison of programmed instruction versus a "conventional" method (Nash, Muczyk, and Vettori, 1971; Hall and Freda, 1982). The consistent result through both reviews is that, while programmed instruction can bring students to a particular level of mastery in a shorter time, the level of retention is really no better. Note that most of these studies were conducted in educational settings, and the dominant criterion measure was a paper-and-pencil achievement test. Virtually no such comparative evidence exists in the occupational context.

Formative Evaluation. Given the size of the training enterprise, there is probably a considerable amount of informal, nonexperimental investigation of where a training program went wrong and how it could be improved. However, very little research of this kind makes its way into the literature. The classic paper of Glickman and Vallance (1958), which used the critical incident method to describe errors made by recent graduates of Navy technical training, still deserves to be emulated. The critical incident method seems well suited to the diagnosis of training deficiencies or unintended consequences. Another study that might well be copied is reported by Downs (1985), who carried out a survey of retraining problems experienced by skilled workers in a sample of firms in the United Kingdom. A team of interviewers spent an entire day at each organization, interviewing both trainers and trainees. One sample finding was that teaching electronic trouble-shooting, in contrast to mechanical trouble-shooting, requires much more attention to basic electronics than anyone had realized. In the absence of an intuitive understanding of why a malfunction occurred (which most people seemed to have for mechanical but not electronic problems), the trainee would often not accept (and retain) the instructor's explanation of the cause of an electronic malfunction. A second sample finding was the widespread lack of pretesting of training materials for new equipment. In general, the results of this interview survey seem to provide information that would be highly useful for the designers and the users of retraining programs. A job family by job family evaluation of training difficulties would be a valuable research effort.

Training for Specific Skills or Knowledges. In the past, research themes have focused on the method (for example, programmed instruction, behavior modeling) or on a general problem area (for example, management development, skills training). During recent times, however, increasing research attention is being devoted to how best to teach a specific skill. Such research implies that there are generic skills or domains of knowledge that are of special importance, and that special attention should be devoted to understanding the capabilities to be taught and how best to teach them.

The dominant example of such skill-specific research examines training for general problem-solving and decision-making skills. There is an abundance of theory about what problem solving and decision making are (Taylor, 1965; MacCrimmon and Taylor, 1976;

Simon, 1975), and improving problem solving through training has received considerable attention in university, public school, and industrial settings. It is one area in which the interest of such diverse fields as organizational training, instructional psychology, computer science, management science, cognitive psychology, and child development have come together (Bransford, Sherwood, Vye, and Rieser, 1986). The common themes in this work are (1) to provide a valid description of what problem solving is; (2) to make valid distinctions between levels of proficiency, as in what distinguishes experts from novices; and (3) to identify common errors that inhibit effective problem solving. The research and theory directed at these considerations has led to a number of innovative university courses in general problem solving in graduate schools of business (Rubinstein, 1980). Notice that the emphasis here is really on a "theory" of the content to be taught.

Other skill domains for which a conceptual specification of training content is possible are leadership (for example, Fiedler and Chemers, 1984; Vroom and Yetton, 1973) and goal setting (Locke and Latham, 1984). A new and potentially valuable skill is self-regulation of such motivational antecedents as feedback, perceived expectancies, and ability evaluations (Manz, 1986; Kanfer and Gaelick, 1986).

Training Design. Within industrial-organizational psychology, research on training design is concerned principally with the specification of training needs (see, for example, Wexley, 1984; Latham, 1988) and the management of motivational antecedents such as feedback (Komaki, Heinzmann, and Lawson, 1980). Both the assessment of needs and the design of feedback have become much more sophisticated during the past few years, and generalized instrumentation for the former (Yukl, 1987) and general principles of application for the latter (Ilgen, Fisher, and Taylor, 1979) are becoming available. In fact, a concern for the effective design of motivational conditions in the training situation has undergone a rebirth stemming both from principles of behavior analysis and social learning theory (Latham, 1988).

In instructional psychology, on the other hand, research on training design plays a much larger role. Entire books have been written on the topic (for example, Gagné and Briggs, 1979), and the list of design parameters is much longer. The following list is intended to be a reasonable summary of the design parameters that have been prominent in the instructional psychology literature:

- Specification of training (behavioral) objectives.
- Specification of training content in terms of its hierarchical structure and sequencing.

- Specification of prerequisites for training.
- Enhancement of individual differences that facilitate learning (for example, increased self-efficacy).
- Adaptation to individual differences that interact with training methods (aptitude treatment interactions).
- Management of learner motivation.
- Matching of the capability to be mastered with the instructional method.
- Management of practice and feedback.

Learning Processes. In addition to its interest in training design, instructional psychology has become intensely concerned with the cognitive processes that explain learning or mastery. These research topics reveal how cognitive psychology has influenced basic research on learning in the context of classroom instruction. Again, perhaps a sample list of research topics will serve to make a long story short.

- The study of attentional processes has received considerable emphasis and is concerned with parameters such as selective attention, divided or multimodality attention, and gaining and maintaining attention.
- Considerable work is directed at the role of cognitive schemata in coding and storing information. For example, what rules or heuristic devices are the most valuable transformations for particular knowledge domains such that useful knowledge is better retained in memory and more successfully accessed?
- Memory and retention processes have continued to be important research topics, and considerable research is still devoted to promoting increased retention.
- A new development related to the above is the study of controlled versus automatic processing (Schneider and Shiffrin, 1977)—the distinction between tasks that become "automatic" when mastered (and thereafter do not require deliberate attention) versus tasks that always require the conscious application of cognitive resources (that is, they must always be under conscious control). The two tasks may require different learning events.
- Also of recent interest is the study of meta-cognitions, or the extent to which individuals are aware of and can control their own cognitive strategies. For example, do people correctly perceive when they should be "creative"?

In general, research in these areas is carried out in a relatively basic context and is still a considerable distance from practical application.

Some Conclusions

The preceding discussion was intended to lead to the following conclusions:

- By definition, and appropriately so, the effects of training and development are several steps removed from productivity. The effectiveness of training should be judged in terms of how well it meets its specific objectives. The degree to which successful training outcomes can influence productivity are a function of job and organization design. Other chapters in this volume speak to these issues.
- There is no doubt that training and development can influence performance and thereby productivity. Both naturalistic observation and research support this conclusion. The crucial question is neither whether training is necessary nor whether it works. The answer is yes to both. The more relevant questions are how to identify training objectives that are most in need of attention and how to design training programs and training environments to attain these objectives in the most effective manner. Therefore, a major frontier is to be found in research on training designs.
- We already know some things about good training design, and there are a number of promising areas that can be developed. While some of this work comes from industrial-organizational psychology, most of the research activity and much of the excitement is to be found in instructional psychology.

Given these conclusions, the remainder of this chapter attempts to be prescriptive about what we already know and can use and what we should be excited about researching further relative to training design.

A Basic Framework

The prescriptions summarized in the remainder of this chapter are organized within a particular conceptual framework. Its goal is to specify the parameters of the training function that should be taken into account when designing any training or development program.

The framework itself is not new; it stems from the work of the educational psychologists who first began to consider problems of instruction prescriptively. More specifically, the work of Briggs (1970, 1977), Gagné (1968, 1977), Glaser (1976), and others forms the basis of what follows, although these researchers should not be held accountable for this particular rendition.

A Paradigm Shift. In my opinion, one of the most important papers ever published in the field of training and development, and largely unrecognized as such, is Gagné's (1962) paper in the *American Psychologist,* entitled "Military Training and Principles of Learning." Its message sounds almost simple-minded, but its implications are profound and go far beyond the confines of military skills training. The paper should be read, reread, and read again by everyone.

Gagné's paper made one fundamental point: by far the highest-priority question for designers, users, and investigators of training is, What is to be learned? That is, what (specifically) should a training program try to accomplish, and what should the training content be? Alongside this fundamental consideration, questions about which method to use—for example, computer-assisted instruction versus lecture—are almost trivial. For Gagné, the question of what is to be learned also takes precedence over the traditional questions addressed by research in learning, such as whether massed versus distributed practice is more effective. Unfortunately, answering this primary question is a difficult and painstaking task. It does not deal in high-tech bells and whistles and has little glamour associated with it. In the marketplace, it is a thankless task to argue that beating one's head against this question is far more important than using computerized instruction, having well-appointed training facilities, or stocking a library with the latest videotapes.

A Training Design Model. The question of what is to be learned leads to a series of additional questions in a particular sequence. This sequence of questions and the guidelines for answering them constitute a *training design model.* It asserts that any training design must consider each step in turn. The steps are summarized below and considered in more detail in the next section.

- *Analyzing Goals and Job Design.* Recognize, describe, or restate the operative goals of the organization in which the training and development effort is taking place. Are the training goals consistent with the organization's goals? If not, why not, and what do we do about the conflict? Next comes a consideration of whether the jobs in question are designed so that their performance outputs are directly relevant for the critical goals of the organization. If they are not, devoting training to such functions is of little value.

- *Determining Training Needs.* We must ask which of the relevant performance factors constitute the highest priority training needs. Where is the performance deficient? What performance components will become critical in the future?
- *Specifying Training Objectives.* The statement of needs must be translated into a complete set of specific training objectives, stated in terms of desired job performance, which constitutes the formal description of what is to be learned.
- *Specifying Training Content.* The objectives dictate the specifications for training content, which is composed of the knowledges and skills that, if mastered, will permit competent performance of the objectives.
- *Specifying Learning Methods and Learning Media.* Decisions about the methods for teaching content break down into two issues: what learning methods are appropriate, and what learning "media" should be used to execute the learning events.
- *Accounting for Individual Differences.* Determine whether specific individual characteristics of trainees interact with important parameters of a training program's design so that different programs are needed or additional screening of trainees is required.
- *Specifying the Conditions of Learning.* Design the optimal conditions for learning based on the determination of learning methods and media and individual differences described above, plus an examination of contributions from research on cognition, motivation, and abilities.
- *Evaluating Training Outcomes.* Design the evaluation of training effects. The model, as is noted in the next section, is very concise and directive in this regard.

Note that the points at issue move from an almost operant perspective (what are the specific behaviors of interest?), to the cognitive concerns of instruction psychology (what conditions facilitate learning?), to the traditional industrial/organizational psychology concern for how training effects should be evaluated. In no sense will this chapter try to reflect a conflict between the operant point of view and cognitive explanations of behavior. The training and development enterprise needs them both, as well as a constant concern for valid and reliable measurement.

Prescriptions from a Model of Training Design

The model will now be considered in more detail, and each
major parameter will be discussed in terms of what it prescribes for
training design, what current research has to say about the issues it
identifies, and what future research might be particularly interesting.

Some of the points should seem new, and some will seem old
hat. Before dismissing the latter, ask whether a particular design step
is usually considered in most training efforts in the form specified
here, or whether we interpret frequent lip service as a bona fide
consideration of a substantive issue. For example, it is the conventional wisdom to say that training must have objectives, but how
frequently are objectives described in anything approaching the
format outlined below?

The fundamental question of what is to be learned is answered
in the organizational training and development context in part by
considering three prior issues: goal analysis, job design, and needs
assessment. These are not unfamiliar to personnel psychologists.

Analyzing Goals and Job Design

What are the organization's operating goals, and what are their
implications for training content in specific jobs? For example, if a
sales organization wishes to develop a variety of new markets quickly,
that implies different things for sales training than if that same
organization wants to stabilize its current markets and develop a core
of long-term repeat customers. Also, it is at this stage that current or
potential goal conflicts must be recognized. If different management
factions are at war over the above marketing goals, the training
operation could get caught in the middle. Given the operative goals
of the organization, how should jobs be defined and structured to best
contribute to goal accomplishment? For example, how big an R & D
operation should there be? What kinds of research positions are
needed? This kind of analysis is necessary to ensure that if a training
program is designed to increase performance on a critical job factor,
performance on this factor will in fact have something to do with the
goals of the organization. If the goals of an educational institution
emphasize research and virtually ignore undergraduate instruction,
conducting seminars for faculty on the design of undergraduate
courses will have little relevance. The time should be spent teaching
grant writing and similar skills.

Models and procedures for goal analysis and job design are
really not within the boundaries of this chapter. The chapters by

Berlinger, Glick, and Rodgers; Ledford, Lawler, and Mohrman; Goodman, Devadas, and Hughson; McLagan; and Banas all take up these issues in varying degrees. The McLagan chapter, in particular, proposes a systematic method for describing current and future goals and for analyzing jobs to make them commensurate with the organization's goals. Quality circles and joint labor-management planning can also be used for this purpose. Much of the literature on organization development (French and Bell, 1984) is also applicable.

Regardless of the chapter in which goal analysis and job design fall, questions about those subjects cannot really be avoided. In the training context, they will be answered one way or another, if only by default. When an organization buys a training program off the shelf from a vendor, it has implicitly asserted that the content of the program does not create goal conflicts and is consistent with a relevant job design.

Determining Training Needs

This aspect of training design is one of the most traditional topics in the training literature. The current scene is described in Wexley (1984), Wexley and Latham (1981), Goldstein (1986), and Latham (1988). However, for the purposes of the present chapter, the conventional use of the phrase *determining training needs* includes too many different issues, such as organizational analysis, job analysis, task analysis, and person analysis. From the perspective of this chapter's model of training design, *determining training needs* is defined to be the identification of the components of job performance that are relevant for the organization's goals and that would benefit if they were enhanced through training. Thus needs analysis is task-oriented and is intended to describe the observable elements of performance that training could improve. Identification of the KSAs (knowledge, skills, and abilities) that control a particular performance component is a part of *content* design.

Training needs exist in a number of contexts. For example, current job holders may be deficient in terms of what their performance should be, and the primary purpose of their training is to remedy the discrepancy. In a different context, if eligibility for promotion is a function of high performance on particular performance components, training on those components may be offered to anyone wanting to be considered for promotion. Also, certain components of performance not yet a part of the job may be forecast to be critical for organizational functioning in the future; for example, training may be needed for dealing with new kinds of outcomes or new

equipment. Finally, training may be needed for performance components that must be executed in totally new environments, as when
NASA was faced with training people to drive a car on the moon.

Ideally, a needs assessment would have two major steps: a
description of the components of effective performance and identification of the components that would benefit from training. Saying
this makes virtually all task-oriented job analyses and criterion
development methods relevant. So what's new? The frontiers can be
found in the use of multiple methods, particularly a more creative use
of the critical incident method, and in generating management
accountability for the results of the assessment.

A prototype is the U.S. Army's Selection and Classification
Project (Campbell, 1986). Three job analysis methods were used: a
specification by management of the tasks the job was designed to
include; a survey of job incumbents, using a questionnaire composed
of several hundred task elements; and a series of critical incident
workshops. The first method described what incumbents should do,
the second described what they actually did, and the third defined high
performance and low performance. The three methods complemented
each other and provided a very complete picture of each job in the
study. Both the methods and results were reviewed by management at
several critical stages. The format of the review was a group decision
meeting in which the agenda was clearly understood to be a decision
as to whether the analytical description of the job was acceptable or
whether it needed further work of a specific nature. In this way,
management participation and accountability were generated. Similar
procedures are outlined by Ford and Wroten (1984) and Goldstein,
Macy, and Prien (1981).

Many variations can be played on the three-part theme. For
example, the McLagan chapter later in this volume advocates a Delphi
approach, which uses panels of relevant experts to generate the "what
should be done" assessment, both under current conditions and under
forecast future conditions. There is nothing to prevent asking judges
for hypothetical critical incidents that might be expected under future
conditions. Using critical incidents in a forecasting mode would force
the judges to express desired and not-desired performance in very
concrete terms. Most needs assessment work has emphasized general
descriptions of training needs via interviews or surveys of job
incumbents and has made very little use of systematic management
specification or critical incidents, both of which are in fact more
directly relevant for training purposes than job description surveys of
incumbents.

Once the components of performance are identified, they must be ordered in terms of their relative need for training. Multiple methods are again necessary, as well as management accountability for the final result. This step should be given no less attention than should the development of performance measures for selection research. In fact, it is very much like it. The critical incidents should be categorized as they are in the BARS (Behaviorally Anchored Rating Scales) technique, and the clusters, or dimensions, each defined by a large number of performance examples, can be evaluated by multiple groups of judges in terms of training priorities. The negative incidents provide a direct specification of the most serious errors that have occurred in the high-priority categories.

Two additional kinds of evidence would significantly aid future needs assessments. First, we must do much more toward developing substantive "theories of performance" similar to those for abilities, personality, and interests. That is, for a particular population of jobs, where *population* is defined as a common latent structure for performance, what are the major components of performance, how should they be defined, what are their interrelationships, and what are their antecedents? Most BARS development takes the first step toward such a theory when the dimensions are proposed as the first definition of the latent structure (Campbell, Dunnette, Arvey, and Hellervik, 1973). However, research cannot stop with one method and one set of measures. For example, the Army Selection and Classification Project (Campbell, 1987) proposed a five-factor latent structure for a population of entry-level skilled jobs. Each factor was assessed with more than one method, alternative factor models were submitted to a confirmatory test, and a variety of the other variables were related to each of the five factors. This is nothing more than the construction of a theory of performance from the perspective of construct validation, but is is sorely lacking in the performance domain.

A notable exception is in the description of management, supervisory, and leadership performance, where standardized descriptions of components now exist. Anyone doing needs assessment for management development or supervisory training should seek guidance from the work on dimensions of leadership performance, an excellent and thorough summary of which is provided by Yukl (1987). Additional construct validation work would further enhance the meaning and the usefulness of the taxonomy that Yukl has developed.

A second theme is an emerging line of research on assessment of training needs in particular populations. A survey by Downs (1985) is an example. This study illustrates what can be learned from the assessment of general training needs in an occupation or category of occupations. If such research were expanded, it would provide a much

194 Productivity in Organizations

broader foundation from which to attack productivity problems via training. A similar theme is concerned with the training needs of demographic subgroups, particularly women (Berryman-Fink, 1985), minorities, and older individuals (Tucker, 1985). Prior work by Triandis and colleagues (Triandis, Feldman, Weldon, and Harvey, 1975) provides an excellent model to follow. If such needs analyses could be interpreted in the context of an overall performance model for the jobs in question, this model would become an even more valuable aid for the planning and design of training.

Specifying Training (Behavioral) Objectives

Once training needs are agreed upon, they must be translated into specific training objectives. Needs assessments as described above are not statements of objectives. They may identify components of performance in need of training, but they do not specify precisely what the trainee should be able to do after training, or how well.

The specification of specific training, or "behavioral," objectives answers Gagné's question of what is to be learned. They define what the learner should be able to do after finishing the program that he or she could not do before. Behavioral objectives are stated in concrete, observable terms, and they include some indication of the conditions under which the individual should be able to perform them and the level of proficiency the individual should be able to exhibit. This is the very heart of training design. If the behavioral objectives cannot be specified, that implies that the trainer (training manager, teacher, professor) cannot be clear about what to teach. Unfortunately, this is probably the most neglected element in training design.

In practice, it is not an easy task to specify behavioral objectives, which may be one reason people tend to avoid it. Guidelines, instructions, and examples can be found in Briggs (1970), Gagné and Briggs (1979), Mager (1975), and Popham and Baker (1970). Again, the critical incident technique is a useful way to begin. Critical incidents are descriptions of observable things people do, and they can be scaled in terms of the degree of competence they represent. What remains is to determine the level of performance the training program wishes to achieve. For example, a critical incident analysis of graduate student performance might identify detection of certain statistical errors in published papers as a training need. The objectives would then specify the specific errors that a competent performer should be able to identify, and the frequency and conditions under which they should be identified. If the behavioral objective does not include some indication of the desired *level* of performance, the training design cannot proceed in a systematic way.

Another method for translating training needs into behavioral objectives is to systematically observe competent performance. Industrial-organizational psychology simply has not done enough of this basic observational work. While there are a numberr of observational or descriptive studies of what managers and supervisors do (Mintzberg, 1973; Stewart, 1976; Tornow and Pinto, 1976), they are not concerned with what *competent* managers or supervisors do, in concrete, observable terms. Glaser (1982) sees the definition of *competent performance* and the development of methods for its description as one of the primary goals of instructional psychology relative to education. The same should be true for job and occupational training. To get close to home, if we made a concerted effort to specify the behavioral objectives for graduate training in industrial-organizational psychology, where would they fall on the scientist-practitioner continuum? Would there be objectives that specify competent performance in making presentations to management? Writing research proposals? Using a keyboard? Using FORTRAN? Using SAS? Translating research ideas into research questions? Testifying as an expert witness?

Rising above the dirty work of actually generating objectives is one very important meta-issue, which is that each training objective must incorporate the correct "capability." For example, a training course for data analysts could formulate objectives having to do with correctly formatting data files and using the proper commands to run standard data analysis software, or it could adopt objectives for teaching analysts how to solve novel analysis problems. The former has to do with the correct execution of certain mechanical steps, while the latter requires problem solving of a specific technical sort. That is, the capabilities to be learned are different. While this is a rather obvious example, the situations when it is not so obvious could lead to a serious misstatement of the behavioral objectives (Gagné and Briggs, 1979).

Based in part on the work of Bloom and his colleagues (Bloom, Hastings, and Madaus, 1971; Krathwohl, Bloom, and Masia, 1964), Gagné and Briggs have developed a taxonomy of capabilities and have based an entire model for instructional design on this taxonomy. At the most general level, the taxonomy includes five types of capabilities with which a training program could deal. These are cognitive skills, cognitive strategies, verbal information, motor skills, and attitudes. Verbal information is in the taxonomy simply because being able to demonstrate knowledge is a legitimate category of objectives for many training programs. The distinction between cognitive skills and cognitive strategies is a distinction between knowing how to execute structured cognitive tasks (completing an income tax return, computing a correlation coefficient) and solving novel problems. In the organizational training context, it might be useful to add two categories to the list. Based on the work of Fleishman and Quaintance (1984), it seems useful to distinguish psychomotor skills from motor skills. The research summarized in Fleishman and Quaintance suggests that these are two different classes of capabilities that would lead to somewhat different training content and methods. Also, a significant amount of training and development has to do with generating more complete and accurate self-knowledge for the trainee, as when T-groups try to teach you how you act toward other people in certain situations. This category might further be broken down into self-knowledge of intellectual behavior (just how smart are you, anyway?) and interpersonal behavior.

Thinking in taxonomic terms at this stage is intended to help avoid incorporating the wrong capability in the description of a training objective.

In sum, the description of the behavioral objectives is the fundamental step in training design, and probably the most neglected (even in graduate education in the behavioral sciences). Producing objectives to the above specifications requires much cognitive effort, and it is difficult to develop very powerful reinforcement contingencies for maintaining such behavior on the part of training designers. It's too much like eating and exercising properly. We know what works, but there are always very persuasive people who promise much easier solutions.

Specifying Training Content

Training content is dictated by the behavioral objectives. It is composed of the knowledges and skills that the trainee must master to be able to perform the objectives. For example, what content must a graduate student master to write a research proposal, make a presentation to management, or write down a research question? The distinction between behavioral objectives and training content is an important one. It is a distinction between training content and job content.

Besides identifying content elements, the sequence in which they are to be learned must also be specified. If the sequence is not clear, the behavioral objectives or the subject matter is not well enough understood (Gagné and Briggs, 1979). For example, in the name of being able to perform multivariate data analysis, must the meaning of multiple correlation be understood before SPSS can be used to compute it?

Content specifications can be determined from three principal sources. The most common is simply expert judgment. People who "know" the topic specify the training content. Content can also come from more formal theory. For example, in basic skills there are now rather well-developed conceptual descriptions of what arithmetic is (Resnick and Ford, 1981). Closer to home, certain theories of leadership provide a specification of what knowledges and skills must be mastered to enhance performance. Fiedler's "leader match" program (Fiedler and Chemers, 1984) is one example. The Vroom and Yetton (1973) model is another. However, one reason that leadership theory has not progressed further than it has is that a clear description of leadership competence, in the behavioral objectives sense, has never really been provided. Training and development will become more powerful as our taxonomies and substantive understanding of performance phenomena grow. We simply need much more research on what constitutes competent performance in various important domains.

A content area that has an even stronger foundation, both in research and theory, is complex problem solving. The existing literature is large and seriously underexploited in organizational training and development. Frederiksen (1984) provides a useful guide to how course content might be structured. He points out that a number of books have been written about what the content of such a training program should be. Graduate schools in management and management sciences have taught such courses for years. All kinds of organizational spinoffs are possible. An excellent review of the basic research pertaining to the teaching of problem solving is provided by Bransford, Sherwood, Vye, and Rieser (1986).

A major contribution of basic research in cognitive and instructional psychology to the methodology of content specification is the refinement of protocol analysis (Ericsson and Simon, 1984), in which experts are asked to perform the objectives, and a protocol of what they do is generated via observation, verbalization, diary keeping, or other means. The content to be mastered is inferred from the protocol analysis. Protocol analysis has been a valuable tool in the study of complex problem solving (Simon, 1979a; Johnson and Associates, 1981) and could well be used to specify content for a variety of training or development problems.

A genuinely innovative suggestion for how to use protocol analysis in the design of training content is contained in a paper by

Brown and VanLehn (1980). The procedure is based on the notion that many of the mistakes people make in using a skill or strategy are systematic and can be modeled. To model them is to understand them, and to understand them is to be more able to design a remedy. These authors are working in the areas of basic skills, but with a little effort their ideas could be translated into some very creative organizational research. The basic procedure would be to create "gaps" in an instructional sequence (for example, the modeling of a particular learning point might be omitted from the videotapes of a supervisory training course) and then describe how people attempt to fill the gaps. If individuals use systematic or stereotypical ways of performing the missing link, the training designer has learned something very concrete about mistakes that must be corrected. Brown and VanLehn refer to this as generating a theory of "bugs" in a particular content area.

Specifying Learning Methods and Learning Media

Given that a particular body of content is to be learned, the next consideration is the set of learning methods that should be used to teach or promote mastery of the content. In instructional psychology, the term *instructional methods* has come to mean the generic teaching methods or events that a trainer has available. For example, information presentation from teacher to student is a learning method, as is question-and-answer discussion, as is simulation. A generic learning method might be executed through any one of several *media.* For example, information presentation is possible via reading, lectures, or closed-circuit television. The question-and-answer method might be executed in a face-to-face discussion group or by computer-assisted instruction.

There are two critical features of learning methods that training design should attempt to optimize (Gagné and Briggs, 1979; Glaser, 1982; Pintrick, Cross, Kozma, and McKeachie, 1986). First, the instructional events that comprise the method should support or be consistent with the cognitive, physical, or psychomotor processes that lead to mastery. That is, they should not inhibit, conflict with, or be unrelated to the processes involved in mastery of the content. For example, if mastery involves the development of a certain set of heuristic devices, the study method should not conflict with the process by emphasizing rote memorization. Second, the "capability" incorporated in the training objective should be reflected as closely as possible in the training method. For example, if the capability is electronic trouble-shooting (a cognitive strategy), the training method should provide an opportunity for the learner to generate the correct problem-solving strategy.

Designing training methods to be consistent with the relevant learning processes and to incorporate the desired performance capabilities will be successful to the extent that both the theoretical description of learning processes and the functional description of performance capabilities are (1) valid and (2) substantive enough to guide the training design. Are they? The instructional psychology literature exhibits mixed opinions. In the most recent *Annual Review* chapter, Pintrick and colleagues (1986) are not yet willing to characterize such guidelines as design principles.

Admittedly, the state of the art as regards the selection or design of teaching methods does not yield great precision. However, just consistently using the guidelines we already have would contribute significantly to the linkage of training and productivity. A place to start would be Table 8.1, which is taken from Gagné and Briggs (1979).

For example, if a cognitive strategy, such as electronic trouble-shooting, is the capability of interest, the teaching method should provide a series of novel problems as stimulus material. However, the design must also ask whether the training objective is a function of information, and perhaps even motor skill. That is, competent trouble-shooting may require the operation of very delicate equipment or tools.

Going beyond such a checklist is dependent on a more complete description of what the literature on cognitive, psychomotor, and physical performance can tell us. In fact, training and development would benefit considerably from a codification of the existing information. For example, research on cognitive processes shows that the training method should guide the learner to the most appropriate encoding operations for storing information, skills, or strategies in memory. The most useful encoding devices (schemata) seem to be at least partially specific to the subject matter under consideration, and they may also be a function of individual differences in learners. For example, in mastering a physical skill, such as golf, do some learners benefit most from schemata in the form of images to encode and others from verbal generalizations? To the extent that training needs deal with physical skills, the literature in physical education is not out of bounds.

Another principle of method design is that, whatever the capability to be mastered, the learner must be induced to actively "produce" that capability during training. Production facilitates both learning and retention (Perry and Downs, 1985). This is as true for a knowledge capability as it is for a physical or cognitive skill. If a

Table 8.1. Instructional Events and the Conditions of Learning They Imply for Five Types of Learned Capabilities.

Instructional Event	Type of Capability				
	Intellectual Skill	Cognitive Strategy	Information	Attitude	Motor Skill
1. Gaining attention	Introduce stimulus change; variations in sensory mode				
2. Informing learner of objective	Provide description and example of the performance to be expected	Clarify the general nature of the solution expected	Indicate the kind of verbal question to be answered	Provide example of the kind of action choice aimed for	Provide a demonstration of the performance to be expected
3. Stimulating recall of prerequisites	Stimulate recall of subordinate concepts and rules	Stimulate recall of task strategies and associated intellectual skills	Stimulate recall of context of organized information	Stimulate recall of relevant information, skills, and human model identification	Stimulate recall of executive subroutine and part-skills
4. Presenting the stimulus material	Present examples of concept or rule	Present novel problem	Present information in propositional form	Present human model, demonstrating choice of personal action	Provide external stimuli for performance, including tools or implements
5. Providing learning guidance	Provide verbal cues to proper combining sequence	Provide prompts and hints to novel solution	Provide verbal links to a larger meaningful context	Provide for observation of model's choice of action, and of reinforcement received by model	Provide practice with feedback of performance achievement
6. Eliciting the performance	Ask learner to apply rule or concept to new examples	Ask for problem solution	Ask for information in paraphrase, or in learner's own words	Ask learner to indicate choices of action in real or simulated situations	Ask for execution of the performance
7. Providing feedback	Confirm correctness of rule or concept application	Confirm originality of problem solution	Confirm correctness of statement of information	Provide direct or vicarious reinforcement of action choice	Provide feedback on degree of accuracy and timing of performance
8. Assessing performance	Learner demonstrates application of concept or rule	Learner originates a novel solution	Learner restates information in paraphrased form	Learner makes desired choice of personal action in real or simulated situation	Learner executes performance of total skill
9. Enhancing retention and transfer	Provide spaced reviews including a variety of examples	Provide occasions for a variety of novel problem solutions	Provide verbal links to additional complexes of information	Provide additional varied situations or selected choice of action	Learner continues skill practice

Source: Gagné and Briggs, 1979.

training objective concerns knowledge of the new tax law, the training method must induce the trainee to produce that knowledge in some way.

Accounting for Individual Differences

Cronbach and Gleser (1965) have shown that to the extent that one training program (treatment) is not uniformly superior to another for all trainees (there is an interaction between treatments and trainee individual differences), the payoff obtained by adapting the training program to the characteristics of the trainees increases exponentially as the number of different treatments increases. Consequently, the training designer is obligated to consider potential aptitude-treatment interactions when designing a program.

Aptitude-Treatment Interactions. The study of aptitude-treatment interactions (ATIs) in training and educational contexts has generated a very large literature (Cronbach, 1975; Cronbach and Snow, 1977; Green, 1974; Snow and Lohman, 1984), and it continues to grow larger (Pintrick, Cross, Kozma, and McKeachie, 1986). All this is in spite of the fact that the empirical evidence for the ability of ATIs to account for variance in training achievement is limited. Why then continue to pursue the role of individual differences in training design? Perhaps two reasons are sufficient to maintain our interest. First, the more recent research is beginning to produce a particular kind of aptitude–instructional method interaction that may be of some use to organizational training and development. It is best captured in a very significant paper by Snow and Lohman (1984). They review a number of recent studies, including many of their own, and conclude that there is a significant interaction between general academic ability and the complexity or degree of structure of the instructional program. High-ability students benefit more from low-structure, high-complexity programs, while the opposite tends to be true for low-ability students.

The above finding would be reason enough for continuing to worry about ATIs. However, a closer examination of the studies on which it is based makes it even more interesting for our purposes. The structure-complexity construct tends to confound learning methods and learning content. That is, the high-structure methods seem to deal with less complex or lower-level content. Also, it is not perfectly clear whether the individual differences continuum should be called *aptitude* or *prior achievement*. Admittedly, this is a sometime confusing distinction (Humphreys, 1974; Anastasi, 1982), but to the extent that the "aptitude measure" is reflective of recent educational or job *experience*, the interaction is between the level of preexisting knowledge or skill and the difficulty or complexity level of the training content. This is a source of variance that training and development can exploit. In design terms, it says that we should pay much more attention to *measuring* the existing achievement level of potential trainees and tailoring the training content accordingly. This would be useful for human relations training as well as skills training. At the same time, if the training content is cognitive in nature, and the trainees exhibit considerable variance in general cognitive ability, then using a supplemental, highly structured instructional method for low-ability people would also be beneficial. The data reviewed by Snow and Lohman seem robust enough to support such an action. Further, if it is true, as Gardner (1983) suggests, that there is a different aptitude for instruction corresponding to different training content (verbal, quantitative, psychomotor, social interaction), we indeed may have only scratched the surface of the "right kind" of ATI research.

Individual Differences in Motivation. While learner motivation has always been of practical interest, the research interest in motivational issues as they pertain to training and instruction has escalated considerably during the last five years. It has progressed to the point where the most recent *Annual Review* chapters in *both* training and development (Latham, 1988) and instructional psychology (Pintrick, Cross, Kozma, and McKeachie, 1986) devote significant space to the topic. Further, both sources point to many of the same developments as being relevant for their respective domains. Specifically, the motivational parameters of greatest interest are cognitive expectancies, self-efficacy judgments, and trainee attributions of the reasons for success and failure. As discussed in more detail in Chapter Seven, research on these parameters is grounded in the theoretical work of Weiner (1979), Bandura (1977), and Vroom (1964) and has centered around the self-efficacy judgment as the basic building block. The experimental research evidence strongly suggests that achievement during training will be greater to the extent that trainees believe that they are capable of mastering the training content—that is, they have reasonably high self-efficacy (Bandura, 1982; Kanfer and Gaelick, 1986; Frayne and Latham, 1987). However, experimental evidence has also shown other cognitions, captured in a comprehensive model described by Noe (1986), to be important. First, the trainees find themselves in a training program because of someone's assessment of their strengths and weaknesses. Achievement will be greater to the extent that trainees attribute validity to that assessment, which is partly a function of the degree to which it corresponds to their self-assessment (self-efficacy). Second, the trainees must perceive the training environment as responsive to their efforts. That is, even if they have high self-efficacy, achievement of tangible training outcomes must be attributed to trainee effort and ability rather than luck or trainer bias (in other words, training performance is instrumental for training success). Third, the outcomes of training must be judged to have relevance (instrumentality) for job performance. And fourth, an increase in job performance must itself have value (valence) for the participant. A very similar set of self-efficacy, expectancy, instrumentality, and valence notions has been proposed in the education context by Eccles (1983) and Dweck and Elliott (1983), based on research with school children.

The prescriptions for training design that flow from the above are that trainers must assess: (1) trainee attributions of how successful training outcomes can be achieved, (2) the instrumentality of training success for improvements in job performance, (3) the value of better job performance, and (4) trainee self-efficacy. The latter is particularly important, because a lack of self-efficacy for a particular task or activity leads to rejection of the "choice to perform."

An intriguing extension of self-efficacy notions is described by Dweck (1986) in a review of the evidence on how a student's "theory" of ability affects his or her achievement. Dweck postulates two different kinds of student goals and labels them *performance goals* and *learning goals*. The former category entails a desire to obtain favorable judgments or evaluations of achievement, while the latter describes a desire to learn more or to learn something new. Performance goals tend to be adopted by people who believe that abilities are fixed, while learning goals tend to be characteristic of people who believe that abilities are malleable. Consequently, low self-efficacy should lead to avoidance behavior on the part of those who adopt performance goals but would not affect the persistence and the seeking of challenge for people who respond to learning goals. This suggests that one way to deal with the effects of low self-efficacy is to try to change the trainees' goal orientation and their "theory" of the ability in question.

If assessment of the trainee's state reveals a lack of appropriate cognitions, the training designer has two major choices: change the training program or change the trainee. A reasonable prescription is to first examine the training program content itself to determine its correspondence to the content of job performance, its general level of difficulty, and the degree to which evidence of mastery is a function of the trainee's effort rather than other, extraneous variables. If the lack of appropriate cognitions is not a function of training design flaws, pretraining is necessary to alter the trainee's cognitions. Latham (1988) summarizes the techniques and supporting evidence for doing just that. In brief, the techniques are to model the appropriate cognitions, reinforce a set of success experiences, and calibrate the individual's self-set goals to the program's goals. At least some research already conducted on training courses is specifically directed at the self-regulation of the crucial cognitions (Frayne and Latham, 1987).

While the above research is promising, much remains to be done before the systematic assessment of trainee cognitions can become an integral part of training design. Construct-valid procedures for assessing self-efficacy would lead to better diagnosis of training defects, better matching of trainees to training content, and the exploration of a number of intriguing research questions, such as how the degree of self-efficacy relates to training achievement. Based on the theory of need achievement (Atkinson, 1964), we might hypothesize that "moderate" levels of self-efficacy produce the highest achievement. The construct validation process should also consider the possibility that motivational dispositions are, at least in part, a stable aspect of personality and may even account for some of the variance we now label *ability*. In an excellent review of these issues, Messick (1987) works through the evidence that supports various explanations of the significant correlations between measures of ability and measures of typical performance. It is a provocative argument and may lead to some fundamental changes in the way we think about aptitude-treatment interactions.

Finally, with regard to the general exploitation of individual differences, an encouraging result is provided by Savage, Williges, and Williges (1982), who used regression techniques to assign each trainee to one of two training programs so as to maximize the reduction in total training time. The gains were substantial—a 50 percent saving in training time over random assignments—and provide an added incentive for ATI research.

Specifying the Conditions of Learning

Given the description of objectives, the specification of training content, the development of learning methods, and the adaptation of content (and possibly instructional methods) to learner characteristics, the next requirement is to specify the conditions of learning that will best promote mastery and retention. This is the traditional concern of research in learning. Based on the current literature in instructional psychology, the conditions of learning that seem to have the highest priority are stimulating learner interest, using learning events that require "productive" behavior, providing appropriate feedback, and providing opportunities for practice under conditions that promote transfer. Such conditions are meant to be a function of normative principles that apply regardless of the training objectives, content, or method and are not a function of individual differences. Consequently, this particular set of design considerations is, in one sense, "left over" after other design decisions have been made.

A frequent prescription for capturing trainee interest is to begin with a description of the training objectives, assuming that they are relevant to outcomes valued by the trainer. In spite of the philosophical arguments surrounding the presentation of behavioral objectives to students (Kneller, 1972), the weight of the evidence supports their use for obtaining and focusing trainee interest (Duchastel and Merrill, 1973). However, there is also a recurring suggestion in the research literature that high-ability people prefer and seem to benefit more from more general, less detailed, statements of objectives (Snow and Lohman, 1984).

Considerable research by educational and cognitive psychologists illustrates the benefits to achievement and retention of learning events that promote "productive" responses on the part of the learner. A productive response, be it cognitive or physical, is one in which the learner actively uses the training content in some manner rather than passively watching, listening to, or imitating the trainer. Asking questions, reorganizing what the instructor said, thinking of new situations in which something applies, and writing a paper are all productive responses. An example from social interaction modeling is described by Hogan, Hakel, and Decker, (1986). Research on many such strategies is summarized by Perry and Downs (1985). One of the more intriguing methods for encouraging productive responses is to ask that trainees "teach back" the material to someone else as one of the formal requirements of the course.

Feedback has a long and honored history in the study of learning, and with good reason. A great deal of research supports its use, and some (Komaki, Heinzmann, and Lawson, 1980; Locke, 1980) would argue that behavior change is not possible without it. Feedback can come from many sources. The cues may be internal or external to the learner. For example, when the learner writes an exam question or hits a golf ball, the response may just "feel right" (an internal source). If external, the feedback may be primary or secondary. That is, the results of the response itself may provide feedback (primary), as when the learner sees the ball fly toward the hole or students read their own exam responses. Secondary feedback comes from some supplemental source, as when the coach says, "Good shot," or the instructor says, "Good answer." As noted some time ago (Blum and Naylor, 1968), the training designer should utilize all possible sources of feedback. For example, golfers should not be sent out on the practice tee when it is too dark to see where the ball goes. The learning events should not suppress internal or primary sources of feedback that are an integral part of the capability to be mastered.

More recently, Ilgen, Fisher, and Taylor (1979) have summarized a number of additional feedback effects on trainee responses. For design purposes, a summary of the evidence they review suggests that feedback must be accurate, perceived as accurate, perceived as being from a credible source, unhampered by intervening activity, at a level of specificity comparable to the specificity of the goal or objective, and positive. Negative feedback tends to have punishing effects that should be controlled. In essence, the Ilgen, Fisher, and Taylor review provides a checklist that training designers can and should use.

Evaluating Training Outcomes

From the perspective of this model, the evaluation questions are straightforward. Did the training or development program lead to proficiency on the behavioral objectives? If not, was the cause of the failure (1) inappropriate or missing content, (2) a poor choice of learning events, (3) trainees who did not satisfy the prerequisites, or (4) inadequate learning conditions? Performance on the objectives may be assessed by supervisory ratings, observer ratings, job sample tests, or critical incidents. While the measurement method must be subjected to the usual requirements of reliability and validity, the fundamental point is that the content of the criterion measures is given directly by the statement of training objectives. Archival records of effectiveness or other measures of overall job performance are not appropriate.

Qualifications and Caveats

The above discussion specifically asserts that every training effort will address this list of major issues, if only by default. That is, goals will be considered, needs will be identified, objectives will be formulated, content will be chosen, methods and media will be used, trainees will be selected, the training will take place under some set of conditions, and decisions will be made about its relative worth. At one extreme, each step in the design process could be given very careful and systematic attention by the organization paying the bill. That would take time, money, and expertise. At the other extreme, the potential sponsor could simply respond to the lure of advertising and buy packaged programs from vendors. That would take less time, perhaps less expertise, and maybe even less money. It is the contention here that the contribution of training to increased productivity via improved individual performance will be aided to the extent that time and effort are devoted to explicit analysis of the above design issues. Devoting even one hour to systematically thinking about these issues should at least make the organization a more sophisticated buyer of off-the-shelf offerings.

However, keep in mind that a precise answer about the return on investment for any particular amount of resources devoted to such a design procedure cannot be given. We know from previous research that training produces performance gains. It also seems to be the case that the gain is greater, or at least more consistent, if the training program has a strong conceptual base, incorporates goal setting and feedback, and is well executed. Further, research in education provides evidence that incorporating these design features can enhance achievement.

Summary of Substantive Prescriptions

Even though more research is needed and most would agree that we have precious few design *principles*, what avenues might the people responsible for training design pursue in the future? The following summary list seems reasonable, keeping in mind that matters of goal analysis and job design are considered elsewhere in this volume.

1. Multiple methods should be used to describe training needs and establish their content validity. Some variant of the Delphi or nominal group technique (Delbecq, Van de Ven, and Gustafson, 1976) using expert panels together with the critical incident technique would provide more complete information and would allow evaluation of the consistency of judgments.
2. The difference between a description of training needs and a description of specific training (behavioral) objectives should be recognized, and the performance capabilities that should result from training should be described. We simply must be more explicit about what we mean by *competent* and *expert* performance. What specific expertise does the organization need? Training designers must do more systematic observation of competent performers.
3. The content of a training or development program must be evaluated in terms of whether a rationale for how mastery on each specific component contributes to performance of the objectives

is provided, the sequence of instruction violates any obvious functional hierarchy, objectives are communicated to the learner, and the capabilities to be mastered in the training program match the capabilities described in the performance objectives.

4. The learning methods must be evaluated in terms of whether they allow the trainer to actively *produce* the desired capability and receive feedback that is accurate, credible, timely, and positive. The training designers should never forget that it is the validity of the method for producing the appropriate capability and providing appropriate feedback that is of fundamental importance. The media by which it is executed (for example, computerization or videotapes) are not of intrinsic importance.

5. If at all possible, trainees should be tested for initial ability and prerequisite knowledge. Most math departments would not allow someone to enter a course in differential equations without minimum mastery of calculus. We seem not to care about such issues in training and development, yet it is an obvious ATI that can be exploited. Further, people who are lower in ability should be offered more structured supplemental training.

6. Recent research strongly suggests that trainee perception of self-efficacy and perceptions of the instrumentality of the program for obtained valued outcomes should be assessed before training begins, and perhaps during training as well. Ideally, the training design should make provisions for dealing with low self-efficacy or instrumentality.

7. Training evaluation should be centered on the degree to which the training objectives have been achieved.

Future Research

Contrary to my somewhat negative view some eighteen years ago, the field of training and development has entered an exciting age, and promises to become even more intense in the future. In general, I think this is because a much richer flow of information and ideas is being injected into the field from cognitive psychology, instructional psychology, social learning theory, behavior analysis, and even individual differences, as in the basic investigation of abilities and performance. As this flow of theory and information intensifies, the field of training and development should become an even more rewarding place to do research and should attract more people to it.

For purposes of better training design, the most interesting research areas are topics such as the following:

- Developing descriptive models of competent or expert performance in specific occupational or job domains.
- Developing a better measurement theory and technology for the assessment of the trainee's current "state." That is, how should this current state be described, and how should it be measured? Current ability and achievement tests don't really do it.
- Developing generic training content in specific, critical content domains such as financial analysis, personnel problem diagnosis, general problem solving, strategic forecasting, use of information technology, and so on. Research should be directed at determining the most critical needs, modeling the structure of the content, and matching the content to learning events. To some degree, such research would mimic the attempt by educators to model the structure of such basic skills as arithmetic and reading comprehension and to develop optimal instructional sequences accordingly.
- Investigating the motivational antecedents of effective trainee performance. We have barely scratched the surface here, and much more remains to be done.
- Investigating the self-regulation of learning, as well as the self-regulation of choice behavior. That is, what aids can be provided for individuals to do their own needs assessment, prerequisite testing, and course selection?

If all goes well, the future impact of training and development on productivity should be greatly enhanced by training programs that are more closely tied to the organization's goals and that are designed to maintain learner interest and achieve mastery in an optimal fashion. The author was born too soon.

References

Anastasi, A. *Psychological Testing.* (5th ed.) New York: Macmillan, 1982.

Atkinson, J. W. *An Introduction to Motivation.* New York: Van Nostrand Reinhold, 1964.

Bandura, A. "Self-Efficacy: Toward a Unifying Theory of Behavior Change." *Psychological Review,* 1977, *84,* 191–215.

Bandura, A. "Self-Efficacy Mechanism in Human Agency." *American Psychologist,* 1982, *37,* 122–147.

Bass, B. M., and Vaughan, J. A. *Training in Industry: The Management of Learning.* Monterey, Calif.: Brooks/Cole, 1966.

Berryman-Fink, C. "Male and Female Managers' Views of the

Communication Skills and Training Needs of Women in Management." *Public Personnel Management*, 1985, *14*, 307-313.

Bloom, B. S., Hastings, J. T., and Madaus, G. F. *Handbook on Formative and Summative Evaluation of Student Learning*. New York: McGraw-Hill, 1971.

Blum, M. L., and Naylor, J. C. *Industrial Psychology: Its Theoretical and Social Foundations*. New York: Harper & Row, 1968.

Bransford, J., Sherwood, R., Vye, N., and Rieser, J. "Teaching Thinking and Problem Solving." *American Psychologist*, 1986, *41*, 1078-1089.

Briggs, L. J. *Handbook of Procedures for the Design of Instruction*. Pittsburgh, Pa.: American Institutes for Research, 1970.

Briggs, L. J. (ed.). *Instructional Design: Principles and Applications*. Englewood Cliffs, N.J.: Educational Technology Publications, 1977.

Brown, J., and VanLehn, K. "Repair Theory: A Generative Theory of Bugs in Procedural Skills." *Cognitive Science*, 1980, *4*, 379-426.

Bruner, J. S. *Toward a Theory of Instruction*. Cambridge, Mass.: Harvard University Press, 1966.

Burke, M. J., and Day, R. R. "A Cumulative Study of the Effectiveness of Managerial Training." *Journal of Applied Psychology*, 1986, *71*, 232-246.

Campbell, J. P. "Personnel Training and Development." *Annual Review of Psychology*, 1971, *22*, 565-602.

Campbell, J. P. *The Army Selection and Classification Project: 1985 Annual Report*. Alexandria, Va.: Army Research Institute for the Social and Behavioral Sciences, 1986.

Campbell, J. P. (ed.). *The Army Selection and Classification Project: 1986 Annual Report*. Alexandria, Va.: Army Research Institute for the Social and Behavioral Sciences, 1987.

Campbell, J. P., and Dunnette, M. D. "Effectiveness of T-Group Experiences in Managerial Training and Development." *Psychological Bulletin*, 1968, *70*, 73-104.

Campbell, J. P., Dunnette, M. D., Arvey, R. D., and Hellervik, L. "The Development and Evaluation of Behaviorally Based Rating Scales." *Journal of Applied Psychology*, 1973, *57*, 15-22.

Campbell, J. P., Dunnette, M. D., Lawler, E. E., III, and Weick, K. E. *Managerial Behavior, Performance, and Effectiveness*. New York: McGraw-Hill, 1970.

Cronbach, L. J. "Beyond the Two Disciplines of Scientific Psychology." *American Psychologist*, 1975, *30*, 116-127.

Cronbach, L. J., and Gleser, G. C. *Psychological Tests and Personnel*

Decisions. (2nd ed.) Champaign, Ill.: University of Illinois Press, 1965.

Cronbach, L. J., and Snow, R. E. *Aptitudes and Instructional Methods: A Handbook for Research on Interactions.* New York: Irvington, 1977.

Decker, P. J., and Nathan, B. R. *Behavior Modeling Training: Principles and Applications.* New York: Praeger, 1985.

Delbecq, A. L., Van de Ven, A. H., and Gustafson, D. H. *Group Techniques for Program Planning.* Glenview, Ill.: Scott, Foresman, 1976.

Downs, S. "Retraining for New Skills." *Ergonomics,* 1985, *28,* 1205–1211.

Duchastel, P. C., and Merrill, P. F. "The Effects of Behavioral Objectives on Learning." *Review of Educational Research,* 1973, *43,* 53–69.

Dweck, C. S. "Motivational Processes Affecting Learning." *American Psychologist,* 1986, *41,* 1040–1048.

Dweck, C. S., and Elliott, E. S. "Achievement Motivation." In P. H. Mussen (ed.), *Handbook of Child Psychology.* Vol. 4 (4th ed.) New York: Wiley, 1983.

Eccles, J. "Expectancies, Values, and Academic Behaviors." In J. T. Spence (ed.), *Achievement and Achievement Motives.* New York: W. H. Freeman, 1983.

Ericsson, K. A., and Simon, H. A. *Protocol Analysis: Verbal Reports as Data.* Cambridge, Mass.: MIT Press, 1984.

Fiedler, F. E., and Chemers, M. M. *Improving Leadership Effectiveness: The Leader Match Group Concept.* (2nd ed.) New York: Wiley, 1984.

Fleishman, E. A., and Quaintance, M. K. *Taxonomies of Human Performance.* Orlando, Fla.: Academic Press, 1984.

Ford, J. K., and Wroten, S. P. "Introducing New Methods for Conducting Training Evaluation and for Linking Training Evaluation to Program Redesign." *Personnel Psychology,* 1984, *37,* 651–665.

Frayne, C. A., and Latham, G. P. "The Application of Social Learning Theory to Employee Self-Management of Attendance." *Journal of Applied Psychology,* 1987, *72,* 387–392.

Frederiksen, N. "Implications of Cognitive Theory for Instruction in Problem Solving." *Review of Educational Research,* 1984, *54,* 363–407.

French, W. L., and Bell, C. H. *Organization Development: Behavioral Interventions for Organization Improvement.* (3rd ed.) Englewood Cliffs, N.J.: Prentice-Hall, 1984.

Gagné, R. M. "Military Training and Principles of Learning." *American Psychologist,* 1962, *17,* 83-91.

Gagné, R. M. "Learning Hierarchies." *Educational Psychologist,* 1968, *6,* 1-9.

Gagné, R. M. "Analysis of Objectives." In L. J. Briggs (ed.), *Instructional Design.* Englewood Cliffs, N.J.: Educational Technology Publications, 1977.

Gagné, R. M., and Briggs, L. J. *Principles of Instructional Design.* (2nd ed.) New York: Holt, Rinehart & Winston, 1979.

Gagné, R. M., and Dick, W. "Instructional Psychology." *Annual Review of Psychology,* 1983, *34,* 261-295.

Gagné, R. M., and Rohwer, W. D., Jr. "Instructional Psychology." *Annual Review of Psychology,* 1969, *20,* 381-418.

Gardner, H. *Frames of Mind: The Theory of Multiple Intelligence.* New York: Basic Books, 1983.

Glaser, R. "Components of a Psychology of Instruction: Toward a Science of Design." *Review of Educational Research,* 1976, *46,* 1-24.

Glaser, R. "Instructional Psychology: Past, Present, and Future." *American Psychologist,* 1982, *37* (3), 292-305.

Glaser, R., and Resnick, L. B. "Instructional Psychology." *Annual Review of Psychology,* 1972, *23,* 207-276.

Glickman, A. S., and Vallance, T. R. "Curriculum Assessment with Critical Incidents." *Journal of Applied Psychology,* 1958, *42,* 329-335.

Goldstein, I. L. "Training in Work Organizations." *Annual Review of Psychology,* 1980, *31,* 229-272.

Goldstein, I. L. *Training in Organizations: Needs Assessment, Development, and Evaluation.* (2nd ed.) Monterey, Calif.: Brooks/Cole, 1986.

Goldstein, I. L. Macy, W. H., and Prien, E. P. "Needs Assessment Approaches for Training Development." In H. Meltzer and W. Nord (eds.), *Making Organizations Humane and Productive.* New York: Wiley, 1981.

Green, D. R. (ed.). *The Aptitude-Achievement Distinction.* New York: CTB/McGraw-Hill, 1974.

Hall, E. R., and Freda, J. S. *A Comparison of Individualized and Conventional Instruction in Navy Technical Training.* Training Analysis and Evaluation Group Technical Report 117. Orlando, Fla.: U.S. Department of Defense, 1982.

Hogan, P. M., Hakel, M. D., and Decker, P. J. "Effects of Trainee-Generated Versus Trainer-Provided Rule Codes on Generalization in Behavior-Modeling Training." *Journal of Applied Psychology,* 1986, *71,* 469-473.

Humphreys, L. G. "The Misleading Distinction Between Aptitude and Achievement Tests." In D. R. Green (ed.), *The Aptitude-Achievement Distinction.* New York: CTB/McGraw-Hill, 1974.

Ilgen, D. R., Fisher, C. D., and Taylor, M. S. "Consequence of Individual Feedback on Behavior in Organizations." *Journal of Applied Psychology*, 1979, *64*, 349–371.

Johnson, P. E., and Associates. "Expertise and Error in Diagnostic Reasoning." *Cognitive Science*, 1981, *5*, 235–283.

Kanfer, F. H., and Gaelick, L. "Self-Management Methods." In F. H. Kanfer and A. P. Goldstein (eds.), *Helping People Change: A Textbook of Methods.* (3rd ed.) Elmsford, N.Y.: Pergamon Press, 1986.

Kneller, G. F. "Behavioral Objectives? No!" (with a reply by R. M. Gagné). *Educational Leadership*, 1972, *23*, 394–400.

Komaki, J., Heinzmann, A. T., and Lawson, L. "Effects of Training and Feedback: Component Analysis of a Behavioral Safety Program." *Journal of Applied Psychology*, 1980, *65*, 261–70.

Krathwohl, D. R., Bloom, B. S., and Masia, B. B. *Taxonomy of Educational Objectives. Handbook II: Affective Domain.* New York: McKay, 1964.

Landy, F. J., Farr, J. L., and Jacobs, R. R. "Utility Concepts in Performance Measurement." *Organizational Behavior and Human Performance*, 1982, *30*, 15–40.

Latham, G. P. "Human Resource Training and Development." *Annual Review of Psychology*, forthcoming.

Latham, G. P., and Saari, L. M. "The Application of Social Learning Theory to Training Supervisors Through Behavior Modeling." *Journal of Applied Psychology*, 1979, *64*, 239–246.

Locke, E. A. "Latham vs. Komaki: A Tale of Two Paradigms." *Journal of Applied Psychology*, 1980, *65*, 16–23.

Locke, E. A., and Latham, G. P. *Goal Setting: A Motivational Technique That Works!* Englewood Cliffs, N.J.: Prentice-Hall, 1984.

MacCrimmon, K. R., and Taylor, R. N. "Decision Making and Problem Solving." In M. D. Dunnette (ed.), *Handbook of Industrial/Organizational Psychology.* Skokie, Ill.: Rand McNally, 1976.

McGehee, W., and Thayer, P. W. *Training in Business and Industry.* New York: Wiley, 1961.

McKeachie, W. J. "Instructional Psychology." *Annual Review of Psychology*, 1974, *26*, 161–193.

Mager, R. F. *Preparing Objectives for Instruction.* (2nd ed.) Belmont, Calif.: Fearon, 1975.

Manz, C. C. "Self Leadership: Toward an Expanded Theory of Self

Influence Processes in Organizations." *Academy of Management Journal*, 1986, *11*, 585-600.

Menges, R. J., and Girard, D. L. "Development of a Research Specialty: Instructional Psychology Portrayed in the Annual Review of Psychology." *Instructional Science*, 1983, *12*, 83-98.

Messick, S. "Structural Relationships Across Cognition, Personality, and Style." In R. Snow and M. Farr (eds.), *Aptitude, Learning, and Instruction*. Vol. 3: *Conative and Affective Process Analysis*. Hillsdale, N.J.: Erlbaum, 1987.

Mintzberg, H. *The Nature of Managerial Work*. New York: Harper & Row, 1973.

Nash, A. H., Muczyk, J. P., and Vettori, F. L. "The Relative Practical Effectiveness of Programmed Instruction." *Personnel Psychology*, 1971, *24*, 397-418.

Noe, R. A. "Trainees' Attributes and Attitudes: Neglected Influences on Training Effectiveness." *Academy of Management Review*, 1986, *11*, 736-749.

Perry, P., and Downs, S. "Skills, Strategies, and Ways of Learning." *Programmed Learning and Educational Technology*, 1985, *22*, 177-181.

Pintrick, P. R., Cross, D. R., Kozma, R. B., and McKeachie, W. J. "Instructional Psychology." *Annual Review of Psychology*, 1986, *37*, 611-651.

Popham, W. J., and Baker, E. L. *Establishing Instructional Goals*. Englewood Cliffs, N.J.: Prentice-Hall, 1970.

Resnick, L. B. "Instructional Psychology." *Annual Review of Psychology*, 1981, *32*, 659-704.

Resnick, L. B., and Ford, W. *The Psychology of Mathematics for Instruction*. Hillsdale, N.J.: Erlbaum, 1981.

Rubinstein, M. F. "A Decade of Experience in Teaching an Interdisciplinary Problem Solving Course." In D. T. Tuma and F. Reif (eds.), *Problem Solving and Education: Issues in Teaching and Research*. Hillsdale, N.J.: Erlbaum, 1980.

Savage, R. E., Williges, B. H., and Williges, R. C. "Empirical Prediction Models for Training Group Assignment." *Human Factors*, 1982, *24*, 417-426.

Schmidt, F. L., Hunter, J. E., and Pearlman, K. "Assessing the Economic Impact of Personnel Programs on Workforce Productivity." *Personnel Psychology*, 1982, *35*, 333-347.

Schneider, W., and Shiffrin, R. M. "Controlled and Automated Human Information Processing." *Psychological Review*, 1977, *84*, 1-66.

Simon, H. A. "The Functional Equivalence of Problem Solving Skill." *Cognitive Psychology,* 1975, *7,* 268–288.

Simon, H. A. "Information Processing Models of Cognition." *Annual Review of Psychology,* 1979a, *30,* 363–396.

Simon, H. A. *Models of Thought.* New Haven, Conn.: Yale University Press, 1979b.

Smith, P. B. "Controlled Studies of the Outcomes of Sensitivity Training." *Psychological Bulletin,* 1975, *82,* 597–622.

Snow, R. E., and Lohman, D. F. "Toward a Theory of Cognitive Aptitude for Learning from Instruction." *Journal of Educational Psychology,* 1984, *76* (3), 347–376.

Stewart, R. *Contrasts in Management.* Maidenhead, Berkshire, England: McGraw-Hill, U.K., 1976.

Taylor, D. W. "Decision Making and Problem Solving." In J. G. March (ed.), *Handbook of Organizations.* Skokie, Ill.: Rand McNally, 1965.

Tornow, W. W., and Pinto, P. R. "The Development of a Managerial Job Taxonomy: A System for Describing, Classifying, and Evaluating Executive Positions." *Journal of Applied Psychology,* 1976, *61,* 410–418.

Triandis, H. C., Feldman, J. M., Weldon, D. E., and Harvey, W. M. "Designing Pre-Employment Training for the Hard to Employ: A Cross-Cultural Psychological Approach." *Journal of Applied Psychology,* 1975, *60,* 44–56.

Tucker, F. D. "A Study of the Training Needs of Older Workers: Implications for Human Resources Development Planning." *Public Personnel Management,* 1985, *14,* 85–95.

Vroom, V. *Work and Motivation.* New York: Wiley, 1964.

Vroom, V., and Yetton, P. *Leadership and Decision Making.* Pittsburgh, Pa.: University of Pittsburgh Press, 1973.

Weiner, B. *Human Motivation.* New York: Holt, Rinehart & Winston, 1979.

Wexley, K. N. "Personnel Training." *Annual Review of Psychology,* 1984, *35,* 519–551.

Wexley, K. N., and Latham, G. P. *Developing and Training Human Resources in Organizations.* Glenview, Ill.: Scott, Foresman, 1981.

Wittrock, M. C., and Lumsdaine, A. A. "Instructional Psychology." *Annual Review of Psychology,* 1977, *28,* 417–459.

Yukl, G. "A New Taxonomy for Integrating Diverse Perspectives on Managerial Behavior." Paper presented at 47th annual meeting of the American Academy of Management, New Orleans, Aug. 1987.

PART THREE

CICICICICICICICI

Multifaceted Interventions
for Influencing Productivity

The methods for influencing productivity that are described in the
four chapters in this part are of a different order than those described
in Part Two. They incorporate more than one "basic" mechanism by
which they try to produce change. In fact, a valid description of the
mechanisms by which they work is often a major issue. Thus the level
of complexity has escalated, the interventions are larger in scope,
things are less easily controlled for systematic study, and the resulting
research findings are less easily interpreted. We are faced with the
band-width versus fidelity problem, which implies that we might have
to settle for more error variance in the results in trade for more
powerful interventions with broader effects. The four chapters
themselves are intended to present a continuum from the relatively
focused to the more broad. Job redesign (Chapter Nine) is certainly the
most focused in scope, in that it concentrates on changing the specific
content of individual jobs (or predicting the effects of such changes).
Quality circles (Chapter Ten) broaden the scope considerably, and
many things are fair game besides the content of individual jobs. Self-
managing teams (Chapter Eleven) go even further and incorporate
even more of the management function. Finally, the intervention
strategy goes the whole way (Chapter Twelve) and considers the effects
of ownership itself. Questions of who manages and who owns run up
against some very relevant political questions that we often try to
ignore but that do not go away. It is time to face them.

217

9

ε3ε3ε3ε3ε3ε3ε3ε3

Job Enrichment
and Performance Improvement

Lisa R. Berlinger
William H. Glick
Robert C. Rodgers

Theoretical explanations of how job enrichment improves performance have stimulated considerable enthusiasm among researchers
and practitioners. These explanations have both intuitive and
practical appeal. Mixed results, however, have generated some
indifference to the theories and to the merits of job enrichment.

Qualitative literature reviews generally conclude that the job
characteristics–performance relationship is tenuous. These reviews
report that some studies find positive effects while others find negative
effects (Aldag, Barr, and Brief, 1981; Griffin, Welsh, and Moorhead,
1981; Locke, 1975; Locke and others, 1980; O'Brien, 1982; Pierce and
Dunham, 1976; Roberts and Glick, 1981; Thomas and Griffin, 1983;
Umstot, Mitchell, and Bell, 1978; White, 1978). Thomas and Griffin
(1983) conclude that "the influence of task characteristics on performance is a study in contradiction" (p. 677). O'Brien (1982) concludes
that the job characteristics model "has not been shown capable of
predicting individual productivity" (p. 398). Griffin, Welsh, and
Moorhead (1981) characterize results of empirical tests of the job
characteristics–performance relationship as "disappointing or incon-
clusive" (p. 656). Locke and others (1980) reach a more cautiously
optimistic conclusion. Performance, they conclude, does improve when
jobs are enriched. The improvement, however, is meager.

Special thanks to Edwin A. Locke, C. Chet Miller, and Yau-de Wang for their
comments and assistance to us in the preparation of this chapter.
Note: Tables 9.1 through 9.4 constitute the appendix to this chapter and
appear at the end of the chapter, preceding the references.

Quantitative reviews, on the other hand, report small but consistently positive results (Guzzo, Jette, and Katzell, 1985; Spector, 1985; Stone, 1986). The most positive quantitative review rated work redesign as one of the most consistently effective psychologically based intervention programs (Guzzo, Jette, and Katzell, 1985).

The purpose of this study is to devleop and test a theory about the job characteristics–performance relationship. When will job enrichment increase performance? When will it have negligible effects? Our approach integrates the theory-building strengths of qualitative reviews with quantitative review techniques. Given seemingly contradictory results from different studies, the qualitative reviews have suggested theoretical and methodological arguments to explain why the job characteristics–performance link is not equally strong under all conditions. These arguments provide the initial components of a theory of the job characteristics–performance relationship. Results from a quantitative review guide the refinement of this theory.

We begin by discussing theories that either support or question the existence of the job characteristics–performance link. A series of arguments are developed that identify the substantive and methodological factors that may influence the strength of observed job characteristics–performance relationships. These hypotheses are tested with meta-analysis, a quantitative review technique for cumulating results across all empirical studies that report data on the job characteristics–performance link. Meta-analysis is particularly appropriate for testing hypotheses about variations in the strength of a relationship, because testing moderator hypotheses requires observation of the job characteristics–performance relationship in a broad variety of contexts while individual researchers typically restrict their investigations to a single, manageable context. Further, testing of moderator hypotheses must be conducted with very large sample sizes (Drasgow and Kang, 1984; Trattner and O'Leary, 1980), which are most easily obtained in quantitative reviews of multiple studies. Results from this meta-analysis suggest to researchers a more comprehensive model of the job characteristics–performance relationship and provide guidance to practitioners who are interested in observing performance gains from job enrichment programs.

Are Job Characteristics Related to Performance?

Theoretically, Yes

Why would we expect enriched jobs to lead to higher performance? Job enrichment, as embodied in the job characteristics model

(Hackman and Lawler, 1971; Hackman and Oldham, 1975, 1976), draws on aspects of needs satisfaction theory and expectancy theory to explain how enriched jobs lead to improved performance. In needs satisfaction terms, people who are given meaningful jobs perform better because doing a meaningful job well satisfies the individual's needs for growth and development. In expectancy theory terms, if an individual (1) expects that working hard will lead to good performance (expectancy), (2) expects that good performance will lead to having higher-order needs fulfilled (instrumentality), and (3) desires self-actualization or satisfaction of higher-order needs (preference or valence), then the individual will be motivated to perform well.

Job enrichment may lead to improved performance for the following reasons, in addition to needs satisfaction and expectancy theory predictions:

- Enriched jobs are not routine and repetitive, so employees will not attempt to avoid work. The reduction in dysfunctional behaviors should improve productivity.
- Restructuring jobs into meaningful units may uncover hidden inefficiencies that result from the extra coordination necessary when work is broken down into "efficient" units. Higher quality as well as increased output may result.
- Any change in the work forces everyone to rethink the structure and flow of tasks. New methods may be discovered of performing work functions, yielding higher productivity (Griffin, 1982b; Hackman and Oldham, 1980).

In summary, enriched jobs are theoretically related to higher-quality performance as well as to higher-quantity output and better overall work effectiveness. Unfortunately, the effects of system changes are rarely reported, so it is not possible to disentangle outcomes caused by system changes from outcomes caused by the motivational effects of enriching jobs.

Theoretically, Probably No

Few researchers have doubted that improved performance *should* be an outcome of enriched jobs. This link has been questioned, however, in a general critique of needs satisfaction models (Salancik and Pfeffer, 1977). Enriched jobs are presumed to be more motivating because individuals anticipate greater satisfaction of their higher-order needs. Salancik and Pfeffer (1977) question this model for two reasons. First, if needs satisfaction motivates performance, the satiation of needs should reduce subsequent motivation and performance. Satisfaction of needs through job enrichment therefore could not sustain high levels of performance. This critique of needs satisfaction models of job enrichment stands in contrast to the assertion that "a person may experience higher order need satisfaction without the strength of desire for additional satisfaction of these needs diminishing" (Hackman and Lawler, 1971, p. 262).

A second argument against expecting a positive job characteristics-performance link (Salancik and Pfeffer, 1977) is the elusive nature of the causal effects of satisfaction on performance (Podsakoff and Williams, 1986; Lawler and Porter, 1967). Salancik and Pfeffer (1977) interpret the job characteristics model as assuming that desirable job characteristics will satisfy needs and, as a consequence, increase motivation. This causal process is questioned because satisfaction is often found to be unrelated to performance. Further, the direction of causality could be reversed (Salancik and Pfeffer, 1977, 1978). Thus Salancik and Pfeffer (1978) conclude that the social context, commitment, and attributional processes are the primary determinants of performance, job perceptions, and job attitudes. Identifiable characteristics of jobs and the degree of needs satisfaction are expected to have a negligible effect on performance.

Theoretically, Under Some Conditions

Generally strong theoretical support for a positive job characteristics-performance link, coupled with contradictory and sometimes puzzling empirical support, has inspired speculation about the cause(s) of the large variation in observed relationships between job characteristics and performance. Theories naturally have boundary conditions. The job characteristics-performance relationship is likely to be weaker or nonexistent in some situations and stronger in others. For example, when employees do not have the ability to perform a complex job, when employees distrust management, or when employees are assigned job functions that simply cannot be made more meaningful, enriching jobs would not be expected to increase performance. If employees distrust management, they may feel that they are being asked to do more work for the same compensation. Rather than feeling pride in their work and a concomitant satisfaction of growth needs, employees may conclude that job enrichment efforts are exploitative (Gomberg, 1973; Fein, 1974).

Other boundary conditions have elicited more attention and an occasional heated debate. Boundary conditions that limit the generalizability of the job characteristics-performance relationship include growth need strength, incumbent perceptions of job characteristics, range restriction, cognitive consistency of the raters, the type of performance, job change, pretest-posttest design, random assignment, and laboratory versus field setting. We first turn to a brief treatment of growth need strength.

Growth Need Strength. The strength of higher-order needs, growth need strength, was explicitly identified in the job characteristics model as a critical moderator of the job characteristics–performance relationship (Hackman and Lawler, 1971; Hackman and Oldham, 1976, 1980). Job characteristics are not expected to be motivating for employees who have weak needs for growth and development. Rather, job characteristics are expected to have the most positive effects on performance among individuals with strong needs for growth.

Incumbent Perceptions of Job Characteristics. The most controversial issue that has perplexed job characteristics researchers is whether to focus on incumbent perceptions of job characteristics or on characteristics of the actual ("objective") job. Although the job characteristics model distinguishes between perceptions and actual job characteristics (Hackman and Lawler, 1971; Hackman and Oldham, 1975, 1976), many researchers inappropriately comingle perceptions and characteristics of the actual job (Roberts and Glick, 1981). Characteristics of the actual job are observable and can be manipulated independently of perceptions held by job incumbents. Job perceptions are determined by characteristics of the actual job and by other factors, such as social cues, social comparison processes, self-perception (Salancik and Pfeffer, 1978), and perceptual job redefinition (Hackman, 1969).

Incumbent perceptions and attitudes are pivotal in most social-psychological explanations. The job characteristics model places incumbent perceptions as an intervening step between characteristics of the actual job and outcomes (Hackman and Oldham, 1976, 1980). Although job incumbents' perceptions are affected by the actual jobs, job incumbents both physically and cognitively redefine their jobs to be consistent with their needs and values (Hackman, 1969). Incumbent perceptions are a direct causal antecedent to outcomes, while objective characteristics are an indirect antecedent. Thus the use of perceived measures provides a more direct assessment of the job characteristics model as a psychological model (Glick, Jenkins, and Gupta, 1986; Taber, Beehr, and Walsh, 1985). Hackman and Lawler emphasize that "it is not [the job's] objective state which affects employee attitudes and behavior, but rather how they are experienced by the employees" (1971, p. 264).

Focusing on incumbent perceptions, however, may "confound

personal needs and preferences of the performer with the objective characteristics of the task" (Schwab and Cummings, 1976, p. 24). This confounding may inflate the estimates of the "true" relation between job characteristics and performance. Thus, if we are interested in job characteristics that are observable situational characteristics that can be manipulated, incumbent ratings are clearly inferior to other measures of job characteristics (Roberts and Glick, 1981; Salancik and Pfeffer, 1977, 1978).

Independent measures of job characteristics are preferred for practical reasons as well. Objective assessments of jobs are not influenced by the needs or characteristics of any particular job incumbent. When management decides to enrich a type of job, the redesign efforts are most easily and consistently guided by a single definition of the job. Although incumbent perceptions may be relevant, independent assessments of actual job characteristics may be more useful.

Although job perceptions and actual job characteristics may be interesting for different purposes, they are not interchangeable (Hackman and Oldham, 1980; Roberts and Glick, 1981). The effects of actual job characteristics on performance are mediated by perceptions. Thus we should expect the job characteristics–performance relationship to be much stronger for incumbent perceptions of job characteristics than for other measures of job characteristics.

Range Restriction. The job characteristics model is concerned with the variation across, not within, jobs (Hackman and Lawler, 1971; Hackman and Oldham, 1980). Many studies, however, collect data from only one occupational group or one type of job. This practice restricts the variation in job characteristics, the independent variable, and limits the external validity of the results (Mitchell, 1985). Specifically, restricting the range of the independent variable reduces the strength of the observed relationship between job characteristics and performance. Thus sampling within only one type of job should reduce the magnitude of the expected correlation.

The effects of range restriction are more complex and theoretically important when considered in conjunction with incumbent perceptions than with more independent measures of the actual job characteristics. Job titles and detailed task analyses are often used as categorical measures of differences in objective job characteristics (Caldwell and O'Reilly, 1982; Glick, Graham-Moore, and Schilhabel, 1984; Hackman and Lawler, 1971; O'Reilly, Parlette, and Bloom, 1980). When researchers report results for a single job or job family, the variation in actual job characteristics is severely restricted. Although this range restriction in actual job characteristics probably also reduces the variation in job perceptions, several studies have noted substantial variation in incumbent perceptions in the same job (Caldwell and O'Reilly, 1982; Glick, Graham-Moore, and Schilhabel, 1984; O'Reilly, Parlette, and Bloom, 1980). Given the psychological nature of the job characteristics model, the variation in job perceptions may be related to performance even when objective differences between jobs are held constant. Thus, assuming that job perceptions mediate the relationship between actual job characteristics and performance, and assuming that job perceptions are a function of both actual job characteristics and other factors, we can predict that restricting the range of actual job characteristics will reduce severely the observed job characteristics–performance relationship. Range restriction will have a more moderate effect on the relationship between incumbent perceptions of job characteristics and performance.

This set of arguments provides a novel comparison of the use of incumbent perceptions versus independent measures of job characteristics. If, as predicted, the job characteristics–performance relationship is positive for all conditions, and if the dampening effects of range restriction are much stronger for actual job characteristics than for incumbent perceptions, the job characteristics model will be supported. These results would indicate that job perceptions intervene between actual job characteristics and performance and that the relationship between incumbent perceptions and performance is based partially on other sources of variance in incumbent perceptions (Hackman, 1969; Hackman and Lawler, 1971; Hackman and Oldham, 1976, 1980; Salancik and Pfeffer, 1978).

Cognitive Consistency of Raters. A recurring issue in critiques of the job characteristics literature is the potential bias caused by the tendency of raters to be cognitively consistent (Roberts and Glick, 1981; Schwab and Cummings, 1976; Spector, 1987). When a predictor and an outcome variable are measured by the same method (usually questionnaires answered by job incumbents) and/or with similarly worded questions, the tendency of individuals to be consistent will result in an observed relationship between the two variables that is due primarily to common methods variance (Roberts and Glick, 1981; Schwab and Cummings, 1976). While common methods variance may be a major threat to the validity of job characteristics studies that examine outcomes such as satisfaction (Spector, 1987), it is less likely to be a problem with performance outcomes, for two reasons. First, cognitive consistency has a weaker effect on performance than on attitudes such as satisfaction (Glick, Jenkins, and Gupta, 1986). In an attempt to remain cognitively consistent in response to a questionnaire or interview, job incumbents (and other raters) may reevaluate their level of satisfaction, but performance level is anchored in more observable behaviors. Second, job characteristics and satisfaction are often assessed with similarly worded and formatted questions, while performance is measured with different types of questions. Thus, although cognitive consistency may be very problematic for job characteristics–satisfaction research, cognitive consistency is less likely to create common methods variance in job characteristics–performance research.

Type of Performance. There are conflicting arguments for examining different performance-related characteristics, such as effort, quality, quantity, and overall performance. The argument for focusing on effort is similar to the argument for perceived job characteristics. The job characteristics model is a psychological model that links most closely the job incumbent's perceptions of job characteristics with the level of effort exerted on the job. Thus the most direct test of this link in the model requires a focus on effort rather than on other performance-related characteristics. Theoretically, we should expect job characteristics to be most strongly related to effort. Lack of ability, reduced demand for products, the physical structure of equipment, and other factors may constrain the strength of the relationship between job characteristics and other performance characteristics.

The job characteristics model also links job enrichment with more observable behaviors. Observable performance has been interpreted in terms of quality of performance, quantity of output, and overall performance. Although the original formulation of the model did not distinguish among these dimensions, initial results suggested that employees associate job enrichment more strongly with high-quality work, because it provides a greater opportunity to accomplish something meaningful (Hackman and Lawler, 1971).

Overall performance may be preferable to either quality or quantity, because it incorporates all dimensions or facets of job performance. Managers are most interested in overall performance because they rarely like to see increases in quality being offset by decreases in quantity of output, or vice versa. Specific characteristics of job performance also tend to emphasize the accomplishment of a single task. When jobs are enriched, several tasks may be combined to increase variety, identity, and significance. Completion of the new tasks reduces the time available to work on the old task and may decrease performance on that specific task. Overall performance, however, reflects performance on all tasks. Thus overall performance measures should reflect larger effects than a measure that evaluates a single dimension of job performance.

Job Change. The job characteristics model focuses on the comparison of the initial and final characteristics of the job to predict performance (Hackman and Oldham, 1976). It does not attribute unique motivational effects to the process of change. Thus enriching the jobs of current employees is expected to increase performance because the new jobs are more enriched, not because a change occurred.

Griffin, Bateman, Wayne, and Head (1987), however, recently argued for a dynamic model of the antecedents and consequences of job perceptions. They claim that changing jobs has a different effect than initially assigning individuals to different jobs. Although they do not explain why dynamic effects should be different than static effects, three rationales exist. First, changing a job creates a Hawthorne effect in addition to the static effect of performing a different job (Salancik and Pfeffer, 1978). The positive expectations of researchers and managers are probably communicated to employees when the job redesign process occurs (Salancik and Pfeffer, 1978). Employees are led to expect the new jobs to be better than their current jobs, especially when employees participate in the change process. These expectations are likely to increase performance.

Second, employees' perceptions of their jobs are affected by a social comparison process (Salancik and Pfeffer, 1978; Oldham and Miller, 1979). Employees who perform only one version of the job will compare their current job with either co-workers' jobs or with less comparable jobs that they may have performed in the past. During a job change, however, employees are exposed to both enriched and unenriched versions of the same job. Thus they have a stronger point of reference for interpreting the characteristics of the final job than employees initially assigned to that final job. The strongest possible social comparison is an employee's own experiences with a different version of the same job before the change. Due to this stronger point of reference, employees involved in a job change are likely to hold more polarized perceptions of the job. The stronger the contrast between jobs in this social comparison, the stronger the effects on performance. Thus enriching the jobs of current employees should increase performance above the level of employees who were initially assigned to the enriched jobs.

Third, changing jobs will increase performance for nonmotivational reasons (Hackman and Oldham, 1980). Hidden inefficiencies in the work flow may be exposed when the job is restructured, and making the work more efficient may lead to higher productivity. In addition, as unenriched jobs are enriched into meaningful units, the amount of coordination needed is reduced. Quality, quantity, and overall performance may increase as errors and inefficiencies caused by the difficulties of coordinating many people and functions are reduced. Thus the relationship between job characteristics and performance will be stronger following a job change.

Pretest-Posttest Design. When a job change occurs, there is also a better point of reference for interpreting current performance. The individual's performance may be compared with his or her performance on the similar job, before the job change. This pretest versus posttest comparison should reveal much stronger relationships between job characteristics and performance, because extraneous differences between subjects are held constant. An individual's performance on the posttest can be compared with performance on the prior job rather than the performance of other individuals assigned (randomly or nonrandomly) to a different job. In a pretest-posttest design involving a job change, between-subjects influences are eliminated. Thus the job characteristics–performance link will be much stronger in pretest-posttest designs than in posttest-only designs.

Random Assignment. Observed job characteristics–performance relationships are likely to vary across experimental versus cross-sectional or correlational research designs also (Mitchell, 1985; Roberts and Glick, 1981). Job characteristics researchers using experimental rather than cross-sectional methodologies are answering different questions. Cross-sectional research addresses the question, Are job characteristics and job performance related? Experimental designs, however, emphasize the question of causality. Both questions are important, but the observed strength of the job characteristics–performance relationship may vary across research designs. Experimental designs use random assignment of subjects or groups of subjects to experimental conditions in order to eliminate or reduce the potentially confounding effects of extraneous factors. Cross-sectional designs do not have this control. Thus extraneous, unmeasured factors may confound and either increase or decrease the observed job characteristics–performance relationship in cross-sectional designs lacking random assignment.

Random assignment also has unpredictable effects on the strength of the observed job characteristics–performance relationship because random assignment studies employ only a few levels of job characteristics. The magnitude of differences between enriched and unenriched conditions varies considerably among random assignment studies, and these differences are hard to compare with the full spectrum of differences among all jobs in a cross-sectional study. Thus it is impossible to predict whether random assignment will increase or decrease the strength of the observed job characterstics–performance relationship.

Laboratory Versus Field Setting. A further research design issue that critics often raise in social science research is the classic distinction between laboratory and field research (Locke, 1986). Criticisms of field research focus on frequent weaknesses of field research: low construct validity, confounding by extraneous factors, nonrandom selection of research sites and subjects, nonrandom assignment of treatment conditions, and inability to assess causality (see, for example, Locke, 1986; Mitchell, 1985). Similarly, criticisms of lab studies emphasize the common weaknesses of lab studies: artificiality, weak manipulations, limited generalizability, small sample sizes, low construct validity, short duration of studies, and the exclusion of important organizational, social, and motivational factors (see, for example, Locke, 1986; Stone, 1986; Webster and Kervin, 1971).

These criticisms provide conflicting arguments for expecting a stronger job characteristics–performance relationship in the laboratory versus the field. Some of the more important arguments are incorporated in previous sections on random assignment, cognitive consistency, and incumbent perceptions of job characteristics. These arguments are not unique to the contrast between laboratory and field research designs. The remaining arguments for laboratory versus field may explain the diverse results in Stone's (1986) comparison of laboratory versus field studies of the job characteristics–performance relationship. We agree, however, with Campbell's (1986) conclusion that the laboratory versus field controversy is a straw issue. Although tentatively included as a potential moderator of the strength of observed job characteristics–performance relationships, we do not expect the laboratory versus field contrast to affect this relationship after researchers control for more focused, substantive boundary conditions introduced in previous sections.

Summary

A qualitative review of the literature reveals theoretical arguments and mixed empirical support for a positive relationship between job characteristics and performance. The strength of this relationship appears to vary across a number of boundary conditions. Based primarily on the job characteristics model (Hackman, 1969; Hackman and Lawler, 1971; Hackman and Oldham, 1976, 1980), theoretical arguments have been developed that predict stronger observed job characteristics–performance relationships under these

conditions: when growth need strength is high; incumbent perceptions of job characteristics are used; there is no range restriction on job
characteristics, particularly when independent measures of actual job
characteristics are used; the performance measure captures overall
performance or effort, rather than just quantity or quality of
performance; and/or incumbents recently experienced a change in the
design of their jobs. Previous literature suggests that the observed job
characteristics–performance relationship may be inflated due to
cognitive consistency (if a single observer or job incumbent provides
all data), lack of random assignment to conditions, and a variety of
factors related to the use of a laboratory versus field design. There are
countervailing theoretical arguments, however, that question the
strength or directionality of these expectations. Thus the net effect of
these moderators on the strength of the job characteristics–performance relationship is an empirical question. A final prediction is that
enhanced controls in pretest-posttest comparisons will reveal stronger
relationships between job characteristics and performance.

The arguments above provide the components of an initial
theory of the relationship between job characteristics and performance. These arguments are tested below in a quantitative review of
the empirical literature.

Methodology

Sample

Studies reporting data on the job characteristics–performance
relationship were located using a variety of search techniques.
Bibliographic cites found in the job design literature reviews were
scanned to locate appropriate studies. The reviews included Aldag,
Barr, and Brief (1981), Brief and Aldag (1978), Griffin, Welsh, and
Moorhead (1981), Guzzo, Jette, and Katzell (1985), Locke (1975), Locke
and others (1980), O'Brien (1982), Pierce and Dunham (1976), Roberts
and Glick (1981), Spector (1985), Stone (1986), Thomas and Griffin
(1983), Umstot, Mitchell, and Bell (1978), and White (1978). In
addition, we identified the names of journals that were most likely to
publish job design research from our bibliographic reviews. Tables of
contents and abstracts were reviewed to locate studies that reported
data on the relationship between job characteristics and performance.
*Academy of Management Journal, Administrative Science Quarterly,
Human Relations, Journal of Applied Psychology,* and *Organizational Behavior and Human Performance* (now *Organizational Behavior*

and Human Decision Processes) were reviewed from 1971 to mid 1987. *Academy of Management Review, Journal of Occupational Behavior,* and *Journal of Occupational Psychology* were also examined, beginning with their first year of publication. Additional citations were located with the assistance of colleagues.

One criticism of meta-analysis has been labeled the "file drawer problem" (Rosenthal, 1979). It arises because we cannot tell how many studies have been conducted but not published. The concern is that studies reported in the literature may not be representative of the studies done, because nonsignificant results are less likely to be published. The file drawer problem is less of an issue in the job characteristics–performance literature than elsewhere, however, because the primary focus of many of the studies located for our analysis was the job characteristics–satisfaction relationship. Many findings on the relationship between job characteristics and performance that might have otherwise remained in someone's file drawer were accepted for publication based on the strength of the job characteristics–satisfaction findings.

Thirty-nine empirical studies were identified that reported a relationship between performance and any or all job characteristics. Some studies reported results for two or more independent groups. These included Cherrington and England (1980), who reported data from three independent groups; Earley (1985) and Gardner (1986), who both reported data on two independent experiments; Hackman and Lawler (1971), who reported correlations for two independent subsamples and the total sample; and Orpen (1979), who reported data from two independent groups. Thus there are forty-five independent samples.

Several studies reported performance data using objective and subjective data sources. Other studies reported outcome data for several types of performance indicators. Because these constituted theoretically relevant moderators, multiple results from the same study were treated as independent samples. For example, if a study reported the relationship between quality of performance as well as quantity of performance and job characteristics, both correlations were included in the analysis. Each of the correlations was treated as an independent estimate of the relationship between job characteristics and performance, yielding sixty-nine correlations for the forty-five independent samples. The total sample size associated with the correlations was 13,403. The size of the individual samples from the studies ranged from 23 to 985.

This approach increased our sample size, making a systematic examination of all twelve moderators feasible. The disadvantage of this approach is that each effect estimate could not be drawn from independent samples. No single study had an unusually large sample size, so the potential bias that resulted from treating multiple observations from the same study population as independent observations in several of the studies was minimal. The inclusion of nonindependent observations is preferable to the alternatives of averaging across moderators or arbitrarily dropping some observations (Hedges and Olkin, 1985).

Measures

Based on our initial theory of the relationship between job characteristics and performance, for each empirical study we coded the strength of the observed job characteristics–performance relationship and ten potential boundary conditions that may moderate this relationship.

Job Characteristics–Performance Relationship. Quantitative estimates of the strength of the relationship between job characteristics and performance were reported in a variety of statistics, including *t*-tests, correlations, *F*-tests, and group means. Whenever possible, these statistics were all converted to a common metric, the correlation coefficient, using techniques outlined in Hunter, Schmidt, and Jackson (1982) and Glass, McGaw, and Smith (1981). Because fewer than half of the studies reported reliabilities for either job characteristics or performance, we did not report analyses that corrected for attenuation.

Multiplicative motivating potential scores (MPS) were used when no other data on the relevant relationships were available (for example, Joyce, Slocum, and Von Glinow, 1982; Oldham, Hackman, and Pearce, 1976). If a study did not report a correlation between job characteristics and performance but did report the correlation between the individual job characteristic scales and performance and the intercorrelations among the scale items, a composite was calculated (Hunter, Schmidt, and Jackson, 1982). Because this composite includes a correction for attenuation, and all other correlations in our analyses are uncorrected, we uncorrected the composite for attenuation. Thus sixty-nine correlations between job characteristics and performance were extracted from the available studies. Table 9.1 lists the studies, sample sizes, and correlations between job characteristics and performance.

Growth Need Strength. The mean value for growth need strength on the "would like" format of the Job Diagnostic Survey (JDS) was used whenever reported (Arnold and House, 1980; Hackman and Lawler, 1971; Hackman and Oldham, 1975; Pierce, Dunham, and Blackburn, 1979). Hackman and Lawler (1971) reported the mean for the upper and lower thirds of the sample. The mean of the two numbers was taken and used as the mean growth need strength for the whole sample (labeled Hackman and Lawler [1971]2 in Tables 9.1–9.4). In most cases, however, the mean growth need strength for the sample was not available, so we attempted to get a best estimate from the description of the job or jobs in each study. Descriptions were classified into one of nine categories of jobs used by Hackman and Oldham (1980) to report normative data for the Job Diagnostic Survey. The descriptions in the studies were compared to the descriptions in the *Dictionary of Occupational Titles* for Hackman and Oldham's (1980) categories. For studies that examined one job, the mean growth need strength from Hackman and Oldham's (1980) normative data for that job was assigned to the study. If a study examined jobs from more than one category and reported the percentage of people in each job group, a weighted mean growth need strength for the study was determined. If the proportion of people in each job category could not be determined but the job categories could be determined from the descriptions, a mean growth need strength was computed for the sampled categories. In all cases, the means used were from the "would like" format of the JDS. In some cases, the job categories could not be determined from the descriptions of the sample in the study, and for these studies, growth need strength was coded as missing. Table 9.2 lists the studies and coding of each moderator.

Incumbent Perceptions of Job Characteristics. Studies were coded to indicate whether the job characteristics for the reported statistics were from the job incumbent (labled yes, coded 1) or from some other source (labeled no, coded 0). It should be noted that some studies manipulated jobs or collected reports of job characteristics but reported the job characteristics–performance relationship based on incumbent reports. These studies were coded as using incumbent reports.

Range Restriction with Incumbent Perceptions. Range restriction was coded for two different situations: those studies in which incumbent perceptions of job characteristics were used and those in which the job characteristics were collected from some other source. When incumbent perceptions were used, studies were coded dichotomously to note whether there was range restriction by indicating whether data were collected from one occupation group or family of jobs (labeled yes, coded 1) or from more than one job (labeled no, coded 0). If a study used independent reports of the job characteristics, the variable was labeled no.

Range Restriction with Nonincumbent Measures. Studies that used the reports of someone other than the job incumbent were coded dichotomously to indicate whether data were collected on one occupation group or family of jobs (labeled yes, coded 1) or more than one family of jobs (labeled no, coded 0). Studies that used incumbent reports were labeled no on this variable.

Cognitive Consistency. Studies that collected information on both job characteristics and performance from the same source (for example, job incumbents) were coded to indicate the potential for a cognitive consistency bias (labeled yes, coded 1), while studies that collected the job characteristics data from a different source than that from which they collected the performance data were coded as not having a congnitive consistency bias (labeled no, coded 0).

Type of Performance. The type of performance was coded as four dichotomous variables: studies that reported only effort, studies that reported only quantity of output, studies that reported only quality of output, and studies that used some overall performance measure. This last category included studies that reported performance as some combination of at least quantity and quality and/or other measures of overall performance.

Job Change. Studies were coded to indicate whether a change took place on any of the jobs in the study. Those studies that did report a job change (labeled yes, coded 1) included studies that enriched the job of the experimental group even if the control group's jobs remained unchanged, as well as studies where all jobs in the study were enriched. Studies that were correlational or that compared two or more groups without a job change for any workers were labeled no (coded 0) for this variable. In all reported cases of job change, the change was designed to enrich the job.

Pretest-Posttest Design. Studies were coded to indicate whether a pretest-posttest design was used (labeled yes, coded 1) or not (labeled no, coded 0). Some studies that collected pretest data did not use the data in their analyses to control for pretest differences in performance. These studies were coded as not using pretest-posttest designs.

Random Assignment. Studies that used random assignment of subjects or groups to conditions were labeled as having random assignment (labeled yes, coded 1), while studies that did not randomly assign subjects or groups to conditions were labeled no (coded 0).

Laboratory Versus Field Setting. Studies that were done in the lab (in a nonwork situation in which subjects were aware that they were not working on a real job) were labeled as lab studies (coded 1), while studies that examined real jobs or what the subjects believed to be real jobs were labeled as field studies (coded 0).

Analysis

Meta-analysis is a method of systematically cumulating the results of existing studies. The correlations that had been collected were transformed to Fisher's z's (Hedges and Olkin, 1985). A weighted average of the z's was then computed across the sixty-nine samples to determine our best estimate of the job characteristics–performance relationship.

For our results to be consistent with the results of qualitative reviews, the average correlation should have been small but positive and the observed variation across studies should have been large and unexplained by sampling error alone. Thus the mean and variation of the sample correlations were examined following Hedges and Olkin (1985) and Hunter, Schmidt, and Jackson (1982). Expecting to find a positive but small average correlation and large, unexplained variation across study results, we examined the effect of each of our theoretical moderators on the job characteristics–performance correlations. These effects were examined in bivariate regressions and in multiple regression analyses (Hedges and Olkin, 1985). A stepwise regression procedure was used for theory trimming, to identify the most parsimonious model (Duncan, 1975; Heise, 1969).

Results

The sample size weighted mean of the sixty-nine correlations between job characteristics and performance is .21 ($p < .001$), with a total sample size of 13,403 observations. The job characteristics–performance correlations extracted from the studies ranged from $-.48$ to .75 (see Table 9.1). Using the meta-analytical procedures of both Hedges and Olkin (1985) and Hunter, Schmidt, and Jackson (1982), we ruled out the possibility that this variation in the correlations was due to the use of small samples. Although some sample sizes were as low as 23 (Locke, Sirota, and Wolfson, 1976), the average sample size for the job characteristics–performance correlations was 194. Thus only a very small fraction of the observed sample variance was attributable to sampling error variance. The random effects estimate of the variance of the population correlations is substantial (.04) and may be a consequence of the hypothesized moderators.

The independent effects of each moderator on the job characteristics–performance correlation are shown in Table 9.3. Combining the estimated intercepts, bivariate regression coefficients, and selected values of moderators produces the expected Fisher's z's. These z's can be transformed back to an expected job characteristics–performance correlation for different conditions. For example, when incumbent perceptions of job characteristics are used, the predicted job characteristics-performance correlation is .20. When other measures of job characteristics are used, the predicted correlation is .27. The predicted correlation in the lab is -.02, while correlations of .22 should be expected in field research. Similar point estimates can be derived for each moderator.

These bivariate regression results, however, are potentially confounded by correlations among the moderators. Table 9.4 shows the means, standard deviations, and correlations among these moderators. These results indicate that research conducted in the lab tended to use quantity measures of performance (r = .45) and random assignment (r = .40). Pretest-posttest designs were used in only 6 percent of the observations (weighted mean = .06) and tended to be employed with nonincumbent measures of job characteristics (r = -.57), range restriction with nonincumbent measures of job characteristics (r = .78), and changes in jobs (r = .76).

Given this clear potential for confounding of the bivariate regression results, a stepwise multiple regression analysis was employed. The stepwise regression was useful for exploratory trimming of our theory of the relationship between job characteristics and performance. The best-fit model consisted of seven variables: growth need strength, range restriction with incumbent perceptions, range restriction with nonincumbent measures, cognitive consistency, overall performance, pretest-posttest design, and random assignment. This model predicted 47 percent of the variation in job characteristics-performance correlations. This indicates remarkable predictive validity of the model. The lack-of-fit test was nonsignificant, however, indicating that the model does not fit the data completely (Hedges and Olkin, 1985). A more complex model of the job characteristics-performance relationship is necessary to accurately fit the data. Unfortunately, post hoc outlier analyses (Hedges and Olkin, 1985) and the examination of outlier cases (Farr, 1976; Griffin, 1983) did not suggest any additional moderators or improvements to the model.

The parameter estimates (and standard errors) for our best model of the job characteristics–performance relationship are as follows:

$$
\begin{array}{lll}
& \text{Growth} & \text{Range Restriction} \\
Z_{\text{job characteristics-performance}} = -.50 + .11 \ \text{Need} & -.13 \ \text{with Incumbent Reports} \\
(.07) \ \text{Strength} & (.05) \ \text{of Job Characteristics}
\end{array}
$$

$$
\begin{array}{lll}
& \text{Range Restriction} & \\
-.50 \ \text{with Nonincumbent Measures} & +.10 \ \text{Cognitive} \\
(.16) \ \text{of Job Characteristics} & (.05) \ \text{Consistency}
\end{array}
$$

$$
\begin{array}{lll}
& \text{Pretest-} & \\
+.10 \ \text{Overall} & +.63 \ \text{Posttest} & +.42 \ \text{Random} \\
(.04) \ \text{Performance} & (.14) \ \text{Design} & (.13) \ \text{Assignment}
\end{array}
$$

Conclusion

Consistent with previous qualitative and quantitative reviews, these results indicate that, on average, job characteristics are correlated with performance ($r = .21$). We are much more successful than previous reviews, however, in explaining and predicting the variation in the observed job characteristics–performance relationships ($R^2 = .47$).

Although the directionality of some of the bivariate regression results were counter to our predictions, all effects in the final model were in the expected directions. (Countervailing arguments predicted either positive or negative effects of random assignment.) These results provide remarkable support for both the job characteristics model (Hackman and Lawler, 1971; Hackman and Oldham, 1976, 1980) and critics of job characteristics research (Roberts and Glick, 1981; Salancik and Pfeffer, 1977, 1978; Thomas and Griffin, 1983). The job characteristics model is a two-stage model of motivation that posits job perceptions as a necessary link between objective job characteristics and performance. Many criticisms of job characteristics research have focused on the failure to distinguish these two links in theoretical interpretations of results (Roberts and Glick, 1981; Salancik and Pfeffer, 1978). The current results provide clear support for the two-stage model in the difference in magnitude of the two range restriction effects. Range restriction with nonincumbent measures of job characteristics directly affects the objective job characteristics–performance relationship but affects job perceptions only indirectly. Thus observing the job characteristics–performance relationship within a single type of job rather than a broad spectrum of jobs influences more negatively the relationship between objective job characteristics and performance ($b = -.50$) than the relationship between job perceptions and performance ($b = -.13$). This confirms the importance of maintaining the distinction between incumbent perceptions of job characteristics and independently observable characteristics of the jobs (Roberts and Glick, 1981; Taber, Beehr, and Walsh, 1985). Job perceptions are affected by objective job characteristics and other factors, such as social cues (Salancik and Pfeffer, 1978).

This study also confirms Spector's (1985) finding that growth need strength moderates the job characteristics–performance relationship. The importance of growth need strength, however, is underestimated in both Spector (1985) and the current study. Both meta-analyses commit an unavoidable ecological fallacy (Glick and Roberts, 1984; Mossholder and Bedeian, 1983). Rather than capturing individual-level growth need strength in the analyses, the meta-analyses average growth need strength for each sample. This averaging severely underestimates the variation in growth need strength and consequently underestimates the importance of growth need strength as a moderator of the job characteristics-performance relationship.

Although the motivational model of the job characteristics-performance relationship is supported by most of these findings, one disconfirming result is the nonsignificant effect of effort in both the bivariate and multiple regressions. We expected the use of effort as the performance variable to be associated with a stronger job characteristics-performance relationship, because effort is the most psychological of the performance variables. Failure of the data to support this expectation may be due to the infrequent use of effort as a performance measure and/or the importance of nonmotivational factors that are associated with job characteristics (Griffin, 1982b; Hackman and Oldham, 1980).

For practical implications, the average correlation between job characteristics and performance appears to validate prior reviews (Roberts and Glick, 1981; Pierce and Dunham, 1976; Umstot, Mitchell, and Bell, 1978) that downplay the importance of job characteristics for increasing performance but emphasize the utility of job characteristics for managing satisfaction. Consistent with prior reviewers, we found an average job characteristics-performance correlation of .21. This is lower than the average job characteristics-satisfaction correlations of .63 reported by Stone (1986) and .29 reported by Loher, Noe, Moeller, and Fitzgerald (1985).

We found, in contrast with conclusions reached in previous quantitative reviews of job characteristics studies, that the average correlation of .21 obscures a tremendous potential for job characteristics to enhance performance. Using the final model of the job characteristics-performance relationship and transforming the predicted Fisher's z to r, we can derive estimates of the expected correlation under specific conditions of interest to researchers and practitioners. For example, practitioners can expect a correlation between job characteristics and performance of .45 if they implement a job characteristics program for individuals with low growth need strength (averaging 3.0 on the JDS) in a single type of job, randomly assign individuals to conditions, control for preenrichment performance, and evaluate performance using an overall performance measure such as supervisory ratings. Among individuals with a higher average growth need strength (6.1 on the JDS), the same job enrichment program would result in a job characteristics-performance correlation of .68. For most practitioners, these estimates are more interesting than the estimate of a .21 correlation averaged across all studies.

These predictions are more consistent with Ford's (1969) early assessment of the AT&T study than more recent pessimistic appraisals of job enrichment. Ford reported that "85% of employees respond favorably to job enrichment" (Locke, 1975, p. 470). Our findings suggest that job enrichment in actual work situations can yield significant improvements in performance. Assuming that a job enrichment program is relatively inexpensive to implement, the potential return on investment is very impressive.

The estimated coefficients in the overall model of the job characteristics–performance relationship must be used cautiously. Few, if any, studies have actually examined the job characteristics-performance relationship under some of the interesting combinations of conditions. Thus additional empirical research is necessary to validate and improve the accuracy of this model. In particular, future studies should combine pretest-posttest designs with random assignments of individuals and groups to conditions. Future research should emphasize causal inferences from controlled studies with a greater emphasis on assessing both motivational and nonmotivational effects of job characteristics.

Appendix to Chapter Nine: Tables 9.1 Through 9.4.

Table 9.1. Reported Correlations Between Job Characteristics and Performance.

Study (Year)	Sample Size	Corre- lation	Study (Year)	Sample Size	Corre- lation
Abdel-Halim (1983)	229	.18	Hackman & Lawler	188	.07
Arnold & House (1980)a	87	.04	(1971)2a		
Arnold & House (1980)b	87	.41	Hackman & Lawler	188	.18
Bishop & Hill (1971)	48	-.37	(1971)2b		
Brass (1979)	140	.33	Hackman & Lawler	188	.23
Breaugh (1985)	97	.35	(1971)2c		
Brief & Aldag (1976)a	77	.08	Hackman & Lawler	67	.01
Brief & Aldag (1976)b	77	-.05	(1971)3a		
Cherrington & England (1980)1	929	.15	Hackman & Lawler (1971)3b	67	.06
Cherrington & England (1980)2	985	.23	Hackman & Lawler (1971)3c	67	.09
Cherrington & England (1980)3	930	.15	Hackman & Oldham (1975)a	355	.14
Earley (1985)1	96	.21	Hackman & Oldham	355	.13
Earley (1985)2	40	.23	(1975)b		
Earley, Hanson, & Lee (1986)	337	.27	Hall, Goodale, Rabino- witz, & Morgan (1978)a	153	.23
Evans, Kiggundu, & House (1979)	327	.21	Hall, Goodale, Rabino- witz, & Morgan	153	.39
Fahr & Scott (1983)a	60	.40	(1978)b		
Fahr & Scott (1983)b	60	-.02	Hogan & Martell (1987)	208	.44
Fahr & Scott (1983)c	60	-.17	Huber & Hyer (1984)	42	.07
Farr (1976)	90	-.48	Joyce, Slocum, & Von	193	.20
Gardner (1986)1	27	.22	Glinow (1982)		
Gardner (1986)2	27	.04	Katz (1978)	89	.24
Glick, Jenkins, & Gupta (1986)a	509	.33	Kozlowski & Hultz (1986)	438	.33
Glick, Jenkins, & Gupta (1986)b	509	.11	Locke, Sirota, & Wolfson (1976)	23	.41
Gould (1979)a	133	.24	Oldham, Hackman, &	201	.16
Gould (1979)b	133	.40	Pearce (1976)		
Greene (1981)	389	.30	O'Reilly (1977)	298	.05
Griffin (1980)a	351	.04	Orpen (1979)1	36	-.08
Griffin (1980)b	88	-.08	Orpen (1979)2	36	-.10
Griffin (1982a)	86	.46	Pierce, Dunham, &	254	.17
Griffin (1983)	351	.75	Blackburn (1979)a		
Hackman & Lawler (1971)1a	67	.03	Pierce, Dunham, & Blackburn (1979)b	254	.20
Hackman & Lawler (1971)1b	67	.11	Pierce, Dunham, & Blackburn (1979)c	254	.20
Hackman & Lawler (1971)1c	67	.06	Seers & Graen (1984)	101	.26
			Sims & Szilagyi (1976)a	766	.25

Table 9.1. Reported Correlations Between Job Characteristics and Performance, Cont'd.

Study (Year)	Sample Size	Corre- lation	Study (Year)	Sample Size	Corre- lation
Sims & Szilagyi (1976)b	33	.24	Thanrenou & Harker (1984)d	92	.10
Sims & Szilagyi (1976)c	33	.24			
Steers & Spencer (1977)	115	.11	Umstot, Bell, & Mitchell (1976)a	42	-.16
Thanrenou & Harker (1984)a	166	.04	Umstot, Bell, & Mitchell (1976)b	42	.07
Thanrenou & Harker (1984)b	166	.13	Wall, Clegg, & Jackson (1978)	47	.41
Thanrenou & Harker (1984)c	92	.01	White & Mitchell (1979)	41	.01

Note: The numbers 1, 2, and 3 are used following study years to denote multiple independent samples within a study. The letters *a*, *b*, and *c* are used to denote multiple nonindependent samples within a study.

Table 9.2. Study Characteristics.

Study (Date)	Growth Need Strength	Incumbent Perceptions of Job Characteristics	Range Restrictions With: Incumbent Perceptions	Range Restrictions With: Noncumbent Measures	Cognitive Consistency	Type of Performance	Job Change	Pretest-Posttest Design	Random Assignment	Lab/Field
Abdel-Halim (1983)	—[a]	Yes	No	No	No	Overall	No	No	No	Field
Arnold & House (1980)a	6.1	Yes	Yes	No	No	Overall	No	No	No	Field
Arnold & House (1980)b	6.1	Yes	Yes	No	Yes	Overall	No	No	No	Field
Bishop & Hill (1971)	4.9	No	No	Yes	No	Quality	Yes	Yes	Yes	Field
*Brass (1979)	—	Partial	No	No	No	Overall	No	No	No	Field
Breaugh (1985)	5.9	Yes	No	No	No	Quality	No	No	No	Field
*Brief & Aldag (1976)a	6.1	Yes	Yes	No	Yes	Quality	No	No	No	Field
Brief & Aldag (1976)b	6.1	Yes	Yes	No	No	Overall	No	No	No	Field
Cherrington & England (1980)1	5.6	Yes	No	No	No	Overall	No	No	No	Field
Cherrington & England (1980)2	5.6	Yes	No	No	No	Overall	No	No	No	Field
Cherrington & England (1980)3	5.6	Yes	No	No	No	Overall	No	No	No	Field
Earley (1985)1	5.6	No	No	Yes	No	Quantity	Yes	No	Yes	Lab
Earley (1985)2	6.1	No	No	Yes	No	Quantity	Yes	Yes	Yes	Field
Earley, Hanson, & Lee (1986)	5.9	Yes	No	No	No	Overall	No	No	No	Field
Evans, Kiggundu, & House (1979)	5.9	Yes	Yes	No	Yes	Overall	No	No	No	Field
Fahr & Scott (1983)a	5.6	Yes	Yes	No	Yes	Overall	No	No	No	Lab
Fahr & Scott (1983)b	5.6	Yes	Yes	No	Yes	Quantity	No	No	No	Lab
Fahr & Scott (1983)c	5.6	Yes	Yes	No	Yes	Quality	No	No	No	Lab
Farr (1976)	4.9	No	No	Yes	No	Quantity	No	Yes	Yes	Lab
Gardner (1986)1	5.3	Yes	Yes	No	No	Quantity	No	No	No	Lab

Study											
Gardner (1986)2	5.9	Yes	Yes	No	No	Overall	No	No	No	Lab
*Glick, Jenkins, & Gupta (1986)a	5.7	Yes	No	No	Yes	Effort	No	No	No	Field
*Glick, Jenkins, & Gupta (1986)b	5.7	No	No	No	Yes	Effort	No	No	No	Field
Gould (1979)a	5.9	Yes	No	No	No	Overall	No	No	No	Field
Gould (1979)b	5.9	No	No	No	No	Overall	No	No	No	Field
Greene (1981)	5.6	No	No	Yes	No	Overall	Yes	Yes	No	Field
*Griffin (1980)a	5.3	Yes	Yes	No	No	Overall	No	No	No	Field
*Griffin (1980)b	5.3	Yes	Yes	No	No	Overall	No	No	No	Field
Griffin (1982a)	5.3	Yes	Yes	No	No	Quantity	No	No	No	Field
Griffin (1983)	5.5	No	No	No	No	Overall	Yes	Yes	Yes	Field
Hackman & Lawler (1971)1a	6.8	Yes	No	No	No	Quantity	No	No	No	Field
Hackman & Lawler (1971)1b	6.8	Yes	No	No	No	Quality	No	No	No	Field
Hackman & Lawler (1971)1c	6.8	Yes	No	No	No	Overall	No	No	No	Field
Hackman & Lawler (1971)2a	5.9	Yes	No	No	No	Quantity	No	No	No	Field
Hackman & Lawler (1971)2b	5.9	Yes	No	No	No	Quality	No	No	No	Field
Hackman & Lawler (1971)2c	5.9	Yes	No	No	No	Overall	No	No	No	Field
Hackman & Lawler (1971)3a	5.1	Yes	No	No	No	Quantity	No	No	No	Field
Hackman & Lawler (1971)3b	5.1	Yes	No	No	No	Quality	No	No	No	Field
Hackman & Lawler (1971)3c	5.1	Yes	No	No	No	Overall	No	No	No	Field
*Hackman & Oldham (1975)a	5.6	Yes	No	No	No	Quality	No	No	No	Field
*Hackman & Oldham (1975)b	5.6	Yes	No	No	No	Quantity	No	No	No	Field

Table 9.2. Study Characteristics, Cont'd.

Study (Date)	Growth Need Strength	Incumbent Perceptions of Job Characteristics	Range Restrictions With: Incumbent Perceptions	Range Restrictions With: Non-incumbent Measures	Cognitive Consistency	Type of Performance	Job Performance Change	Pretest-Posttest Design	Random Assignment	Lab/Field
Hall, Goodale, Rabinowitz, & Morgan (1978)a	—	Yes	No	No	Yes	Effort	Yes	No	No	Field
Hall, Goodale, Rabinowitz, & Morgan (1978)b	—	Yes	No	No	Yes	Overall	Yes	No	No	Field
Hogan & Martell (1987)	—	Yes	No	No	Yes	Overall	No	No	No	Field
Huber & Hyer (1984)	5.5	No	No	Yes	No	Overall	No	No	No	Field
Joyce, Slocum, & Von Glinow (1982)	5.9	Yes	Yes	No	Yes	Overall	No	No	No	Field
Katz (1978)	6.1	Yes	Yes	No	No	Overall	No	No	No	Field
Kozlowski & Hultz (1986)	6.0	Yes	No	No	No	Overall	No	No	No	Field
Locke, Sirota, & Wolfson (1976)	5.6	No	No	Yes	No	Quantity	Yes	No	Yes	Field
Oldham, Hackman, & Pearce (1976)	5.6	Yes	Yes	No	No	Overall	No	No	No	Field
O'Reilly (1977)	—	No	No	No	No	Overall	No	No	No	Field
Orpen (1979)1	5.6	Yes	No	No	No	Overall	Yes	No	No	Field
Orpen (1979)2	5.6	Yes	No	No	No	Overall	Yes	No	No	Field
Pierce, Dunham, & Blackburn (1979)a	5.7	Yes	No	No	Yes	Effort	No	No	No	Field
Pierce, Dunham, & Blackburn (1979)b	5.7	Yes	No	No	No	Effort	No	No	No	Field
Pierce, Dunham, & Blackburn (1979)c	5.7	Yes	No	No	No	Overall	No	No	No	Field
Seers & Graen (1984)	5.6	Yes	No	No	No	Overall	No	No	No	Field

Study									
*Sims & Szilagyi (1976)a	6.0	Yes	No	No	No	Overall	No	No	Field
*Sims & Szilagyi (1976)b	6.0	Yes	No	No	No	Overall	Yes	No	Field
*Sims & Szilagyi (1976)c	6.0	Yes	No	No	No	Overall	Yes	No	Field
Steers & Spencer (1977)	5.9	Yes	Yes	No	No	Overall	No	No	Field
Thanrenou & Harker (1984)a	6.1	Yes	Yes	Yes	No	Overall	No	No	Field
Thanrenou & Harker (1984)b	6.1	Yes	Yes	No	No	Overall	No	No	Field
Thanrenou & Harker (1984)c	6.1	Yes	Yes	Yes	No	Overall	No	No	Field
Thanrenou & Harker (1984)d	6.1	Yes	Yes	No	No	Overall	No	No	Field
Umstot, Bell, & Mitchell (1976)a	5.6	Yes	Yes	No	No	Quantity	No	No	Lab
Umstot, Bell, & Mitchell (1976)b	5.6	No	No	Yes	Yes	Quantity	No	Yes	Lab
Wall, Clegg, & Jackson (1978)	5.3	Yes	Yes	No	No	Overall	No	No	Field
White & Mitchell (1979)	5.4	No	No	Yes	Yes	Quantity	No	Yes	Lab

Note: The numbers 1, 2, and 3 are used to denote multiple independent samples within a study. The letters a, b, and c, are used to denote multiple nonindependent samples within a study.

aData that could not be collected are noted with dashes.

*An asterisk before a study indicates that information from more than one article was used to determine characteristics of the sample. The primary article and supplemental sources are:

- Brass, 1979: Brass, 1981; Brass, 1985.
- Brief and Aldag, 1976: Brief, Aldag, and Jacox, 1978.
- Glick, Jenkins, and Gupta, 1986: Jenkins and Nadler, 1977; Jenkins, Nadler, Lawler, and Cammann, 1975.
- Griffin, 1980: Griffin, 1981.
- Hackman and Oldham, 1975: Hackman and Oldham, 1976; Oldham and Miller, 1979.
- Sims, Szilagyi, and Keller, 1976: Sims and Szilagyi, 1976; Bechtold, Sims, and Szilagyi, 1981.

Table 9.3. Bivariate Regressions of Job Characteristics–Performance Correlations on the Moderators.

Moderators	Unstandardized Regression Coefficient[a]	Intercept	R^2
Growth need strength	.07**	-.19	.01
Incumbent perceptions of job characteristics	-.08**	.28	.03
Range restriction with incumbent perceptions	-.10***	.23	.05
Range restriction with non-incumbent measures	.19***	.20	.09
Cognitive consistency	.02	.21	.00
Type of performance			
Effort	.00	.21	.00
Quantity	-.14***	.23	.05
Quality	-.07**	.21	.01
Overall performance	.08***	.16	.04
Job change	.24***	.19	.16
Pretest-posttest design	.36***	.19	.23
Random assignment	.25***	.20	.09
Lab/field	-.24***	.22	.07

[a]*p < .05; **p < .01; ***p < .001.

Table 9.4. Means, Standard Deviations, and Correlations Among Job Enrichment–Performance Correlation and Potential Moderators.

Variables	Number of Samples	Means	S.D.	1	2	3a	3b	4	5a	5b	5c	5d	6	7	8
Job Enrichment–Performance	69	0.21	2.53												
Moderators															
1. Growth need strength	63	5.73	3.76												
2. Incumbent perceptions of job characteristics	69	0.82	5.11	0.21											
3. Range restrictions with:															
a. Incumbent perceptions	69	0.20	5.51	0.11	0.22										
b. Nonincumbent measures	69	0.09	3.92	-0.28*a	-0.68***	-0.15									
4. Cognitive consistency	69	0.22	5.75	0.14	-0.01	0.25*	-0.16								
5. Type of performance															
a. Effort	69	0.13	4.65	-0.04	-0.14	-0.19	-0.12	0.58***							
b. Quantity	69	0.08	3.79	-0.14	-0.08	-0.02	0.20	-0.13	-0.12						
c. Quality	69	0.06	3.16	-0.02	0.02	-0.04	-0.04	-0.05	-0.10	-0.09					
d. Overall performance	69	0.73	6.11	0.11	0.14	0.17	-0.02	-0.32**	-0.60***	-0.49***	-0.44***				
6. Job change	69	0.11	4.25	-0.17	-0.47***	-0.17	0.72***	0.00	-0.02	0.03	-0.05	0.02			
7. Pretest-Posttest design	69	0.06	3.38	-0.19	-0.57***	-0.13	0.84***	-0.14	-0.10	-0.04	-0.02	0.11	0.76***		
8. Random assignment	69	0.06	3.92	-0.27*	-0.53***	-0.12	0.78***	-0.13	-0.09	-0.30*	-0.01	-0.12	0.52***	0.54***	
9. Lab/field	69	0.04	2.72	-0.20	-0.18	0.16	0.30	0.06	-0.08	0.45***	0.03	-0.25*	0.05	-0.05	0.40***

Note: All values are weighted by sample size in the calculation of these statistics.
a*p < .05; **p < .01; ***p < .001.

References

Abdel-Halim, A. A. "Effects of Task Characteristics on Subordinate Responses to Participative Decision Making." *Academy of Management Journal*, 1983, *26*, 447–484.

Aldag, R. J., Barr, S. H., and Brief, A. P. "Measurement of Perceived Task Characteristics." *Psychological Bulletin*, 1981, *90*, 415–431.

Arnold, H. J., and House, R. J. "Methodological and Substantive Extensions to the Job Characteristics Model of Motivation." *Organizational Behavior and Human Performance*, 1980, *25*, 161–183.

Bechtold, S. E., Sims, H. P., Jr., and Szilagyi, A. D., Jr. "Job Scope Relationships: A Three-Wave Longitudinal Analysis." *Journal of Occupational Behavior*, 1981, *2*, 189–202.

Bishop, R. C., and Hill, J. W. "Effects of Job Enlargement and Job Change in Contiguous but Nonmanipulated Jobs as a Function of Worker Status." *Journal of Applied Psychology*, 1971, *55*, 175–181.

Brass, D. J. "Effects of Relationships Among Task Positions on Job Characteristics, Interpersonal Variables, and Employee Satisfaction and Performance." *Dissertation Abstracts*, 1979, *33*, 5498. Unpublished doctoral dissertation, Business Administration, University of Illinois at Urbana-Champaign, 1979.

Brass, D. J. "Structural Relationships, Job Characteristics, and Worker Satisfaction and Performance." *Administrative Science Quarterly*, 1981, *26*, 331–348.

Brass, D. J. "Technology and the Structuring of Jobs: Employee Satisfaction, Performance, and Influence." *Organizational Behavior and Human Decision Processes*, 1985, *35*, 216–240.

Breaugh, J. A. "The Measurement of Work Autonomy." *Human Relations*, 1985, *38*, 551–570.

Brief, A. P., and Aldag, R. J. "Correlates of Role Indices." *Journal of Applied Psychology*, 1976, *61*, 468–472.

Brief, A. P., and Aldag, R. J. "The Job Characteristic Inventory: An Examination." *Academy of Management Journal*, 1978, *21*, 659–670.

Brief, A. P., Aldag, R. J., and Jacox, A. "A Study: The Impact of Task Characteristics on Employee Response in Hospital Nursing." *Nursing Administration Quarterly*, 1978, *2*, 107–114.

Caldwell, D. F., and O'Reilly, C. A., III. "Task Perceptions and Job Satisfaction: A Question of Causality." *Journal of Applied Psychology*, 1982, *67*, 361–369.

Campbell, J. P. "Labs, Fields, and Straw Issues." In E. A. Locke (ed.), *Generalizing from Laboratory to Field Settings*. Lexington, Mass.: Lexington Books, 1986.

Cherrington, D. J., and England, J. L. "The Desire for an Enriched Job as a Moderator of the Enrichment-Satisfaction Relationship." *Organizational Behavior and Human Performance*, 1980, *25*, 139–159.

Dictionary of Occupational Titles. (4th ed.) U.S. Training and Employment Service. Washington, D.C.: U.S. Government Printing Office, 1977.

Drasgow, F., and Kang, F. "Statistical Power of Differential Validity and Differential Prediction Analyses for Detecting Measurement Nonequivalence." *Journal of Applied Psychology*, 1984, *69*, 498–508.

Duncan, O. D. *Introduction to Structural Equation Models.* Orlando, Fla.: Academic Press, 1975.

Earley, P. C. "Influence of Information, Choice, and Task Complexity upon Goal Acceptance, Performance, and Personal Goals." *Journal of Applied Psychology*, 1985, *70*, 481–491.

Earley, P. C., Hanson, L. A., and Lee, C. "Relation of Task Complexity, Task Strategies, Individual Differences, and Goals to Performance." *Academy of Management Proceedings*, 1986, pp. 184–188.

Evans, M. G., Kiggundu, M. N., and House, R. J. "A Partial Test and Extension of the Job Characteristics Model of Motivation." *Organizational Behavior and Human Performance*, 1979, *24*, 354–381.

Fahr, J., and Scott, W. E., Jr. "The Experimental Effects of 'Autonomy' on Performance and Self-Reports of Satisfaction." *Organizational Behavior and Human Performance*, 1983, *31*, 203–222.

Farr, J. L. "Task Characteristics, Reward Contingency, and Intrinsic Motivation." *Organizational Behavior and Human Performance*, 1976, *16*, 294–307.

Fein, M. "Job Enrichment: A Reevaluation." *Sloan Management Review*, Winter 1974, pp. 69–88.

Ford, R. N. *Motivation Through the Work Itself.* New York: American Management Association, 1969.

Gardner, D. G. "Activation Theory and Task Design: An Empirical Test of Several New Predictions." *Journal of Applied Psychology*, 1986, *71*, 411–418.

Glass, G. V., McGaw, B., and Smith, M. L. *Meta-Analysis in Social Research.* Beverly Hills, Calif.: Sage, 1981.

Glick, W. H., Graham-Moore, B. E., and Schilhabel, L. "Antecedents and Consequences of Perceptions of Job Characteristics: An Empirical Test of Two Theories." Paper presented at the 44th annual meeting of the Academy of Management, Boston, 1984.

Glick, W. H., Jenkins, G. D., and Gupta, N. "Method Versus Substance: How Strong Are the Underlying Job Characteristics-

Attitudinal Outcome Relationships?" *Academy of Management Review*, 1986, *11*, 441-464.

Glick, W. H., and Roberts, K. H. "Hypothesized Interdependence, Assumed Independence." *Academy of Management Review*, 1984, *9*, 772-735.

Gomberg, W. "Job Satisfaction: Sorting Out the Nonsense." *American Federationist*, 1973, *80* (6), 14-19.

Gould, S. "Age, Job Complexity, Satisfaction, and Performance." *Journal of Vocational Behavior*, 1979, *14*, 209-223.

Greene, C. N. "Some Effects of a Job Enrichment Program: A Field Experiment." *Academy of Management Proceedings*, 1981, pp. 281-285.

Griffin, R. W. "Relationships Among Individual, Task Design, and Leader Behavior Variables." *Academy of Management Journal*, 1980, *23*, 665-683.

Griffin, R. W. "A Longitudinal Investigation of Task Characteristics Relationships." *Academy of Management Journal*, 1981, *24*, 99-113.

Griffin, R. W. "Perceived Task Characteristics and Employee Productivity and Satisfaction." *Human Relations*, 1982a, *35*, 927-938.

Griffin, R. W. *Task Design.* Glenview, Ill.: Scott, Foresman, 1982b.

Griffin, R. W. "Objective and Social Sources of Information in Task Redesign: A Field Experiment." *Administrative Science Quarterly*, 1983, *28*, 184-200.

Griffin, R. W., Bateman, T. S., Wayne, S. J., and Head, T. C. "Objective and Social Factors as Determinants of Task Perceptions and Responses: An Integrated Perspective and Empirical Investigation." *Academy of Management Journal*, 1987, *30*, 501-523.

Griffin, R. W., Welsh, A., and Moorhead, G. "Perceived Task Characteristics and Employee Performance: A Literature Review." *Academy of Management Review*, 1981, *6*, 655-664.

Guzzo, R. A., Jette, R. D., and Katzell, R. A. "The Effects of Psychologically Based Intervention Programs on Work Productivity: A Meta-Analysis." *Personnel Psychology*, 1985, *38*, 275-291.

Hackman, J. R. "Toward Understanding of the Role of Tasks in Behavioral Research." *Acta Psychologica*, 1969, *31*, 97-128.

Hackman, J. R. "Work Design." In J. R. Hackman and J. L. Suttle (eds.), *Improving Life at Work.* Santa Monica, Calif.: Goodyear, 1977.

Hackman, J. R., and Lawler, E. E., III. "Employee Reactions to Job Characteristics." *Journal of Applied Psychology* (monograph), 1971, *55*, 259-286.

Hackman, J. R., and Oldham, G. R. "Development of the Job

Diagnostic Survey." *Journal of Applied Psychology*, 1975, *60*, 159–170.

Hackman, J. R., and Oldham, G. R. "Motivation Through the Design of Work: Test of a Theory." *Organizational Behavior and Human Performance*, 1976, *16*, 250–279.

Hackman, J. R., and Oldham, G. R. *Work Redesign*. Reading, Mass.: Addison-Wesley, 1980.

Hall, D. T., Goodale, J. G., Rabinowitz, S., and Morgan, M. A. "Effects of Top-Down Departmental and Job Change upon Perceived Employee Behavior and Attitudes: A Natural Field Experiment." *Journal of Applied Psychology*, 1978, *63*, 62–72.

Hedges, L. V., and Olkin, I. *Statistical Methods for Meta-Analysis*, Orlando, Fla.: Academic Press, 1985.

Heise, D. R. "Problems in Path Analysis and Causal Inference." In E. F. Bogata and G. W. Bohrnstedt (eds.), *Sociological Methodology*. San Francisco: Jossey-Bass, 1969.

Hogan, E. A., and Martell, D. A. "A Confirmatory Structural Equations Analysis of the Job Characteristics Model." *Organizational Behavior and Human Decision Processes*, 1987, *39*, 242–263.

Huber, V. L., and Hyer, N. L. "The Human Factor in Group Technology: An Analysis of the Effects of Job Redesign." *Academy of Management Proceedings*, 1984, pp. 309–313.

Hunter, J. E., Schmidt, F. L., and Jackson, G. B. *Meta-Analysis: Cumulating Research Findings Across Studies*, Beverly Hills, Calif.: Sage, 1982.

Jenkins, G. D., Jr., and Nadler, D. A. "Standardized Observations of Job Characteristics: A Replication and Refinement." In Survey Research Center, University of Michigan, *Effectiveness in Work Roles: Employee Responses to Work Environments, 1977*. DLMA Report 92-26-72-35-3: 219-250. NTIS PB280-669/3G1. Washington, D.C.: U.S. Department of Labor, 1977.

Jenkins, G. D., Jr., Nadler, D. A., Lawler, E. E., III, and Cammann, C. "Standardized Observations: An Approach to Measuring the Nature of Jobs." *Journal of Applied Psychology*, 1975, *60*, 171–181.

Joyce, W., Slocum, J. W., Jr., and Von Glinow, M. A. "Person-Situation Interaction: Competing Models of Fit." *Journal of Occupational Behavior*, 1982, *3*, 265–280.

Katz, R. "The Influence of Job Longevity on Employee Reactions to Task Characteristics." *Human Relations*, 1978, *8*, 703–725.

Kozlowski, S. W., and Hultz, B. M. "Joint Moderation of the Relation Between Task Complexity and Job Performance for Engineers." *Journal of Applied Psychology*, 1986, *71*, 196–202.

Lawler, E. E., III, and Porter, L. W. "Antecedent Attitudes of Effective

Managerial Performance." *Organizational Behavior and Human Performance*, 1967, *2*, 122-142.

Locke, E. A. "Personnel Attitudes and Motivation." *Annual Review of Psychology*, 1975, *26*, 457-480.

Locke, E. A. (ed.). *Generalizing from Laboratory to Field Settings*. Lexington, Mass.: Lexington Books, 1986.

Locke, E. A. Sirota, D., and Wolfson, A. "An Experimental Case Study of the Successes and Failures of Job Enrichment in a Governmental Agency." *Journal of Applied Psychology*, 1976, *61*, 701-711.

Locke, E. A., and others. "The Relative Effectiveness of Four Methods of Motivating Employee Performance." In K. D. Duncan, M. M. Gruneberg, and D. Wallis (eds.), *Changes in Work Life*. New York: Wiley, 1980.

Loher, B. T., Noe, R. A., Moeller, N. L., and Fitzgerald, M. P. "A Meta-Analysis of the Relation of Job Characteristics to Job Satisfaction." *Journal of Applied Psychology*, 1985, *70*, 280-289.

Mitchell, T. R. "An Evaluation of the Validity of Correlational Research Conducted in Organizations." *Academy of Management Review*, 1985, *10*, 192-205.

Mossholder, K. W., and Bedeian, A. G. "Cross-Level Inference and Organizational Research: Perspectives on Interpretation and Application." *Academy of Management Review*, 1983, *8*, 547-558.

O'Brien, G. E. "Evaluation of the Job Characteristics Theory of Work Attitudes and Performance." *Australian Journal of Psychology*, 1982, *34*, 383-401.

Oldham, G. R., Hackman, J. R., and Pearce, J. L. "Conditions Under Which Employees Respond Positively to Enriched Work." *Journal of Applied Psychology*, 1976, *61*, 395-403.

Oldham, G. R., and Miller, H. E. "The Effect of Significant Other's Job Complexity on Employee Reactions to Work." *Human Relations*, 1979, *32*, 247-260.

O'Reilly, C. A. "Personality Job Fit: Implications for Individual Attitudes and Performance." *Organizational Behavior and Human Performance*, 1977, *18*, 36-46.

O'Reilly, C. A., Parlette, G. N., and Bloom, J. R. "Perceptual Measures of Task Characteristics: The Biasing Effects of Differing Frames of Reference and Job Attitudes." *Academy of Management Journal*, 1980, *23*, 118-131.

Orpen, C. "The Effects of Job Enrichment on Employee Satisfaction, Motivation, Involvement, and Performance: A Field Experiment." *Human Relations*, 1979, *32*, 189-217.

Pierce, J. L., and Dunham, R. B. "Task Design: A Literature Review." *Academy of Management Review*, 1976, *1* (4), 83-97.

Pierce, J. L., Dunham, R. B., and Blackburn, R. S. "Social Systems Structures, Job Design, and Growth Need Strength: A Test of a Congruency Model." *Academy of Management Journal,* 1979, *22,* 223–240.

Podsakoff, P. M., and Williams, L. F. "The Relationship Between Job Performance and Job Satisfaction." In E. A. Locke (ed.), *Generalizing from Laboratory to Field Settings.* Lexington, Mass.: Lexington Books, 1986.

Roberts, K. H., and Glick, W. "The Job Characteristics Approach to Task Design: A Critical Review." *Journal of Applied Psychology,* 1981, *66,* 193–217.

Rosenthal, R. "The 'File Drawer Problem' and Tolerance for Null Results." *Psychological Bulletin,* 1979, *86* (3), 638–641.

Salancik, G. R., and Pfeffer, J. "An Examination of Need Satisfaction Models of Job Attitudes." *Administrative Science Quarterly,* 1977, *22,* 427–456.

Salancik, G. R., and Pfeffer, J. "A Social Information Processing Approach to Job Attitudes and Task Design." *Administrative Science Quarterly,* 1978, *23,* 224–253.

Schwab, D. P., and Cummings, L. L. "A Theoretical Analysis of the Impact of Task Scope of Employee Performance." *Academy of Management Review,* 1976, *1,* 23–35.

Seers, A., and Graen, G. B. "The Dual Attachment Concept: A Longitudinal Investigation of the Combination of Task Characteristics and Leader-Member Exchange." *Organizational Behavior and Human Performance,* 1984, *33,* 283–306.

Sims, H. P., Jr., and Szilagyi, A. D. "Job Characteristics Relationships: Individual and Structural Moderators." *Organizational Behavior and Human Performance,* 1976, *17,* 211–230.

Sims, H. P., Jr., Szilagyi, A. D., and Keller, R. T. "The Measurement of Job Characteristics." *Academy of Management Journal,* 1976, *19,* 195–212.

Spector, P. E. "Higher-Order Need Strength as a Moderator of the Job Scope-Employee Outcome Relationship: A Meta-Analysis." *Journal of Occupational Psychology,* 1985, *58,* 119–127.

Spector, P. E. "Method Variance as an Artifact in Self-Reported Affect and Perceptions at Work: Myth or Significant Problem?" *Journal of Applied Psychology,* 1987, *72,* 438–443.

Steers, R. M., and Spencer, D. G. "The Role of Achievement Motivation in Job Design." *Journal of Applied Psychology,* 1977, *62,* 472–479.

Stone, E. F., "Job Scope-Job Satisfaction and Job Scope-Job Performance Relationships." In E. A. Locke (ed.), *Generalizing from Laboratory to Field Settings.* Lexington, Mass.: Lexington Books, 1986.

Taber, T. D., Beehr, T. A., and Walsh, J. T. "Relationships Between Job Evaluation Ratings and Self-Ratings of Job Characteristics." *Academic Press,* 1985, *35,* 27–45.

Thanrenou, P., and Harker, P. "Moderating Influence of Self-Esteem on Relationships Between Job Complexity, Performance, and Satisfaction." *Journal of Applied Psychology,* 1984, *69,* 623–632.

Thomas, J., and Griffin, R. "The Social Information Processing Model of Task Design: A Review of the Literature." *Academy of Management Review,* 1983, *8,* 672–682.

Trattner, M. H., and O'Leary, B. S. "Sample Sizes for Specified Statistical Power in Testing for Differential Validity." *Journal of Applied Psychology,* 1980, *65,* 127–134.

Umstot, D. D., Bell, C. H., and Mitchell, T. R. "Effects of Job Enrichment and Task Goals on Satisfaction and Productivity: Implications for Job Design." *Journal of Applied Psychology,* 1976, *61,* 379–394.

Umstot, D. D., Mitchell, T. R., and Bell, C. H. "Goal Setting and Job Enrichment: An Integrated Approach to Job Design." *Academy of Management Review,* 1978, *21,* 867–879.

Wall, T. D., Clegg, C. W., and Jackson, P. R. "An Evaluation of the Job Characteristics Model." *Journal of Occupational Psychology,* 1978, *51,* 183–196.

Webster, M., Jr., and Kervin, J. B. "Artificiality in Experimental Sociology." *Canadian Review of Sociology and Anthropology,* 1971, *8,* 263–272.

White, J. K. "Individual Differences and the Job Quality-Worker Response Relationship: Review, Integration, and Comments." *Academy of Management Review,* 1978, *3,* 267–280.

White, S. E., and Mitchell, T. R. "Job Enrichment Versus Social Cues: A Competitive Test." *Journal of Applied Psychology,* 1979, *64,* 1–9.

10

CCCCCCCCCC

The Quality Circle
and Its Variations

Gerald E. Ledford, Jr.
Edward E. Lawler III
Susan A. Mohrman

The quintessential quality circle success story tells of a group of workers who struggle with a vexing organizational problem that managers and staff specialists have ignored or been unable to resolve. The group is successful, giving its members a great deal of satisfaction and saving the organization a large sum of money. For example, a quality circle (QC) in an auto assembly plant finds that a supplier's defective tire stems are causing flat tires on cars still in the factory; solving the problem saves the company $225,000 (Cole, 1979). A quality circle at Nashua Corporation realizes that a thinner coating on carbonless paper can improve quality and save $500,000 annually ("Can Quality Boost Your Productivity?" 1981). According to an oft-repeated tale, a Westinghouse white-collar circle saves over $600,000 by suggesting that suppliers be forced to stop overshipments (Arbose, 1980; Bocker and Overgaard, 1982; Dewar, 1982b; Wayne, Griffin, and Bateman, 1986).

Stories such as these have helped fuel an astonishing increase in the use of quality circles in the United States. During the last decade, a variety of societal, economic, and historical forces have converged to turn quality circles into a social movement (Cole, 1982, 1985). In that time, QCs have spread from a few U.S. companies to thousands, and from a few dozen workers to hundreds of thousands. Quality circles doubtless have become the most popular form of participative management in American history.

Social scientists have played minor roles in the quality circle saga. Until recently, they had relatively little to offer in the way of theory or empirical research on QCs. That situation is changing quickly. At the time of this review, some eighteen theoretical, empirical, and review articles on quality circles had been published in refereed scientific journals. The recent scientific literature, in combination with the much larger practitioner literature on quality circles, offers a number of insights into the nature, strengths, weaknesses, and design of QCs.

This chapter will consider several issues. First, we will examine QCs as a social phenomenon. Second, we will review the QC model and its basis in theory. Next, we will review the performance and attitudinal outcomes of QCs, as well as persistence and life cycle issues. Then, we will consider organizational and design contingencies that bear on QC effectiveness. This will be followed by a review of environmental factors that influence effectiveness. Finally, we will examine future directions for research and practice. We will begin by examining why quality circles have become so popular in the United States.

Quality Circles as a Social Phenomenon

History of the QC Movement. A quality circle is a small group of employees from a common work area who get together regularly to identify and generate solutions for problems they encounter in their work situation. Later in this chapter, we will consider specific characteristics of QCs that distinguish them from other types of participative groups. Here we will note that participative decision-making groups of various kinds have been used for decades in the United States. For example, suggestion-making groups resembling quality circles have been used in organizations with Scanlon Plans and other gainsharing plans since the 1930s. However, such groups never became widespread in the United States until the advent of QCs. For this reason, historical accounts of the QC movement (Cole, 1979, 1980b, 1985; Cole and Tachiki, 1984; Dewar, 1982b; Munchus, 1983) have emphasized the Japanese origins of quality circles.

The transformation of Japanese manufacturers from low-cost, low-quality producers to high-quality, high-margin producers is a familiar story. Two Americans, W. Edwards Deming and Joseph Juran, provided some of the tools and much of the advice that helped Japanese industry shift its emphasis toward quality improvement during the 1950s. The Japanese modified American methods, however, so that quality became the responsibility of blue-collar employees as well as engineers and managers.

Starting in 1961, the Japanese Union of Scientists and Engineers (JUSE) helped extend these ideas by advocating the use of quality circles. The number of QCs grew steadily, so that by the late 1970s about 50 percent of Japanese firms with over 30 employees were using small employee decision-making groups. Some 200,000 quality circles, involving 1.7 million employees, were formally registered with JUSE; perhaps four times as many groups were unregistered (Cole, 1979). Yager (1980) estimates that one-fourth of Japanese hourly employees were members of registered or unregistered quality circles.

In 1973, a group from Lockheed's Missile Systems Division visited Japan to learn about Japanese manufacturing methods. They were inspired by the quality circles they saw, and the next year began the first formal quality circles in the United States. Honeywell and later other companies in the aerospace industry followed with their own QC programs. The original proponents of quality circles at Lockheed (including Wayne Reiker, Donald Dewar, and James Beardsley) left the company in 1976 and became well-known private consultants. Although the Lockheed program languished and eventually died, the QC movement took off elsewhere. Later, QCs were reintroduced at Lockheed as well.

The International Association of Quality Circles (IAQC) was formed in 1977, with Dewar as its first president, to foster the spread of the movement. The IAQC began to publish a magazine (*Quality Circles Journal*), to distribute publications, and to conduct conferences and training programs. By 1985, over 7,000 companies were members of IAQC. There also were over 200 registered consultants.

By the late 1970s, U.S. corporations began to experience a whole range of economic, social, and technological pressures on performance that have yet to dissipate. These problems increased the felt need for trying new ways of managing. Of particular importance for the history of quality circles was the emergence of the Japanese as formidable competitors in world markets. Japanese companies took market share away from domestic companies in industry after industry. Attention was focused on management practices that seemingly provided clues to the Japanese success. Two books about Japanese management became best sellers in the early 1980s (Ouchi, 1981; Pascale and Athos, 1981), leading to a flood of articles and books on the topic.

These conditions gave quality circles a major boost. QCs were especially appealing because they were one Japanese management practice that could be adopted quickly, easily, and with relatively little disruption to the organization as a whole. QC programs were marketed as standardized programs, complete with a price tag that included training, support materials, procedures, and consulting assistance. Managers knew what they were purchasing and how much it cost. Because circle programs did not involve everyone, managers controlled the amount of activity and its cost. Finally, many managers were willing to adopt QCs because they did not seriously challenge management authority. It was not uncommon, in our experience, to hear managers say that they had little to lose—that any positive outcome was a bonus, because the organization was investing so little. These circumstances, coupled with widespread reports of QC success, created ever-increasing interest in quality circles.

Incidence of Use. There are no solid data on the total number of quality circles or the total number of QC members in the United States. However, the available data suggest that usage is extensive. One study found that 21 percent of U.S. firms with over 50,000 employees used such programs, and that most had started their programs within the previous two years (Freund and Epstein, 1984). A Conference Board study (Gorlin and Schein, 1984) indicates that forty out of fifty-two companies in the study used QCs. Ingle and Ingle (1983) estimate that some 4,000 American companies use quality circles. Our estimate is that there currently are several hundred thousand QC members in the United States.

Although quality circles can now be found in a great many organizations, the incidence of use is higher in some organizations than others. The QC program in some cases involves only one or two circles, while other companies have made especially extensive use of circles. Approximately 10 percent of Westinghouse employees and 5 percent of Honeywell employees were members of QCs at one point ("Will the Slide Kill Quality Circles?" 1982). IBM, TRW, Westinghouse, DEC, Xerox, and Hughes Aircraft are among other heavy users of the QC approach. Usage across industries is also uneven. The greatest use has been made in the aerospace industry, where QCs began in the United States, and in industries such as autos, steel, and consumer goods that have faced the stiffest competition from the Japanese.

Many observers have suggested that QCs may become just one more short-lived management fad. Although many quality circle programs have died out, as we shall see, there is no persuasive evidence at this point that the overall level of QC use is declining.

What Are Quality Circles?

Design Characteristics of QCs. Most QC programs use a fairly standard set of design features, although each organization tends to do a certain amount of fine-tuning so that the design fits the context in which circles are being implemented. The standard design characteristics of QCs include the following:

1. *Voluntarism.* Membership is voluntary.
2. *Membership.* Members are drawn from a particular work group or department. However, usually not all employees in the work group or department are included in the QC; representatives are chosen if there are more volunteers than there are positions available (usually there are no more than ten members of each circle).
3. *Decision-making power.* The group has the responsibility for making suggestions but does not have the authority to make decisions. It submits suggestions to an appropriate manager or management group, which may be a specially constituted steering committee.
4. *Goals/agenda.* The problem-solving domain is limited to quality- and productivity-related issues and cost reduction. This set of goals is borrowed from Japan, where 90 percent of QCs focused on quality control, productivity, and cost issues (Ishikawa, 1968). In contrast to some other types of decision-making groups, QCs have no broad authority to look at ways in which the organization could operate more effectively or improve employees' quality of worklife. However, advocates of QCs expect the groups to serve a wide variety of indirect goals, such as greater communication within and across organizational units, enriched jobs, increased skill development, and positive changes in such employee attitudes as job satisfaction, organizational commitment, and motivation.
5. *Meetings.* Meetings are usually held on company time. Typical schedules call for either an hour of meeting time per week or two hours biweekly.
6. *Training.* QC members receive training in group process and problem-solving techniques, and in some cases receive training in statistical process control. Standard packages are commonly used that provide between ten hours and a week of training.
7. *Facilitation.* A staff of specially trained facilitators is usually hired to help with training, facilitation of group process at meetings, and performing staff functions associated with the QC process (such as maintaining communication links).
8. *Rewards.* No financial rewards for group suggestions are offered, except through the normal company suggestion process. Recognition awards, such as banquets, trophies, gifts of nominal value, pictures on the wall, and so on, are stressed.
9. *Information sharing.* Usually, the group is provided with no systematic information about company performance, costs, long-range plans, and other matters.

10. *Installation.* QCs exemplify the old saying that participative management is something that the top tells the middle to do for the bottom. The decision to install QCs is usually made at the top of the organization, and then circles are created at the bottom. Only after the program begins to function are middle managers involved in the program, as they are required to respond to suggestions made by the groups.

These design characteristics are similar to those used in the original U.S. quality circle program at Lockheed. They have become standard practice largely on the basis of tradition, not because empirical investigation has demonstrated that these characteristics are better than the alternatives.

The Parallel Organization Model. The nature of quality circle programs becomes much clearer if they are understood as parallel (Stein and Kanter, 1980), collateral (Zand, 1974), or dualistic (Goldstein, 1985) structures that exist side by side with the normal bureaucratic organization. As parallel structures, they are not intended to replace the day-to-day organization, but rather are intended to supplement it by performing functions that a traditional bureaucratic structure is unable to perform well. In particular, a QC program is a parallel structure that is used to initiate change, in contrast to the normal bureaucratic organization, which is oriented toward stability. Some of the QC design characteristics that illustrate the parallel nature of the QC model include use of a limited number of volunteers in a hierarchy of special groups, the lack of decision-making authority granted to QCs, the use of a unique leadership structure (that is, the facilitators), and separation of the organization's financial reward system from the QC effort.

The parallel nature of quality circle programs is a source of certain strengths and some very real weaknesses. The parallel character of QCs enables them to be established relatively quickly, in the form of a discrete program with bounded costs and risks. Indeed, sometimes QCs are advocated on the basis that they do not require much organizational change (see, for example, Yager, 1979). On the other hand, parallel groups such as QCs often have difficulty achieving organizational legitimacy. In a real sense, they are parasites on the normal organization; QCs depend on the normal organization for personnel, time, information, and money. Like parasites of other kinds, QCs tend to arouse defenses in their hosts. We will consider these points further when we examine the effectiveness of quality circles, and their sustainability.

Theoretical Basis for Claims of QC Effectiveness. Is there a theoretical basis for the belief that quality circles can be effective in increasing productivity and generating other desirable outcomes? This question has not been a major concern to most quality circle proponents. Quality circles have been developed by and for practitioners, and the evolution of QC practice has not been linked very closely to social science theory or research. Quality circle proponents have relied on a familiar set of quasi-theoretical ideas that are loosely tied to research, as well as on "common sense" (see Ferris and Wagner, 1985).

One such quasi-theoretical idea is that employee participation can lead to the acceptance of change, to better understanding and consequently more effective implementation of new ideas, and to increased intrinsic satisfaction. Another idea is that group decisions are often more effective than individual decisions, because multiple viewpoints are represented. Common-sense beliefs that are frequently voiced about participation include "The people closest to the work have the information about how to make improvements" and "People want to contribute more to their organizations." Ferris and Wagner (1985) indicate that assumptions such as these by QC proponents represent oversimplifications of the research evidence. For example, groups are sometimes inferior to individuals in problem solving, the benefits of participation are inconsistently realized and are highly dependent on implementation strategy, and many employees are not interested in participation (see also Miner, 1984; Zander, 1977; Locke and Schweiger, 1979; Miller and Monge, 1986).

It is possible, however, to provide testable theoretical models of QC effectiveness that clarify why quality circles might work and that serve as guides for research and practice. Mohrman has proposed two models (Mohrman, 1982; Mohrman and Novelli, 1985) that help explain why QCs may lead to an increase in productivity. The two models depict different causal paths to productivity improvement that are implicit in the QC literature.

Figure 10.1 depicts the first causal sequence, in which circles meet and generate ideas, the ideas are implemented, and implementation of the ideas leads both to positive changes in employee attitudes (such as satisfaction and involvement) and to improvements in productivity. A number of intervening variables may block or facilitate the steps in this causal chain. First, leadership and facilitation of the group are expected to be crucial in the early stages of group functioning. That is the rationale for providing groups with a specially trained facilitator and, in many cases, for providing extra training to nominal leaders of the group. Second, the group will not function effectively unless the group has sufficient skills, an appropriate performance

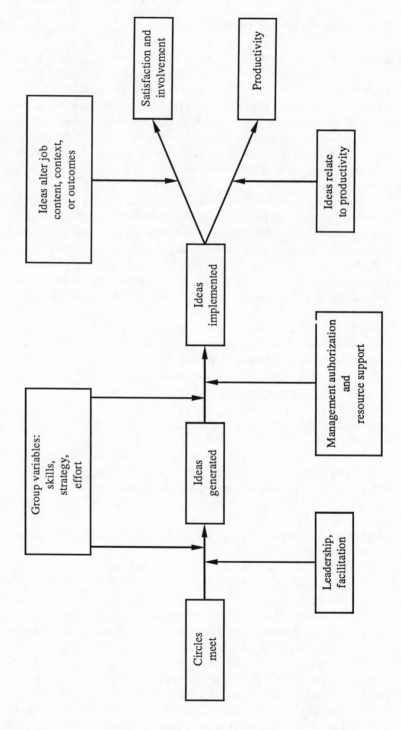

Figure 10.1. Ideas Lead to Productivity and Satisfaction.

strategy, and motivation to exert effort (Hackman and Morris, 1977). Next, management support for the QC is critical—a point emphasized by virtually every writer on the topic of QCs. Without management support, it is impossible to implement the new ideas or to obtain the resources necessary to develop them. If implementation of new ideas does occur, there may be positive, negative, or neutral outcomes. There will be a positive impact on productivity only if the ideas for change are truly relevant to and facilitative of performance. There will be a positive impact on employee attitudes only if the ideas lead to positive changes in the job itself, the job context, or other individual outcomes.

Figure 10.2 captures a second causal sequence that is often used to indicate how QCs affect productivity. Participation in a circle is assumed to result in individual-level outcomes such as job variety, increased skills, recognition from management, feelings of accomplishment and involvement, and social rewards from membership in a team. These feelings and conditions in turn lead to greater motivation and improved performance back on the job, and thus to greater productivity. Indirectly, these feelings and conditions may increase productivity by enhancing job satisfaction, which leads to decreased absenteeism and turnover and finally to improved productivity by lowering costs associated with these withdrawal behaviors (Lawler and Ledford, 1981–82).

Again, a variety of intervening variables may disrupt or facilitate the proposed chain of events. As with the causal chain depicted in Figure 10.1, management responsiveness and group-functioning variables are important, because these factors determine whether good suggestions will be proposed and implemented and consequently whether participants will feel a sense of accomplishment. Equity considerations may be important if employees feel that the outcomes resulting from participation are inequitably distributed (Adams, 1965). Individual differences in growth need strength may moderate the effect of individual-level outcomes on satisfaction, motivation, and task performance (Hackman and Lawler, 1971). It is also reasonable to expect that task performance and therefore productivity gains will be greatest if the skills learned in the circle are directly transferable to the work situation. Even if the individual does experience positive outcomes from being part of a successful circle, this may not lead to increased day-to-day work motivation. Value expectancy theory (Lawler, 1970) predicts that greater effort will be applied to the activity that leads to the positive outcomes—in this case, expending more effort in QC activity.

The number of stages and the number of intervening variables in the two causal models are suggestive of how difficult it is for quality

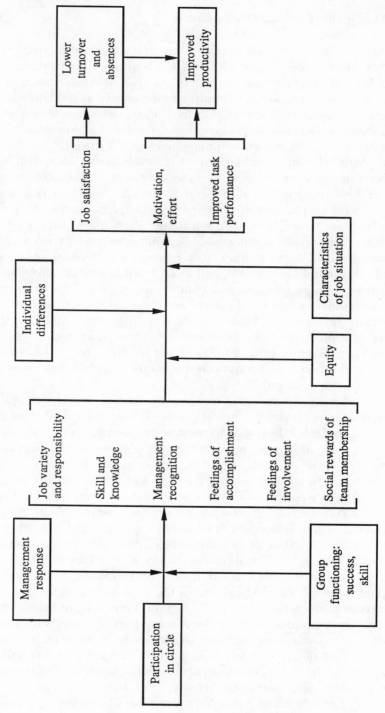

Figure 10.2. The Quality Circle Process Results in Productivity and Satisfaction.

circles to enhance productivity. There are many places for the causal chain to break down or be blocked.

The two models show alternate routes by which quality circles can have a positive effect on productivity. Potentially, both chains can operate at the same time. There are some key differences between the two models, however. The model depicted in Figure 10.1 suggests that QCs may benefit participants and nonparticipants alike, because the outcomes are the result of the implementation of ideas rather than direct participation. The model depicted in Figure 10.2 suggests that direct participation in the quality circle is needed to achieve the outcomes. This is consistent with the research evidence on participation in general (see Coch and French, 1948; Nurick, 1985) and QCs in particular (Mohrman and Novelli, 1985; Rafaeli, 1985). It shows that the attitudinal benefits of participation accrue more to direct participants than to nonparticipants, even if the nonparticipants are indirectly represented in the participative group.

Now that we have considered the conceptual basis for claims that quality circles can enhance productivity and other outcomes, we will examine whether in fact QCs have been shown to achieve such outcomes.

Outcomes of Quality Circles

First, we will examine the outcomes of QCs on their own terms—that is, success as defined in the practitioner literature on QCs. Second, we will consider whether there is specific evidence of the impact of QCs on productivity. Finally, we will briefly review other outcomes of QCs, such as attitudinal changes, that may lead to productivity improvements much less directly.

Reports of Success in the Practitioner Literature. The practitioner literature on quality circles has many shortcomings, but it does not lack for reports of QC effectiveness. The QC literature contains innumerable stirring testimonials, success stories, and claims for astounding levels of return on investment. These stories are not concerned specifically with productivity (defined as a ratio of outputs to inputs), but the kind of cost reductions that are claimed for QCs certainly imply productivity improvements. With a few exceptions, these accounts are directed at practitioners; claims for QC success have rarely rested on research that meets scientific standards.

The literature includes many moving testimonials from those involved in the QC movement. Donald Dewar, the first president of the International Association of Quality Circles, speaks of QCs as ushering in a "new era" in the way organizations are managed, "whereby the people who do hands-on work will be brought into the mainstream and properly recognized as a potentially more powerful and valuable resource" (Dewar, 1982b, p. 1). Rendel (1981) sees QCs as part of what Alvin Toffler has termed the "third wave" of civilization, succeeding the era of the Industrial Revolution. An executive of Hughes Aircraft, quoted by Marks (1986, p. 46), tells why he believes QCs have grown rapidly: "It is a spiritual reason—people want to work together. They are more effective as a team. It increases their knowledge. It increases their communication. It increases their security. It increases their dignity." In conferences, interviews, and meetings, we have heard countless impassioned statements by QC participants and their managers that remind us strongly of religious conversion experiences. Intriguing as such statements are, they cannot substitute for empirical evidence that quality circles actually lead to the claimed changes.

Most success stories concern particular QCs that "hit a home run"—that is, that proposed one solution that saved a huge sum of money. This chapter began with three such success stories. Also popular in the QC literature is the claim, based on an unpublished internal company study, that Lockheed's initial fifteen quality circles saved $2,844,000 in the first two years of operation (for example, Bocker and Overgaard, 1982; Yager, 1979). Proponents also often claim that quality circles generate the kind of high, riskless return on investment (ROI) that no rational manager can ignore. Arbose (1980) considers four companies in which the ROI is estimated at from five to one to ten to one. Yager (1980) indicates that the ROI is "typically" between six to one and ten to one. Ingle and Ingle (1983, p. 209) claim that "based on experience in general, the savings to cost ratio will run about 5:1 (for every dollar invested, the organization receives $5 back). In some cases it is reported as high as 20:1 and as low as 3:1."

There are a number of problems with these success stories and eye-opening ROI reports. First, QC success stories rarely mention how costs and benefits are estimated. This is an important issue, because costs and benefits are hard to estimate. When the estimating procedure is explicit, the figures are usually based on the estimated value of QC suggestions prior to implementation. Thus the savings are "paper" savings that are probably realized only rarely (Lawler, 1986), because many suggestions are actually never implemented or are implemented only after a long period of time (Mohrman and Novelli, 1985; Wayne, Griffin, and Bateman, 1986). Many suggestions are never implemented because they arouse resistance on the part of management, affected employees, or other constituencies. Sometimes suggestions turn out to be impractical or to conflict with other planned changes that were unknown to the circle. Since QCs usually work almost in an information vacuum, this is not uncommon. It may take a long time to implement suggestions that require budget authorization; the QC may have long since disbanded in frustration. Finally, the estimated value of suggestions is often inflated, intentionally or otherwise. Higher estimated savings bring more recognition and management attention, while later findings that the savings are not as high as anticipated are unlikely to produce any negative outcomes for the estimator.

There are other problems with the success stories in the practitioner literature. Stories of huge savings generated by a single group may imply that the overall QC effort is highly successful, when in reality most circles may fail to accomplish anything (Mohrman and Novelli, 1985; Wayne, Griffin, and Bateman, 1986). Finally, there is doubtless a tendency to emphasize success stories rather than failures in the practitioner literature, as there is in the academic literature on organizational change (Mirvis and Berg, 1977). Although some failures have been reported in the practitioner literature (for example, Burck, 1981; Cook, 1982; Metz, 1981; Meyer and Stott, 1985), it is difficult to know from the literature how likely an organization is to experience success rather than failure.

Research on the Impact of QCs on Productivity and Other Outcomes. There is relatively little empirical evidence of the effectiveness of quality circles, as a number of observers have noted (Ferris and Wagner, 1985; Head, Molleston, Sorensen, and Gargano, 1986; Ramsing and Blair, 1982; Wayne, Griffin, and Bateman, 1986). A recent review of the literature was highly critical of the quality of the available studies (Steel and Shane, 1986) and urged that premature conclusions not be drawn on the basis of the existing body of evidence. The reviewers indicated that "the majority of studies constituting the quality circle evaluation literature are, at best, seriously flawed and, at worst, potentially misleading. If the level of scientific rigor found in other field research domains such as job redesign, survey feedback, and goal setting may be employed as a yardstick, then the quality circle literature exhibits generally inferior quality" (pp. 450–451). There is no question that the QC literature could benefit from more empirical investigations. This chapter references some 112 citations that are specifically concerned with quality circles. Of these, over 70 percent (80 references) are directed primarily at practitioners. One indication of the status of the QC literature is that the number of how-to books (seventeen, or 15 percent) is exceeded by the number of refereed journal articles (eighteen, or 16 percent) only if we include in the latter two reviews of how-to books that have appeared in *Administrative Science Quarterly!*

The few evaluation studies measuring performance show no clear trend for or against any productivity effects of quality circle programs (Steel and Shane, 1986). Marks, Mirvis, Hackett, and Grady (1986) collected data from a period six months before to twenty-four months after adoption of a QC program in a machining operation. QC members showed a significant increase in percentage of hours spent on production, efficiency levels, and work quality, and showed a significant decrease in absenteeism. Mohrman and Novelli (1985) tracked six performance measures at four-week intervals from one year prior to the start of a QC program to one year after in a warehouse operation. They found indications of a slightly more positive trend in the experimental unit compared to the control unit on the set of productivity measures (costs, throughput costs, labor costs as a percentage of total costs, overtime costs, absenteeism, and accident rates). Although the effects were slight and may have been due to other organizational changes that were being installed at the time, the data indicate that productivity never declined even temporarily as a result of the program. Jenkins and Shimada (1983), in a study of 450 production personnel, found that productivity was higher on three of four criteria (production quantity, quality, and rework costs) for QC members than nonmembers.

On the other hand, Harper and Jordon (1982) found no significant difference in productivity between ten QC and ten non-QC groups in one organization. Atwater and Sander (1984) conducted an eight-month study of eleven QC and control groups in three U.S. Navy organizations and found no evidence of any significant effect of QCs on absenteeism, number of suggestions, accident rates, or promotions. Overall, then, some studies have found that productivity and other objective measures are positively impacted by QCs, while other studies show no effect. No study shows a serious negative effect on performance measures.

Most of the few available evaluation studies report only attitudinal data. The evidence for attitudinal effects of QCs is equivocal, although slightly more extensive than the evidence for performance effects. Steel and others (1985) studied attitudes in a hospital and a maintenance unit with QC programs. They found significant positive effects on seven of twenty measures in the latter case but no positive effects—indeed, they found negative trends—in the former. Marks, Mirvis, Hackett, and Grady (1986) found positive effects for QC participants relative to control subjects, but only in areas directly related to QC activity (such as suggestions offered, decision-making opportunities, group communication, skills needed for advancement, sastisfaction with opportunities for accomplishment, and satisfaction with opportunities for advancement). Attitudes concerning job characteristics (meaningfulness of work, job challenge, and job responsibility) and organizational communication were unaffected. Similarly, Rafaeli (1985), in a cross-sectional study of 455 QC members and 305 nonmembers in a manufacturing organization, found significant differences favoring members on measures of perceived influence and task variety but no differences on other job characteristics or on job satisfaction. The possibility of selection biases (that is, the possibility that those who volunteered to become participants were more favorable on perceived influence and task variety to begin with) cannot be ruled out in the study. Hocevar and Mohrman (1984), in a cross-sectional study of a police precinct that had QCs, found that QCs were perceived to have a slight positive impact on feelings of involvement, participative decision making, and work systems and procedures. Again, the cross-sectional design makes it impossible to determine the direction of causality. In a cross-sectional study, Wayne, Griffin, and Bateman (1986) found that members of more effective QCs had more favorable attitudinal outcomes (job satisfaction, intrinsic satisfaction, satisfaction with co-workers, and organizational commitment) than members of less effective QCs. This may be an indication that individuals with high morale make better team members, or it may suggest that the level of effectiveness of the QC moderates the impact of QC membership on outcomes, as our earlier model suggested. Finally, Atwater and Sander (1984), Harper and Jordon (1982), and Head, Molleston, Sorensen, and Gargano (1986) found no effects of QCs on attitudinal outcomes such as job satisfaction.

Both Marks, Mirvis, Hackett, and Grady (1986) and Mohrman and Novelli (1985) found evidence of a "buffering" effect of QC membership on attitudes. In both cases, the attitudes of control or comparison groups declined, probably as a result of disruptions imposed by the organization's environment. In the study by Marks and colleagues, attitudes of QC members did not decline as they did in the comparison groups. In the Mohrman and Novelli study, attitudes of QC members declined, but not as sharply as attitudes of nonmembers. This suggests that QC programs can have some desirable effects but are not a strong enough intervention to overcome environmentally imposed adversity.

In addition, Mohrman and Novelli (1985) found that the attitudinal outcomes of former members of QCs were in some cases worse than those of nonmembers. This is an important issue, because it bears on the long-term viability and impact of the parallel organization model. The hope of proponents of the parallel organization model is that the positive benefits of participation will be maintained while membership in QCs is rotated to those who have not previously had the opportunity for participation. If positive effects of membership are lost once membership ceases, the effects of QCs will be quite limited.

Overall, the evidence available so far suggests that QCs do not have very powerful effects on attitudinal outcomes such as job satisfaction and commitment. Negative effects of QCs have less commonly been reported than neutral effects or positive effects. There are some indications that QCs affect attitudes that are directly relevant to the intervention (such as perceived influence), even when they do not show evidence of affecting attitudinal outcomes. A surprising area of neglect in the literature is attitudes toward the intervention itself, including perceptions of how well the intervention was implemented (the equivalent of a manipulation check in laboratory research) and perceptions by participants and nonparticipants of whether the intervention had any impact.

Sustainability of QCs

Persistence and Life Cycle Issues. Even when quality circle programs seem to experience initial success, the programs often die. For example, the famous Lockheed program that helped launch the quality circle movement in the United States died within a few years of its beginning (Burck, 1981), despite claims that it saved millions of dollars for Lockheed. Meyer and Stott (1985) recount their experience with two companies in which the QC effort languished despite early success. In one case, the company realized an estimated $576,000 of annualized savings over the first two years, there was a reported 3-to-1 return on investment, attitudes were very positive, and initial enthusiasm was "to the point of evangelical fervor" (p. 36). Yet after four and a half years, individual circles could not be sustained; the longest running circle survived 2.5 years, and the average age of continuing circles was 1.5 years. Mohrman and Novelli (1985) report a similarly discouraging story of early financial success, fervent testimonials, and stagnant circles. Portis, Fullerton, and Ingram (1985) conducted ten case studies of organizations adopting QCs and found that it was very difficult to sustain circle activity for more than two years. Cook (1982) and Smeltzer and Kedia (1985) also suggest that the failure rate in QC programs is high. In our experience, it is very rare to encounter quality circle programs that survive in pure form for more than five years.

A Model of the QC Life Cycle. An understanding of why it is difficult to sustain quality circle programs can be gained by examining the typical life cycle of a program. Our experience indicates that quality circles go through a series of identifiable phases or stages of development (Lawler and Mohrman, 1985), as shown in Table 10.1. Each phase has its own key activities as well as its own threats to the

Table 10.1. Phases of a Circle Program's Life.

Phase	*Activity*	*Destructive Forces*
1. Start-up	Publicize	Low volunteer rate
	Obtain funds and volunteers	Inadequate funding
	Train	Inability to learn group process and problem-solving skills
2. Initial problem solving	Identify and solve problems	Disagreement on problems
		Lack of knowledge of operations
3. Presentation and approval of initial suggestions	Present and have accepted initial suggestions	Resistance by staff groups and middle management
		Poor presentation and suggestions because of limited knowledge
4. Implementation of solutions	Relevant groups act on suggestions	Prohibitive costs
		Resistance by groups that must implement
5. Expansion and continued problem solving	Form new groups	Member-nonmember conflict
	Old groups continue	Raised aspirations
		Lack of problems
		Expense of parallel organization
		Savings not realized
		Rewards wanted
6. Decline	Fewer groups meet	Cynicism about program
		Burnout

Source: Lawler and Mohrman, 1985.

continuation of the QC program. Quality circle programs that survive the threats of the first stage move to the second stage, and so forth. That is, the organization either drops the program at one of the stages or moves on to the next one.

1. *Start-up*. During the start-up phase, a high level of activity is demanded, and considerable effort needs to be put into a QC program. The program usually begins with a communication program and a call for volunteers. At this point, it is also important to identify who the facilitators will be and to be sure that they are trained and capable. In addition, an intensive training program in group process and problem-solving skills is often conducted for the circle members.

The primary threats to QCs in this phase concern whether anyone will volunteer, whether adequate training will be provided, whether the problem-solving capability of the volunteers will be adequate, whether competent facilitators can be found, and, finally, whether an adequate budget will be made available to allow for meetings, facilitator time, and training. Most quality circle programs deal successfully with this stage and are able to progress to the next phase. Successful completion is aided by the availability of good training packages for QC participants and by the appeal of participating in problem-solving groups for most employees. In fact, the danger is that the high level of enthusiasm will create expectations that cannot possibly be met. Setting up the groups is a relatively straightforward process. Moreover, deficiencies in start-up activities generally do not become apparent until later stages.

2. *Initial problem solving*. In this phase, circles identify the problems that they will work on and begin to come up with solutions. Most groups successfully identify problems and begin problem solving. Once they begin, they may find that they have inadequate business and technical knowledge, but this too can be overcome, through additional training or by adding expertise to the group, sometimes in the form of resource people. Therefore, in most quality circles, early success in problem solving is experienced.

3. *Presentation and approval of initial solutions*. Because QCs are a parallel structure, the results of QC problem-solving activities must be reported back to decision makers in the line organization. This report-back activity is often perceived by the participants and managers alike as the high point of the entire circle process. It is also critical to the evolution of the program. If circles are to succeed, the reporting back must be done well and the line organization must respond quickly, knowledgeably, and, in a significant percentage of the cases, positively to the ideas coming out of the quality circle

program. It is during this phase that the typical QC program encounters the first serious threats to its continuation.

Most of the individuals who have to accept and act on suggestions from QCs are middle managers and staff personnel. In many organizations, they have had little or no role in the program until this point. Indeed, they may have little experience soliciting and responding to ideas from subordinates. They are often presented with ideas that they or other people feel they should have thought of themselves or with ideas that will change their own work activities.

Part of the problem in obtaining adequate responsiveness to QC suggestions is that the people who must respond have competing priorities, and as a result they may not have the time available to respond. In any case, a scenario can develop in which the circles present their ideas and literally no activity follows on the part of the people to whom they were presented. This is particularly likely to happen to circle suggestions that follow the first round of presentations to management. There is often a special urgency to show responsiveness to early suggestions, but subsequent ideas are often received far less positively.

If their ideas are not accepted, QC participants often become discouraged and may feel that the program is a sham, a waste of time, and a management trick. If there is a negative response or no response to a high percentage of circle suggestions, the program usually ends. Individuals in the group become discouraged and stop meeting. They may react against the whole idea of the QC program and believe that management never took the program seriously. If, however, ideas are accepted, the circle moves to the next phase.

4. *Implementation of solutions.* Many initial QC ideas may be accepted, because the pressures for acceptance are quite strong. However, many of these accepted ideas may never be implemented. Those who must devote time, energy, and resources to implementing the suggestions may not be involved in or committed to a circle's suggestions. Engineering, maintenance, and middle management groups are often faced with a choice between continuing their normal activities and picking up on ideas that have been suggested to them by the quality circles. Thus they often lack the necessary motivation to act on the suggestions.

Failure of the organization to implement circle ideas can cause the QC program to lose momentum and die. Although participants are delighted to have their ideas officially approved, this is not sufficient to reinforce QC activity. They need to see implementation of their ideas and receive feedback on the impact of their suggestions. Failure to provide both implementation and feedback will ultimately lead to deterioration and cessation of the program. Many but not all organizations successfully implement some of the ideas of the QC program, make projections of large savings based on them, and move on to the next phase.

5. *Expansion and continued problem solving.* During this phase, the program is often expanded to include new groups. Old groups are either phased out or told to work on new and additional problems. Circle programs require maintenance of and investment in the parallel organization. If the program has gotten this far, there is usually considerable commitment of resources to it, and it becomes a major operating part of the organization. More facilitators are hired, and more groups are started and trained. An administrative structure develops to support circle activities.

The initial success of the program leads to a desire of other people to get into the QC program. Nonparticipants become jealous of participants and wonder why they too cannot have the luxury of meeting and problem solving while others are working. They may also resent the recognition and status accorded to successful QC members. To some degree, this issue can be met by expanding the number of groups, but there almost always is an insider-outsider culture.

At this point, the members of the initial groups often develop aspirations for further development. For example, they may desire greater upward career mobility and/or additional training and technical skills. They may wish to transfer the QC approach back into the everyday activities of the organization. Circle members become uncomfortable with the split between the way they are treated in the parallel organization and the way they are treated in normal day-to-day operations. They ask for more participative management as their sense of competence increases and their aspirations for influence rise.

Some groups run out of problems to solve. Initially, they pick off the easiest ones to solve. They then find themselves in a situation where, with the limited charter and training they have, there is little more they can do. They may react to this by simply going out of existence, or they may try to expand their activities into new topic areas that are out of line with their mandate.

Initial success may also bring requests for financial rewards from the participants. This is especially likely when organizations trumpet QC successes and the high savings they have produced for the organization. Ironically, the more publicly the organization measures and reports on the costs and benefits of the program, the more likely employees are to develop a desire to share in the claimed financial gains.

Expansion may also bring to a head issues of the cost of running the program and the parallel organization needed to operate it. Ultimately, many organizations ask whether the cost in time and money is justified by the savings that have been realized. Partially because circle ideas are not implemented or because there is not sufficient follow-up to ensure continued utilization of new procedures, savings often turn out to be somewhat smaller than had originally been estimated. A combination of disappointment over the smaller actual savings from early ideas and the significant expense of running the QC program often provides the single most serious threat to its continued existence and sets the stage for the decline that usually follows.

6. *Decline.* Although some QC programs and particular circles within a program may survive for years, many others gradually decline. Groups begin to meet less often and become less productive, and the resouces committed to the program are decreased. Often the main reason for group persistence is the social satisfaction the group brings to its members, rather than their problem-solving effectiveness. As the organization begins to recognize this, it cuts back further on resources, and as a result the program starts to decrease in size. The people who all along have resisted the QC program recognize that it is losing power, and they openly reject and resist it. The combination of more effective resistance on the part of middle and staff managers, the decreasing budget, and decreasing participant enthusiasm can lead to the rapid decline and ultimate cessation of the program.

In summary, then, our analysis of the phases that QC programs go through suggests that there are many threats to their continued existence. Because of these threats, it is likely that few programs will be institutionalized and sustained over a long period of time.

Ironically, the demise of QC programs results from the very design feature that makes the QC concept attractive to managers in the first place—namely, its parallel nature. Even in organizations that have maintained some QC activity for as long as ten years, we have found that it remains "extra" and outside of the normal organizational routine. As such, the primary challenge is to maintain energy and enthusiasm among the various parties whose active involvement is essential to circle accomplishments. This is difficult when the work is seen as an extra activity.

Conclusion. Our experience indicates that in the long run, the QC program must be responsible for producing ideas that are implemented and that improve organizational performance if it is to be taken seriously by managers or, for that matter, workers. Human relations victories and increased communication are not enough. Yet several design features of QC programs reduce the likelihood that circles will effect significant changes. First, as an activity that is parallel to the organization, QC activity is not seen as a required part of anyone's job. In busy times, circle activity is often seen as a burden. Second, QCs can accomplish nothing on their own; they have no budget, no authority to implement, no ability to command a response. Indeed, QC programs tend to exclude those who must implement circle suggestions—namely, middle managers and staff personnel. Third, the entire organization is not usually given training in group process and problem-solving skills. Thus the skills of participants remain "special" and potentially nontransferable to the normal organization. Finally, circles are usually tightly restricted in their ability to examine the kinds of issues that may result in truly significant, and thus potentially efficacious, organizational changes. They are generally confined to discovering inefficiencies of method, equipment, and communication within their work area; they are usually denied opportunities to question personnel policies, division of labor and job design, management treatment of employees, the reward system, training, or promotional practices.

Returning to the two models of QC efficacy that were presented in Figures 10.1 and 10.2, it can be seen that there is a common progression of events in QC programs that blocks both causal chains. This set of events can prevent members from experiencing the satisfaction and sense of accomplishment that result from being part of a successful problem-solving and change-implementation process. It can also prevent employees and the organization from experiencing the benefits of successful change.

It appears, then, that the very design of QC programs ensures that their survival is unlikely. This leads us to another issue that has received attention in the literature: whether QCs may serve as a starting point for organizations that are attempting to build a culture of high employee involvement.

QC Programs as a Transition Toward Other Forms of Participation. Some attention has been devoted to whether QCs can serve as a transition vehicle toward other forms of participative management. It is beyond the scope of this chapter to consider this issue in any detail. We can note, however, that there are three ways in which it is possible to move beyond QC programs (Lawler and Mohrman, 1987). One possibility is to develop other types of parallel structures, such as task forces, that permit employee participation in such areas as strategy, organization design, and operations. A second possibility is to move in the direction of self-managing work teams, to which various kinds of responsibilities are delegated (see also Sims and Dean, 1985). A third possibility is to alter various aspects of the organizational context to support QCs more successfully (see also Meyer and

Stott, 1985). We will discuss the implications of the last possibility in the next section.

Design Characteristics and QC Effectiveness

The literature contains only a few serious discussions of the relationship between factors in QC program design and the organizational context that promote or undermine QC effectiveness. Most of the available treatments are relatively narrow in scope, focusing on two or three factors, such as the importance of management commitment to the QC effort. Klein (1981), for example, suggests that important factors in QC success include job security and trust between management and employees. Wayne, Griffin, and Bateman (1986) found that group cohesion and performance norms showed a positive relationship to QCs' ability to make and implement suggestions. Steel and Shane (1986) argue that QC effectiveness depends on compatibility of the intervention and attributes of the organization, the level of QC program demands on tangible and intangible resources, and the type of response desired from participants. Overall, however, there has been little attempt to generate more inclusive models or to build on prior research in considering design contingencies.

A Model of Design Effectiveness. We have proposed and conducted research on a relatively comprehensive framework for assessing design factors that influence QC effectiveness (Mohrman and Ledford, 1984, 1985). The model, shown in Figure 10.3, is based on the assumption that QCs (and other participation groups) must be designed to attain both *internal competence* and *external effectiveness.*

Figure 10.3. General Model of the Effects of Participation Group Design.

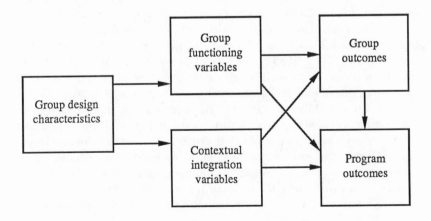

Internal competence is reflected in the groups' functioning and ability to solve problems. Standard QC consulting packages focus most of their effort on group functioning. Specific group functioning variables that may be important for QCs include goal clarity, which is an indicator of group performance strategy; intensity of effort, reflecting motivation; and group skill at problem solving (Hackman and Morris, 1977). High levels of group conflict may also be important as an indicator of destructive group process.

External effectiveness is reflected in the groups' ability to deal effectively with the normal operating organization so that they can sustain themselves and foster the implementation of suggested changes. Our previous analysis of the parallel nature of QCs indicates why we believe that this kind of effectiveness is also crucial. We considered five contextual variables that are repeatedly suggested as important in the QC literature: management responsiveness, recognition given to the QCs and the QC program, support for the program across a broad range of constituencies, communication about the program, and representation of the views of nonmembers in group decisions.

The model considers a number of particular design characteristics of participation groups. These are reflected in the QC model we have previously reviewed. We considered goal characteristics (broad versus narrow goals and use of measurable performance goals), membership characteristics (use of volunteers versus use of intact work groups, and breadth of membership opportunities), use of a facilitator, level of training provided, diversity of membership (variety of organizational constituencies included as members), diversity of outside resource personnel used, methods used to provide recognition of group accomplishments, use of management-level groups to support and assist the participation groups, use of multiple communication channels, record keeping, and meeting frequency.

We conducted a large-scale study of participation groups in nine organizational units of a large multidivisional firm (Mohrman and Ledford, 1984, 1985). The model provided an organizing framework for data collection. This study offered some major advantages in assessing the model and in assessing the importance of specific QC design factors. Most important, the diversity of the participation programs provided us with a naturally occurring field experiment. All nine research sites used a parallel organization model, but there was considerable variation across and within sites on the specific design features that were used. For example, the composition of the groups, kinds of training provided, and level of use of facilitators varied greatly. Some of the organizational units used a traditional QC approach, while others departed significantly from it. The study also embodied some weaknesses. First, the study was cross-sectional rather than longitudinal. Although we conducted interviews, made observations, and examined archival records in order to gain more depth of perspective than often is afforded by questionnaire research, we collected survey data for the study at only one point in time. Thus causality cannot be established firmly in our analyses. Second, perceived outcomes were measured through the questionnaire, but data on objective outcomes of the participation groups or group programs were generally not available. We suspect, however, that until such time as enough solid case-study research has been conducted to permit meta-analysis of the importance of various design characteristics, a study such as the one we conducted is the most practical way to investigate the relative importance of various design factors.

The data provided strong overall support for the model. Contextual integration and group functioning variables were quite strongly related to group and program outcomes. We found support for some but not all of the group design elements in the QC model. We summarized our findings concerning the importance of various design elements in the form of four guidelines (Mohrman and Ledford, 1985). In reviewing them here, we will indicate where others have expressed agreement or disagreement in the literature.

1. Participation groups must include or have access to the necessary skills and knowledge to address problems systematically. This capability was enhanced by the level of training provided to members, managers, and support personnel and the use of a diversity of outside resource personnel on an as-needed basis rather than as group members. These findings are consistent with the QC model and the findings of Steel and others (1985). Level of facilitation was related weakly to success; facilitators were often more important for their role as a communication channel and trainer than for their role as group facilitator. Werther (1982) also argues for the importance of the facilitator role.

2. Formalized procedures enhance the effectiveness of the group. Among the strongest predictors of effective group functioning and contextual integration were number of records kept, number of communication channels, and frequency and regularity of scheduled meetings. These findings are all consistent with the QC model.

3. The groups should be integrated horizontally and vertically with the rest of the organization. The use of multiple communication channels, use of management-level support groups, and use of a

variety of formal recognition award programs were related to contextual integration. Again, these findings are consistent with the QC model, although many QC proponents do not strongly emphasize the formation of management-level support groups. Goldstein (1985), for example, argues against such groups on the grounds that they stifle employee ideas through overcontrol.

4. The groups should be a regular part of the organization rather than special or extra activities. The availability of membership opportunities to all interested employees, the use of intact work groups rather than voluntary special groups, and the use of measurable performance goals by the group all predicted contextual integration and group functioning. This finding is consistent with our critique of the parallel model in general. Our finding about use of volunteers rather than work groups is also consistent with reports about Japanese quality circles by Cole (1979) and Ferris and Wagner (1985). They suggest that U.S. observers have naively believed that membership in Japanese circles is voluntary, when in reality pressure from peers and superiors generates nearly complete work-group participation.

   Taken together, these conclusions suggest that the QC model includes some desirable elements (training, formalization, facilitation support, recognition, and so on), and some that limit the impact of QCs (for example, use of volunteers and limitation of membership opportunities).

   Individual Differences as Moderators of Effectiveness. One issue that has received some attention in the literature is whether there are systematic individual differences between QC participants and nonparticipants. This is an especially important issue in researching QCs, because QC programs usually rely on volunteers. This means that selection biases are a threat to external validity, especially in cross-sectional studies. That is, differences in outcomes between participants and nonparticipants may be due to individual differences that existed before the intervention rather than to QCs.

   At this point, not enough research has been conducted for us to reach firm conclusions about the ways in which QC volunteers tend to differ systematically from nonvolunteers. Several studies have failed to find demographic differences (for example, Dean, 1985), and Wayne, Griffin, and Bateman (1986) found no demographic differences between members of more and less effective QCs. However, Hocevar and Mohrman (1984) found that QC volunteers were older and had greater tenure, although there were no differences in education or time in current job. Brockner and Hess (1986) found that for QC members in a computer manufacturing plant, self-esteem was related to performance measured in terms of ability to initiate changes. Dean (1985) found support for a model predicting QC membership in which those who show greater organizational involvement and who believe QCs will be instrumental in making improvements are more likely to join. Overall, however, there has been no systematic examination of differences between participants and nonparticipants.

Conclusion. There is evidence that a number of factors within the design and organizational context influence QC effectiveness. However, research on these issues is still at a primitive level. Next, we turn our attention outside the organization with a QC program to examine contingencies for effectiveness that are located in the organizational environment.

Environmental Contingencies and QC Effectiveness

A number of observers have discussed environmental contingencies that they believe influence QC effectiveness. These include contingency factors influencing the use of quality circles, cultural factors affecting the suitability of quality circles for Western societies, and the suitability of QCs for different populations of organizations.

Several factors at the environmental or societal level of analysis have been said to influence the use of quality circles. The most impressive research on this issue has been conducted by Cole (1982, 1985), who conducted a multinational comparative study of the diffusion of small-group activity (including QCs) over a period of two decades. He found that diffusion depended on three factors: (1) incentives for innovative management practices that are embedded in the condition of the national labor market, (2) the establishment of well-funded industrial or national-level organizations that are supported by management to communicate methods and to support the change, and (3) the disposition of organized labor toward these changes, and its ability to enforce its preferences. It is interesting that none of these factors strongly favored the diffusion of QC-type group programs in the United States through the 1970s, although conditions during the 1980s have probably become somewhat more favorable. Cole (1985) argues that these factors are the "forest," while specific implementation and design factors that attract so much attention in the literature are the "trees," which have relatively little explanatory power.

Whether or not quality circles are as suitable to U.S. organizations as to Japanese companies is the source of extensive comment in the literature. Proponents generally suggest that QCs have been a major element of the Japanese economic revival during the past twenty-five years, implying that they may similarly be a useful tonic for what currently ails American organizations. On the other hand, a number of observers argue that the uncritical application of this Japanese practice is misguided, for a number of reasons.

First, American national culture may not be as hospitable as Japanese national culture to quality circles. Cole (1979) notes that many Japanese firms with successful, well-established QC programs in Japan do not have such programs in their U.S. subsidiaries, because the Japanese managers doubt that American workers have sufficient commitment to the organization or that American managers are receptive enough to employee suggestions for QCs to work. Ohmae (1982) suggests that the importance of QCs to Japanese success has been overblown in the United States, and that QC success in Japan depended on several preconditions that are not necessarily present in U.S. companies. These preconditions include a work force that is well enough educated to use statistical methods and industrial engineering analyses, management that is willing to trust workers with cost data and other important information, management that is willing to give workers the authority to implement ideas, and workers who are willing to cooperate with each other. A similar set of conditions for success in Japan is mentioned by Ishikawa (1968).

Ferris and Wagner (1985) suggest that organizational differences and differences in orientation may make the United States a less suitable society for QCs than Japan. They speculate that QCs better fit the orientation of Japanese managers toward work groups, as well as the Japanese management style, which Ferris and Wagner characterize as manipulative, paternalistic, and "pseudo-participative," and QCs better suit the collectivist orientation of Japanese workers than the individualistic orientation of American workers. Lawler (1986) notes that Japanese organizations use a form of gainsharing that allows employees to share in company performance improvements and thus indirectly rewards them for their suggestions. Japanese organizations also tend to adopt a lifetime employment policy that protects the jobs of workers who develop labor-saving ideas. Crocker, Chiu, and Charney (1984) outline a wide range of organizational differences between U.S. and Japanese companies, including differences in values, labor-management relations and personnel systems, organizational structure, management style, and decision-making practices. Even though they tend to overstate the differences, as Dean (1987) comments in a review, Crocker and colleagues do believe that QCs can be adapted to fit Western conditions.

Our view is that the differences between Japanese and Western organizations are great enough so that the success of Japanese quality circles says very little about whether the QC approach can be sustained successfully in U.S. companies. QCs are one small part of a rather complex set of management beliefs and practices in Japan. As we have argued, the set of conditions facing U.S. quality circle programs is much less hospitable to their success and long-term survival.

A different environmental issue is whether some types or populations of organizations are more suitable for quality circles than others. As we have noted, QCs are used more in some industries than others; we may add that QCs are used more widely in blue-collar manufacturing than in white-collar organizations. However, no theoretical rationale has been articulated for the relative suitability of QCs to different types of organizations. QCs now are reportedly used with some degree of success in virtually every type of organization, including government agencies (see Blair, Cohen, and Hurwitz, 1982; Chisolm and Munzenrider, 1985), such unlikely places as police departments (Hocevar and Mohrman, 1984) and the U.S. Department of Defense (Horn, 1982; Bryant and Kearns, 1981, 1982), white-collar organizations (McClanahan, 1982; Richards, 1984; Yager, 1980), and service organizations (Ingle and Ingle, 1983; Jenkins and Shimada, 1981), including banks (Wood and Barksdale, 1982; Wood and Richardson, 1982). QCs have also been used in unionized organizations, although sometimes under different names and with modifications appropriate to a collective bargaining setting (Boylston, 1986; Cole, 1979; Crocker, Chiu, and Charney, 1984; Guest, 1979; Lazes and Costanza, 1983; Tavernier, 1981). At this point, there is no basis in the literature for claiming that QCs are more effective in some industries than others.

Future Directions

This chapter has considered the history of the QC approach, the nature of the QC model, the performance and attitudinal outcomes of QCs, the sustainability of QCs, design options and contingencies relevant to QC effectiveness, and environmental contingencies affecting success. We have been concerned with theory, research, and practice, but we have devoted the bulk of our attention to theory. This reflects our belief that the key weaknesses of quality circle practice and research derive from inadequate theory.

We believe that the quality circle topic is ripe for more and better research. Certainly, there is no shortage of potential research sites for exploring the kinds of issues we have raised in this chapter. Thousands of QC programs that were established in the early 1980s are now reaching the end of their life cycle. This is the point at which some managers begin to ask thoughtful questions about what they should do next, yet this is the point at which programmed, prepackaged QC programs are no longer helpful. Such conditions can make for the alliance of research and practice to the advantage of both.

We summarize our findings in an unusual form: as a set of specific recommendations about the types of information that should be included in future research reports on quality circles. We are concerned here with the factors that prior research and theoretical analysis indicate may be responsible for any observed pattern of results in a QC program. These cannot always be controlled for in individual studies. However, following these recommendations will permit research users to assess threats to validity in individual studies and to conduct sounder analyses across studies. Specifically, studies of quality circles should report the following:

1. *Design characteristics of QCs.* Design characteristics of the QC program should be described, especially with respect to any deviations from the standard QC model. This is essential to future cross-case analyses that attempt to assess the importance of different features of the QC model.

2. *Age of the QC program, average age of the circles studied, and life cycle stage of the QC program.* Our discussion indicates that the life cycle stage of QC programs and QC groups can have a major impact on attitudes toward QCs and beliefs about their effectiveness. Qualitative description is required to indicate whether the QC process seems to be following a standard life cycle, and to locate the program in the life cycle.

3. *Assessment of QC implementation.* Ideally, assessment involves qualitative description and simple descriptive statistics about the implementation process, including mention of whether outside consultants were used—and if so, whether they used the standard QC approach; indication of the percentage of employees in the organization who are currently and were previously participants; and description of suggestion activity, include the rate of suggestion making and examples of key suggestions made by circles, and the fate of these suggestions. This kind of description is needed in order for researchers to understand specifically what intervention is being assessed; to say that "quality circles" were studied does not provide enough information.

4. *Attitudinal data.* Both attitudinal outcome variables (such as job satisfaction and organizational commitment) and variables more closely linked to the intervention (such as job characteristics,

feelings of involvement, and feelings of accomplishment) should be measured. Selection of variables should be guided by theoretical models such as those presented in Figures 10.1 and 10.2. Moreover, it is very important to assess attitudes toward the intervention itself; this is a necessary component of assessing the nature and strength of the intervention. Finally, it is essential to collect attitudinal data from current participants, former participants, and those who have never participated in QCs, because prior studies suggest that there are systematic differences in the attitudes of these groups. Collecting data from nonparticipants is usually easy to do in organizations with QC programs, given that typically only a minority of employees are direct participants in QCs.

5. *Performance data.* In light of the goals of QCs, no assessment is complete without collection of performance data on productivity and quality. Any reports concerning cost savings or cost-benefit ratios should be explicit as to method for calculating savings, benefits, and costs.

6. *Year data were collected, environmental conditions facing the organization (for example, rapid technological change and economic conditions), type of organization, and nationality of employees.* These factors can permit assessment of important environmental contingencies across studies.

We anticipate that if researchers adhere to these recommendations in future research reports, the potential for accumulation of knowledge across studies will be vastly enhanced.

References

Adams, J. S. "Inequity in Social Exchange." In L. Berkowitz (ed.), *Advances in Experimental Social Psychology.* Vol. 2. Orlando, Fla.: Academic Press, 1965.

Alexander, C. P. "A Hidden Benefit of Quality Circles." *Personnel Journal,* 1984, *63*, 54–59.

Amsden, D. M., and Amsden, R. T. (eds.). *QC Circles: Applications, Tools, and Theory.* Milwaukee, Wis.: American Society for Quality Control, 1976.

Arbose, J. R. "Quality Control Circles: The West Adopts a Japanese Concept." *International Management,* Dec. 1980, pp. 31–39.

Atwater, L., and Sander, S. *Quality Circles in Navy Organizations: An Evaluation.* Technical Report NPRDC TR 8453. San Diego, Calif.: Navy Personnel Research and Development Center, 1984.

Baird, J. E., Jr. *Quality Circles: Leader's Manual*. Prospect Heights, Ill.: Waveland Press, 1982.

Baird, J. E., Jr., and Rittoff, D. J. *Quality Circles: Facilitator's Manual*. Prospect Heights, Ill.: Waveland Press, 1982.

Barra, R. J. *Putting Quality Circles to Work: A Practical Strategy for Boosting Productivity and Profits*. New York: McGraw-Hill, 1983.

Blair, J. D., Cohen, S. L., and Hurwitz, J. V. "Quality Circles: Practical Considerations for Public Managers." *Public Productivity Review*, May/June 1982, pp. 9–19.

Bocker, H. J., and Overgaard, H. O. "Japanese Quality Circles: A Managerial Response to the Productivity Problem." *Management International Review*, 1982, *22* (2), 13–19.

Boylston, B. C. "Employee Involvement and Cultural Change at Bethlehem Steel." In J. M. Rosow (ed.), *Teamwork: Joint Labor-Management Programs in America*. Elmsford, N.Y.: Pergamon Press, 1986.

Brockner, J., and Hess, T. "Self-Esteem and Task Performance in Quality Circles." *Academy of Management Journal*, 1986, *29* (3), 617–623.

Brooks, G., and Linklater, J. R. "Statistical Thinking and W. Edwards Deming's Teaching in the Administrative Environment." *National Productivity Review*, 1986, *5* (3), 271–280.

Bryant, S., and Kearns, J. *The Quality Circle Program of the Norfolk Naval Shipyard*. Washington, D.C.: U.S. Office of Personnel Management, 1981.

Bryant, S., and Kearns, J. "Workers' Brains as Well as Their Bodies: Quality Circles in a Federal Facility." *Public Administration Review*, 1982, *42*, 144–150.

Burck, C. G. "What Happens When Workers Manage Themselves?" *Fortune*, 1981, *104* (2), 62–69.

Burns, J. E. "Honeywell Quality Circles Boom—Part of a Growing American Trend." *Industrial Management*, 1982, *24*, 12–14.

"Can Quality Circles Boost Your Productivity?" *Purchasing*, May 14, 1981, pp. 77–80.

Chisolm, R. F., and Munzenrider, R. F. *Final Report: Evaluation Study of Quality of Work Life in the Clearfield County, PA. PENNDOT Organization*. Middletown, Pa.: Center for Quality of Working Life, Pennsylvania State University (Capitol Campus), 1985.

Coch, L., and French, J. R. P. "Overcoming Resistance to Change." *Human Relations*, 1948, *1*, 512–532.

Cole, R. E. "Made in Japan—Quality-Control Circles." *Across the Board*, 1979, *16* (11), 72–77.

Cole, R. E. "Learning from the Japanese: Prospects and Pitfalls." *Management Review*, 1980a, *69*, 22–28.

Cole, R. E. *Work, Mobility, and Participation: A Comparative Study of American and Japanese Industry.* Berkeley, Calif.: University of California Press, 1980b.

Cole, R. E. "Diffusion of Participatory Work Structures in Japan, Sweden, and the United States." In P. S. Goodman (ed.), *Change in Organizations: New Perspectives on Theory, Research, and Practice.* San Francisco: Jossey-Bass, 1982.

Cole, R. E. "The Macropolitics of Organizational Change: A Comparative Analysis of the Spread of Small-Group Activities." *Administrative Science Quarterly*, 1985, *30*, 560–585.

Cole, R. E., and Tachiki, D. S. "Forging Institutional Links: Making Quality Circles Work in the U.S." *National Productivity Review*, 1984, *3*, 419–420.

Cook, M. H. "Quality Circles—They Really Work, But . . ." *Training and Development Journal*, Jan. 1982, pp. 4–6.

Cox, J., and Dale, B. G. "Quality Circle Members' Views on Quality Circles." *Leadership and Organization Development Journal*, 1985, *6* (2), 20–23.

Crocker, O. L., Chiu, J. S. L., and Charney, C. *Quality Circles: A Guide to Participation and Productivity.* New York: Facts on File, 1984.

Dailey, J. J., Jr., and Kagerer, R. L. "A Primer on Quality Circles." *Supervisory Management*, 1982, *27*, 40–43.

Dean, J. W., Jr. "Toward a Model of Member Satisfaction with Quality Circles." Unpublished working paper, Pennsylvania State University, 1984.

Dean, J. W., Jr. "The Decision to Participate in Quality Circles." *Journal of Applied Behavioral Science*, 1985, *21*, 317–327.

Dean, J. W., Jr. "Review of O. L. Crocker, J. S. L. Chiu, and C. Charney, *Quality Circles: A Guide to Participation and Productivity.*" *Administrative Science Quarterly*, 1987, *32*, 151–153.

Deming, W. E. "Improvement of Quality and Productivity Through Action by Management." *National Productivity Review*, 1981–82, *1* (1), 12–22.

Dewar, D. *The Quality Circle Handbook.* Red Bluff, Calif.: Quality Circle Institute, 1982a.

Dewar, D. *The Quality Circle Guide to Participation Management.* Englewood Cliffs, N.J.: Prentice-Hall, 1982b.

"Editor to Readers: Quality Circles." *Personnel Journal*, 1981, *62* (6), 424–435.

Ferris, G. R., and Wagner, J. A., III. "Quality Circles in the United

States: A Conceptual Reevaluation." *Journal of Applied Behavioral Science,* 1985, *21* (2), 155-167.

Freund, W., and Epstein, E. *People and Productivity: The New York Stock Exchange Guide to Financial Incentives and the Quality of Work Life.* Homewood, Ill.: Dow Jones-Irwin, 1984.

Fujita, Y. "Participative Work Practices in the Japanese Auto Industry: Some Neglected Considerations." *Quality Circles Journal,* 1983, *6,* 15-19.

Gillett, D. "Better QCs: A Need for More Manager Action." *Management Review,* 1983, *72,* 19-25.

Goldstein, S. G. "Organizational Dualism and Quality Circles." *Academy of Management Review,* 1985, *10,* 504-517.

Gorlin, H., and Schein, L. "Innovations in Managing Human Resources." New York: Conference Board, 1984.

Graf, L. A. "Suggestion Program Failure: Causes and Remedies." *Personnel Journal,* 1982, *61,* 450-455.

Griffin, R. W., and Wayne, S. J. "A Field Study of Effective and Less Effective Quality Circles." *Academy of Management Proceedings,* 1984, pp. 217-221.

Gryna, F. M., Jr. *Quality Circles: A Team Approach to Problem Solving.* New York: AMACOM, 1981.

Guest, R. H. "Quality of Work Life: Learning from Tarrytown." *Harvard Business Review,* 1979, *57,* 76-87.

Hackman, J. R., and Lawler, E. E., III. "Employee Reactions to Job Characteristics." *Journal of Applied Psychology* (monograph), 1971, *55,* 259-286.

Hackman, J. R., and Morris, C. "Improving Group Performance Effectiveness." In J. R. Hackman, E. E. Lawler, III, and L. Porter (eds.), *Perspectives on Behavior in Organizations.* New York: McGraw-Hill, 1977.

Harper, S. E., and Jordon, G. L. *The Utility of Quality Circles in U.S. Manufacturing Companies.* Technical Report N00014-82-C0139. Alexandria, Va.: Office of Naval Research, U.S. Department of Defense, 1982.

Head, T. C., Molleston, J. L., Sorenson, P. F., and Gargano, J. "The Impact of Quality Circles on Employee Task Perceptions." *Group and Organization Studies,* 1986, *11* (4), 360-373.

Hesterman, E. W. "Model for Implementing a Participatory Program in Statistical Process Control Areas." *Personnel,* 1986, *63* (11), 53-58.

Hocevar, S. P., and Mohrman, S. A. "Quality Circles in a Metropolitan Police Department." Center for Effective Organizations

Publication 60-84. Los Angeles: University of Southern California, 1984.

"Honeywell Quality Circles: Part of a Growing American Trend." *Journal of Organizational and Behavior Management*, 1981-82, *3*, 97-101.

Horn, L. J. *Effects of Quality Circles on Productivity Attitudes of Naval Air Rework Facility Production Employees.* Technical Report 82-120-7, Mobilization and Defense Management Technical Report Series, Fort Leslie J. McNair. Washington, D.C.: Industrial College of the Armed Forces, 1982.

Imberman, W. "Why Quality Circles Don't Work." *Canadian Business*, 1982, *20* (11), 24-27.

Ingle, S. *Quality Circles Master Guide: Increasing Productivity with People Power.* New York: Prentice-Hall, 1982a.

Ingle, S. "How to Avoid Quality Circle Failure in Your Company." *Training and Development Journal*, 1982b, *36*, 54-59.

Ingle, S., and Ingle, N. *Quality Circles in Service Industries: Comprehensive Guidelines for Increased Productivity and Efficiency.* Englewood Cliffs, N.J.: Prentice-Hall, 1983.

Ishikawa, K. *QC Circle Activities.* Tokyo, Japan: Union of Japanese Scientists and Engineers, 1968.

Jenkins, K. M., and Shimada, J. "Quality Circles in the Service Sector." *Supervisory Management*, 1981, *26*, 2-7.

Jenkins, K. M., and Shimada, J. "Effects of Quality Control Circles on Worker Performance: A Field Experiment." Paper presented at the 43rd annual meeting of the Academy of Management, New York, 1983.

Juran, J. M. "The Quality Circle Phenomenon." *Industrial Quality Control*, 1967, *23*, 329-336.

Kanariek, A. "The Far Side of Quality Circles." *Management Review*, 1981, *70* (10), 16-17.

Kanter, R. *The Change Masters: Innovations for Productivity in the American Mode.* New York: Simon & Schuster, 1983.

Kelly, J. "Quality Circles in Fort Collins: A Municipal Perspective and Experience." *Public Personnel Management*, 1985, *14* (4), 401-408.

Klein, G. D. "Implementing Quality Circles: A Hard Look at Some of the Realities." *Personnel*, 1981, *58*, 11-20.

Kleinberg, E. M. "How Westinghouse Adapts Quality Circles to Sales Management." *Industrial Marketing*, 1981, *66*, 82, 84.

Kolodny, H. "Review of M. Robson, *Quality Circles: A Practical Guide.*" *Administrative Science Quarterly*, 1984, *29*, 156-158.

Lawler, E. E., III. "Job Attitudes and Employee Motivation: Theory, Research, and Practice." *Personnel Psychology*, 1970, *23*, 223-337.

Lawler, E. E., III. *High-Involvement Management: Participative Strategies for Improving Organizational Performance.* San Francisco: Jossey-Bass, 1986.

Lawler, E. E., III, and Ledford, G. E., Jr. "Productivity and the Quality of Work Life." *National Productivity Review,* 1981-82, *1* (1), 23-36.

Lawler, E. E., III, and Mohrman, S. A. "Quality Circles After the Fad." *Harvard Business Review,* Jan./Feb. 1985, pp. 65-71.

Lawler, E. E., III, and Mohrman, S. A. "Quality Circles After the Honeymoon." *Organizational Dynamics,* 1987, *15,* 42-54.

Lazes, P., and Costanza, T. "Cutting Costs Without Layoffs Through Union-Management Collaboration." *National Productivity Review,* 1983, *2* (4), 362-370.

Locke, E., and Schweiger, D. "Participation in Decision-Making: One More Look." In B. Staw (ed.), *Research in Organization Behavior.* Vol. 1. Greenwich, Conn.: JAI Press, 1979.

McClanahan, J. S. "More Quality Circles Sporting White Collars." *Industry Week,* 1982, *213,* 28-29, 32.

Marks, M. L. "The Question of Quality Circles." *Psychology Today,* Mar. 1986, pp. 33-46.

Marks, M. L., Mirvis, P. H., Hackett, E. J., and Grady, J. F., Jr. "Employee Participation in a Quality Circle Program: Impact on Quality of Work Life, Productivity, and Absenteeism." *Journal of Applied Psychology,* 1986, *71,* 61-69.

Mento, A. J., and Steel, R. P. "Conducting Quality Circles Research: Toward a Comprehensive Perspective." *Public Productivity Review,* 1985, *9* (1), 35-48.

Metz, E. J. "Caution: Quality Circles Ahead." *Training and Development Journal,* 1981, *35* (8), 71-85.

Meyer, G. W., and Stott, R. G. "Quality Circles: Panacea or Pandora's Box?" *Organizational Dynamics,* Spring 1985, pp. 34-50.

Miller, K. L., and Monge, P. R. "Participation, Satisfaction, and Productivity: A Meta-Analytic Review." *Academy of Management Journal,* 1986, *29* (4), 727-753.

Miner, F. C. "Group Versus Individual Decision Making: An Investigation of Performance Measure, Decision Strategies, and Process Losses/Gains." *Organizational Behavior and Human Performance,* 1984, *33,* 112-124.

Mirvis, P. H., and Berg, D. *Failures in Organization Development and Change.* New York: Wiley, 1977.

Mohrman, S. A. *The Impact of Quality Circles: A Conceptual View.* Paper presented at the Bureau of National Affairs Conference on

Current Directions in Productivity—Evolving Japanese and American Practices, Houston, May 13, 1982. Center for Effective Organizations Publication G83-5. Los Angeles: University of Southern California, 1982.

Mohrman, S. A., and Lawler, E. E., III. "Quality of Work Life." In K. Rowland and G. Ferris (eds.), *Personnel and Human Resource Management*. Greenwich, Conn.: JAI Press, 1984.

Mohrman, S. A., and Ledford, G. E., Jr. *The Design of Employee Participation Groups: Guidelines Based on Empirical Research*. Center for Effective Organizations Publication 84-14-62. Los Angeles: University of Southern California, 1984.

Mohrman, S. A., and Ledford, G. E., Jr. "The Design and Use of Effective Employee Participation Groups." *Human Resource Management*, 1985, *24*, 413–428.

Mohrman, S. A., Ledford, G. E., Jr., Lawler, E. E., III, and Mohrman, A. M. In C. L. Cooper and I. T. Robertson (eds.), *International Review of Industrial and Organizational Psychology 1986*. New York: Wiley, 1986.

Mohrman, S. A., and Novelli, L., Jr. "Beyond Testimonials: Learning from a Quality Circles Programme." *Journal of Occupational Behavior*, 1985, *6*, 93–110.

Morland, J. *Quality Circles*. London: Industrial Society, 1981.

Mroczkowski, T. "Quality Circles, Fine—What Next?" *Personnel Administrator*, June 1984, pp. 173–184.

Munchus, G. "Employer-Employee Based Quality Circles in Japan: Human Resource Policy Implications for American Firms." *Academy of Management Review*, 1983, *8*, 255–261.

Nurick, A. J. *Participation in Organizational Change: The TVA Experiment*. New York: Praeger, 1985.

O'Donnell, M., and O'Donnell, R. J. "Quality Circles—The Latest Fad or a Real Winner?" *Business Horizons*, 1984, *27*, 48–52.

Ohmae, K. "Quality Control Circles: They Work and They Don't." *Wall Street Journal*, Mar. 29, 1982.

Ouchi, W. *Theory Z: How American Business Can Meet the Japanese Challenge*. Reading, Mass.: Addison-Wesley, 1981.

Pascale, R. T., and Athos, A. G. *The Art of Japanese Management*. New York: Simon & Schuster, 1981.

Patchin, R. I., and Cunningham, R. *The Management and Maintenance of Quality Circles*. Homewood, Ill.: Dow Jones–Irwin, 1983.

Portis, B., Fullerton, D. J., and Ingram, P. R. "Effective Use of Quality Circles." *Business Quarterly* (School of Business Administration, University of Western Ontario), Autumn 1985, pp. 44–47.

Positive Personnel Practices. *Quality Circles: Participants' Manual.*
    Prospect Heights, Ill.: Waveland Press, 1982.
"Productivity and Morale Sagging? Try the Quality Circle Ap-
    proach." *Personnel,* 1980, *57,* 43-45.
"QCs Show Change." *Personnel Journal,* 1981, *58,* 12.
Rafaeli, A. "Quality Circles and Employee Attitudes." *Personnel
    Psychology,* 1985, *38,* 603-615.
Ramsing, K. D., and Blair, J. D. "An Expression of Concern About
    Quality Circles." *Academy of Management Proceedings,* 1982, pp.
    323-327.
Rendel, E. "Quality Circles: A 'Third Wave' Intervention." *Training
    and Development Journal,* 1981, *35,* 28-31.
Richards, B. "White-Collar Quality Circles and Productivity."
    Training and Development Journal, Oct. 1984, pp. 92-98.
Robson, M. *Quality Circles: A Practical Guide.* Aldershot, Hampshire,
    England: Gower, 1982.
Ross, J. E., and Ross, W. C. *Japanese Quality Circles and Productivity.*
    Reston, Va.: Reston, 1982.
Schuster, M. "Cooperation and Change in Union Settings: Problems
    and Opportunities." *Human Resource Management,* 1984, *23,* 145-
    160.
Seelye, H. N., Stewart, E. C. P., and Sween, J. A. "Evaluating Quality
    Circles in U.S. Industry: A Feasibility Study." Arlington, Va.: Office
    of Naval Research, U.S. Department of Defense, 1982.
Seelye, H. N., and Sween, J. A. "Critical Components of Successful
    U.S. Quality Circles." *Quality Circle Journal,* Feb. 1983, pp. 14-17.
Sims, H. P., Jr., and Dean, J. W., Jr. "Beyond Quality Circles: Self-
    Managing Teams." *Personnel,* 1985, *62,* 25-33.
Smeltzer, L. R., and Kedia, B. L. "Knowing the Ropes: Organizational
    Requirements for Quality Circles." *Business Horizons,* 1985, *28* (4),
    30-34.
Soyka, D. "Honeywell Pioneers in Quality Circle Movement." *World
    of Work Report,* 1981, *6,* 65-67.
Steel, R. P., and Shane, G. S. "Evaluation Research on Quality Circles:
    Technical and Analytical Implications." *Human Relations,* 1986,
    39, 449-468.
Steel, R. P., and others. "Factors Influencing the Success and Failure
    of Two Quality Circle Programs." *Journal of Management,* 1985,
    11, 99-119.
Stein, B. A., and Kanter, R. M. "Building the Parallel Organization:
    Creating Mechanisms for Permanent Quality of Work Life."
    Journal of Applied Behavioral Science, 1980, *16,* 371-386.

Takeuchi, H. "Learning from the Japanese." *California Management Review*, 1981, *23*, 5–19.

"Talking in Circles Improves Quality." *Industry Week*, Feb. 1977, pp. 62–64.

Tavernier, G. "Awakening a Sleeping Giant: Ford's Employee Involvement Program." *Management Review*, 1981, *70*, 15–20.

Thompson, P. C. "Quality Circles at Martin Marietta Corporation Denver Aerospace/Michoud Division." In R. Zager and M. P. Rosow (eds.), *The Innovative Organization: Productivity Programs in Action*. Elmsford, N.Y.: Pergamon Press, 1982.

Thompson, P. C. *Quality Circles: How to Make Them Work in America*. New York: AMACOM, 1982.

Turban, E., and Kamin, J. Y. "Cost-Benefit Analysis of Quality Circles." *Engineering Costs and Production Economics*, 1984, *8*, 199–209.

Wayne, S. J., Griffin, R. W., and Bateman, T. S. "Improving the Effectiveness of Quality Circles." *Personnel Administrator*, Mar. 1986, pp. 79–88.

Werther, W. B. "Quality Circles: Key Executive Issues." *Journal of Contemporary Business*, 1982, *11*, 17–26.

White, D. D., and Bednar, D. A. "Locating Problems with Quality Circles." *National Productivity Review*, 1984–85, *4*, 45–52.

"Will the Slide Kill Quality Circles?" *Business Week*, Jan. 11, 1982, pp. 108–109.

Wolfe, D. R., Hauck, W. C., and Varney, G. H. "Quality Circles: The U.S. Experience." *Proceedings of the Annual Midwest Academy of Management*, 1983, *26*, 169–178.

Wood, O. G., Jr., and Barksdale, W. C., Jr. "How Quality Circles Can Be Effective in the Lending Function." *Journal of Commercial Bank Lending*, 1982, *64*, 54–59.

Wood, O. G., Jr., and Richardson, J. H., Jr. "Quality Circles Begin in Bank Operations." *Bankers Magazine*, 1982, *165*, 12–14.

Wood, R., Hull, F., and Azumi, K. "Evaluating Quality Circles: The American Application." *California Management Review*, 1983, *26*, 37–53.

Yager, E. "Examining the Quality Control Circle." *Personnel Journal*, 1979, *58*, 682–684, 708.

Yager, E. "Quality Circle: A Tool for the '80s." *Training and Development Journal*, 1980, *34*, 60–63.

Yager, E. "The Quality Circle Explosion." *Training and Development Journal*, 1981, *35*, 98–105.

Zand, D. "Collateral Organization: A New Change Strategy." *Journal of Applied Behavioral Science*, 1974, *10*, 63–89.

Zander, A. "Group Motivation and Performance." In A. Zander (ed.), *Groups at Work*. San Francisco: Jossey-Bass, 1977.

Zemke, R. "Honeywell Imports Quality Circle as Long-Term Management Strategy." *Training*, 1980, *17*, 91–94.

11

ΣΣΣΣΣΣΣΣΣΣΣ

Groups and Productivity: Analyzing the Effectiveness of Self-Managing Teams

Paul S. Goodman
Rukmini Devadas
Terri L. Griffith Hughson

In this chapter, we review what we know now and what we need to know about how groups can improve productivity in organizations. The discussion is organized around a specific kind of work group, self-managing teams. We focus on this type of group intervention because (1) it is a relatively new type of intervention to improve group effectiveness, (2) self-managing teams will continue to be a major strategy in redesigning work in the future, (3) there is some evidence about the effectiveness of these teams, and (4) this intervention is a comprehensive form of change that includes modification of goals, work, job allocation, group problem solving, pay systems, and so on.

The chapter is organized into two sections. We begin with a review of self-managing groups and address the following questions.

- What are self-managing groups?
- What are the assumptions underlying the use of these groups?
- What are the effects of these groups on productivity?
- What are the critical issues in understanding the effectiveness of self-managing groups?

The second section of the chapter discusses some broader theoretical issues about changing groups to increase productivity and other organizational effectiveness indicators.

Definition

Concepts such as *self-managing teams, autonomous work groups, semiautonomous work groups,* and *QWL* (quality of work-life) *teams* are often used interchangeably. In this section, we present a conceptual way to delineate these various concepts, the historical origins of self-managing groups, and some examples of actual interventions.

Self-managing teams are groups of individuals who can self-regulate work on their interdependent tasks. The key elements of such teams are (1) *groups* (versus dyads or organizations) in which there typically is face-to-face interaction, (2) a physically defined *area,* (3) a whole set of *interdependent tasks,* and (4) group members who have *control* over the management and execution of these tasks. *Management* refers to activities such as planning, directing, organizing, staffing, and monitoring. *Control* means that group members have authority and responsibility to initiate the management activities. The *whole set of tasks* refers to all the interdependent activities required to produce a definable product. (Note that the product is most likely a definable part of the production process, not the completed product that goes to the customer.) In a manufacturing context, this set of tasks would begin with the acquisition of raw materials and proceed through the transformation process to shipping, including all the auxiliary activities, such as quality control and maintenance.

Self-managing teams differ from traditional work groups primarily in who controls the critical managing processes and the set of tasks the group works on. In a traditional work group, the first-line manager does the planning, organizing, directing, staffing, and monitoring processes. In addition, the traditional work group does the core production activities, while support activities, such as receiving, quality control, and maintenance, are completed by other groups. For example, in a study of traditional and self-managing teams in a coal mine (Goodman, 1979), the traditional crew members were told who should do what job and when, while self-managing team members performed these managerial functions in addition to doing the specific jobs (for example, bolting). In the traditional crews, the members performed only the core production jobs, while all the support jobs were included as part of the work of the self-managing team.

The terms *autonomous work groups* and *self-managing teams* seem to be used interchangeably, and we do not see any conceptual difference between these two concepts. The distinction between *autonomous work groups* and *semiautonomous work groups* seems to be a matter of the number of "production" tasks the group is responsible for managing and executing. For example, in one plant studied by the senior author, both autonomous and semiautonomous teams were used. The primary difference was whether the team performed support activities (for example, receiving, materials, quality control, maintenance) that were related to but outside of the major production or transformation activities. The semiautonomous teams managed and performed the major production activities, and other support groups performed quality control and maintenance tasks.

The last definitional distinction concerns the terms *self-designing* and *self-managing* (see Hackman, 1982). Self-designing teams have control over the design of the team itself—that is, what tasks should be done and who should belong to the team. In the self-managing team, the tasks and personnel are given, and the team executes the tasks. These last two distinctions, between autonomous and semiautonomous and self-designing and self-managing, highlight two dimensions that can be controlled by the group. The first dimension deals with the extent to which the group controls all the relevant production processes (maintenance versus production) to complete the whole task. The second dimension deals with the extent to which the group controls its own design. For the remainder of the chapter, we will use the term *self-managing teams* to refer to both dimensions. That is, self-managing teams will always be involved in managing and executing tasks. They will differ in the number of subtasks they control and in whether they control the design and membership in their group.

Historical Antecedents

Before we turn to some examples of self-managing teams, it is probably useful to acknowledge some of the antecedents of this type of group. The group dynamics movement, led by Kurt Lewin (1951), is clearly a precursor to the emergence of self-managing teams. In that work, there is a blend of theory, action research, and forms of participation that appears in all the interventions of self-managing teams.

Other themes emerged from the group dynamics movement that influenced the development of self-managing teams. Research on the antecedents and consequences of group cohesiveness (Seashore, 1954) is relevant to understanding self-managing teams. High levels of cohesiveness characterize most self-managing teams. Similarly, research on forms of group participation in group decision making

(Maier, 1963; Coch and French, 1968; Vroom, 1964) also bears on the development of self-managing teams.

Probably the most powerful intellectual antecedent of self-managing teams comes from the socio-technical tradition (see Trist, 1963). Here the focus is on trying to find a way to optimize both the social and technological systems. Trist and Bamforth's (1951) seminal paper describes the emergence of early forms of self-managing teams in a British coal mine. Many of the current examples of self-managing teams find their intellectual tradition in this early work. Indeed, researchers in the socio-technical tradition have been the major advocates of self-managing teams.

Over the last three decades, there has been growing commitment to the concept of participation, both in theory and in practice (Locke and Schweiger, 1979). While the concept of participation has many possible definitions and forms, the basic idea is that participation represents a shift toward sharing control and power. The underlying assumptions are that providing employees with more control, information, and responsibility is a valuable activity in its own right and that, on a more practical side, it improves worker satisfaction and productivity. It should be clear from our definition of self-managing teams that the design of these groups represents a substantial shift in control and power. Group members not only are involved in decisions about production, but they may also have control over group design and membership. The broad movement toward greater forms of participation clearly provides a context for the development of self-managing teams.

Some Examples

Three examples of self-managing work groups will sharpen our understanding of the meaning of this concept. The Topeka case was selected because it is probably the best-known example of the use of self-managing teams in a U.S. organization. The Rushton case was selected because it is the most comprehensive evaluation of a self-managing team intervention. The confectionery case was selected because it is the most recent well-documented account of self-managing teams. In this section, we describe only the nature of these self-managing teams. In a subsequent section, we reveal the positive and negative results.

Topeka. The Topeka work system (Walton, 1972) is one of the earliest self-managing teams in a U.S. company. In 1968, General Foods decided to open an additional pet food plant at a new location. At that time, the existing manufacturing facility was experiencing a number of problems due to employee alienation from work. Indifference and inattention on the part of employees led to frequent plant shutdowns, and there were many instances of sabotage and violence. Management therefore decided to design the new plant in an innovative way to counteract these problems, and the plant went into operation in January 1971.

Most of the changes were designed by a small group of managers, facilitated in their endeavors by consultations with experts and visits to plants of other organizations that had implemented or were in the process of implementing new work methods.

The new plant was characterized by the following design:

1. *Goals.* The change program had two broad goals: to improve productivity and to enhance the quality of worklife.
2. *Focal unit.* The focal unit of analysis was the work team, which consisted of from seven to fourteen operators and a leader. There were six teams in the whole plant, and two teams—a processing team and a packaging team—worked each shift. The processing team was responsible for handling raw materials and for the actual conversion of the raw materials to the finished product, while the other team dealt with the packaging, warehousing, and shipping of the pet food.
3. *Self-managing teams.* These teams were given collective responsibility for large portions of the production process, which included a natural set of interdependent tasks.
4. *Support functions.* Maintenance, personnel functions, quality control, and so on were not separated but built into the teams' responsibilities.
5. *Supervisor's role.* In the old plant, supervisors planned, directed, and controlled work of the operators. In the new system, there was no supervisor—only a team leader, whose job was primarily to facilitate team development and group decision making.
6. *Training.* The early development of the plant took over two years. During this time, employees were given skill training and education regarding the team philosophy of the new organization.
7. *Hiring.* The team was given responsibility for screening and selecting employees to replace those who were leaving. It could also nominate its members to serve on plantwide committees.
8. *Job flexibility.* In the older plant, individuals were permanently assigned to specific jobs. At Topeka, the team assigned tasks to individuals, and these tasks could be reassigned at a later date. Movement was controlled by the team.

9. *Pay*. A "pay for learning" system was instituted. Pay increases depended on how many tasks an individual operator mastered in his or her team, and later in the whole plant. Thus there were four basic pay rates: the starting rate, the rate for mastering the first job, the rate for mastering all jobs within the team's responsibility, and, finally, the plant rate. In the old plant, pay increases were based on movement up the job hierarchy.

10. *Grievances*. Grievances were handled by the team itself. Management did not specify any rules when the plant began operation; these were expected to evolve over time and through experience.

11. *Other changes*. Employees were encouraged to teach and learn from one another. The pay system did not hinder this sharing of skills and knowledge, because there was no limit on the number of people who could qualify for those higher pay rates. Attempts were also made to minimize status differences by having a common decor throughout the plant, an open parking lot, and so on. Finally, responsibilities for challenging and unchallenging tasks were evenly distributed among the teams. Housekeeping tasks were assigned to everyone.

Rushton. The Rushton Quality of Work Project is one of the most comprehensively evaluated adoptions of self-managing teams (Goodman, 1979). It is of historic interest that this project was conducted in a coal mine and that the change team in this project was headed by Eric Trist. The classic article on self-managing teams was written by Trist and Bamforth (1951) about work in an English coal mine.

The Rushton Mining Company, located in Pennsylvania, operated a midsized mine producing steam coal for a major electrical utility. In late 1973, management and the union decided to explore new ways of organizing work at the mine. The president of the mine was concerned with attracting young miners to Rushton in the future. The problem was that younger, better-educated miners brought higher expectations to the job, yet the current state of mining was not congruent with these expectations. The union was primarily interested in finding new ways to change work in order to improve safety. The parties involved at the initiation of the project included management, the union, a consulting team headed by Eric Trist, and an independent evaluation team (Goodman, 1979).

The basic structure of the program that evolved from the consulting team and a labor-management committee included:

1. *Goals*. There were five major goals: increased safety, increased productivity, higher earnings, greater job skills, and increased job satisfaction.

2. *Focal unit.* The major unit of analysis was the section. By focusing on the section instead of the crew (for example, in terms of performance evaluation), less between-crew competition and more cooperation was expected.

3. *Autonomous work groups.* The responsibility for daily production and for directing the work force was delegated to the crew.

4. *Foreman's job.* With responsibility delegated to the men in the crew, the foreman was no longer responsible for production. The foreman's prime responsibility was safety. This change was introduced because the research team felt that there was a basic contradiction between safety and production objectives. In addition, the foreman was to become more involved in planning activities and in integrating the section with the rest of the mine.

5. *Job switching.* All men were expected to exchange tasks and learn other jobs within their crews, so that the crew would be multiskilled. That is, the crew would develop the flexibility to be able to staff any job. Movement between jobs did not require bidding, as would be the case under the regular contract.

6. *Pay.* All members of the experimental section received the same pay rate, and it was the top rate for the crew. The rationale for the high rate was that the men had increased responsibility for production and maintenance of equipment. Also, they had agreed to learn to perform multiple skills.

7. *Additional crew members.* The traditional crew consisted of six production men. In the experimental section, two support men (to lay track, transport supplies, and so on) were added to the crew. These two support men had traditionally been drawn from the general labor force and been assigned to a section only when support work was needed.

8. *Joint committee.* A small labor-management committee (five members from each side) was instituted seventy-five days after the experiment began, to supervise the daily operation of the program. The larger labor-management committee remained intact; its responsibilities were to deal with broader policy issues.

9. *Grievances.* Grievances were not initially processed through the traditional machinery. The expectation was that grievances would be resolved within the experimental section. If they were not, they were to be brought to the joint committee. Failure to resolve the grievance at this point would lead to the use of the traditional grievance machinery.

10. *Training.* A major part of the change effort was to move the men toward being professional miners. A training program on safety

practices, ventilation, roof control, and other potential problems
was to be a major part of the change effort.

11. *Allocation of financial gains.* No gainsharing plan was worked
out in the initial agreement. Rather, some general principles
were established. If no gains resulted, the company would
assume all the costs from the experiment. If gains did occur, the
company would be reimbursed, and the remaining gains would
be allocated between labor and management.

Confectionery Company. The third and last example comes
from a report by Wall, Kemp, Jackson, and Clegg (1986) on the use
of self-managing teams in a new plant of a large, multisite, British
nonunionized confectionery company. We selected this case because it
represents the most recent, well-evaluated published account of the use
of self-designing teams.

As was the case in the Topeka project, the initiation of a new
factory was the stimulus for thinking about new ways to organize
work. The senior management of the confectionery company, with a
consultant from the Tavistock Institute, began a planning process to
create a new factory and a new form of work. The structure took the
following form.

1. *Focal unit.* The focal unit was a work group comprising from
eight to twelve people.
2. *Nature of work tasks.* Groups were responsible for allocating jobs,
reaching production and quality targets, solving local production
problems, recording production data, organizing breaks, collecting raw materials, delivering finished goods, calling for engineering support, and selecting and training new recruits.
3. *Supervision.* The post of the supervisor did not exist.
4. *Training.* Training was given to the new work teams on how the
factory would be organized and managed.
5. *Other changes.* Consistent with providing shop-floor employees
with substantial autonomy, the factory had a single eating
facility, no time clocks, monthly payment by credit transfer, and
a flat (three-level) managerial structure.

It will be useful now to see how our conceptualization of self-
managing teams fits with the three model descriptions of self-
managing teams. Our basic definition referred to a team in which
members have control over the management and execution of a set of
interdependent tasks. The degree of self-management, we said,
depends on the number of tasks (support and production) the group

controls and the degree to which the group controls its own design and its membership. This definition seems to characterize some aspects of these three examples. It also permits the identification of differences in degree of self-management. For example, the Topeka teams seemed to have greater control over more of the support activities than the Rushton teams. The confectionery teams seemed to have more control over the membership in the groups than the Rushton teams. In all three cases, management was the primary controller of the initial design or structure of the teams.

The problem with our definition is that it focuses only on control within the group and not on the other structural changes that characterize these three cases. In all these cases, there were basic philosophical and value changes. In the Topeka case, for example, there was a clearly articulated philosophy that emphasized human development and business performance and was based on the value of variety of work, freedom from close supervision, membership in teams, opportunity to learn, and so on. This philosophy needed to be articulated and accepted prior to designing self-managing teams. In all of the cases, there were organizational changes that were independent of the teams but essential to the effective functioning of the teams. For example, in the Rushton case, the single-rate pay system reinforced the idea that everyone had common responsibilities and agreed to learn the different jobs in the crew. A very extensive training system provided the knowledge for the teams to better manage their work. The joint labor-management committee provided a mechanism to coordinate across the three-shift operation, given the change in the supervisors' roles. In the confectionery case, the common dining area and elimination of time cards were important symbols that reinforced the change in autonomy and responsibility delegated to the shop-floor employees.

What is the critical message? It is difficult to think about changing control in the work team without thinking about the correlated changes in the organization. One cannot design a system in which workers have greater responsibility and authority over work without changing the pay and training system. Initiating major changes in some parts of an organization (for example, work group) requires concomitant changes in other aspects of the organizational structure if the change is to have some long-run viability (Lawler, 1982).

Our conceptualization of self-managing groups stands, but it does not completely characterize the three cases we have described. Indeed, the cases are really examples of multiple system interventions at the group level, where *one* of the core changes is self-managing teams. It is unlikely that management could introduce self-managing teams into a traditional organization without corollary changes in that organization and expect them to survive.

In this sense, self-managing teams are different from other new forms of work organization. Quality circles (see Chapter Ten) are problem-solving teams that exist in conjunction with the regular forms of work. They do not require major modifications in pay or authority systems. Labor-management steering committees are set up to find new ways to organize work and to legitimize labor-management cooperation outside the traditional collective bargaining arena. Both quality circles and labor-management committees are important innovations, but they exist in addition to the regular design of work. Self-designing teams change the actual way work is managed and executed. In addition, they require concomitant changes in the organizational structure.

As we move to examining some of the assumptions and results of self-managing teams, the reader should note that we are talking about (1) groups that control many of the production and support processes, (2) groups that control the design of and membership in their group, *and* (3) organizations in which there have been substantial changes in training, pay systems, and so on to support the shift in control to group members. The point is that most self-managing interventions are part of a larger system intervention.

Basic Assumptions

Why should self-managing groups be more effective than more traditional work groups performing the same tasks? Also, why should they be more effective than groups using other forms of participation (for example, quality circles)? We can approach these questions by examining the theory underlying self-managing groups. Hackman (1982) is a major contributor to the work-group literature, and his model of work-group effectiveness is a good way to organize this discussion. At the core of this model (Figure 11.1) are three process criteria: effort, knowledge, and the appropriateness of task performance strategies. Increases in these three criteria, given task configurations, should improve the overall effectiveness of the group. The basic levers to change the process criteria are group design, organizational context, and group synergy. (See Figure 11.1 for definitions.) Self-managing groups bring about direct changes in group design and organizational context, which in turn should bring about changes in group synergy; all three factors should affect the process criteria.

Figure 11.1. An Overview of the Normative Model of Group Effectiveness.

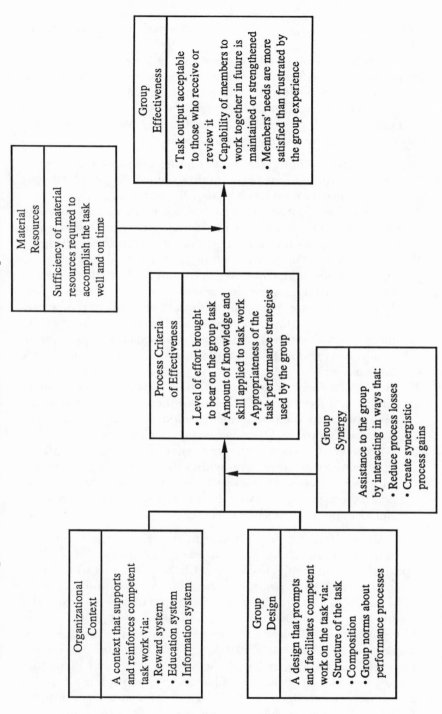

Source: Hackman, 1982.

Let us now move to a specific case to trace out the expected effects on group performance of the changes in structure and process incorporated in the self-managing groups. We will use the Rushton case and focus on a specific effectiveness dimension. The following are changes in design, organizational context, and group synergy that should have improved safety-related behaviors.

1. The knowledge of workers about mining and safety practices was increased through intensive training. Knowledge about safety is a precondition for improving safety behaviors.
2. Many of the negative incentives related to safety activities were removed. A major problem in mining is close supervision and constant pressure for production from the foreman. By changing the foreman's role to concentrate on safety and buffering the foreman from production pressures from his boss, this source of tension between the supervisor and worker was removed.
3. New social arrangements, in the form of department conferences and labor-management meetings, provided frequent feedback to the workers about their performance (for example, discussion of accidents, violations). Without feedback, it is difficult to change one's behavior.
4. New rewards were introduced. Workers were given more responsibility and more pay. The department conferences provided an opportunity for the management, union officials, or the research team to recognize and reinforce changes in behavior.
5. Greater group synergy or cohesiveness was created by greater opportunities for interaction within the team, greater opportunities for decision making, greater control over their environment, and more mechanisms to resolve intra- and intercrew differences (for example, department conferences).

If we return to the Hackman model (Figure 11.1) using the Rushton case as an example, we can trace through the effects of this type of change on group effectiveness. Changes in the structure of the group (that is, greater control, responsibility, opportunity to make decisions, and so on) directly affected the amount of effort expended and the level of group synergy. The problem-solving opportunities in the groups permitted selection of new task performance strategies. The changes in the organizational context (for example, pay system, meetings, and training) affected the level of effort and knowledge directed toward safety behaviors. Changes in group synergy probably directly impacted the level of effort and adherence to task performance strategies. Changes in these process criteria in turn should have improved group effectiveness criteria such as safety.

Understanding the theoretical mechanisms underlying self-managing teams is a precondition for understanding their effectiveness.

Do Self-Managing Teams Improve Effectiveness?

Determining the effectiveness of self-managing teams is no trivial task. Much has been written about the problems of assessing the effects of these organizational interventions (see Goodman, Ravlin, and Schminke, 1987). It is not appropriate to explore these issues in detail here, but it is necessary to specify some minimum conditions for answering the question, Do self-managing teams improve effectiveness? The minimal critical conditions for assessment include:

1. A theory that permits tracing through the effects of the group design, organizational context, and group variables on group effectiveness indicators.
2. Data on relevant outcome measures (for example, productivity).
3. Data over a sufficient time frame to assess the longer-term consequences of the change.
4. An analysis model and procedure that can separate out the effects of change and nonchange variables on the relevant effectiveness criteria.
5. Some comparison group to assess the incremental effects of the change.

While these criteria are quite straightforward and represent standard scientific approaches to assess effects of change, they are absent in most studies of organizational change. Indeed, in a comprehensive review of the organizational design literature, Macy and others (1986) document 1,100 naturalistic studies. Although 835 presented some empirical data, only 6 percent of these had both "longitudinal empirical data and the necessary sample sizes, means, [and] significance testing . . . to perform a reasonable meta-analysis of these studies." The data available reveal a bias toward collecting attitudinal versus hard productivity data. The point is this: there are not many well-designed studies that evaluate the impact of self-managing groups.

Our strategy is to look at two types of data: some of the individual firm studies of self-managing teams and some of the recent meta-analyses that include self-managing teams. These different types of data should provide some insights into whether self-managing teams improve organizational effectiveness.

Individual Firm Studies. The advantage of the individual studies is that we have a detailed picture of the nature of the self-managing teams and their effects on different criterion variables. We selected individual cases not for their empirical rigor but rather because they represent the range in data available on self-designing teams.

The Topeka plant was one of the earliest U.S. plants to introduce self-managing teams. Does it satisfy our five criteria for assessing effectiveness of the change program? (1) There is an underlying theory that guided the design; (2) data are reported on a number of outcome variables, such as commitment, productivity, employee satisfaction, and diffusion of the work innovations; (3) data, gathered by different investigators, are available from the time the plant went into operation in January 1971 until 1981; (4) there was no analysis model that separated out the effects of self-managing teams from other causal variables (however, qualitative evidence is presented to eliminate a few of the alternative explanations for the results); and (5) no explicit control groups were used, but the existing older manufacturing facility and a plant that came up after Topeka served as bases for comparison. Walton (1982) reports the following results on Topeka:

1. *Commitment.* In the initial years, commitment was very high, but it started declining gradually from 1974 onward. According to Walton, this decrease in commitment was due to a lack of correspondence between requirements of the technology and the available problem-solving capabilities. In other words, the plant "reached an operational steady-state in 1974 when the absence of a number of externally stimulated changes . . . helped perpetuate a skill surplus and promote a sense of stagnation" (p. 269). Topeka introduced new products and began expansion in 1978, and commitment started rising again.

2. *Productivity.* There was an increase in productivity every year except one. Product quality was high, and overhead costs were low.

3. *Worker attitudes.* Satisfaction expressed by the employees followed a trend similar to commitment. In the initial stages, employees expressed a number of positive attitudes, but this was followed by a period of decline. The decline, however, lasted only a short period before employee satisfaction started rising again.

4. *Indirect effects.* There were positive and negative consequences. On the positive side were higher pay and job security than were found in comparable organizations. On the negative side was friction between higher-level Topeka managers and support personnel at headquarters; as a result of this friction, all but one of the original Topeka managers left.

The Rushton Quality of Work Experiment is one of the most comprehensive evaluations of any of the work innovation projects initiated in the last ten years. In terms of our five criteria, there were (1) a theory to explain the effects of the intervention, (2) data on multiple outcome variables measured by different methods, (3) data over a three-year period, (4) an analysis model that separated out the effects of the intervention from alternative causal variables, and (5) the use of control groups. The results for the Rushton project fall into six categories.

1. *Attitudes.* Positive job attitudes in sections adopting self-managing teams increased during the first twenty months of the project. Miners felt that they had greater opportunities to make decisions, jobs offered more variety, the crews were more productive and innovative, and so on. After the self-designing team concept was extended to the whole mine, there was a gradual deterioration of attitudes toward the baseline levels of 1973. (This point will be discussed later.)
2. *Safety.* There was general agreement among union, management, and federal safety inspectors that safety improved in the mining sections adopting self-managing teams. Indicators included accidents, violations, and independent ratings of safety.
3. *Skills.* Job skills substantially increased in all sections using self-managing teams.
4. *Productivity.* The best estimate is that there was a slight positive effect on productivity on the order of 3 to 4 percent. These differences are not statistically significant, and we must be cautious about this estimate. The reader should note, however, that there are no other studies of self-managing teams that have provided as detailed econometric analyses of productivity effects.
5. *Benefits versus costs.* Analyses of the production benefits versus the investment costs of introducing and operating self-managing teams indicate that benefits slightly exceeded costs.
6. *Indirect effects.* There were positive and negative consequences. On the positive side, there were improvements in communication and coordination, and new talent was recognized and promoted among the employees. In general, there were qualitative improvements in labor-management relations. On the negative side, there were increased levels of stress for first-line and middle managers as well as greater conflict within the union.

The most recent comprehensive evaluation of self-managing teams appears in a study of a *confectionery plant* by Wall, Kemp,

Jackson, and Clegg (1986). In terms of our five criteria, this study uses
(1) a theory; (2) data on multiple outcome variables; (3) data at six,
eighteen, and thirty months after the start-up of the plant and the self-
managing group concept; (4) an analysis plan to separate out the
effects of alternative explanations; and (5) a comparison group. The
results from this study indicate:

1. *Job attitudes.* Workers in self-managing groups reported higher
    levels of work complexity and involvement than workers in
    conventional groups. In terms of leadership, the former group
    reported higher levels of consideration and tolerance for freedom.
2. *Job satisfaction and motivation.* Workers in self-managing
    groups exhibited greater levels of intrinsic satisfaction. Extrinsic
    job satisfaction increased for the short rather than the long term.
    There were no clear effects for intrinsic job motivation, organi-
    zational commitment, or mental health.
3. *Productivity.* The researchers were not able to systematically
    compare productivity measures across the self-managing and
    conventional groups. Qualitative data indicate that there were no
    differences between the two types of work performance.
4. *Turnover.* There was higher turnover in the self-managing
    groups. This was attributed to differences in labor markets
    between self-managing sites and conventional sites. However,
    there was also a higher number of disciplinary dismissals in the
    self-managing teams. One rationale for this difference is that the
    managers at the new plant were under pressure to produce.
    Because there were no supervisors in the self-managing teams to
    deal with or shield problem employees, and because the teams did
    not want to discipline, higher management, when apprised of the
    problem employee, dismissed that individual. This did not occur
    in conventional groups.
5. *Indirect effects.* There were positive and negative effects. On the
    positive side, employees at the self-managing site preferred that
    form of work to conventional work, preferred not having to use
    a time clock, and preferred their new working conditions. On the
    negative side, managers experienced more stress in operating this
    type of work system.

    What can we learn from these microstudies? First, self-
managing groups do change organizational effectiveness outcomes.
Second, the effects are greater on the attitude or quality of life
indicators than on business criteria such as productivity. This is in
part due to the fact that these variables are more frequently measured.

Third, the effects on attitudes are not uniform. In the Rushton study, attitudes varied over time with the viability of the self-managing groups. In Wall, Kemp, Jackson, and Clegg (1986), some attitude variables changed, while others did not. Fourth, the rigor of the research design affects the reported results. The more rigorously designed studies showed more modest or no results.

Meta-Analysis

Meta-analysis of organizational change studies represents another source of data about the effectiveness of self-managing teams. These data are different from the microstudies we presented, because they provide a quantitative way to assess the effects of variables over a large number of different studies. In addition, the data will position self-management against other forms of work innovation so that we can get some information on its relative effectiveness. Also, the meta-analysis will include more studies than were presented in our microanalysis, and there will be nonoverlapping studies, because we looked at studies that were not available at the time of the meta-analysis or did not fit the "rigor" required for the meta-analysis.

Macy and others (1986) conducted the most recent and most comprehensive meta-analysis of work innovation field projects. Their analysis is based on fifty-six innovation projects conducted between 1970 and 1981. The small number of studies reflects the lack of rigor in most of the 1,000 or more studies published in this area (Macy and others, 1986, pp. 15–16). Each study is coded in terms of the major action levels (for example, type of change strategy), moderator variables (for example, size of firm, use of consultants, type of control groups), and dependent variables (for example, quantity of output, absenteeism, QWL indicators). Findings from this analysis relevant to our investigation include the following. Self-managing groups have a positive impact on productivity. The impact on productivity is generally larger than for other types of interventions, and self-managing teams exhibit a negative association with general satisfaction and job satisfaction. This later finding seems quite at odds with the theory and results from other studies on self-managing groups. Basically, we expect a positive association, not about attitudes in general (see Wall, Kemp, Jackson, and Clegg, 1986) but about attitudes related to more variety, control, responsibility, and so on. Given that we expect positive associations with attitudes specific to the intervention, it is not clear whether the negative association with general satisfaction needs explanation. It is surprising that job satisfaction was not positively associated with self-managing teams.

A meta-analysis by Guzzo, Jette, and Katzell (1985) focused on the effectiveness of eleven intervention strategies at improving productivity. The basic findings are that large-scale socio-technical interventions have a greater-than-average impact on productivity and little impact on withdrawal criteria. Other results across all techniques indicated that the impacts of these interventions were moderated by organizational context (that is, effects were greater in small organizations) and by research designs (for example, effects of the intervention were weaker with more stringent controls) and when the measurement interval increased. A possible problem with this meta-analysis is that the substantive intervention we focused on within the analysis was labeled "large-scale socio-technical intervention," which is not identical to the concept of self-managing teams. However, self-managing teams have their origin in socio-technical theory, and the self-managing team interventions we presented were all large-scale interventions.

There have been other meta-analyses. Roitman and Gottschalk (1984) studied the effects of socio-technical design, job enrichment, and quality circles on productivity and QWL indicators. However, the small number of studies in their analysis precluded examining the separate effects of these three types of interventions. Pasmore, Francis, Haldeman, and Shani (1982) reviewed 134 socio-technical studies. However, their criteria with respect to methodological issues for selecting studies are quite general. For example, a case study in which the researcher simply stated that there was an increase in productivity and a study with data reported for experimental and control groups would be considered equivalent. The key figure in this review is the percentage of studies reporting improvements (regardless of size) in costs, productivity, and attitudes. While the reviewers' analysis points to positive effects of self-managing teams on productivity, attitudes, turnover, and so on, the variability of the quality of studies included in this review and the method of reporting results make this review nonequivalent to the other meta-analyses.

What have we learned about the effectiveness of self-managing teams? First, there are not many studies of sufficient quality to provide a robust answer to that question. The Macy and others (1986) meta-analysis identified fifty-six studies, Guzzo, Jette, and Katzell (1985) found eleven, and Roitman and Gottschalk (1984) found three. Second, in the available studies, the focus has been more on measuring attitude change than on productivity, cost, or other economic data. Third, the results are conditioned by the rigor in the design. The more rigorous the design, the harder it is to identify clear, significant results. For example, Wall, Kemp, Jackson, and Clegg (1986) have shown that the selection of control groups has an important bearing on confirming or disconfirming hypotheses about self-managing teams. Lastly, longitudinal designs are absent in many of these studies, yet the critical question is whether these studies are viable over time. Goodman (1979), Guzzo, Jette, and Katzell (1985), and Wall, Kemp, Jackson, and Clegg (1986) present evidence that the effectiveness of these interventions changes over time. Measuring at one point in time will not be informative. Unfortunately, we have found only three studies (Goodman, 1979; Walton, 1972; and Wall, Kemp, Jackson, and Clegg, 1986) that measure the effects of self-managing teams over time.

Given these constraints on our information, we can make the following observations from the micro- and meta-analyses of self-managing teams:

1. *Productivity.* The meta-analyses indicate that self-managing teams do increase productivity. There is also some indication that this type of intervention has a stronger impact on productivity than do other interventions. In the microanalysis, there were small positive effects of self-managing teams on productivity.

   The difference in productivity effects between self-managing teams and other interventions can be explained by the differences between the interventions. The self-managing team interventions typically are large-scale, multiple system interventions. One cannot compare that type of change with a team-building or a goal-setting intervention. The latter are one part of the multiple system intervention.

   The real magnitude of productivity effects is much harder to assess. There are very few studies (see Goodman, 1979) that use analytical techniques to separate out the effects of the intervention from other causal variables. To assess productivity, we need to know what factors (for example, technological) affect productivity independent of the intervention, how these factors affect productivity, how the intervention affects productivity, and whether the intervention affects these other causal variables and then indirectly affects productivity. One cannot answer these by simply comparing productivity changes against a baseline. Our best judgment, looking across all the studies, is that self-managing groups have a modest impact on productivity.

2. *Attitudes.* Self-managing teams do change attitudes of team members, but the change is in attitudes specific to the intervention. Thus we would expect to see changes in beliefs and attitudes about responsibility, control, and job variety but not about general satisfaction or general commitment to the organization.

Indeed, the studies that measured attitudes over time found changes in these specific attitudes rather than attitudes in general.
3.   *Withdrawal.* There are no clear trends in the effects of self-managing teams on absenteeism or turnover.
4.   *Safety.* There are data (Walton, 1972; Goodman, 1979) indicating that self-managing groups can improve safety.
5.   *Cost-benefit analysis.* Unfortunately, there has been very little work (see Goodman, 1979) in this area. Yet it is important, because we need to know more than whether self-managing groups increase productivity. It could be possible, for example, that although productivity might increase, the costs of obtaining that increase might be greater than the productivity benefits. The real benefit, however, of doing this analysis is not the results; rather, the analysis forces the researcher to think broadly of the overall effectiveness of the intervention.

Could Self-Designing Groups Be More Effective?

While we have indicated some of the positive consequences of self-designing teams, the results are probably not as robust as we might have expected. Because this book is about productivity, let us explore some explanations of why self-managing teams have not had major impacts on increasing productivity. If the reader disagrees with the above assumption, the explanations can be thought of in terms of how we can make self-managing teams more effective in regard to productivity. There are four important explanations.

Joint Optimization of the Social and Technical Systems. Self-managing teams are the product of socio-technical theory (Pasmore, Francis, Haldeman, and Shani, 1982). The basic tenet of that theory is the joint optimization of the social and technical systems. This principle claims that organizational effectiveness will be enhanced if management designs both the social and technical systems jointly in some optimum way rather than focusing solely on the technical or the social system. What is interesting is that the thrust of most of the self-managing team interventions has been on modifying the social system to fit the technological system, not on jointly optimizing both the social and technical systems. This point of view is not new. Kelly (1978) and Roitman and Gottschalk (1984) note that the self-managing team interventions are primarily changes in the social system to fit the existing technical system. Our argument is that if socio-technical theorists were really concerned with joint optimization, productivity effects might be more pronounced. In other words, if the multiple system interventions using self-managing teams grappled more with alternative ways to change the technical system, we might see more dramatic changes in productivity.

Linkages and Diffuse Linkages. In the simplest form, the basic theoretical rationale for self-managing teams is that if workers are given control over a whole task, they will be more motivated to perform that task. Greater opportunities for responsibility, variety, control, and so on will motivate workers to work harder and smarter. But to work harder and smarter on what? The instrumental behaviors that link effort and knowledge to the performance criteria are not clearly identified. Contrast self-managing teams with a Scanlon Plan. The latter type of intervention provides workers greater opportunities for control, participation, and responsibility. But these changes in potential motivation and knowledge are *structurally linked* to productivity improvement through a bonus plan and a committee system. There is no such linkage in self-managing groups among the design change, the motivation and knowledge change, and specific criteria such as productivity. So it is not surprising that we do not see robust productivity changes. To create these changes, one needs to ask, What are the instrumental behaviors that will increase productivity in a given technological system? Then how do we channel the increased effort and knowledge from self-managing teams to these instrumental behaviors?

Cohesiveness. A basic assumption underlying self-managing teams is that the design will enhance the level of group cohesiveness, which in turn will increase group performance and satisfaction. While the popular view is that cohesiveness positively relates to group performance, the empirical literature does not support this belief (Goodman, Ravlin, and Schminke, 1987). Indeed, a careful review of the early theory on cohesiveness (Seashore, 1954) shows that the links between cohesiveness and performance are problematic. Remember, for cohesiveness to affect performance, visible standards about performance must be available, deviant behavior must be observed, the group must induce pressure, the deviant worker must conform, and the conforming behavior must be instrumental for performance. Our argument (see Goodman, Ravlin, and Schminke, 1987) is that these five conditions are not necessarily inherent in self-managing teams. An illustration from the Rushton case may be helpful. In that intervention, the self-managing teams were very cohesive. However, there were no agreed-upon standards. There was deviant behavior that was punished and changed, but the behavior had to do with whether team members would rotate jobs, not whether production standards would be achieved.

The basic argument is that links between self-managing teams, cohesiveness, and productivity are not inherently strong. Such links could be purposefully designed into these interventions, but that is not typically the case.

Ceiling Effects. In all the studies we have reviewed on self-managing teams, there has been little consideration given to optimum settings for these interventions. It is unlikely that self-managing teams would be effective in all settings. Basically, they create an opportunity for new releases of energy, skill, and problem-solving activity. If the technology or organizational context constrains the use of these three factors, there will be a ceiling effect on the impact of self-managing teams on productivity. For example, in the Rushton case, variation in productivity was greatly affected by the quality of the machinery and physical conditions (for example, good roof). These factors were exogenous to the variables in the intervention. Not only did these factors account for substantial variation in productivity, they also constrained the opportunity of the self-managing teams to affect productivity. The point is this: one reason we may not find major impacts of self-managing teams on productivity is that the initiators of these changes may not have selected the optimum sites in terms of technological and organizational constraints.

Linking Groups and Productivity: Some General Strategies

In this section, we want to review some general strategies for linking groups and productivity. We move from focusing exclusively on self-managing teams to examining a set of strategic issues for designing more productive work groups. Our orientation is to improve both theory and practice about designing effective work groups.

Theory Specification. We will not be able to design more productive or effective groups unless the level of theoretical specification is improved. This point was made earlier, in the discussion of the results of self-managing teams. The basic theoretical assumption underlying self-managing teams is that changing levels of control, responsibility, involvement, task, variety, and so on would change levels of motivation and knowledge, which in turn would affect productivity. That assumption is much too general and does not inform us about the links or instrumental behaviors for translating effort into increased performance. In a review of the current models of group performance, Goodman, Ravlin, and Argote (1986) argue that most of the models are too general, do not specify functional relationships, and in general are not in a form to confirm or disconfirm. If we want to understand how to design more productive groups, we need to move to finer-grained models that link group design and productivity changes. The Hackman model presented earlier in this chapter provides a good start. It outlines the major classes of variables that one should consider in examining or changing group effectiveness. In its current form, that model would identify the general classes of variables across all groups.

Goodman, Ravlin, and Argote (1986) argue that one has to move from this type of heuristic model to a specification of the role of technology in order to develop a viable model of performance. *Technology* refers to a system of four components—equipment, materials, physical environment, and programs—involved in acting on and/or changing an object from one state to another. These components provide the constraints and patterns for group activity. To develop a viable model of group performance, we need to know in detail how the technological system works. The model that links group design and productivity in a coal mine is not the same model we would use to estimate productivity variations in teams in the auto industry. A major problem in most models of group performance is the failure to specify the role of technology.

The importance of technological specification can be pointed out in another way. One critical dimension in the Hackman model is the concept of appropriate task performance strategies. He argues that increasing levels of effort or knowledge will not impact effectiveness unless the appropriate task strategies are implemented. Where do these strategies come from? How can we learn what the appropriate strategies are? The major way to identify these strategies is to develop an intimate knowledge of the technology. Inherent characteristics of the technology will indicate to a large extent the appropriate task strategies.

The following is a brief illustration of how to move to a more technological specification. Coal mining is done in crews of from eight to ten workers. The basic production process is the transportation of coal from the face to an end user (utility company). There are three major pieces of equipment (continuous miner, bolter, cars). The work flow is highly interdependent, physical conditions are important, and equipment outside of the crew (for example, conveyor belts) affect performance. The question we want to ask is, How does the technological system affect performance independent of the organizational context, group synergy, or the structure and composition of the group? We answer that question by writing down a model that identifies how the critical components of the technological system should affect productivity. Table 11.1 lists the major variables in the technological system for explaining variation in coal-mining crew

Table 11.1. Technological Model for Coal Mining.

Delay Times For:	Expected Sign	Magnitude
Continuous miner	–	***
Car	–	*
Bolter direct	–	***
Bolter indirect	–	*
Inside equipment	–	**
Outside equipment	–	**
Number of cars	–	*
Seam height	+	*
Physical conditions	+	**

productivity, expected signs of the variables, and expected magnitude of the coefficients. The table or model says that machine down time is a major predictor of between-crew performance. The amount of down time is influenced by the type of machine, age, time since last overhaul, and so on—factors that tend to be exogenous to the group. Also, the number of cars, seam height, and physical conditions all explain between-crew productivity.

Why develop such a model? Because it forces us to think about the critical parts of the technological system. This is a very different way to model group performance than is found in the literature. In mining, the continuous miner is the critical piece of equipment. Down time in the continuous miner has a more important impact on productivity than car down time. The implication is that the quality of the continuous miner, the maintenance strategy for this machine, the manning of this position, and so on will have a major impact on production. If we had to guess, the quality of machine and maintenance program would probably dominate the effect of the skill of the operator, given that operators have to be certified (ensuring at least minimum skill) to operate the equipment.

The purpose of this illustration is the following: (1) If we want to increase productivity, we need a thorough understanding of the technological system. (2) There are critical points or levers (Goodman, 1986) in any technological system that have greater impacts on productivity than other factors in the production system. Some of these are within the group's control; others are not. (3) If we really want to affect productivity, we need to focus on changing the levers. If down time on the continuous miner is a major key in coal mining, we can concentrate on developing more effective maintenance programs (typically exogenous to the group) or focusing group efforts and knowledge on increasing "up time" on the continuous miner. This is a much more specific strategy than saying group design will lead workers to work harder or smarter. The critical levers need to be identified and effort and knowledge focused on enhancing these specific levers. Different technologies require different models and levers.

The Intersection of Human, Organizational, and Technological Variables. A review of most models of work-group performance (see Goodman, Ravlin, and Argote, 1986) will show that the majority of variables concern some aspect of human conditions (for example, knowledge, skill, composition) and organizational conditions (for example, reward system, information system). In addition, most models assume that the antecedents of group performance (reward system, group structure, technology) affect group performance through their impact on group process. These positions are not surprising, given that current research on groups in organizations has been influenced by the strong focus on process in laboratory studies of group performance. Also, because most of the work is done by psychologists, we would expect that more attention would be given to the human and organizational variables. The issue is whether this major emphasis on human and organizational variables in group performance models is justifiable.

One alternative position is that the human and organizational factors play only a minor role in influencing performance in groups. Variables in the technological system are more important in affecting productivity variation and in providing constraints on the role of human and organizational variables. The quality of the equipment, the inventory policy, and the quality of exogenous support services really determine why some groups are more effective than others. For example, in our research on coal-mining crews, we estimated the effect of the technological system (Table 11.1) and a simple labor component (number of workers) on crew productivity. This type of model explains a reasonable amount of variation in production ($R^2 = .60$) over a variety of different companies. When we began to differentiate the labor component in terms of "human" variables, such as absenteeism and familiarity with the job, these did contribute significantly to explaining production variance, but only to a minor degree. The point is this: in this technological system, the technology variables really have a major impact. The same issue was true in the Rushton case, discussed earlier. Let us assume that the self-designing team intervention was put in place successfully. The crews involved in the experiment became powerful cohesive groups. But still in this context, the factors that really impacted crew productivity were outside the control of the groups. Groups with better equipment and in better conditions produced more. There was not much room for the intervention to make a significant and lasting impact on productivity. The technological systems provided major constraints.

The issue is not that we live in a technologically deterministic world. The real issue is *not to assume that human and organizational factors do make a difference.* It would probably be better *to assume they do not make any difference and then look for the points where they do.*

What are the factors that should make a difference in determining the intersection between technological and human variables?

1.   The amount of discretion in the transformation process.
2.   Whether the technology makes performance sensitive to variations in human effort, skill, and so on.
3.   Whether the redesign of the technological system is controlled by the group.
4.   Whether there are major exogenous factors affecting performance.

Let us illustrate how these factors would fit into the Rushton case. In that example, there were major exogenous factors that affected performance (for example, physical conditions). The redesign of the technology was not controlled by the group. The technology was more sensitive to the skills of the continuous miner operator and the mechanics than to levels of effort. There is little discretion during regular operations; but there is discretion during down time, in the transformation process. The picture then is not one where human and organizational variables can make a big difference. The key "window" focuses on the intersection between continuous miner, its operator, and the mechanic. Also, during down time, groups have considerable discretion to do nothing, to do indirect production activities that need to be done later, or to work on the down-time problem. The point is this: that these two intersections are the key ways human and organizational factors can make a difference in this particular technological system.

From this example, we can also see that the effects of antecedent factors are not simply mediated through group process. Factors such as technology directly affect group performance and group process. Group process, in turn, can modify technological components (for example, through working effectively during down time), which in turn will affect performance.

The basic idea in this argument is that we should move away from the view that human factors and group process are the primary tools to understanding group productivity. Rather, one should begin with the four criteria (above) to determine (1) the degree to which human factors and group process may make a difference and (2) the specific *intersections* where this difference will be important. This truly would be an important contribution to theory and practice.

Creating Long-Term Change. A major challenge in designing more effective work groups is not to find some optimum design configuration but rather to create change where the effects are viable over time. If we go back to our review of the literature on self-managing groups, we can find examples of successes, but we can also find examples where these successes were not sustained over time. This issue is not unique to designing groups. A major theme in all the work innovation projects over the last decade is the problem of sustaining change over time (Goodman and Dean, 1982). Thus the problem of sustaining change in work design projects is of critical importance.

The reasons for the failure of self-managing teams and other new work organization designs over time include withdrawal of initial sponsor, insufficient training, stress and burnout of first-line and middle managers, lack of sharing of financial gains, lack of top management commitment, threats to union viability, failure to diffuse projects, unrealistic expectations of benefits, and declining economic conditions (see Trist and O'Dwyer, 1982; Walton, 1972; Goodman and Dean, 1982). There has rarely been one factor that affected viability of these work redesign efforts; rather, it is a combination of these factors. The dilemma we face is that we have knowledge of how to design groups, and to make them more effective, yet at the same time there are very few examples of group design efforts that have stood the test of time. The research and practical challenge is to better understand the process of sustaining long-term change. One problem with the existing literature is that it contains a long listing of variables that explain reasons for long-term viability. A more parsimonious approach is necessary.

A model by Goodman and Dean (1982) describes five processes that are critical for sustaining long-term change.

1. *Socialization.* The process by which people continually learn and adapt to new group redesign projects is critical for long-term viability. The problem in early self-managing group work was that training was oriented primarily to "starting up the project" as opposed to teaching what was necessary to help the project evolve over time.

2. *Commitment.* The process by which all the relevant actors commit to and support new institutions, such as self-managing teams, is also critical. A problem with many of the group design projects we reviewed was that there was only partial commitment and the commitment process was not sustained over time.

3. *Reward allocations.* The attractiveness of the reward system is also important. Over time, we would expect certain rewards to be less attractive and new types of rewards to be initiated. A problem in many of the work design efforts was that the reward system was not recalibrated over time.

4. *Diffusion.* The spread of new institutions (for example, self-managing teams) to other parts of the organization is also critical. The structure of these new forms of work organization requires legitimation and infrastructure to support these new activities. Diffusion helps fulfill these two requirements.

5. *Sensing and recalibration.* The new group designs are by nature dynamic. The structure of a self-managing team should evolve over time. A problem with some of the early self-managing team projects was that there was no mechanism to feed back information on the change process or to redesign the group. Unless some sensing and recalibration mechanism exists, it is unlikely that the change activity will persist.

In addition to these five processes, a set of criteria are presented by Goodman and Dean to measure the degree of institutionalization of the change effort.

While this and other (see Walton, 1972) theoretical perspectives are available for understanding long-run change in group structure, none of these frameworks has been empirically tested. One important avenue is to begin testing these frameworks. The reason for doing this is not simply to enhance theory but also to develop principles that will help us introduce long-term effective change in work groups.

Conclusion

In this chapter, we have presented the concept of self-managing teams, delineated the underlying theory, summarized the research findings, and identified factors that facilitate or inhibit the effectiveness of self-managing groups.

The basic findings are that self-managing groups positively affect productivity, but the magnitude of effect is not well known. There are not a large number of well-designed evaluations of self-managing teams. In terms of attitudes, most studies report effects on specific attitudes rather than on general attitudes about work (for example, job satisfaction). The data on withdrawal behaviors are not as robust, and there has been only one comprehensive cost-benefit analysis. Overall, the effects of self-management productivity are positive and stronger than those of alternative interventions (see our earlier discussion of meta-analysis).

Self-managing teams can be more effective if the following four steps are taken. First, the theoretical linkages in self-managing team theory need to be more specific. We have argued that changing work-group design to increase knowledge and effort will not increase productivity unless the linkages between effort, knowledge, and productivity are delineated. Most theoretical statements about self-managing teams do not specify these linkages. The key to finding the linkages comes from a thorough understanding of the technology, because the linkages reflect the unique aspects of a given technology.

Second, most self-managing team interventions focus primarily on the social system. Innovations in technology would provide another strategy for self-managing teams to increase productivity.

Third, more attention should be given to the selection of sites for self-managing team interventions. Sites where technology provides greater amounts of discretion to the group and where performance is sensitive to variations in human effort and skill will have higher probabilities of success.

Fourth, in designing self-managing teams, more attention needs to be focused on long-term viability. There is evidence that some self-managing interventions, while having initial success, do not persist over time. Long-run viability needs to be considered early in the design of these groups.

Self-managing teams represent a relatively new form of work design. There are not a lot of well-documented cases; there is much to be learned. The results of this design are promising: self-managing teams do increase productivity. The potential effectiveness of self-managing teams has not yet been realized, however. Some of the ideas in this chapter represent strategies for improving the effectiveness of self-managing teams.

An appropriate way to conclude this discussion is to speculate on the development of self-managing teams in the future. We think there will be a slow but increasing proliferation of self-managing teams. We use the word *slow* because self-managing teams are very complex organizational interventions that need to be congruent with organizational values and technology, and they are therefore constrained in terms of their application.

There will be increasing use of self-managing teams for several reasons. First, the cultural trend toward more participation and employee involvement will continue. Second, many organizations that have experimented with less complex forms of groups, such as quality circles, will begin to explore new forms of group design. The argument is that if an organization is committed to employee involvement efforts, there are evolutionary forces that move it from simpler to more complex interventions (that is, self-managing teams). New technology will be another factor contributing to the growth of self-managing teams. For example, the development and spread of computer-integrated manufacturing is changing the nature of work. In this type of technology, there are major forces toward greater integration, more flexibility, and faster reaction time. These attributes are congruent with and should encourage the development of self-managing teams across traditional boundaries. Most of the current teams generally fall within a particular work boundary rather than integrating across boundaries.

With the growth of self-managing teams, there will be changes in form. For example, most self-managing teams now are in a production setting at the level of the employee. We expect more growth of these teams in nonmanufacturing environments. Also, we expect these teams to be found more frequently at the managerial level. For example, as new technology blurs traditional organizational boundaries, we would expect teams to be organized by areas. The areas would be made up of autonomous managerial teams linked to more traditional, shop-floor self-managing teams.

We also expect greater use of self-managing teams in service or support settings. Airline crews, sales teams, and maintenance teams seem ripe for this self-management intervention. For example, sales teams involved in technologically advanced products require expertise from a variety of areas. Given the nature of the interdependent task and the professional level of the participants, self-managing teams seem a natural intervention (see Gladstein, 1984).

The increasing power of information systems is creating the option for new organizational forms that should be attractive for self-managing teams. For example, we have observed the emergence of satellite organizations. The satellite organization is made up of a small core organization, where the main information systems reside, and a series of autonomous production organizations. Each of these satellites, which produces a part of the product, is independently owned but linked contractually and through information systems to the core organization. This particular form of organization, which is made up of linked *autonomous* units, seems to be a natural setting for the emergence of new self-managing teams.

Other changes in technology should also influence the form of self-managing teams. Telecommuting (Hughson and Goodman, 1986), for example, may change the form of self-managing teams. In this chapter, all of the self-managing teams are face-to-face groups. Telecommuting permits work outside of the traditional boundaries. We expect that, as telecommuting continues to grow, we may see the development of self-managing teams whose members are linked through computer networks.

We can conclude with the following observations: self-managing teams are in place in the United States and other industrialized countries. There are strong forces—from cultural values about participation, the evolution of new forms of employee involvement, and changes in new technology—that will support the growth and redesign of self-managing teams.

References

Coch, L., and French, J. R. P., Jr. "Overcoming Resistance to Change." In D.. Cartwright and A. Zander (eds.), *Group Dynamics: Research and Theory*. (3rd ed.) New York: Harper & Row, 1968.

Gladstein, D. L. "Groups in Context: A Model of Task Group Effectiveness." *Administrative Science Quarterly*, 1984, *29* (4), 499–517.

Goodman, P. S. *Assessing Organizational Change: The Rushton Quality of Work Experiment*. New York: Wiley-Interscience, 1979.

Goodman, P. S. "Impact of Task and Technology on Group Performance." In P. S. Goodman (ed.), *Designing Effective Work Groups*. San Francisco: Jossey-Bass, 1986.

Goodman, P. S., and Dean, J. W., Jr. "Creating Long-Term Organizational Change." In P. S. Goodman (ed.), *Change in Organizations: New Perspectives on Theory, Research, and Practice*. San Francisco: Jossey-Bass, 1982.

Goodman, P. S., Ravlin, E. C., and Argote, L. "Current Thinking About Groups: Setting the Stage for New Ideas." In P. S. Goodman (ed.), *Designing Effective Work Groups*. San Francisco: Jossey-Bass, 1986.

Goodman, P. S., Ravlin, E. C., and Schminke, M. "Understanding Groups in Organizations." In B. M.. Staw and L. L. Cummings (eds.), *Research in Organizational Behavior*. Vol. 9. Greenwich, Conn.: JAI Press, 1987.

Guzzo, R. A., Jette, R. D., and Katzell, R. A. "The Effects of Psychologically Based Intervention Programs on Work Productivity: A Meta-Analysis." *Personnel Psychology*, 1985, *38*, 275–291.

Hackman, J. R. "The Design of Work Teams." In J. W. Lorsch (ed.), *The Handbook of Organizational Behavior.* Englewood Cliffs, N.J.: Prentice-Hall, 1982.

Hughson, T. L., and Goodman, P. S. "Telecommuting: Corporate Practices and Benefits." *National Productivity Review,* Autumn, 1986, pp. 315–324.

Kelly, J. E. "A Reappraisal of Socio-Technical Systems Theory." *Human Relations,* 1978, *31,* 1069–1099.

Lawler, E. E., III. "Increasing Worker Involvement to Enhance Organizational Effectiveness." In P. S. Goodman (ed.), *Change in Organizations: New Perspectives on Theory, Research, and Practice.* San Francisco: Jossey-Bass, 1982.

Lewin, K. *Field Theory in Social Science.* New York: Harper & Row, 1951.

Locke, E. A., and Schweiger, D. M. "Participation in Decision-Making: One More Look." *Research in Organizational Behavior.* Vol. 1. Greenwich, Conn.: JAI Press, 1979.

Macy, B. A., and others. "Meta-Analysis of United States Empirical Organizational Change and Work Innovation Field Experiments: Methodology and Preliminary Results." Paper presented at the 46th annual meeting of the National Academy of Management, Chicago, Aug. 1986.

Maier, N. R. F. *Problem-Solving Discussion and Conferences: Leadership Methods and Skills.* New York: McGraw-Hill, 1963.

Pasmore, W., Francis, C., Haldeman, J., and Shani, A. "Sociotechnical Systems: A North American Reflection on Empirical Studies of the Seventies." *Human Relations,* 1982, *35,* 1179–1204.

Roitman, D., and Gottschalk, R. "Job Enrichment, Socio-Technical Design, and Quality Circles: Effects on Productivity and Quality of Work Life." Unpublished manuscript, Michigan State University, 1984.

Seashore, S. E. *Group Cohesiveness in the Industrial Work Group.* Ann Arbor, Mich.: Institute for Social Research, 1954.

Trist, E. L. *Organizational Choice.* London: Tavistock Publications, 1963.

Trist, E. L., and Bamforth, K. W. "Some Social and Psychological Consequences of Long-Wall Methods of Coal Getting." *Human Relations,* 1951, *4,* 3–38.

Trist, E., and O'Dwyer, C. "The Limits of Laissez-Faire as a Socio-Technical Change Strategy." In R. Zager and M. P. Rosow (eds.), *The Innovative Organization: Productivity Programs in Action.* Elmsford, N.Y.: Pergamon Press, 1982.

Vroom, V. *Work and Motivation.* New York: Wiley, 1964.

Wall, T. D., Kemp, N. J., Jackson, P. R., and Clegg, C. W. "Outcomes of Autonomous Workshops: A Long-Term Field Experiment." *Academy of Management Journal,* 1986, *29,* 280–304.

Walton, R. E. "How to Counter Alienation in the Plant." *Harvard Business Review,* Nov./Dec. 1972, pp. 70–81.

Walton, R. E. "The Topeka Work System: Optimistic Visions, Pessimistic Hypotheses, and Reality." In R. Zager and M. P. Rosow (eds.), *The Innovative Organization: Productivity Programs in Action.* Elmsford, N.Y.: Pergamon Press, 1982.

12

ЄЭЄЭЄЭЄЭЄЭЄЭЄЭЄЭЄЭ

New Developments in Profit Sharing, Gainsharing, and Employee Ownership

Tove Helland Hammer

While employers are searching for new ways to increase worker productivity and reduce labor costs, some old established programs designed to do the same are being rediscovered. Profit-sharing, gainsharing, and employee stock ownership plans, which have been around in modest numbers in small pockets of industry for decades, are enjoying a revival. In this chapter, I will describe the programs, the reasons why they have become so popular, and what is known about their effects on labor productivity and organizational effectiveness.

The conceptual anchor for the chapter is the labor exchange, or the trade between worker and employer of pay (wages and benefits) for effort. (The word *worker* means the same thing as *employee*—that is, someone who trades labor for wages. It includes blue-collar and white-collar workers, professionals, and low-level management. While, strictly speaking, higher-level managers and corporate officers are also employees, I consider members of those groups to be the employer's representatives for the purposes of this chapter and do not include them on the *worker* or *employee* side when I discuss the employee-employer relationship or the labor-management relationship.) I argue that worker productivity is a political issue, a major source of conflict between labor and management. Because so much of the research literature on motivation, productivity, and organizational effectiveness in industrial psychology treats worker effort as a

I want to acknowledge extensive comments from George Milkovich on an earlier version of this chapter.

politically neutral topic (a perspective that I believe is incorrect), I begin with an analysis of the labor exchange to demonstrate how and why it is conflictive. The programs of gainsharing and ownership will be analyzed within the context of the labor exchange, with emphasis on how they redefine its terms.

The first two sections of the chapter contain the analysis of the labor exchange, or the wage and effort bargain (see Begin and Beal, 1985), and a discussion of recent changes in this bargain. This is followed in the third section by descriptions and evaluations of profit-sharing, gainsharing, and employee stock ownership programs. In the fourth section, I review gainsharing research and present a model that shows how the components of gainsharing programs influence productivity outcomes. The fifth section contains descriptions of different employee ownership forms and the empirical research evaluating them. In the last section, I will discuss the validity of the assumptions underlying the use of gainsharing and worker ownership plans and return to their importance in the current efforts of employees and employers to redefine the wage and effort bargain.

The Labor Exchange and Worker Productivity

The commodity being traded in the labor exchange is labor power—that is, an individual's ability and willingness to exert effort toward the tasks specified by the employer. If we assume that both parties want to maximize their own benefits in the exchange, the question for the employer is how to extract the maximum amount of labor (effort) from the purchased labor power, and for the worker, how to get the best price for the effort he or she is willing to expend. The labor exchange is the result of a bargain between employee and employer. It need not be a formal contract, or collectively bargained. In most employment situations, however, it is a formal agreement between an individual worker and an employer that specifies the wages and fringe benefits to be paid by the employer for time worked or amounts produced. The agreement usually does not contain provisions about exact amounts of effort expected from the employee.

In general, it is easier to specify wages and fringe benefits than it is to quantify worker effort. Therefore, a large part of official bargaining consists of operationally defining worker effort to have it match the purchase price. In the absence of formal collective bargaining, the terms of the labor exchange are shaped by a series of formal and informal events around job structures and performance standards (including negotiations, past practices, speedups, slow-downs, motivation programs, reward systems, and so on), in which workers and employers try to maximize their respective outcomes and minimize the extent of exploitation of one group by the other.

We do not need to use a Marxian analysis of labor under capitalism to be able to see that the labor exchange is a primary source of labor-management conflict. However, for Marxian theorists, this conflict is inevitable, a result of fundamentally opposed interests of employers and employees at the wage nexus (see, for example, Bachrach and Baratz, 1970; Bendix, 1965; Lukes, 1974). Simplified, their arguments are as follows: employers have a direct economic interest in reducing the purchase price of labor to maintain or increase the amount of profits (capital maximization). Workers, on the other hand, have a direct interest in raising the price of labor, a goal that can be a threat to the employers' profits (especially if the increased labor costs cannot be passed on to consumers). Employees certainly have no interest in exerting extra effort beyond that which they perceive has been fairly bought, because that would be noncompensated, or surplus, labor. Therefore, the two interest groups are locked in a struggle for control over pay and performance, and they use a variety of overt and covert power tactics to gain advantage. From the radical perspective, employer programs to improve worker productivity are part of an arsenal of tactics used to alter the terms of the labor exchange by extracting more surplus value from labor. Because labor is always at a power disadvantage in this model, in the long run workers are unable to withstand the exploitation.

There are, of course, other schools of thought on the nature of employee-employer relations. Fox (1973) includes, in addition to the radical view, the pluralist and unitarist perspectives in his theory of conflict.

Pluralists hold a more moderate view of labor-management conflict. They see organizations as consisting of a variety of groups and coalitions, some with divergent interests, some with common goals. While there is conflict, it can give way to collaboration and compromise when it is regulated through bargaining and negotiations that follow established rules. For example, pluralists recognize the potential for conflict caused when employers, believing that there are vast untapped reserves of worker productivity in the pool of labor power they have purchased, start up QWL programs, quality circles, or work redesign to release these reserves, without first adjusting wages and benefits. But the pluralists believe that equity can be restored through accepted conflict management techniques and through bargaining. The pluralist view requires more of a power balance between the bargaining parties.

In contrast, the unitarists assume a true communality of interests between employers and employees, or management and labor. They consider labor-management conflict over anything connected with work in organizations, including the labor exchange, as undesirable and avoidable. To unitarists, the employer's goals are also the workers' goals, and therefore there is no need to worry about power differentials. In an open, trusting relationship based on communality of interests, there will be no exploitation for private gain.

For those of the radical and pluralist perspectives, worker productivity is not a politically neutral issue. It is anchored in interest-group differences, power differentials, and conflict. For the unitarists, productivity carries no political message. Of course, for those with opposing views, the position that productivity is a neutral subject is in itself a political statement, a message that serves the interests of the power holders—namely, the employers and their representatives, the management (Baritz, 1960).

The benefit of gainsharing, profit-sharing, and worker stock ownership plans is the recognition inherent in them of the trade between pay and performance. Their basic premise is that employees' contributions to organizational effectiveness beyond accepted and established levels will be returned to them in the form of money, either as a bonus in addition to fixed wages and benefits, or as stock dividends. This promise also says that other positive outcomes for the employee that can follow from the introduction of the plans—such as increased job satisfaction and intrinsic motivation from participation in decision making, feelings of self-worth as a capital owner, and so on—are not substitutes for pay in the redefined labor exchange.

The Search for New Wage and Effort Bargains

The growing popularity of gainsharing and profit-sharing plans, and to some extent worker stock ownership plans, has come primarily from the real or perceived needs of employers to control labor costs and increase productivity.

Unions, accustomed to a quarter century (1950–1975) of wage and benefit gains, were faced with threats of plant closures and movement of jobs to nonunionized locations or overseas and had to negotiate wage freezes or actual cuts. But in a large number of these cases, the unions traded economic concessions for stock ownership (particularly in the airlines) and the chance to share in their employer's future profits. And in trade for relaxation of job-control rules, introduction of productivity improvement programs, and reductions in wages and benefits from concessions came gain- and profit-sharing plans. Gainsharing, in particular, has been introduced into union contracts to allow workers to make whole what was lost in wage concessions (McKersie, 1986).

Concession bargaining, worker stock ownership, labor cost containment, and productivity improvement programs have not occurred only among economically pressed employers. Examples of novel concession bargaining can be found in the airline industry, where both financially strong and weak carriers have negotiated two-tier wage structures with their unions to reduce labor costs (Cappelli, 1985; Walsh, 1987). Innovative and successful gain- and profit-sharing programs and employee stock ownership plans are part of the compensation package in many financially healthy companies (for examples, see Lawler, 1986; Levering, Moskowitz, and Katz, 1984; Rosen, Klein, and Young, 1986).

While some of the spread of worker ownership is due to economic constraints on employers, it has resulted primarily from employers taking advantage of recently enacted tax laws designed to encourage widespread share ownership. A series of changes in the tax laws, beginning in 1974 and continuing through 1984, have given companies strong financial incentives to adopt a particular form of worker ownership, the employee stock ownership plan (ESOP).

In a recent study of the transformation taking place in American industrial relations, Kochan, Katz, and McKersie (1986) found that programs such as gainsharing and employee stock ownership are part of a new system of work organization and worker involvement, where the emphasis is on the use of work teams, joint labor-management problem solving, delegation of management tasks to workers, and so on. In these "high-involvement systems" (Lawler, 1986; McKersie, 1986), performance-based pay and company stock distributions are not isolated programs introduced into the organization to improve effectiveness. They are part of a whole package of workplace redesign that has changed work processes and authority structures as well as the equations for calculating wages and benefits. Kochan, Katz, and McKersie (1986) argue that the redesigned workplace is part of a human resource management strategy that developed slowly in nonunionized firms during the 1960s, grew visibly and rapidly during the 1970s, and spread to the unionized sector of the economy in the early 1980s.

The transformation of industrial relations from a rigid, rule-based, "job-control unionism" system, with industry-wide pattern bargaining aimed at taking labor costs out of competition, to a system with company-based negotiations, flexible job classifications, and managerial choice in the design of work and compensation packages, has given the employer much more flexibility in shaping the wage and effort bargain. The result is less standardization across firms in both work process designs and wage and benefits programs. As we shall see, gainsharing, profit-sharing, and employee stock ownership plans can be tailored to fit the ideosyncratic needs of individual organizations, and they come in a wide variety of forms.

In summary, what gainsharing, profit-sharing, and stock ownership plans do is to translate into action the idea that employees who contribute effort to productivity gains and company profits over and above expected (standard) performance levels will be compensated for it. Turned around, this means that the incentive of economic gain should act to release the extra effort necessary to generate it and create sufficient surplus value for employees and employers to share. These are simple statements. However, the programs themselves are not simple. They often have multiple components and multiple causes, each of which can have separate effects on worker motivation and productivity. The psychological processes that translate conditions of employment and work experiences into behaviors and attitudes are complex, and the contingent relationships between the programs, worker effort, and financial gains are not always clear. And, despite their implied statement about both employees' and employers' rights to share in profits generated by collaboration, the programs are not always conflict-free.

So far, there has been very little theoretical or empirical work done to define the nature of the relationships between the programs and their outcomes. It is an open field for the application of motivation and group process theories and organizational change models.

Relationships Between Profit Sharing, Gainsharing, and Employee Ownership

A common goal of profit sharing, gainsharing, and employee stock ownership is greater organizational profits (or effectiveness). The plans differ on the means to accomplish this, and on whether, in practice, they are work incentive programs or worker benefit plans. They share the basic assumption that workers have untapped energy and talent that will be released in the employer's service once contingencies between the release and personal economic gain are established. This assumption is the foundation for a number of organizational intervention and change programs that require labor-management collaboration (Brett and Hammer, 1982). By and large, it is untested, except for inferences made about its veracity when such programs succeed.

Profit Sharing. This is by far the oldest and most frequently used of the programs. It originated sometime during the first half of the nineteenth century and is used in an estimated 350,000 firms in the United States (Doyle, 1983). Profit sharing is any procedure whereby an employer pays to regular employees current and deferred sums based on company profits, in addition to existing established wages. The plans usually come in one of three forms:

1. Cash or current distribution plans, which provide for the payment of profits according to some predetermined formula to all participants shortly after profits have been determined, usually quarterly or annually.
2. Deferred plans, which place earned profits in individual workers' accounts to be paid out at retirement, permanent disability, or death.
3. Combination plans, in which a portion of profits to be shared is paid out immediately to employees and the rest is put in individual escrow accounts.

The majority of U.S. profit-sharing plans are deferred plans, used by organizations as supplements to, or substitutes for, pension plans. As such, they are covered by the Employee Retirement Income Security Act (ERISA) of 1974.

While the motivation for installing profit-sharing plans is to provide a direct incentive for employees to work as effectively as possible, the use of profit sharing as a benefit plan tends to discourage worker involvement in reducing costs and improving profits. It is usually management personnel, not workers, who act as trustees in the management of the investment of the funds accumulating through profit sharing. And where profit shares are paid out directly, a firm's profit levels are often too far beyond the influence of individual workers to be linked to work behavior. In addition, the relationship between work behavior and outcome attainment is too tenuous for most profit-sharing plans to have a motivating effect on worker productivity (see Lawler, 1986; McKersie, 1986).

There are exceptions to this observation. The Profit Sharing Research Foundation publishes case studies of successful profit-sharing plans and presents arguments for combining profit sharing with a participative management style to increase employees' understanding of the importance of profits, their effect on it, and how increased profits benefit them. But beyond these case studies, there is little research done to test the hypothesis that profit sharing increases worker motivation, effort, and performance.

Gainsharing. The term *gainsharing* is often used to refer to programs or plans that combine employee involvement with a financial formula for distributing monetary bonuses based on improvements in organizational performance (Bullock and Lawler, 1984; Lawler, 1986). This definition would include profit-sharing plans. The term is used here in a narrower sense—in part to distinguish it from profit sharing—as the label for productivity improvement programs that focus on reducing costs (also called cost-reduction programs).

Schuster (1985) identifies three significant differences between gainsharing and profit sharing. First, with gainsharing, rewards are based on some measure of productivity instead of on a global profitability measure. Gainsharing programs aim to measure and reward workers for those aspects of organizational performance that are under their control. Second, in gainsharing, productivity measurement and bonus payments are frequent events, distributed monthly or quarterly, in contrast to the annual measures and rewards of profit-sharing plans. The frequency of the gainsharing bonus is a better reinforcer of increased worker effort, and it helps establish perceptions of behavior-outcome contingencies. Third, gainsharing plans are current distribution plans, in contrast to most profit-sharing plans, which have deferred payments. This means that gainsharing plans are true incentive plans, not benefit plans.

McKersie (1986) separates gainsharing from profit sharing by defining them as motivational and organizational equity plans, respectively. He argues that the purpose of gainsharing is to improve performance of specific organizational units by increasing worker motivation, while profit sharing has as its purpose the equitable distribution of organization-level gains. Profit-sharing plans are more of a mechanism for "sharing the fruits" (McKersie, 1986, p. 7).

In summary, gainsharing plans operate closer to the worker at the point of production. People are rewarded for their own behavior (or rather, the behavior of employees as a group) and should be able to see the relationship between their effort, the improvements in productivity, and their personal outcomes. The redefined terms of the wage and effort bargain should be more clearly perceived and understood by labor and management, if not always completely agreed upon.

Employee Ownership. There are three forms of employee ownership: cooperatives, buyouts, and employee stock ownership plans (ESOPs). Because they are the most common ownership form, ESOPs are briefly summarized here.

An ESOP is a benefit plan through which employees receive

company stock. In most plans, the employer contributes stock (or cash to purchase stock) to a special trust for distribution to individual accounts of participating workers. Allocation of stock in the typical ESOP is based on relative compensation, but seniority can also be included in the distribution formula. The basic ESOP is quite similar to a profit-sharing plan, except that workers receive stock in the employer, and the plan does not have to depend on company profits. The logic behind an ESOP, when used as a benefit or incentive plan, is to give workers a financial and psychological interest in ownership and company growth. In theory, as shareholders they can directly affect the value of their property through their work efforts (as can, of course, a number of other factors affecting the stock prices). This contrasts with profit-sharing plans, where the funds are placed in a wide range of investments, and benefit payments are not directly linked to the value of the employer's stock. The use of ESOPs as additions to, or substitutes for, pension plans has the same limiting motivating potential as profit-sharing deferred benefit plans.

Like profit-sharing plans, ESOPs also come in a variety of forms. The legislation covering both (particularly ERISA, 1974, and the Deficit Reduction Act of 1984) is complex, and the administrative details of the plans are burdensome.

Gainsharing

For the reasons noted earlier, gainsharing is more directly related to individual behavior and should be a potentially more valuable research area than profit sharing. Consequently, profit sharing as an intervention will not be considered further.

Of the different gainsharing plans, the Scanlon Plan is the best known and the one to have received the most research attention. Other programs, such as the Rucker and Improshare Plans, have not been studied extensively. However, a fair amount of descriptive material is available to allow a comparison of the different plans' features.

It should be noted that gainsharing plans bearing the same name take on many forms, because the plans are tailored to meet the needs of the organizations in which they are installed (see Cummings and Molloy, 1977; Frost, Wakeley, and Ruh, 1974; Schuster, 1984b; Lawler, 1986). The common features of gainsharing plans are a management philosophy of worker participation in decision making and two structural characteristics: a bonus payment formula and a committee system established to facilitate worker participation and adopt productivity improvement suggestions when worker involvement is part of the plan design.

The Scanlon Plan. The Scanlon Plan was developed in the 1930s by Joseph Scanlon, a union leader in the steel industry, as a mechanism to turn around financially threatened plants. It gained widespread attention several years later when data showed that it could also make financially healthy companies healthier. (The history of the plan can be found in Davenport, 1950; Frost, Wakeley, and Ruh, 1974; Goodman, Wakeley, and Ruh, 1972; White, 1979.)

The philosophical foundation given to the plan is the premise that all people have needs for psychological growth and development and are capable of and willing to fulfill those needs in their employer's service if they are allowed the opportunity to participate in organizational decision making and if they are equitably compensated for the participation (see Frost, Wakeley, and Ruh, 1974; Lesieur, 1958; McGregor, 1960). This philosophy follows the basic unitarist line, with the exception of the caveat stipulating a financial return to the employee for the effort and intelligence generated through need fulfillment.

From the plan's philosophy comes the structure that allows participation to take place: a series of shop-floor (and office) level *production committees* with rank-and-file representation that meet periodically to evaluate and act on suggestions contributed from individual employees on methods to improve productivity and eliminate waste, and plantwide *screening committees* with joint union-management representation that act on suggestions exceeding certain cost limits, adjudicate work-group boundary disputes caused by suggestions, review current business problems and formulate general long-range plans for improving productivity, and administer the bonus plan.

The bonus component is designed to reward cooperation and to create a unified interest group working toward common goals. Bonuses are therefore paid on a plantwide basis, monthly or quarterly. The common Scanlon Plan formula uses the ratio of labor costs to the sales value of production to calculate deviations from a base or norm period. Productivity will have increased if the sales value of production has increased at a faster rate (or decreased at a slower rate) than labor costs. (For details on the use of the formula, see Geare, 1976; Nightingale and Long, 1984; Puckett, 1958; Schuster, 1984b.) It is not unusual to find expanded formulas in operation that include other factors over which workers have control, such as materials and energy (see Frost, Wakeley, and Ruh, 1974). Usually, the bonus pool generated through labor cost savings is split twenty-five–seventy-five between the company and its work force (which includes *all* employees). From the employee portion, a percentage is kept in reserve to offset time periods without productivity gains. At the end of the fiscal year, the remainder of the reserves is distributed to the work force.

Implicit in the Scanlon Plan is a recognition of organized labor. The plan is used primarily in unionized firms to build and strengthen labor-management cooperation, and it functions best with a strong local union and a management that accepts collective bargaining as a legitimate mechanism for controlling labor-management conflicts and solving interest-group disputes (Driscoll, 1979).

The Rucker Plan. The Rucker Plan, designed by Allen Rucker in the 1930s, covers hourly employees and involves a more sophisticated measure of productivity improvement but a less developed participative philosophy and structure. The bonus formula is a ratio that expresses the amount of production required for each dollar of the company's total payroll. Production value is calculated as the difference between the selling price of products and the costs of materials, supplies, and services (again, see Geare, 1976; Nightingale and Long, 1984; Schuster, 1984b, for more details and calculation examples). Of the labor cost savings, 75 percent is distributed to the workers while 25 percent is kept in a reserve pool to offset poor months. The remainder of this pool is then released to the workers at the end of the year.

The Rucker Plan has a similar structure for participation to the Scanlon Plan, but it emphasizes participation less. Some plans may have both production and screening committees; other plans have just the screening committee.

Improshare. A more recent addition to gainsharing plans, Improshare was developed by an industrial engineer, Mitchell Fein. Like the Scanlon Plan, it measures only labor costs, but it uses engineered time standards to calculate a base productivity factor. Its bonus formula is a ratio that includes the number of units produced to number of hours worked; thus it is a straight labor productivity measure (see Nightingale and Long, 1984; Schuster, 1984a, for examples). The formula can be applied to whole organizational units or groups within them. Productivity gains are split fifty-fifty between the company and its employees. Distributions are usually made on a weekly basis, which makes connections between performance and rewards more immediate than under the Scanlon and Rucker Plans.

There is no philosophy of participation inherent in the Improshare Plan. However, it is possible for organizations to add participative structures to their tailor-made version of it, and some do so (Schuster, 1984b; Lawler, 1986). Information about the exact number of companies that have tried Improshare is not available, but a recent estimate of at least 150 is given by Lawler (1986).

On Theories About Gainsharing

Gainsharing is a practice in search of profits and in need of theory. The literature has ample descriptions of various plans, prescriptions for what to do to make them succeed, and what not to do to avoid failure. The question of why they work (or do not work), or how they work, has been raised only infrequently. It is possible that theory on gainsharing is hard to come by because knowledge about the effects of contingent rewards is well developed in learning theory and in cognitive models incorporating learning theory principles. Thus it may seem obvious how the programs work. However, the gainsharing philosophy, at least in Scanlon Plans, goes far beyond individual workers' subjective expected utility calculations. A brief review of the available models, all of which come from the Scanlon Plan literature, follows.

Theoretical explanations for Scanlon Plan success in the 1970s centered on the relative importance of worker participation and bonus payments. Frost, Wakeley, and Ruh (1974) gave most of the weight to the presumed intrinsic value of participation, which was reinforced by bonus payments and workers' perceptions of being equitably rewarded for extra effort. Geare (1976) argued to the contrary: employees exert extra effort to improve organizational productivity because they get paid for it. For Geare, participation had an auxiliary effect because it focuses on the day-to-day activities of immediate concern to workers. Cummings and Molloy (1977) listed a number of motivational features of the plan that emphasize benefits made available by participation (skill utilization, fulfillment of higher-order needs, worker control over the labor process). In addition, they argued, gainsharing works because it increases labor-management trust and two-way communication, improves work-group cohesion and group pressure on individuals to perform, and reinforces worker effort by bonus payments. The extrinsic rewards help to strengthen worker perceptions of effort-reward contingencies and beliefs about labor-management equity.

Goodman and Moore (1976) moved beyond lists of general motivators and global worker responses to them to focus on a subset of psychological processes believed to operate in gainsharing. They used expectancy theory to explain workers' beliefs about the personal utility of the Scanlon Plan, assuming that subjective expected utilities would determine the extent of active participation in gainsharing programs. They were not able to predict perceptions of effort-performance (in their case, *effort* meant *participation*) and performance-outcome contingencies from a series of individual, interpersonal, and organizational-level variables. There are no further published accounts of expectancy theory as a model of how gainsharing works.

Theory development has not advanced much beyond the vague and elementary causal statements when we move into the 1980s. Bullock and Lawler (1984) developed a rudimentary model to analyze information from case studies of Scanlon Plans, which predicts plan success from the separate effects of structural variables (what is done in implementing the plan), implementation factors (how it is done), and situational variables (where it is done). However, their model is more a heuristic device for cataloging existing information and is not intended as an explanation of why the plans work or not.

The most extensive and well-designed evaluation research on the effectiveness of gainsharing plans is the recent work of Schuster (1983b, 1984a, 1984b, 1985). Unfortunately, he brings us no closer to a theoretical understanding, because his research is designed primarily to test models of labor-management collaboration. Gainsharing programs are a subset of such programs. In fact, Schuster admits to the frustration of not knowing what it is that makes the plans successful and believes that it cannot be determined from present research data. He suggests, tentatively, that an organizational commitment model may be a better fit to the data than an expectancy model, but such a model has not yet been developed (Schuster, conversation with the author, February 13, 1986).

Research on the Outcomes of Gainsharing

Early Research. Empirical research on gainsharing plans is focused on Scanlon Plans. Quite detailed reviews of the early research, which is primarily case studies, are available in Schuster (1983a), Bullock and Lawler (1984), and Geare (1976) and will not be summarized here. In general, the findings are positive, showing that gainsharing is accompanied by improvements in productivity and labor relations. However, these studies are poorly designed and lack detailed statistical analyses of data used in the evaluation.

Schuster (1983b) also reviews attitude studies conducted by Ruh and his colleagues (Goodman, Wakeley, and Ruh, 1972; Ruh, Wallace, and Frost, 1973; White and Ruh, 1973) to explain how the Scanlon Plan works to increase worker effort. The results strengthen a central finding from the case studies: participation is an important feature in Scanlon Plan success. Otherwise, the data shed little light on the process questions. Neither the attitude surveys nor the case studies contain information to support the hypothesis that participation influences gainsharing plan effectiveness by releasing an untapped reservoir of worker talent and energy.

Recent Research. Recent studies move gainsharing research beyond evaluations of single cases. White (1979) used a sample of twenty-three firms to examine the importance to Scanlon Plan success of worker participation, top management support for worker participation in a gainsharing program, and company size. He found positive correlations between plan success, which was measured by judges' ratings and by whether gainsharing was still used or had been discontinued, and employees' reports of the extent of participation, as well as managerial attitudes toward worker participation.

Bullock and Lawler (1984) used thirty-three published and unpublished cases as the basis for a study describing characteristics of Scanlon Plans (unpublished cases included eleven doctoral dissertations and master's theses and one senior honor thesis completed at MIT, the academic "home" of the Scanlon Plan, from 1950 to 1961). They focused on the identification of three sets of variables hypothesized to influence Scanlon Plan success: structural factors (financial formulas, bonus shares distributed to employees, participative mechanisms used), implementation factors (presence and roles of external consultants and internal change agents, degree of worker involvement in implementation planning), and situational factors (company size, union status, technology, management style).

The results showed that two-thirds of the programs were reported as successful, with improvements in productivity, quality, cost reduction or customer service, worker attitudes, and quality of worklife. Improvements in labor-management relations and communications and cooperation between workers and managers were reported in over half the cases. In all but three cases, bonus payments and pay increases were granted based on performance improvements. The majority of plans (73 percent) used formal participative structures.

Of the situational factors believed to facilitate or hamper gainsharing plans, organization size was not important, corroborating data from White's (1979) study, but technology mattered; all but two plans were installed in manufacturing operations. Data on management style, available in eleven cases, showed that most managements were participative rather than autocratic.

More than half of the plans in the Bullock and Lawler (1984) study produced some tangible benefits to the employer, but the researchers were unable to discover what kinds of structures and processes worked best to create the results. They hypothesize that gainsharing works because it transforms individual workers, engaged in separate tasks and unaware of their interrelationships to the rest of the organization, into groups of workers with a much broader understanding of and commitment to the organization. It is the sense of a community of people and purpose that encourages employees to work smarter, even harder. This interpretation follows the original propositions about the Scanlon Plan set forth in Frost, Wakeley, and Ruh (1974).

Schuster (1983b, 1984a, 1984b) examined the effectiveness of gainsharing plans as part of a larger study of labor-management cooperation programs. Included in his sample were nine Scanlon, seven Rucker, and eight Improshare Plans, on which monthly productivity data, employment levels, and absenteeism and turnover data were collected for a period of from five to six years (Schuster, 1984b). In addition to the effectiveness measures, information was collected on methods of bonus payments, company strategies to build employee acceptance of the plans, and worker participation structures. Schuster's studies contain the best published evaluation data available on gainsharing plans on a case basis.

In the research sample, twenty-eight firms had some form of financial sharing provision (gainsharing plans and one profit-sharing plan). Of the firms for which productivity data were available, about half showed significant improvements in productivity (measured as employee output) after the introduction of the plan. In the rest, productivity was either unchanged or it declined.

Two-thirds of the firms used a plantwide distribution of bonuses, while the rest distributed bonuses to work groups. The productivity improvements occurred more often in firms with plantwide bonus systems, and Schuster (1984b) concludes that plantwide distribution is preferable to group-based distribution, in part because feelings of inequality are created when work groups receive different bonus payments.

The effects of participation are less clear. Of the seventeen sites with both employee involvement in decision making and productivity data, eight had positive changes in productivity levels after plan implementation, seven had no change, and two showed declines.

Detailed, plan-specific data are available on six Scanlon Plans, five Rucker Plans, and one Improshare Plan (Schuster, 1983b, 1984b) that allow some comparisons across plan type. They show that the Scanlon Plan appears to do the best, and keeps on doing well the longest. It is not clear whether this is due to the bonus formula, the high level of worker participation, or some unknown other factor(s).

Schuster concludes that the Scanlon Plan differs from other gainsharing plans in the organizations' commitment to and institutionalization of a high level of worker involvement.

The analysis of cases in which gainsharing failed in Schuster's study demonstrates the importance of preserving labor and management equity in gainsharing. When there are very few bonus payments, programs are not successful. When management "adjusts" or "manipulates" the bonus formula without consulting (and obtaining the agreement of) labor, cooperation ceases. When management does not demonstrate its commitment to worker involvement, and—where the work force is unionized—does not work honestly with the union leadership, programs do poorly.

A Comment on Gainsharing Research. Because methodologically adequate research on gainsharing is scant and not theory-driven, it is difficult to draw confident conclusions from the empirical literature. Nevertheless, two features stand out in the empirical evaluations of gainsharing plans (in particular, of Scanlon Plans): the presence of worker participation as an almost necessary condition for success, and the absence of the wage and effort bargain as a variable of importance in explaining both successes and failures.

Given the integral part that bonus payments play in the design of these programs, and the fact that the Scanlon Plan originated in the trade union movement, where the wage and effort bargain is the crux of labor-management relations, the very secondary role ascribed to the distribution of gains in the explanations offered for productivity improvement data seems more like a decision to neglect it (Bachrach and Baratz, 1970) than a reflection of its actual power. This is probably due to the strong philosophical commitment that early Scanlon Plan followers had to participation as a solution to interest-group conflict (see Frost, Wakeley, and Ruh, 1974; McGregor, 1960). Unfortunately, the belief that worker participation is highly desirable in itself and has very high utility as a work motivator has put a disproportionate amount of research attention on it as a primary cause of productivity improvement (the exception to this is Geare, 1976), and may have served to restrict the field of alternative hypotheses.

A Theoretical Model of the Roles of Participation and Productivity Bonuses in Gainsharing

The research findings suggest that both bonus payments and participation have been important factors in successful gainsharing programs. It is unlikely, however, that the documented productivity improvements have resulted solely from increases in intrinsic motivation and employee perceptions of labor-management equity. Figure 12.1 presents a model that describes how the bonus and participation components of gainsharing plans may operate to influence productivity levels.

The productivity bonus appears twice in the model: first as a promised outcome in a redefined labor exchange; second, as payments to employees following productivity gains. The bonus serves to secure employee acceptance of an organizational change that will, by definition, require more worker effort—physical, mental, or both. It is the promise of equity in the contractual relationship between employer and employee (the wage and effort bargain) that creates the initial acceptance of gainsharing programs.

The functions served by worker participation depend in part on the nature of the participation—on whether it is direct or indirect, restricted to short-range decisions about the immediate work situation or encompassing long-range decisions about the organization's goals and policies, the degree of control (from none to self-management) employees have over decision making, and the level at which participation takes place (from the shop floor to the board room) (Bernstein, 1976; Dachler and Wilpert, 1978). It is difficult to state exactly where the participation found in gainsharing programs falls on these four dimensions, because the nature of the participation appears to vary considerably, both between formal gainsharing plans and within plans. The large number of tailor-made plans adds to the variety of ways employees are involved in managerial decision making (Lawler, 1986; Schuster, 1984b). The only element common to the participation in the different plans is the area of decision making; workers are involved in short-range decisions about the labor process and the factors immediately surrounding it—the "nuts and bolts" of work performance.

In the traditional Scanlon Plan, participation is both direct, through the suggestion system open to all plan participants, and indirect, through representatives on production and screening committees. The degree of control that employees exercise in the decision-making process differs between the direct and indirect participation, however. Participation by suggestion making is involvement, not influence—what Bernstein (1976) calls "consultation." In contrast, worker representatives on the committees that evaluate and decide on implementation of the suggestions have both involvement and influence. They operate at the level of "coinfluence," where managers may veto decisions made by workers, but seldom do so (Bernstein, 1976). Of course, if there is a large number of production committees in an organization, a larger percentage of the work

Figure 12.1. The Roles of Worker Participation and Productivity Bonuses in Gainsharing Programs.

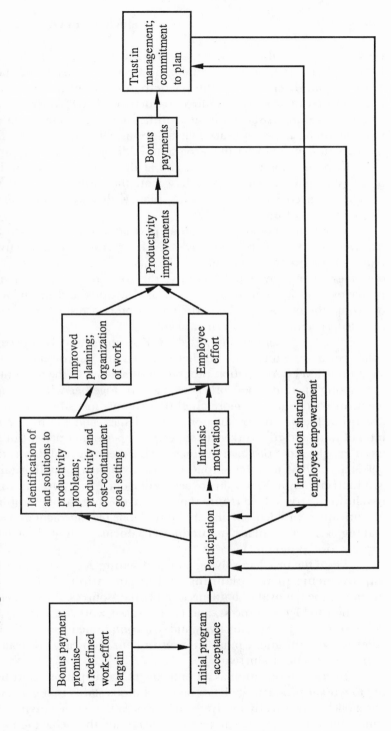

force experiences direct participation with both involvement and influence—a situation that should generate more satisfaction and a sense of empowerment in the participatory program than in a program that involves only indirect participation (IDE International Research Group, 1981). While it is difficult to be certain from the research literature, it appears that a substantial amount of worker participation in gainsharing programs is direct (see, for example, Rosenberg and Rosenstein, 1980), and at the coinfluence level. The model shown in Figure 12.1 is based on the assumption that the employees covered by a gainsharing plan with participation experience the direct form.

From the model, we see that participation—direct worker involvement in and influence over work process and productivity issues—leads to three outcomes. The first is the identification of obstacles to improved productivity, the solution to performance problems, and agreement on work-related actions and behavior to overcome the obstacles. The participation process results in a set of accepted, specific work performance goals.

This argument is supported by Rosenberg and Rosenstein's (1980) research, which showed that productivity improvements in a shop-floor-level participation program were related to the amount of "managing" activity the workers engaged in together with management. In particular, the more often participants met, the more their discussion focused on production-related issues, and the higher the ratio of rank-and-file workers to supervisory personnel present in the meetings, the more productivity increased. Rosenberg and Rosenstein (1980) argue that it is the output of participation activity that raises productivity, not how employees experience the participation psychologically. (By *output*, they mean the organized problem identification, problem solving, and joint labor-management decision making that takes place in productivity-focused shop-floor-level participation programs.)

From the problem-solving and goal-setting activities follow (1) improvements in the planning and organization of the work, including the removal of bottlenecks and other sources of inefficiency from the production process, and (2) increased worker effort toward the attainment of the productivity and cost-containment goals. Worker effort to perform and a more efficient organization of work lead to improvements in productivity.

Intrinsic motivation as an outcome of participation contributing to worker productivity has a more nebulous status in a gainsharing model. Intrinsically motivated behavior is the set of activities for which there is no apparent reward other than the behavior itself.

Actions are motivated by people's need to feel competent and self-directed in dealing with their environment (Deci, 1975). If we accept the hypothesis that involvement in and influence over organizational decision making is intrinsically motivating, workers will be motivated to participate, but they will not necessarily be more motivated to do the work they are supposed to do at the point of production. The model therefore has a feedback loop from the experienced intrinsic motivation back to participation, but not a direct causal arrow from participation to an intrinsic motivation to engage in other forms of work.

Two arguments can be raised against this line of reasoning. The first is that participation can be viewed as an integral part of the job—a form of vertical job loading (Herzberg, 1966). The intrinsic motivation experienced as workers participate influences the work people do at the point of production. Thus intrinsic motivation belongs in a model that explains how gainsharing with participation operates to improve productivity.

It is true that in a formal participation program, worker involvement in decision making is part of the job and requires effort for which employees are compensated. But if we want to explain the processes that link participation to productivity, we need more precise descriptions of the psychological properties of our variables. In the present case, we need to separate the components of the job—that is, the *work* people are paid to do—into those directly related to, and necessary for, the production process, and those auxiliary to it. Participation is an important auxiliary function. The primary job can be done without it, but the job may be done better with it. As long as the basic work process remains the same, with participation only added to it, intrinsic motivation will not be a direct cause of work performance.

The second argument is based on the assumption that the basic jobs people do will be changed where there is gainsharing. From the evidence presented on the emergence and adoption of a new industrial relations model by Kochan, Katz, and McKersie (1986), Lawler (1986), and McKersie (1986), it appears that gainsharing is accompanied by, or accompanies, changes in job design. If the basic work process changes to include broader job scopes, longer work cycle times, decision making, and worker autonomy (the hallmarks of socio-technical systems theory [Hackman and Oldham, 1980; Trist, 1981]), participation will be a fully integrated part of the labor process. It can then be argued that the whole job, of which participation is a part, is intrinsically motivating. That will mean that intrinsic motivation can be a direct cause of worker performance. Of course, when participation is a component of "high-involvement management," it will be difficult to separate its effects on the intrinsic motivation to work from the effects of other job components.

A third outcome of worker participation is the empowerment of nonmanagerial employees through their access to management-level information. Effective worker participation creates pressure on management to open communication and share information with labor. Information is power in organizations (Bacharach and Lawler, 1980), and extensive information sharing decreases traditional labor-management power gaps. It is easier to build mutual trust and commitment to common economic interests between labor and management when power is more evenly distributed. This is consistent with the pluralist view of labor-management collaboration.

Trust in management and commitment to gainsharing are further strengthened by the payment of bonuses. The monetary gains, and employee trust and commitment, reinforce participation. Over time, a new culture may emerge, as Lawler (1986) suggests and Schuster (1984b) implies.

The model shows how participation and productivity bonuses work together to facilitate and improve worker performance. It is also possible to have the same positive outcomes from participation without gainsharing, as long as employees can be induced to participate and convinced to adjust their expectations about the ratio of wages to effort. Rosenberg and Rosenstein (1980) demonstrated empirically that the addition of productivity bonuses to a shop-floor participation program led only to a modest increment in productivity beyond that provided by participation. Similarly, gainsharing by itself can influence performance levels if the promise of bonus payments leads to worker acceptance of higher work performance goals and management takes action to improve the planning and organization of work. The actual bonus payments balance the wage and effort bargain and reinforce the increased effort levels.

Summary

Research has demonstrated that gainsharing can have positive effects on economic outcomes for both employees and employers. The use of more sophisticated research designs and statistical analyses of criterion data in the evaluation research contributes considerably to the confidence one can have in these plans.

A number of research questions are still unanswered. Some are primarily practical: for example, What kinds of plans, or combination of plan components, work best under what circumstances (see Bullock and Lawler, 1984)? The most important empirical question is still how gainsharing works to improve labor productivity. It is better to ask how than why, because the why seems to lead to studies that pit predictors against one another. Instead of investigating whether participation is more important than bonus payments, research should examine how they interact to jointly create labor productivity. The model presented here can perhaps guide such endeavors. There is no longer a need for more exploratory research on gainsharing.

A useful research design can be the longitudinal case study with repeated quantitative measures of both predictors and criteria over several years. Recent research on models of union-management collaboration demonstrates both the utility and the necessity of long-term observation and assessment (Hammer and Stern, 1986). Schuster's (1983b; 1984a) analyses of productivity trend data support this argument.

Employee Ownership

Employee ownership in the United States dates back 200 years. Initially, it took the form of producers' cooperatives—industrial firms owned, managed, and operated by workers (Aldrich and Stern, 1983; Jones, 1979; Shirom, 1972). A modest number of cooperatives still exist, some of which have lasted since the 1930s, but no current information is available on exact numbers (Rosen, Klein, and Young, 1986). In a historical study, Aldrich and Stern (1983) found only 800 producers' cooperatives in existence between 1840 and 1940.

A second form of worker ownership is the joint partnership. In the United States, partnerships have resulted primarily from employee buyouts, in which workers, managers, and nonworker members of a community buy plants scheduled for closure to avoid job loss (Hammer, Stern, and Whyte, 1983). Rosen, Klein, and Young (1986) estimate that there have been between sixty and seventy buyouts since 1970, supposedly covering some 50,000 jobs ("Employees Bought 60 Companies in the Past 10 Years," 1983). Most buyouts have occurred since 1980; they have included such large firms as the 8,000-employee Weirton Plant of National Steel and the 3,000-employee Rath Packing Company.

The third form is the trust, or the ESOP, which is by far the most popular.

Producers' Cooperatives. Most producers' cooperatives were formed for practical economic reasons—to create jobs and provide job security in periods of economic distress and industrial conflict (Aldrich and Stern, 1983; Berman, 1967; Russell, 1985). A few originated in their founders' political and philosophical commitment to worker ownership and control (Gunn, 1984), but the large majority of cooperatives have profit maximization (financial returns to owners) as the primary goal.

The cooperatives are characterized by equality of ownership and decision-making rights. Each worker-owner usually owns one share, all shares are held within the firm (no public trading is allowed), and owners are required to sell their shares back to the company upon resignation or retirement. Usually, a company charter specifies that differences between worker-owners in compensation and influence be minimized and dictates that the firm be democratically run (see Bernstein, 1976; Gunn, 1984, for examples).

Buyouts. Buyout firms have all originated in the need to save jobs and local community tax bases. They have appeared in two waves. The first occurred during the early to middle 1970s through divestitures, as conglomerates tried to sell or close relatively unprofitable plants or plants in the wrong line of business. These were financially viable firms, and some were quite healthy (Stern and Hammer, 1978). They were converted to employee ownership through the joint partnership mechanism, whereby each investor bought as many shares of stock as he or she wanted, or could afford, and gained immediate possession of the shares, together with the right to vote them on the basis of one share, one vote. Usually, this meant that shares and votes were distributed unequally across employee-owners and their non-worker partners.

The second wave of buyouts involved firms in more serious financial trouble, into which immediate infusion of capital was necessary. In these cases, jobs were saved by a combination of worker equity contributions, bank loans, government loans and grants, wage and benefit cuts, and reduced employment. The ownership structure was usually the trust. Ownership was limited to employees and was distributed equally across them. In some cases, workers and managers had immediate rights to vote their stock (or to direct trustees in voting it); in other cases, a period of vesting was necessary before employee-owners could control their shares (Whyte and others, 1983).

ESOPS. Employee ownership through a traditional ESOP covers ten million workers ("Employee Ownership Plans Jumped to 6800," 1985). The U.S. General Accounting Office (1987) located around 4,800 active plans by March of 1986, and Rosen, Klein and Young (1986) estimate that there are 7,000 firms with ESOPs. These figures are growing rapidly.

The popularity of ESOPs comes in large measure from their immediate financial utility to the employer: they are used to raise capital, to lower corporate taxes, to avoid costly pension plan obligations, and as barter in concession bargaining to lower labor costs.

There are considerable tax advantages to ESOPs for the employer. The employer's contributions are tax-deductible, and the amount of cash contributed each year can vary (although there is an upward limit of 25 percent of the payroll of ESOP participants). Two forms of ESOPs, called TRAYSOPs and PAYSOPs, permitted parts of the cost of stock ownership to be deducted directly from the corporate tax bill. These tax-credit ESOPs were eliminated in the Tax Reform Act of 1986, however. As corporate financing vehicles, ESOPs can be leveraged in the following manner: The employer sets up an employee stock ownership trust (ESOT), which borrows funds from a lender (often a bank). The loan is usually guaranteed by the corporation. The ESOT invests the amount borrowed in newly issued common stock of the employer at fair market value. The employer contributes cash to the ESOT, which is used to pay back the loan. For the employer, both principal and interest payments are tax-deductible. The shares contributed to employees' accounts are not currently taxable, but they are taxed when distributed.

ESOPs are also used as a means to motivate workers and build organizational commitment. Stock ownership is believed to merge worker and employer interests, and to improve labor effectiveness because employees are now working for themselves. In addition, some employers have set up ESOPs because they have a philosophical commitment to widespread share ownership and (usually) worker involvement in managerial decision making. A 1983 survey by the National Center for Employee Ownership found that 7 percent of all ESOP firms are ideologically based.

The ESOP is not without problems for both employers and workers. For the company, if new shares are issued it means a dilution of current shareholders' equity. For workers, it means that their future economic welfare is more closely tied to the fortunes of the employer, which, under certain circumstances, is not financially prudent. Unionists, who have traditionally been antagonistic to worker ownership, both in principle and practice, have been particularly opposed to the replacement of pension plans by ESOPs. Under current law, an employer can exclude unionized workers from participation in an ESOP.

Theoretical Models

Where ESOPs are installed for their immediate financial incentives, there is little, if any, attention paid to whether and how stock ownership will influence worker behavior. The motivational properties of what is essentially a fringe benefit plan are not of primary interest. But when an employer sets up an ESOP to improve worker productivity and organizational effectiveness, the interest in evaluation of its effects increases. Two theoretical models describe the effects of share ownership on company performance and on worker productivity, commitment, involvement, motivation, and job satisfaction.

The *direct financial effects model* predicts that when workers become stockholders, they will seek to increase the worth of their stock by working harder and smarter, reducing materials waste and energy costs, and attending work regularly. Once improvements in productivity are translated into increased stock values, worker-owners will work still harder in a self-reinforcing spiral (Burck, 1976). Worker-owners will direct their individual and collective behavior toward the capitalist's goal of profit maximization rather than the wage laborer's goal of higher wages and fringe benefits. Under these circumstances, worker participation and control are irrelevant issues (Copeman, 1975; Bradley and Gelb, 1983)

The *control effects model* predicts that the positive effects of worker ownership can be obtained only through worker participation and self-government. As participation becomes more intensive and covers more issues and more levels of the organizational hierarchy, the more effective it will be.

Evidence for the Effectiveness of Employee Ownership

There are a number of studies of economic performance in ESOP firms and producers' cooperatives. Economic assessment of the buyouts are more complicated, because a number of the firms have, or have had, severe financial difficulties, and because different criteria have been used in the assessment (organizational survival, number of jobs saved, impact on local community economic conditions, and so on—see Stern, Wood, and Hammer, 1979).

Cooperatives, buyouts, and ESOP firms are not comparable entities. They differ from each other on two important dimensions: the extent of worker control and worker contributions of equity. In cooperatives, worker ownership equals worker control; in buyouts and ESOPs, the relationship is weak or nonexistent. In cooperatives and buyouts, workers have purchased their shares either directly, with personal savings and/or loans, or through payroll deductions. In ESOPS, stock ownership is a gift from the employer.

For worker-owners in cooperatives, there are at least three factors that can impact worker behavior and attitudes: personal financial commitment and responsibility, participation in and control over decision making, and value of the financial returns from stock ownership. In the buyouts, there are two: equity responsibility and expected (and sometimes even experienced) financial returns. For the ESOP participants, expected and experienced financial returns are the motivation.

Of course, these differences between the three types of employee ownership do not hold in all cases. Some ESOPs allow extensive worker involvement, and some buyouts provide at least modest amounts (for examples, see Strauss and Hammer, forthcoming). Despite this caveat, it is useful to examine the studies of the different ownership forms separately.

Producers' Cooperatives. The economic evaluations of the cooperatives cover three dependent variables: economic performance, firm survival, and job creation. Because of the ownership structure and organizational charters (equal distribution of capital ownership and formal authority), an additional success criterion is often the extent of workplace democracy (Bernstein, 1976; Gunn, 1984).

Research on well-established cooperatives—such as the ply-wood factories in the Pacific Northwest, the San Francisco Scavenger firms, and the Mondragon cooperatives—shows that profitability of these firms is certainly equal to, and frequently surpasses, the average profitability of their respective industries (Bellas, 1972; Berman, 1967; Russell, 1985; Thomas and Logan, 1982).

Early evaluations of the cooperative movement concluded that worker-owned firms were economically unviable and short-lived (Webb and Webb, [1921] 1975). Recent research based on extensive archival records, however, shows that many producers' cooperatives in the United States lasted over fifty years, which is beyond the life span of most conventional organizations (Aldrich and Stern, 1983; Jones, 1979). Of the thirty plywood cooperatives started in the 1930s and 1940s, some have closed, some have been bought by private capital, but twelve remain in business (Bellas, 1972; Greenberg, 1984). Among the European cooperatives, the Mondragon group's growth from one small firm in 1956 to eighty-some companies, providing employment for 18,000 worker-owners, supports the hypothesis that worker-owned firms can compete successfully against their conventional counterparts in economic and political systems that favor the conventional firm (Bradley and Gelb, 1983; Thomas and Logan, 1982).

Of course, sometimes producers' cooperatives fail. Some go under in a blaze of publicity, as did the 1970s Benn cooperatives in

Britain (Coates, 1976). The more spectacular failures have often been due to the fact that the firms were seriously underfunded at their start, and without access to loan capital (Lockett, 1980). Gunn (1984), in an economic evaluation of cooperatives and buyouts in the United States, identifies a number of the financial constraints on the cooperative firms.

A major problem facing the U.S. cooperatives is not financial survival but survival as true producers' cooperatives with worker self-management. There is considerable deviation from the democratic ideal in a number of these firms. Particularly threatening is the hiring by worker-owners of nonowning wage labor without participation rights, to buffer seasonal fluctuations in employment levels and to avoid diluting the existing high share values (Gunn, 1984; Russell, 1985).

Buyouts. Economic evaluation research on the buyout firms is quite primitive. Cross-sectional research is difficult, because the firms are spread over a large number of industries, the numbers are small, and many firms have been employee-owned for only a few years. Case studies show that buyouts appear to be successful at first: profits increase, worker productivity improves, absenteeism rates go down, and turnover declines (for summaries, see Long, 1980; Strauss, 1982; Whyte and others, 1983). There are several causes: (1) wages, benefits, and staffing levels have been cut, which lowers labor costs; (2) plants spun off from parent corporations no longer contribute toward corporate overhead; and (3) there is an initial enthusiasm and cooperative spirit among both labor and management—a euphoria of success that is channeled into effort and performance. Eventually, disillusionment sets in, followed by conflict, and the euphoria becomes alienation (Whyte and others, 1983). Often, work performance and absenteeism return to prebuyout levels, and grievance filing and industrial action increase (Hammer, Landau, and Stern, 1981; Hammer and Stern, 1986; Meek, 1988).

ESOPs. With ESOPs, there are no sample restrictions to limit the opportunity for interfirm studies. According to various economic evaluations, ESOP firms have been more profitable than comparable non-ESOP firms (Conte and Tannenbaum, 1978), been more productive (Marsh and McAllister, 1981), increased employment faster (Rosen and Klein, 1986; "Majority Employee-Owned Companies," 1983), and enjoyed higher sales growth, net operating margin, book value per share, and return to equity (Wagner, 1984). However, other studies of company performance are less encouraging. Tannenbaum, Cook, and Lochmann (1984), for example, found no significant differences between ESOP and conventional companies in profits, productivity, or technological adaptiveness for the years 1976 to 1982. But the ESOP firms had a significantly higher survival rate over this period than the conventional firms.

The research to date has not determined whether ESOP firms become more prosperous as a result of employee ownership (the direct financial effects model) or whether prosperous firms are more likely to establish ESOPs to begin with. A longitudinal study of productivity and profitability of ESOP companies, designed to disentangle cause from effect, is now being conducted by the U.S. General Accounting Office, but the results are not available yet.

The numerous studies of attitudinal and behavioral change under employee ownership report mixed results. Some conclude that such factors as motivation, job satisfaction, perceived worker influence, and organizational commitment have improved; others find no significant differences (for summaries, see Strauss, 1982; Tannenbaum, 1983; Kruse, 1984). According to Rosen, Klein, and Young (1986), the most recent and extensive of these studies (covering workers in thirty-seven diverse ESOP firms), employee satisfaction with the ESOP, commitment to the organization, and turnover intentions were significantly influenced by (1) the size of the company's contribution to the ESOP (the amount of stock the participants received), (2) management's philosophical commitment to worker ownership, and (3) the company's communications program about the ESOP. Whether the ESOP owned a large percentage of company stock, whether the stock carried voting rights, the reasons why the ESOP was established in the first place, and stock returns did not affect worker attitudes. The researchers concluded that when employee stock ownership is viewed as a fringe benefit, as opposed to a means of saving jobs or a mechanism for living out a corporate philosophy, the financial benefits matter a great deal.

To explain these results, Klein (1987) tested three different models of worker satisfaction with ESOPs. An intrinsic satisfaction model suggests that the simple fact of share ownership will have positive effects on worker attitudes. She found no support for this hypothesis. Instead, the relationships in the Rosen, Klein, and Young (1986) study could be explained by (1) an instrumental satisfaction model, which states that share ownership influences attitudes by creating opportunities for worker participation in decision making (the equivalent of the indirect effects model), and (2) an extrinsic satisfaction model, which links attitudes directly to the financial outcomes of ESOPs.

As was the case with gainsharing, we return to a possible conclusion about the joint effects of money and participation instead of to the more politically controversial one about participation being (or not being) a moderator in the ownership-attitude relationship.

Summary

The evaluation research presents an encouraging picture of employee stock ownership. An equity stake in the company coupled with information about the firm's financial fortunes and employees' role in creating economic health is positively correlated with economic performance and worker attitudes, at least on the firm level.

But while share ownership can be used effectively to build worker commitment to organizational goals and increased efforts to reach them, it is unlikely that such positive effects will materialize in the absence of some mechanism that makes workers aware that they have an equity stake in the company. There is no evidence supporting the hypothesis that a stock account existing as a deferred benefit will influence worker behavior and attitudes. There must be an awareness of the ownership beyond a lump sum at retirement. Worker participation can be such a mechanism, as can a good communications program.

It is difficult to be precise about the meaning of the employee ownership data—especially from ESOP firms—because the research is at the level of the firm and we want to make inferences at the level of the worker. So far, very little research on the psychological processes that define the meaning of stock ownership to employees has been conducted. Almost all of the individual-level studies have been done on buyouts, where the focus has been on a variety of variables: the internal distribution of power, the establishment and functions of participative structures, worker behavior and attitudes, and labor-management conflict. Again, the buyouts are special cases, with a more complex set of variables explaining behavior than what we find in the ESOPs. Some of the lessons from the buyout studies are relevant to all firms with ownership, such as the need to grant participation rights to worker-owners when they expect it, the necessity of labor-management trust, and the importance of worker access to financial information to guide decisions about work behavior.

What is clearly needed in the ESOP research are performance evaluation studies on the individual worker-level to allow a more precise explanation for the firm-level research data.

Conclusion

Productivity gainsharing and employee stock ownership can have sustained positive effects on worker productivity and company economic performance. The research findings supporting this statement are more ample and convincing in the employee ownership field than they are in gainsharing. In part, this is because more theoretically grounded model testing studies have been done on producers' cooperatives, buyouts, and ESOPs by researchers in economics, sociology, psychology, and industrial relations. Gainsharing research has been largely atheoretical, and has not been the beneficiary of research attention from several disciplines.

That is not to say that we are saved from reading glowing accounts of employee ownership's many virtues, and impassioned defenses of capital diffusion, worker participation, and organizational redistribution of power. At times, championship of "the worker as owner" is as much based on political and ideological beliefs about how property should be distributed in society, and what rights are attached to, and who should manage, property, as it is based on empirical evaluations of effectiveness in spurring economic survival and growth.

The problem one faces in the employee ownership and gainsharing literature is the separation of fact from wishful thinking, both with respect to causes and consequences and to the processes that explain the causal links. A considerable amount of work remains to be done on both gainsharing and employee ownership before we will know with some certainty how and when (that is, under what conditions) these programs, with their many variants, will influence worker productivity and other work-related behaviors and attitudes.

The main deficiency in gainsharing research has been the absence of tight conceptual frameworks to guide empirical investigation. There are three loosely defined models, or potential models, of the path(s) between gainsharing plans and their outcomes mentioned in the literature: the intrinsic motivation model, an organizational commitment model, and a cultural change model.

I have already dismissed the intrinsic motivation model as an adequate explanation of the effects of gainsharing programs on worker productivity. The commitment model exists more as a suggestion for a possible explanatory network than as a set of hypotheses. It is not clear how it would function to affect worker productivity. The original commitment model (Steers, 1977) specifies that commitment will influence job performance because it increases the amount of effort people exert on the job. The model does not dictate that the extra effort will be directed toward productive work, and, as it happens, the empirical relationships between commitment and job performance are weak (Steers and Porter, 1983). A commitment model of gainsharing would have to specify how a willingness to exert effort on behalf of the organization will be directed at containing or cutting labor costs and other productivity-improving activities.

A cultural change model is even less satisfying, because culture, if it is a meaningful hypothetical construct, is an organizational, not an individual, attribute. Unless it is specified how the organization's culture functions at the level of the individual worker in the form of perceptions, beliefs, or attitudes related to job performance, it is difficult to see much merit in such a model.

A fourth possibility is the model described in this chapter that combines employees' acceptance of a redefined wage and effort bargain with the tangible outcomes of direct shop-floor participation. I believe this to be a more accurate representation of how effective gainsharing works, because it recognizes as psychologically meaningful the political nature of the employee-employer relationship and the necessity to explain how we arrive at both behavioral intentions and productivity facilitators. Whether it is a valid model will, of course, depend on the outcomes of empirical testing.

In the case of employee ownership, we know the most about the firms that matter least to the economy as a whole: the cooperatives. The bulk of worker share ownership is in the ESOPs, where a number of questions await answers, including the crucial economic one of whether an ESOP is a cause or an effect of company profitability. Other unknowns at this time are whether a direct effects model will be sufficient to explain individual worker (as opposed to firm) productivity, whether the indirect model will be a better fit, and whether economic returns and participation both contribute significantly to worker performance.

The direct and indirect effects models have been used successfully to explain worker satisfaction toward ESOPs. They do well when data are aggregated to the firm level. It would be of great interest to see what happens with the worker as the unit of analysis.

In their present state, the direct and indirect effects models are too broad to be used to predict behavior at the individual level. The psychological processes that could turn economic returns and participation into behavioral intentions still have to be identified. The central variables operating when employees are owners will be similar to the ones identified in the gainsharing model—that is, the development of solutions to productivity-related problems and task goals— but the mechanisms used to arrive at those states of the firm and the worker will be more varied than they are in gainsharing programs. For example, the models must describe the effects of indirect participation coupled with communication programs, or long-range education of worker-owners (used by the Mondragon and some of the U.S. producers' cooperatives), in addition to, or in place of, direct participation. Further, the role of equity ownership in the creation and maintenance of work behavior norms will be a factor in an employee ownership–worker productivity model.

When conducting research on employee ownership, we must understand that cooperatives, buyouts, and ESOPs are separate phenomena. If they are treated as the same independent variable, some crucial differences that can influence employee behavior and attitudes will be missed. These are the presence or absence of structures that ensure ultimate worker control over the enterprise (including the form that worker participation takes) and the presence or absence of personal equity contributions to the firm. Research on individual and work-group productivity, absenteeism, commitment, job satisfaction, and so on must incorporate into the models that guide the empirical work those variables dictated by the ownership form.

Ten years ago, employee stock ownership was viewed by many as a transient phenomenon of faint importance, unlikely to spread and not worth serious investment of research resources. By now, it is clear that both the phenomenon and the research are here to stay. The research has helped to bring to the foreground a number of interesting practical and theoretical issues of importance beyond the population of worker ownership firms, such as the utility and psychological meaning of worker participation, the effects of different distributions of intraorganizational power, the dynamics of labor-management collaboration, and the role of expectations, or psychological contracts, in improvements and declines of worker productivity. The research has become more sophisticated, both conceptually and methodologically, and is conducted by a number of researchers free from obvious political and philosophical commitments to ownership as a cause. Of course, neither the research nor the theory development is free from problems, but the field itself is alive and well.

It is more difficult to be optimistic about the present state and the future of gainsharing research. Schuster's work in this field is certainly encouraging, as he has demonstrated the utility of time-series models in longitudinal comparative case studies. Unfortunately, there is no evidence of a widespread research effort on what is a very interesting topic. It is possible that gainsharing may more easily capture the imagination of industrial relations scholars if it is seen as a component in the new industrial relations model put forward by the MIT research groups (Kochan, Katz, and McKersie, 1986; Piore and Sabel, 1984). But it would be a mistake for psychologists to leave the study of gainsharing to others. A number of important psychological questions about the relationships between gainsharing and worker productivity will not be answered by industrial relations researchers and labor economists, because they will not be asked.

Most programs of productivity improvement rest on the assumption that it is possible to create a common interest group from labor and management, at least temporarily. It is through the recognition of a communality of interests that coalitions will be formed between separate interest groups.

Labor-management cooperation in areas related to organizational effectiveness has usually had a common economic interest as the stimulus. Such programs as gainsharing, profit sharing, and (to a more limited extent) employee stock ownership have been means for translating the common purpose into joint action.

The fact that labor-management collaboration to increase worker productivity and organizational effectiveness is possible, and quite often works well, does not mean that a permanent common interest group has been created, however. The unitarist perspective on labor-management relations, with its hope for prosperity through industrial peace, cannot be met as long as there are wage labor and a wage and effort bargain. To assume that any organizational intervention will be the mechanism through which employees' and employers' interests will merge is to put demands on program structures and processes that cannot be satisfied. The unitarist perspective will inevitably lead to disappointment, because programs of gain- and equitysharing, work redesign, worker participation, and so on will not remove conflict. They can only serve to suppress conflict for periods of time.

We will view these programs more realistically if we accept a pluralist perspective of labor-management relations. The pluralist view means a recognition of the limitations of organizational interventions and an acceptance of the often-elaborate support systems necessary to sustain them. It is possible to get productivity improvement through gainsharing and worker ownership when a set of conditions is met—first and foremost, equity in the wage and effort bargain. Successful implementation does not demand the absence of divergent political interests.

References

Aldrich, H., and Stern, R. N. "Resource Mobilization and the Creation of U.S. Producers' Cooperatives." *Economic and Industrial Democracy*, 1983, *4*, 371–406.

Bacharach, S. B., and Lawler, E. J. *Power and Politics in Organiza-*

tions: The Social Psychology of Conflict, Coalitions, and Bargaining. San Francisco: Jossey-Bass, 1980.

Bachrach, P., and Baratz, M. S. *Power and Poverty, Theory and Practice.* London: Oxford University Press, 1970.

Baritz, L. *The Servants of Power.* New York: Wiley, 1960.

Begin, J. P., and Beal, E. F. *The Practice of Collective Bargaining.* Homewood, Ill.: Irwin, 1985.

Bellas, C. J. *Industrial Democracy and the Worker-Owned Firm: A Study of Twenty-One Plywood Firms in the Pacific Northwest.* New York: Praeger, 1972.

Bendix, R. *Work and Authority in Industry: Ideologies of Management in the Course of Industrialization.* New York: Wiley, 1965.

Berman, K. V. *Worker-Owned Plywood Companies: An Economic Analysis.* Pullman: Washington State University Press, 1967.

Bernstein, P. *Workplace Democratization: Its Internal Dynamic.* Kent, Ohio: Kent State University Press, 1976.

Bradley, K., and Gelb, A. *Worker Capitalism: The New Industrial Relations.* London: Heineman Educational Books, 1983.

Brett, J. M., and Hammer, T. H. "Organizational Behavior and Industrial Relations." In T. A. Kochan, D. J. B. Mitchell, and L. Dyer (eds.), *Industrial Relations Research in the 1970s: Review and Appraisal.* Madison, Wis.: IRRA, 1982.

Bullock, R. J., and Lawler, E. E., III. "Gainsharing: A Few Questions, and Fewer Answers." *Human Resource Management,* 1984, *23,* 23–40.

Burck, C. "There Is More to ESOP Than Meets the Eye." *Fortune,* 1976, *93,* 128–133.

Cappelli, P. "Competitive Pressures and Labor Relations in the Airline Industry." *Industrial Relations,* 1985, *24* (3), 316–338.

Coates, K. *The New Worker Cooperatives.* Nottingham, England: Spokesman Books, 1976.

Conte, M., and Tannenbaum, A. S. "Employee Owned Companies: Is the Difference Measurable?" *Monthly Labor Review,* 1978, *101,* 22–28.

Copeman, G. H. *Employee Share Ownership and Industrial Stability.* London: Institute of Personnel Management, 1975.

Cummings, T. G., and Molloy, E. S. *Improving Productivity and the Quality of Work Life.* New York: Praeger, 1977.

Dachler, H. P., and Wilpert, B. "Conceptual Dimensions and Boundaries of Participation in Organizations: A Critical Evaluation." *Administrative Science Quarterly,* 1978, *23* (1) 1–39.

Dahrendorf, R. *Class and Class Conflict in Industrial Society.* Stanford, Calif.: Stanford University Press, 1959.

Davenport, R. "Enterprise for Every Man." *Fortune,* 1950, *41* (1), 51–58.

Deci, E. L. *Intrinsic Motivation.* New York: Plenum Press, 1975.

Doyle, R. J. *Gainsharing and Productivity.* New York: AMACOM, 1983.

Driscoll, J. W. "Working Creatively with a Union: Lessons from the Scanlon Plan." *Organizational Dynamics,* 1979, *8,* 61–80.

"Employee Ownership Plans Jumped to 6800." *Daily Labor Report,* April 3, 1985, p. A5.

"Employees Bought 60 Companies in the Past 10 Years, Conference Board Reports." *Daily Labor Report,* July 18, 1983, p. A2.

Fox, A. "Industrial Relations: A Social Critique of Pluralist Ideology." In J. Child (ed.), *Man and Organization.* London: Allen & Unwin, 1973.

Frost, C. F., Wakeley, J. H., and Ruh, R. A. *The Scanlon Plan for Organization Development: Identity, Participation, and Equity.* East Lansing: Michigan State University Press, 1974.

Geare, A. J. Productivity from Scanlon-Type Plans. *Academy of Management Review,* 1976, *1* (3), 99–108.

Goodman, P. S., and Moore, B. E. "Factors Affecting Acquisition of Beliefs About a New Reward System." *Human Relations,* 1976, *29* (6) 571–588.

Goodman, R., Wakeley, J., and Ruh, R. "What Employees Think of the Scanlon Plan." *Personnel,* 1972, *49* (5), 22–29.

Greenberg, E. "Producers' Cooperatives and Democratic Theory: The Case of the Plywood Firms." In R. Jackall and H. M.. Levin (eds.), *Worker Cooperatives in America.* Berkeley: University of California Press, 1984.

Gunn, C. E. *Workers' Self-Management in the United States.* Ithaca, N.Y.: Cornell University Press, 1984.

Hackman, J. R., and Oldham, G. R. *Work Redesign.* Reading, Mass.: Addison-Wesley, 1980.

Hammer, T. H., Landau, J. C., and Stern, R. N. "Absenteeism When Workers Have a Voice: The Case of Employee Ownership." *Journal of Applied Psychology,* 1981, *66* (5), 561–573.

Hammer, T. H., and Stern, R. N. "A Yo-Yo Model of Cooperation: Union Participation in Management at the Rath Packing Company." *Industrial and Labor Relations Review,* 1986, *39* (3), 337–349.

Hammer, T. H., Stern, R. N., and Whyte, W. F. "Can You Buy Your Job?" In W. F. Whyte and others (eds.), *Worker Participation and Ownership: Cooperative Strategies for Strengthening Local Economies.* Ithaca, N.Y.: ILR Press, 1983.

Herzberg, F. *Work and the Nature of Man.* New York: New American Library, 1966.

IDE International Research Group. *Industrial Democracy in Europe.* Oxford, England: Clarendon Press, 1981.

Jones, D. "U.S. Cooperatives: The Record to Date." *Industrial Relations,* 1979, *18,* 342–357.

Klein, K. J. "Employee Stock Ownership and Employee Attitudes: A Test of Three Models." *Journal of Applied Psychology,* 1987, *72* (2), 319–332.

Kochan, T. A., Katz, H. C., and McKersie, R. B. *The Transformation of American Industrial Relations.* New York: Basic Books, 1986.

Kruse, D. *Employee Ownership and Employee Attitudes.* Norwood, Pa.: Norwood Press, 1984.

Lawler, E. E., III. *High-Involvement Management: Participative Strategies for Improving Organizational Performance.* San Francisco, Calif.: Jossey-Bass, 1986.

Lesieur, F. G. (ed.). *The Scanlon Plan: A Frontier in Labor-Management Cooperation.* Cambridge, Mass.: MIT Press, 1958.

Levering, R., Moskowitz, M., and Katz, M. *The One Hundred Best Companies to Work for in America.* Reading, Mass.: Addison-Wesley,1984.

Locke, E. A., and Schweiger, D. M. "Participation in Decision-Making: One More Look." In B. M. Staw (ed.), *Research in Organizational Behavior.* Vol. 1. Greenwich, Conn.: JAI Press, 1979.

Lockett, M. "Worker Cooperatives as an Alternative Organizational Form: Incorporation or Transformation?" In D. Dunkerley and G. Salaman (eds.), *The International Yearbook of Organization Studies,* Boston: Routledge & Kegan Paul, 1980.

Long, R. J. "Job Attitudes and Organizational Performance Under Employee Ownership." *Academy of Management Journal,* 1980, *23,* 726–737.

Lukes, S. *Power: A Radical View.* London: Macmillan, 1974.

McGregor, D. *The Human Side of Enterprise.* New York: McGraw-Hill, 1960.

McKersie, R. B. "The Promise of Gainsharing." *ILR Report,* 1986, *24* (1), 7–11.

"Majority Employee-Owned Companies: A Survey of Characteristics and Performance." *Employee Ownership,* 1983, *3,* 1–2.

Marsh, T. R., and McAllister, D. E. "ESOP Tables: A Survey of Companies with Employee Stock Ownership Plans." *Journal of Corporation Law,* 1981, *6* (3), 613–617.

Meek, C. B. "Employee Ownership, Worker Participation, and

Economic Impact: A Case Study of the Rath Packing Company."
In W. F. Whyte and C. Craypo (eds.), *Evaluation Research on Federally Assisted Employee Buyouts.* Washington, D.C.: Economic Development Administration, 1988.

Nightingale, D. V., and Long, R. J. *Gain and Equity Sharing.* Ottawa, Canada: Ministry of Labour, 1984.

Piore, M. J., and Sabel, C. *The Second Industrial Divide.* New York: Basic Books, 1984.

Puckett, E. S. "Measuring Performance Under the Scanlon Plan." In F. G. Lesieur (ed.), *The Scanlon Plan: A Frontier in Labor-Management Cooperation.* Cambridge, Mass.: MIT Press, 1958.

Rosen, C., and Klein, K. J. "Job Creating–Performance of Employee Owned Companies." *Monthly Labor Review,* 1986, *106,* 15–19.

Rosen, C., Klein, K. J., and Young, K. M. *Employee Ownership in America: The Equity Solution.* Lexington, Mass.: Lexington Books, 1986.

Rosenberg, R. D., and Rosenstein, E. "Participation and Productivity: An Empirical Study." *Industrial and Labor Relations Review,* 1980, *33,* 355–367.

Ruh, R. A., Johnson, R. G., and Scontrino, M. P. "The Scanlon Plan, Participation in Decision-Making, and Job Attitudes." *Journal of Industrial and Organizational Psychology,* 1973, *1* (1), 36–45.

Ruh, R. A., Wallace, R. L., and Frost, C. F. "Management Attitudes and the Scanlon Plan." *Industrial Relations,* 1973, *12,* 282–288.

Russell, R. *Sharing Ownership at the Workplace.* Albany: State University of New York Press, 1985.

Schuster, M. H. "The Impact of Union-Management Cooperation on Productivity and Employment. *Industrial and Labor Relations Review,* 1983a, *36,* 415–430.

Schuster, M. H. "Forty Years of Scanlon Plan Research: A Review of the Descriptive and Empirical Literature." In C. Crouch and F. Heller (eds.), *International Yearbook of Organizational Democracy.* 1983b, *1,* 53–71.

Schuster, M. H. "The Scanlon Plan: A Longitudinal Analysis." *Journal of Applied Behavioral Science,* 1984a, *20* (1), 23–28.

Schuster, M. H. *Union-Management Cooperation: Structure, Process, and Impact.* Kalamazoo, Mich.: Upjohn Institute, 1984b.

Schuster, M. H. "Gainsharing Issues for Senior Managers." Unpublished manuscript, School of Management, Syracuse University, 1985.

Shirom, A. "The Industrial Relations System of Industrial Cooperatives in the United States, 1880–1935." *Labor History,* 1972, *13,* 533–551.

Steers, R. M. "Antecedents and Outcomes of Organizational Commitment." *Administrative Science Quarterly*, 1977, *22*, 46–56.

Steers, R. M., and Porter, L. W. "Employee Commitment to Organizations." In R. M. Steers and L. W. Porter (eds.), *Motivation and Worker Behavior*. New York: McGraw-Hill, 1983.

Stern, R. N., and Hammer, T. H. "Buying Your Job: Factors Affecting the Success or Failure of Employee Acquisition Attempts." *Human Relations,* 1978, *31* (12), 1101–1117.

Stern, R. N., Wood, K. H., and Hammer, T. H. *Employee Ownership in Plant Shutdowns: Prospects for Employment Stability*. Kalamazoo, Mich.: Upjohn Institute, 1979.

Strauss, G. "Workers' Participation in Management: An International Perspective." In B. M. Staw and L. L.. Cummings (eds.), *Research in Organizational Behavior*. Vol. 4. Greenwich, Conn.: JAI Press, 1982.

Strauss, G., and Hammer, T. H. *Worker Participation in the United States*. Geneva, Switzerland: International Labour Organization, forthcoming.

Tannenbaum, A. S. "Employee-Owned Companies." In L. L.. Cummings and B. M. Staw (eds.), *Research in Organizational Behavior*. Vol. 5. Greenwich, Conn.: JAI Press, 1983.

Tannenbaum, A. S., Cook, H., and Lochmann, J. "The Relationship of Employee Ownership to the Technological Adaptiveness and Performance of Companies." Unpublished manuscript, Institute for Social Research, Ann Arbor, Michigan, 1984.

Thomas, H., and Logan, C. *Mondragon: An Economic Analysis*. London: Allen & Unwin, 1982.

Trist, E. "The Evolution of Sociotechnical Systems." In A. Van de Ven and W. Joyce (eds.), *Perspectives on Organizational Design and Behavior*. New York: Wiley-Interscience, 1981.

U.S. General Accounting Office. *Employee Stock Ownership Plans: Benefits and Costs of ESOP Tax Incentives for Broadening Stock Ownership*. Report to the Honorable Russel B. Long, U.S. Senate. Washington, D.C.: U.S. General Accounting Office, 1987.

Wagner, I. "Report to the New York Stock Exchange on the Performance of Publicly Traded Companies with Employee Ownership Plans." Unpublished manuscript, National Center for Employee Ownership. Cited in C. Rosen, K. J. Klein, and K. M. Young, *Employee Ownership in America: The Equity Solution*. Lexington, Mass.: Lexington Books, 1984.

Walsh, D. J. "Two-Tier Wage Structures in the U.S. Airline Industry." Unpublished master's thesis, New York State School of Industrial and Labor Relations, Cornell University, 1987.

Webb, S., and Webb, B. *A Constitution for the Socialist Common-wealth of Great Britain.* Cambridge, Mass.: Cambridge University Press. (Originally published 1921.)

White, J. K. "The Scanlon Plan: Causes and Correlates of Success." *Academy of Management Journal,* 1979, *22* (2), 292–312.

White, J. K., and Ruh, R. A. "Effects of Personal Values on the Relationship Between Participation and Job Attitudes." *Administrative Science Quarterly,* 1973, *18* (4), 506–514.

Whyte, W. F. "Worker Participation: Ownership and Control." Paper presented at the 9th World Congress of Sociology, Uppsala, Sweden, 1978.

Whyte, W. F., and others. *Worker Participation and Ownership: Cooperative Strategies for Strengthening Local Economies.* Ithaca, N.Y.: ILR Press, 1983.

PART FOUR

Implementing Organization-Wide Productivity Innovations

The two chapters in this section are very different than what has gone before. They are written by two practicing behavioral scientists, not academicians, and the chapters are intended to illustrate different truths. U.S. organizations have not had a strong record of success for implementing personnel programs when the intervention is viewed as a stand-alone "program" that can be bought and implemented with little additional effort on the organization's part, much as they might install a new air-conditioning system. Chapters Thirteen and Fourteen provide descriptions of work that is intended to change the way the organization manages itself in a very fundamental way. The two authors describe what they do in this regard. They come from somewhat different academic traditions, but they both illustrate the scope of what it takes to truly implement what many of the previous chapters have talked about from a theoretical or research perspective. The two chapters do not review a great deal of literature or research evidence, but we make no apologies for that. They show another, and very important, side of applying industrial-organizational psychology to productivity problems. All the relevant parties must become involved, must come face to face with the organization's goals and values, and must be held accountable for the method and results of the intervention. "Plausible deniability" is not a recourse.

13

CECECECECECECE

Flexible Job Models:
A Productivity Strategy
for the Information Age

Patricia A. McLagan

In the information age, human resource management, organization development, and job design must be flexible, provide appropriate guidance for decision making under uncertainty, and reflect strategies and future needs of the business. The flexible job modeling approach is intended to provide such products through an approach to organization development and job design that has these features:

- Systematically forecasts future organizational requirements.
- Views the organization as an open social system that is constantly changing in response to outside influences. That is, human resource management cannot be designed for the status quo.
- Focuses on outputs (products, services, programs, information) as the *major* building blocks of organization design, rather than positions, organization structure, or type of technology.
- Identifies both the job performance requirements and the individual capabilities needed to produce the outputs of a job.
- Views job design as a process of assigning or reassigning outputs to jobs based on (1) the organization's current and future needs; (2) the current capability, motivation, and development priorities of individuals; and (3) the current capabilities, motives, and development priorities of others in the organization or work team.
- Supports a view of job evaluation that places individuals in broad salary bands based on the overall types of outputs they produce. This allows maximum flexibility in job design without requiring constant adjustments in the compensation structure.

- Treats a description of performance goals as the job description, thus eliminating the traditional job description process and allowing for job design flexibility.
- Provides a conceptual framework for integrating all human resource functions related to organization and job design, development, performance management, selection/placement, and career management.
- Provides managers and the workers themselves with the information they need to fully participate in defining their jobs, managing performance, and guiding development.
- Is easily updated as organization strategies and conditions change.

As should be inferred from the above list, flexible job design is a strategy for change that can be applied to the redesign of a particular job, a specific department, or the entire organization. The focus can be as narrow or broad as is warranted by the needs of the organization.

Key Components of Flexible Job Design

The flexible job modeling approach has its conceptual foundations in the literature of instructional design (Gagné and Briggs, 1979), goal setting (Locke, Shaw, Saari, and Latham, 1981), and participation (Maier, 1973). It is a procedure that leads an organization through a series of steps to specify precisely what outcomes it wants to produce and the kinds of jobs and job holders that will be required to produce those outcomes. The emphasis is on using participative methods and a very specific and concrete language to facilitate the precise description of what an organization wants to do. The central theme is analogous to Gagné's (1962) dictum concerning instruction and training: for Gagné, the fundamental question is not about what training techniques or methods will be used, but about what is to be learned. It is only by knowing the precise objectives of training that we can make reasonable inferences about the content of training, and only after specifying the content of training does it make sense to ask what methods will best promote mastery.

A similar framework can be applied to organization development and job design. The fundamental questions are these: (1) What is to be produced (that is, specific outcome goals), and (2) What must be mastered (by people in the organization) to meet these objectives? Only after these design questions are answered can questions of method be addressed (that is, better selection, training, or management techniques). As was the case with individual training, putting the question of content before method sounds simple-minded, but it is fundamental. This order of events is violated time and time again in human resource management. The promises of this or that "program" are no substitute for a careful and painstaking examination of the more fundamental issues.

Flexible job modeling attempts to address these design questions systematically, by using panels of experts at each stage and by incorporating management involvement and accountability at each step. That is, the organization itself must do the major design work, must participate completely, and must accept accountability for the final design. The remainder of this chapter gives a brief description of how this approach proceeds.

The flexible job design methodology produces five major products:

1. A statement of assumptions about the current and future context within which the business must operate or jobs must be designed.
2. Output menus that specify the desired outputs from a group or function.
3. Competency menus that specify the knowledge, skills, and abilities required to produce the outputs.
4. Generic job or role models.
5. Individual job models.

Context Assumptions. We first make the prior assumption that job design, as it is described in this chapter, is a major vehicle for accomplishing an organization's goals. However, to use job design intelligently, we must take future conditions and strategic requirements into account. This is a major challenge in a dynamic environment: when past performance cannot adequately describe future requirements, on what basis do we infer those future requirements? The flexible job design approach incorporates a step we refer to as the description of "context assumptions." These are statements that describe highly probable future conditions that will affect the job or organization being analyzed. The statements may be predictions about strategy ("Our key markets will be . . ."), structure ("The organization will decentralize, increasing the number of profit centers"), technology ("All major office functions will be automated by . . ."), or about such factors as work-force demographics or values, the legal/regulatory environment, the competitive environment, and so on. These assumptions about future conditions are derived from a series of carefully structured sessions with panels of expert judges. Depending on the context domain under consideration (for example, legal-regulatory, manufacturing technology, and so on), the best available expert judges are chosen for the panel. The process of achieving consensus among the expert panel members is much like a Delphi forecasting procedure. What is crucial here is that it is identified as an explicit step in flexible job design, and significant time is devoted to it.

The description of context assumptions then becomes a major source of information for describing the work that must be done. It also provides a basis for predicting the competencies that must be present in the organization in order to meet future requirements.

Output Menus. An output menu is a list of *all* the outputs (products, services, programs, information) that the organization must provide to external individuals or groups, or that individuals in the organization must provide to each other to accomplish the organization's operating goals.

Output menus do not define individual job requirements. They provide a comprehensive list of the products, services, or information that must ultimately become individual or team accountabilities to achieve the organization's goals. Outputs on the menu are stated at the level of generality judged to be most useful in describing any individual job's outputs to any other job or group in or outside the organization.

There are two major ways to categorize outputs on the menu: by core discipline and/or by span of control. Core disciplines are categories that have a common underlying subject matter, or "body of knowledge" (for example, engineering is a core discipline, with interrelated research methodologies, concepts, theoretical bases). (See Table 13.1 for a sample output menu by discipline.) Categorization of outputs by "span of control" draws on Elliott Jaques's (1961) and others' assertion that the value of jobs (or outputs) corresponds to the relative impact of the decisions (or judgments) that must be made about them. In the flexible job design methodology, there are six broad categories of levels of outputs, ranging from narrow to broad decision impact, defined as outputs whose judgments relate to:

1. Simple, discrete, prescribed tasks ("a clean floor").
2. Semiskilled operations that are to be performed ("entries").
3. Statements about how existing processes will be used ("course designs").
4. Broad resource allocations ("department budget").
5. Action and program priorities ("business plan").
6. Broad organizational goals or objectives ("strategic goals").

Because higher levels of outputs have broader, longer-lasting impact on the organization, they have higher value. This simple

Table 13.1. Sample Output Menu by Discipline.

Managerial Outputs	*Training and Development Outputs*
• Work climate	• Needs analyses
• Performance feedback	• Evaluation processes
• Development support	• Facilitated cases
• Department's operating plans	• Learning objectives
• Organization's strategic goals	• Instructor guides
• Business plan	• People with new skills or knowledge
	• Course designs
Finance Outputs	*Engineering Outputs*
• General ledger entries	• Technical standards
• Inspected receipts	• Equipment designs
• Invoices	• Stress analyses
• Expense allocations	• Operating guidelines
• Variance reports	
• Cost analyses	

classification scheme provides a framework for evaluating jobs that allows for maximum flexibility of job content as well as comparable worth decisions. An individual's overall job may be placed at a level that corresponds to the major output level for which the organization expects to use the individual's skills. The specific job content may then draw on the full range of outputs at that level (and across disciplines) without requiring a reclassification for salary purposes. Also, an individual's job content may change as needed by simple reassignment of outputs (job responsibility change), addition of outputs (job enlargement), reduction of outputs (job reduction), addition of outputs from the next level for developmental reasons (developmental assignment), and so on. If such a menu can be described, it opens major options for nonhierarchical career movement. It also provides a basis for salary decisions: salary ranges can be established for each level. Within those ranges, base salary may rise to reflect increased depth or breadth of output capability.

Output menus are derived and updated by another panel of expert judges, composed of experts in the core disciplines, and by management representatives who are responsible for the priorities, work requirements, and job categories in the part of the organization each represents. The menus identify outputs in the context of current as well as future requirements. For example, in a large telecommunications company, fifteen engineers who were known for their technical leadership developed the engineering section of an output menu for their company. Context assumptions that they and their management developed were part of their decision structure.

Competency Menus. A competency is a personal capability that is critical to the production of a quality output or outputs. A competency menu lists all the competencies that are important for the successful production and delivery of the entire range of an organization's outputs (those that are delivered within and outside the system). Competencies may be stated as broad areas of knowledge or skill (for example, "listening skill," "analysis skill," "physical strength," "industrial-organizational psychology knowledge") or as relatively discrete and specialized areas of competence or skill (for example, "upper-body strength," "survey questionnaire development skill").

Broad knowledge and skill statements are more appropriate expressions of competency requirements as the outputs of the position increase in their breadth of impact and in the degree to which problem solving and decision making are the product. Thus task descriptions are less useful than descriptions of the broad knowledge and skills that a performer will draw on to make judgments and decisions about appropriate actions to take. An exhaustive competency menu would contain a finely grained list of the key skills and knowledge required for producing a job's outcomes. However, in our work it is most common for the menu to describe broad knowledge and skills, thus relegating finer levels of competency identification to the "generic model" or "individual job model" stages described in later sections. (For example, "knowledge of the organization" may be required across a broad range and across levels of outputs, but "knowledge of the engineering organization structure" may be required only in selected parts of the organization.)

We have found five categories of competencies to be useful in menu development. Three are skill or capability categories: physical, inter- and intrapersonal, and cognitive process. Two are knowledge categories: broad business/industry knowledge and specialist knowledge.

These categories and their contents draw on a broad range of taxonomies and models, including Bloom's taxonomies (Krathwohl, Bloom, and Masia, 1964), Fine's structural job analysis categories (Fine and Wiley, 1971), Gardner's theory of multiple intelligence (Gardner, 1983), and (for detailed specialist knowledge) theories and models from individual disciplines.

The panel method is again used to derive a competency menu for an organization from a series of carefully structured judgments by management representatives, incumbents in key positions, experts in the core discipline, and job analysis experts. They draw from and expand on a generic list of knowledge and skills. The final menu may contain fifty or more broad knowledge and skill competencies that relate to the full range of outputs and to the context assumptions. In addition, the menu may include behavioral indicators for each competency, which provide tangible illustrations of different levels of mastery (much like the behavioral anchors used with behaviorally anchored rating scales).

Generic Job Models. A generic job model is a general description of or framework for a role or job. The generic job model usually does not totally describe any one person's job. Rather, it specifies the outputs and the competencies that are the most likely and generally desirable requirements of people in that role or job.

Management representatives, and others who are knowledgeable about the work to be done, develop the generic job model by pulling relevant outputs and competencies off the menus. They do so after identifying the relevant context assumptions for the position they are describing. The final model must reflect these assumptions. The level of outputs in the generic job model determines the salary range appropriate for the position. The prototype also serves as a basis for career planning and selection as well as a guide for individual job design and objective setting.

Individual Job Models. Individual job designs are becoming, and must continue to become, more individualized and flexible. This presents major problems for traditional job design methodologies, which hold the individual constant while developing job descriptions that can accommodate many personalities. In today's environment, individuals often *shape* their jobs. As they work, they broaden and deepen or reduce the scope of their output responsibilities. Because of their competencies, others include them in task forces, give them special assignments, and ask them to play different roles. In addition to the individual's own influence on job requirements, jobs are also affected by strategies and external conditions, capabilities of others in the work or support team, available resources and technologies, and so on. An individual's actual job will therefore probably vary from the generic model for the position.

In spite of these dynamics, it is still important for incumbents and their managers and colleagues to be clear about job requirements and roles. The individual job model helps them perform this purpose.

It is a list of the outputs an individual is expected to produce and the competencies that will be used during a specified performance period. The model thus becomes a set of objectives and therefore a guide to specific individual performance for a predetermined period.

The individual job model may use a generic job model as a guide. It may draw from menus of outputs and competencies. But it may also include unique or customized outputs to reflect unique requirements that could not be anticipated by "menu developers" or other people outside the individual's immediate work group. For example, a general output of a market researcher might be "market analysis," but a specific output *next year* for a specific market analyst might be "analysis of the southern market."

Individuals, their managers, and perhaps their customers work together to specify context assumptions and create job models that reflect the actual requirements of the job for a specified time period. These may be subject to review by consultants and coordinating groups or managers, to assure that all key organization performance areas are adequately covered. Because the profiles are based on the organization's requirements (menus, assumptions, generic job models) as well as the unique context requirements of the job, they are both future-oriented *and* defensible as job-relevant. They also help individuals focus attention on *output,* not activity, as the "raison d'être" of their job.

A Case Example: The ASTD Competency Study

In 1981, the American Society for Training and Development (ASTD) commissioned a competency study of the training and development field (McLagan, 1983; McLagan and Bedrick, 1983). The intention was to develop tools and procedures to guide the job design of training and development positions, permit more systematic career management, facilitate self-development for training professionals, inform the design of postgraduate programs, and enhance the management of the training and development function for current and future practitioners of training and development. Ninety professionals, academic and nonacademic, nominated by ASTD leaders as experts in training and development used a modified Delphi technique to identify thirty-four context assumptions—or predictions about the conditions that would have the most impact on the field through 1990. These context assumptions included:

- Increased importance of technical/computer competencies.
- Increased effort (dollars and time) toward improving productivity.
- Increased number of teachers seeking jobs in industry rather than educational institutions.
- Increased dominance of information processing as the major learning model.
- More dual-career families.
- Increased average age of work force.
- Increased need for business/industry to operate in an international environment.

The Professional Development Committee of the ASTD then worked with over 500 experts in the field in a series of Delphi panels to identify the key outputs of the training and development function, both currently and in the future, given the agreed-upon context assumptions. The result was a taxonomic menu of 102 outputs. The same expert panels also used a modified Delphi procedure to develop a basic competency menu for people in the training and development field. This menu identified and defined 31 knowledges and skills. At the same time, three levels of proficiency were described in behavioral terms for each competency, by generating critical incident–like descriptions of each level of mastery or performance. This step provided a rather detailed specification of competent performance as a training and development specialist. Finally, the experts and the ASTD Professional Development Committee identified 15 roles associated with training and development work through 1990, each role describing a coherent set of responsibilities/activities that was relatively independent (functionally speaking) of the other roles. The total of 15 was intended to describe all the major parts of the profession. This step was, in effect, a cluster analysis of outputs into roles by expert judgment. The judges identified the outputs and competencies for each role, thus creating "generic job (role) models." Table 13.2 provides an illustrative model for the role of evaluator, including the relevant outputs and competencies drawn from the taxonomic menus of 102 outputs and 31 basic competencies.

Individual training and development professionals are now using the study products to design and describe their own jobs. They either select relevant individual outputs and competencies from the menus (and thus bypass the generic role models), or they select the role or roles that make up their job. In either case, the outputs and competencies are the building blocks for describing an individual's

**Table 13.2. Sample Generic Job Model for the Training and
Development Role of Evaluator.**

Evaluator role: the role of identifying the extent of a program's, service's, or
product's impact.

Key outputs for this role (this role produces the following):

- Instruments to assess individual change in knowledge, skill, attitude, behavior, results.
- Instruments to assess program and instructional quality.
- Reports (written and oral) of program impact on individuals.
- Reports (written and oral) of program impact on an organization.
- Evaluation and validation designs and plans (written and oral).
- Written instruments to collect and interpret data.

Key competencies for this role (the following competencies are critical for
people to perform the outputs for this role):

- Competency identification skill
- Computer competence
- Data reduction skill
- Performance observation skill
- Presentation skill
- Questioning skill
- Research skill
- Writing skill

---

work. They make it possible to be flexible in individual job design but
to retain a relatively small and stable list of job elements.

ASTD plans on five-year updates of the context assumptions,
outputs, and competencies. However, individual job designs are able
to change as frequently as necessary within that time frame, because
the emphasis in the study was on menus, not individual job descriptions or job titles.

Uses of Flexible Job Models

Flexible job modeling is useful in five broad categories of
application: performance management, training and development,
career management, human resource planning, and organization and
job design. While the precise form of the implementation process may
vary depending on such factors as the organization's structure,
management climate, and existing systems (for example, strategic
planning procedures), the basic applications are as follows.

Performance Management. Flexible job models can be used as
a basis for goal and objective setting, performance observation,

ongoing and periodic feedback, and rewards and recognition. The emphasis on *outputs* is particularly useful for these applications (see Table 13.3). The individual's goals or objectives can be drawn from the output menu and/or from generic job models, or from an individual's and manager's own knowledge and forecasts of job requirements. The goal-setting process produces a list of the outputs on the menu that the individual will be accountable for during a specified performance period. Goals also include the critical criteria and measures that must be met to assure that internal and/or external customers are satisfied with the quality of products and services.

With this method, goals and objectives do not specify *how* the performer will work—unless the "how" is a critical requirement for reasons of safety, values, ethics, customer satisfaction, or strategic contribution (for example, a pilot must "work step by step through a preflight checklist before takeoff," or a salesperson must produce orders "that order processors can read," or a nuclear equipment operator must follow specific procedures). Nor is it necessary that all goals be objectively measurable. The key measurement question in this systems-oriented approach is, What qualities, subjective or objective, must the output possess in order to satisfy its receivers? Objectivity of measurement does not drive the selection of goals; the needs of the organization and of the output's "receivers" do.

Table 13.3. Sample Output-Focused Performance Goals.

| | *Performance Goals for a Supervisor* | |
Output	*Critical Criteria That the Output Must Meet*	*Measures/Indicators (How We Will Know That the Criteria Have Been Met)*
Production plan	• Is complete by Aug. 1 • Reflects input from sales and marketing • Minimizes equipment downtown • Is approved by plant manager	• Opinion of plant manager • Opinion of sales manager • Actual equipment downtown due to production plan
Development support for employees	• Employees have a written development plan • Employees know what their needs are • The manager plays an active support role	• Sampling reviews of employee plans • Opinions of employees

In this scenario, performance feedback focuses on the quality of what the individual is producing and has produced. *Ongoing* feedback is essential, and the outputs and criteria listed as the individual's or group's goals are the targets for this feedback.

Outputs are also the focus of attention during periodic performance appraisals. The appraisal question becomes, To what extent did your outputs meet the previously agreed upon quality criteria? Quality is the standard. Internal or external customers play a major role in determining that standard. The job model also provides a useful basis for analyzing the causes of performance problems. The key questions become these: To what extent are the individual's outputs meeting the needs of the people who must use them? What evidence, objective and subjective, leads to this conclusion? Where are the strengths and problems? What competencies are contributing to success or failure? How can competency deficiencies be remedied? What failures in output were not under the control of individual competencies?

Finally, flexible job models produce descriptions of performance requirements that support an accomplishment-focused approach to rewards and recognition. Individuals and managers can acknowledge and reward successful output production. This keeps the focus on performance accomplishments and the extent to which the accomplishments support the strategic requirements and values of the business as well as satisfy the needs of the internal and external customers.

Because they do not prescribe activities, output-focused performance goals provide direction without unduly restricting judgment or innovation. This means that a traditional source of performance discipline and control, the specification of work procedures and actions, does not exist, except where it is critical to quality (then the procedure is a criterion of the output). Instead, discipline and control must occur through (1) increasing the amount of communication about overall business goals and assumptions, (2) training individuals in output-focused planning and goal setting, rewarding personal goal accountability and commitment, (4) increasing the flow of feedback to assure that the individual has timely information for making appropriate adjustments in goals and in the actions for achieving them, (5) assuring that people in coordinating roles (for example, managers) are accountable for the overall outputs of the group they manage, and (6) assuring that performance management is defined and rewarded as a shared responsibility, which requires that both individuals and their managers have the skills and attitudes necessary for creating and sustaining a high-accountability, open-performance environment. If, as the design for flexible job modeling stipulates, there is wide involvement in the development of the job model, then increasing communication about goals and assumptions, training in output-focused planning, and commitment to goal accountability will be facilitated by the model-building procedure itself.

Training and Development. Flexible job models provide a common language and focus for use in all phases of individual and group development: needs analysis, the design of learning experiences, and development itself. Because the impact of development actions is not felt until the future, the anticipatory quality of menus and generic models makes them an especially appropriate basis for this application. Job models and menus may be used for group or individualized development actions. For example, the training and development staff can convert the menus and generic job models into diagnostic questionnaires and then use the data collected with them as a basis for forecasting group development needs. These needs forecasts can focus on either outputs or competencies. Both generate information about common strengths and improvement areas. Needs analyses that examine output quality have an added advantage of providing useful operational information to management; weak output quality may signal an organizational deficiency other than knowledge or skill.

Needs analysis results provide guidelines for the design of learning programs and materials and for the design of on-the-job developmental actions. Designers must plan on improving the specific competencies associated with the outputs or competencies that the analysis has identified as weak. This helps avoid the waste that characterizes less targeted approaches.

The models and menus also support self-directed development. Individuals can use generic job models or their own job models as a basis for gathering data about their own strengths and weaknesses. While the organization may provide diagnostic tools for people in specific categories of jobs or roles (for example, supervisor, salesperson, engineer, general manager), the prototype models or individualized job profiles themselves may be a succinct enough basis for self-diagnosis and for gathering feedback from others. Individuals may then use the job models as checklists for selecting learning experiences: reading materials, courses, expert advisers, and so on. Even when the organization does not provide formal diagnostic tools and organized learning activities, individuals can engage in self-designed, focused development that relates to the broader needs of their jobs and the business itself. Generic job models or individual job models are thus a key link between job and organization requirements and the individual's own development actions.

Career Management. Job models have unique implications for career management, individual career planning, human resource planning, and selection. This is true because the components of the model reflect future requirements and conditions. Also, because the output and competency menus describe taxonomies of critical job elements and are not tied to specific jobs, the menus provide a relatively stable foundation for career planning. Individuals who develop the capability to deliver specific kinds of outputs or master specific competencies should be able to perform in any job where those elements are important. The point is this: in the future, many jobs as we know them may not exist. But their elements or outputs may be "reorganized" into new patterns. Career planning should prepare people to be able to deploy their capabilities across the spectrum of jobs that will exist in the future.

Human Resource Planning. In this context, human resource planning becomes a process of forecasting key outputs and competencies and assuring that people who are capable of providing key outputs are available when the organization needs them. It is *not* a process of forecasting which boxes on today's organization chart will or won't be filled. In the future, organization and job restructuring will likely occur with greater frequency to support new initiatives and to assure the best deployment of current talents. Thus management can use the output and competency menus to communicate their view of tomorrow's most probable requirements. They can update the menus and generic job models as part of their strategic planning exercise and thus provide a dynamic framework for individual and organizational planning. They can do this without committing to a specific organization structure or job design.

Generic models for roles and positions can also be used to guide selection, promotion, and other job assignments. The key selection task is finding individuals who possess the competencies needed to perform in a particular role or position or whose capabilities relate to a critical mass of the outputs their units and teams will be asked to provide.

Output and competency menus, generic job models, and individual job models can provide individuals and the organization with tangible targets for career and staffing plans. The utility of these tools will depend on the thoroughness and care with which they were developed and on the ability of human resource professionals, managers, and employees to stop thinking about careers as movements from job to job on the organization chart. They must start thinking about the organization as a dynamic, open system in which organization needs, team capabilities, and individual competence will determine an individual's unique output configuration at any point in time.

Organization and Job Design. With this application, we come full circle. Flexible job modeling is primarily a job and organization design process. In this methodology, the organization is first described as an open system that will pursue its goals in a dynamic future. The management of the organization chooses its goals, markets, and products. These choices place the organization in a specific competitive economic environment. These choices also define the domain of subsystem outputs that must be produced in order to accomplish the larger organizational purposes.

The first organization design problem is to define the system and subsystem outputs that must be produced to assure the highest quality performance of the system. A second design problem is to determine the value of each output and thus assess how much the organization is willing to pay for the skills and other resources used in its production. A third problem is to determine the best mix of resources to accomplish each output. Yet a fourth design issue is to organize accountabilities for those outputs and thus assure optimum use of available human resources.

Again, the procedure used by flexible job modeling to address these design problems is to identify the appropriate experts and guide them through some variant of the Delphi procedure. For example, if the first problem is to define the organization's critical outputs, the managers and technical people most responsible for outputs at that level must agree to serve on the expert panel, and they must be prepared to commit a significant amount of time to group discussions of the issues and to generating specific, concrete descriptions of outputs that will go through at least one or two rounds of Delphi-type revision. Thus the procedure literally forces the parties to come face to face with their most critical issues, to make their judgments explicit (they must write them down or describe them in detail orally), to compare their concrete, explicit ideas with the ideas of other experts, and to come to a consensus (or maintain a divergent view) based on an explicit rationale. Such a procedure is consistent with many decades of research on group problem solving dealing with its effects on commitment and solution quality (for example, Maier, 1967; Vroom, 1976).

The process requires considerable effort and involvement on the part of the people in the organization. In that sense, it is not cheap. It also requires considerable facilitation skills. Outputs of the facilitator's role include obtaining management commitment to the process and showing managers that this approach confronts directly the major issues of the business and is therefore an integral part of their management responsibility.

If the commitment of top management can be achieved, flexible organization and job design is a total-system design process. The output and competency menus describe the productivity requirements for the whole organization. The elements on the menus are allocated and reallocated as individual accountabilities. This allocation and reallocation process leads to individual job designs that can both support the organization's needs and fully utilize team and individual competencies.

Job Models and Productivity/Quality Strategies

Productivity and quality programs have several broad goals: (1) to assure that all resources are focused on the organization's current and long-term objectives, (2) to assure that products and services meet the customer's quality requirements, (3) to assure that the most appropriate resources are available and fully employed, (4) to prevent waste, (5) to create an atmosphere of continuous improvement, and ultimately (6) to assure that the organization is financially viable, competitive, and capable of sustaining its own growth. Flexible job models represent a way of thinking about work and provide a major tool designed to support these goals.

First, they help focus all resources on the current and long-range goals of the enterprise. The context assumptions predict the future conditions that will affect the goals and work of the organization and of individual organizational units.

Second, the focus is on productivity in meeting the (internal or external) customers' needs, not on performing activities. Flexible job models define work in terms of outputs. Key questions to describe an individual's or a team's work include the following: Who are our customers? What should I/we provide them? What are their quality requirements? The output menus portray the organization as a productive enterprise. Everyone, at every level in the organization, has responsibility for or contributes to one or more of the outputs on the organization's menu. And that contribution is expected to provide value to the customer.

Third, flexible job modeling helps assure that the most appropriate human resources are available and fully employed. Individuals are assigned or take on responsibilities based on their competence to perform. Because outputs, not individual job descriptions, are the basic building blocks of job design, individual jobs can be highly flexible and draw on unique individual competencies to assure optimal use of the competencies available in the team.

The same issues apply for forecasting future human resource needs, although an additional question becomes important: What additional competencies will we need, and how will we develop/ acquire them? The flexible job design methodology provides the tools and frameworks for answering all these important resource questions.

Fourth, the flexible job models can help prevent waste. Major waste often occurs when people pursue tasks as ends rather than developing better ways of producing the outputs that are the real purpose of the job. Flexible job models clarify what should be produced, what its qualities must be in order to satisfy the customer, and what competencies will support performance. The models thus help focus attention on the productive requirements of the job and on the need to assure that everything individuals do supports constructive goals.

Fifth, flexible job models help create an atmosphere of continuous improvement. Because the focus is on ends rather than means, new ways of working are always possible. For example, floor sweepers who see their job as "sweeping the floor" are limited to innovations in *sweeping* technology. On the other hand, sweepers who see their job as "producing a clean floor" can draw on a far broader range of innovation: they might suggest floor mats, air cleaners, or even new, cleaner work processes for people who are working in the area.

Finally, the flexible job modeling methodology helps management better describe and assess the cost-value equation. Because everyone's work is described as outputs, it is possible to put a value on each output (for example, on a clean floor, on a positive work climate, or on an engineering drawing). If the cost of producing the output exceeds its value, appropriate people must decide whether to change the requirements, ask someone else to produce the output, stop producing it, or produce it in another way.

Flexible job modeling is a productivity and quality tool. Perhaps more important, it provides people everywhere in the organization with a way of thinking that helps them effectively manage their jobs. Individuals who use it continually ask, What conditions will affect my work in the future? Who are my customers? What do I need to provide them? What will their requirements be? How will I know the requirements have been met? What competencies will I need so that I can meet their needs?

Organizations whose people continually ask and answer these

questions are well on their way toward accomplishing their productivity and quality goals.

Conclusion

Job analysis, job design, and job description are cornerstone
processes in industrial-organizational psychology. However, traditional approaches to job and organization design, which examine past
behavior and specific tasks, are often not the most appropriate in
today's dynamic environment.

The conditions that today's managers face are fundamentally
different than those that gave rise to existing job analysis purposes and
methodologies. The new work environment requires new approaches
to the design of work—approaches that assure optimum and flexible
utilization of human capabilities in service to the strategic goals of the
enterprise. Managers and employees themselves are looking for job
design methodologies to accomplish these ends. Flexible job modeling
is a systems approach to job and organization design that addresses the
needs of an increasingly dynamic and open workplace.

References

Fine, S., and Wiley, W. *An Introduction to Functional Job Analysis.*
Kalamazoo, Mich.: Upjohn Institute, 1971.

Gagné, R. M. "Military Training and Principles of Learning."
American Psychologist, 1962, *17,* 83–91.

Gagné, R. M., and Briggs, L. J. *Principles of Instructional Design.*
New York: Holt, Rinehart & Winston, 1979.

Gardner, H. *Frames of Mind: The Theory of Multiple Intelligence.*
New York: Basic Books, 1983.

Jaques, E. *Equitable Payment.* New York: Wiley, 1961.

Krathwohl, D. R., Bloom, S., and Masia, B. *Taxonomy of Educational
Objectives: The Classification of Educational Goals. Handbook II.
Affective Domain.* New York: McKay, 1964.

Locke, E. A., Shaw, K. N., Saari, L. M., and Latham, G. P. "Goal
Setting and Task Performance: 1969–1980." *Psychological Bulletin,*
1981, *90,* 125–152.

McLagan, P. A. *Models for Excellence: The Conclusions and Recom-
mendations of the ASTD Training and Development Competency
Study.* Washington, D.C.: American Society for Training and
Development, 1983.

McLagan, P. A., and Bedrick, D. "Models for Excellence: The Results

of the ASTD Training and Development Competency Study."
Training and Development Journal, June 1983, pp. 10–20.

Maier, N. R. F. "Assets and Liabilities in Group Problem Solving."
Psychological Review, 1967, *74,* 239–249.

Maier, N. R. F. *Psychology in Industrial Organizations.* (4th ed.)
Boston: Houghton Mifflin, 1973.

Vroom, V. H. "Leadership." In M. D. Dunnette (ed.), *Handbook of
Industrial and Organizational Psychology.* Skokie, Ill.: Rand
McNally, 1976.

14

ᔓᔓᔓᔓᔓᔓᔓᔓᔓᔓ

Employee Involvement: A Sustained Labor/Management Initiative at the Ford Motor Company

Paul A. Banas

The purpose of this chapter is to describe a sustained joint labor-management initiative in employee participation that has stimulated a significant cultural change in a major industrial corporation. It is neither a complete documentary nor a controlled experiment. Rather, it is one person's account, as a participant-observer and consultant. As a result, it is a combination of personal recollections and factual evidence and is meant to accurately reflect the efforts of the thousands of people, including employees, union leaders, and managers, who have been involved in making employee involvement a way of life at the Ford Motor Company.

What Is Employee Involvement?

Philosophically, employee involvement begins with a belief on the part of the union and management that employees want more out of work than extrinsic rewards and that the two parties, working together, can create a work environment in which employees can achieve job satisfaction by directing their ingenuity and creativity toward improving their work and overall work environment. It assumes that when given the opportunity, employees want to develop their full capabilities and participate in the success of the company. It is a three-way partnership—a recognition by employees, the union, and management that their common interests can best be served when there are common goals and mutual benefits.

Operationally, in the early stages of employee involvement at Ford, the term *employee involvement* was defined very narrowly. It referred to a group of employees getting together with their supervisor to identify and solve work-related problems. As a result, the focus was on the formation of problem-solving groups. However, as the parties became more experienced with the process, the definition was broadened to include participation in other processes usually reserved for management, such as planning, goal setting, communicating, and decision making. Also, the form of employee involvement began to take different shapes as the definition expanded. These changes will be discussed in greater detail later in this chapter.

Employee involvement at Ford has created a long-term, major change in Ford's basic management style and in the union-management relationship. Probably the most difficult task for both union leadership and management has been to keep a balanced perspective when they are expected to be adversarial on certain issues and then work jointly on employee involvement. In several situations, the employee involvement process has been recessed until a particular issue or the conflict could be resolved. Parties to the process do not believe that employee involvement is the panacea that will resolve all issues.

Although employee involvement is a product of contract negotiations and as such could be considered a joint *program*, strenuous efforts have been made by both the union and management to refer to it as a *process*. The main reason is that, historically at Ford, a *program* has connoted an activity that has a beginning and an end. The objective is to make employee involvement a continuous process.

Origins of Employee Involvement at Ford

Discussions between the Ford Motor Company and the United Automobile Workers (UAW) about joint efforts to support greater participation of employees go back to 1973. However, employee involvement, as a systematic, viable joint union-management initiative, had its principal origins in the 1979 negotiations. During these negotiations, the company and the union discussed at length the potential benefits of increased involvement of employees in matters affecting their work. The parties concluded that employee involvement held great promise for aiding and expanding efforts of the company and union to make work a more satisfying and stimulating experience. They felt that it could enhance employee creativity, contribute to improvements in the workplace, support goals of achieving the highest-quality products, heighten efficiency, and reduce unwarranted absenteeism. As a result of these discussions, a Letter of Understanding was signed in October 1979 committing the union and the company to a process labeled *employee involvement.*

To provide leadership and focus for the goals agreed upon in the 1979 negotiations, a National Joint Committee on Employee Involvement (NJCEI) was established and given the following responsibilities:

- Review and evaluate existing programs that involve improving the work environment of Ford employees represented by the UAW.
- Develop new concepts and pilot projects, including actions that encourage employee participation in identifying and solving work-related problems, in actions directed at minimizing the disruptive effect of unwarranted absenteeism on employees and operations, and in examination of alternative work schedules.
- Maintain records of its meetings, deliberations, and all projects and evaluations it conducts.
- Make reports to the company and the UAW on the results of its activities.

In November 1979, Philip Caldwell, then president of the company, articulated top management policy with a Policy Letter on Employee Involvement, which applied to all employees of the company and which provided guidelines to management on how they were expected to operate. The essence of this policy is captured in the first paragraph, which reads as follows: "It is the policy of the Company to encourage and enable all employees to become involved in and contribute to the success of the Company. A work climate should be created and maintained in which employees, at all levels, can achieve individual goals and work satisfaction by directing their talents and energies toward clearly defined Company Goals."

Background Events. This was not the first time that the company and the union had engaged in joint programs. A precedent had been established over the years in such areas as apprenticeship, health and safety, employee orientation, and alcohol and drug abuse. Over the years, the company had also introduced training programs for managers in participative management; various plants had experimented with job enrichment; a company-wide Salaried Employee Opinion Survey Program had been instituted to enhance communication; assessment centers for selection of first-line supervisors incorporated ability to relate to employees as an important criterion; a few plants had experimented with organizational development techniques that encouraged employee participation. The primary factor missing was the catalyst to make participation the preferred way of management throughout the company. The joint UAW-Ford employee involvement process was designed to be that catalyst.

In November 1978, a Human Resources Study Team recommended that management attention and the necessary resources be focused on improving productivity within manufacturing by developing a work environment in company plants and offices that fostered increased involvement and improved satisfaction. Specifically, the study team recommended that a corporate policy be established that explicitly stated that it is the responsibility of all levels of management to develop a work environment in which employees are encouraged, to the fullest extent practicable, to participate in resolving job problems and to contribute to decisions that affect their work. The team also recommended that each manufacturing division be asked to implement at least one employee involvement pilot program.

In October 1978, Philip Caldwell made the following statement at a meeting of the top executives of the company: "Our strategy for the years ahead will come to nothing unless we ask for greater participation of our workforce. Without motivated and concerned workers, we're not going to lower our costs as much as we need to— and we aren't going to get the product quality we need."

In that same year, in a report to top management, a Durability, Quality, and Reliability (DQR) Taskforce identified the following problem: "The entire hourly and salaried workforce are not involved in problem solving. In particular, it is believed that DQR could be improved through the planned involvement of employees, particularly hourly, on a voluntary (and paid) basis in work-related problem solving activities as an integral part of the ongoing way of doing business."

At the same time that these kinds of pronouncements were being made, a few plants were already taking action. At the Indianapolis plant, a consultant was hired to assess the readiness of the plant for employee involvement. Because Indianapolis had developed a reputation for enlightened and innovative management, it was no surprise that the plant was ready to step forward as the first plant to implement employee involvement. A management steering committee was formed and a plan of action was developed, focusing on the creation of problem-solving groups among hourly employees. A few months later, the union joined in the effort, and the Indianapolis plant was selected as the pilot site for introducing employee involvement.

A few months after Indianapolis initiated its project, four additional plants implemented forms of employee involvement and five other plants initiated planning for implementation. A corporate ad hoc committee was formed to coordinate efforts, to facilitate information exchange, and to initiate further planning for implementation. One of the committee's first actions was to disseminate guidelines for the implementation of employee involvement. They pointed out that employee involvement projects took time and should proceed in increments. They emphasized the importance of planning, having adequate funding, forming a joint union-management steering committee, starting with a pilot group, and systematically monitoring progress. It was also recommended that a professional consultant be used to help guide the process. The committee further recommended, as had the 1978 study team, that each manufacturing division should be asked to implement at least one employee involvement pilot program.

All of these actions, which took place prior to the signing of the Letter of Understanding and the Policy Letter, set the stage for the introduction of employee involvement within the company.

Implementation Strategy

Building on the earlier work of the ad hoc committee and the plants, the NJCEI developed an implementation strategy. The elements of the strategy were identified as top union/management support, a common language, knowledge and understanding, implementation guidelines, local ownership, adequate resources and funding, and education and training.

Top Union/Management Support. As a demonstration of top union/management support, teams of NJCEI representatives visited plants to explain employee involvement, discuss its relationship to UAW-Ford collective bargaining agreement, and provide guidelines for implementation. The teams consisted of a union leader, a corporate staff labor relations representative, and a corporate staff personnel research consultant. As a rule, they were accompanied by a UAW regional representative.

Prior to a joint meeting of plant management representatives and local union leadership, separate meetings were held by both groups to deal with any sensitive questions or potential problems. These separate meetings were particularly valuable where the parties had a history of a strong adversarial relationship. When the joint meeting took place, both parties were more receptive to the joint presentations and to initiating a pilot employee involvement project. The following principles formed the basis for the comments made at these meetings by union leaders and the staff labor relations representatives:

- Employee involvement projects were to be separate from collective bargaining agreements. They were not to be a substitute for the grievance procedure or other contractual provisions.
- Participation of represented employees was to be strictly voluntary.
- Projects were to be based on local circumstances and needs.
- Elected union representatives were to be involved in the development and implementation of local projects.
- Programs were to evolve in a reasonable and prudent manner over a period of time.
- There was to be no single program offered to work for everybody or for all locations.
- Local management or union leadership was to be given license to terminate a project at any time.

The role of the staff personnel research consultant at the joint meeting was to present suggested guidelines for implementation of employee involvement. These guidelines will be presented later in the chapter.

Once employee involvement was launched, local initiatives were given a boost by periodic visits by the cochairs of the NJCEI. These visits were especially important in that they gave employees a chance to showcase their accomplishments. These visits proved to be valuable at a later stage in the employee involvement process as a way of revitalizing programs that had lost some of their momentum.

To further reinforce the importance of employee involvement to the company, the chairman, the president, and other senior executives emphasized the value of employee involvement whenever they visited a Ford facility. Indeed, the number of visits by senior management to company facilities was increased substantially in order to promote employee involvement and to recognize employee accomplishments. This left little doubt in the minds of the employees at all levels about the commitment of top management.

Common Language, Knowledge, and Understanding. A great deal of time and effort were spent in communicating with management, union leaders, and employees. Communications included presentations to management, union, and employee groups, NJCEI newsletters, and explanatory brochures. These communications dealt with the philosophy of employee involvement; its definition; its benefits; the role of the employee, union, and management; guidelines for launching the employee involvement process; and the use of consultants.

Employee Involvement Guidelines. The goal of the employee involvement guidelines was to provide direction and at the same time allow for maximum autonomy, to encourage local ownership. Although the Letter of Understanding and the Policy Letter set the parameters under which these joint initiatives would be carried out, it was the responsibility of the local parties to determine what would be done, how it would be done, when it would be done, and at what rate. The guidelines were developed as a framework for carrying out these responsibilities.

The guidelines addressed the eight elements, or steps, that were considered essential to the successful launching of employee involvement in each location or part of the business.

Step 1. *Union and management support.* Key factors in gaining joint support at the local level were the Letter of Understanding, the Policy Letter, and the visits by representatives of the NJCEI. The parties were also encouraged, as a supplement to these sources, to visit other Ford facilities as well as other companies, so that they could learn from the experience of their peers. In discussions held with local parties, it was emphasized that employees would assess union and management support not by their words but by their actions, such as genuine labor-management participation on the joint steering committee, the extent to which time was made available for employee involvement activities, and the disposition of recommendations made by problem-solving groups. Although the union management and leadership were committed to employee involvement, both parties had agreed to put the decision to launch employee involvement in the hands of the local parties. It was believed that this was necessary to promote local ownership and commitment.

Step 2. *Guidance of a joint steering committee.* The essential functions of the steering committee were to set objectives, conduct an organizational diagnosis, develop local guidelines, assign responsibilities, manage communications, implement pilot projects, provide ongoing support, and resolve problems. If they wanted outside assistance, it was also their responsibility to select a consultant. Experience indicated that the most effective steering committees consisted of three or four members of both the union bargaining committee and management, with the unit chair and the senior management person serving as cochairs. Given what was expected of the steering committee, it was recommended that they assign someone to function as a full-time employee involvement coordinator.

Step 3. *Diagnosis of the organization.* The phrase *diagnosis of the organization* refers to the process of gathering information about the work relationships and the work environment in order to determine the readiness of the organization for employee involvement, to identify the factors that would facilitate or impede attainment of objectives, and to provide benchmark data to be used later in evaluation. This diagnosis was an integral part of preparing the organization for the introduction of employee involvement. Steering committees were strongly urged to use outside expert assistance in planning and conducting the diagnosis.

Step 4. *Selection of a pilot site.* The steering committee was advised to use the following criteria in their selection of a pilot site:

- *Receptive climate.* Supervisors, union representatives, and employees at the site selected should be generally receptive to participating in the pilot project.
- *Stable work group.* To the extent possible, a site should be selected where supervision and union representation would be relatively stable, so that employees would not be likely to be bumped.
- *Self-contained unit.* The site should have an identifiable product that results from the interrelated efforts of a single work group or unit.

Step 5. *Preparation of the organization.* Prior to the introduction of employee involvement in any organization, there is usually a great deal of uncertainty among supervision, committee members, and employees about employee involvement and how it might affect them. In particular, misperceptions about employee involvement may lead supervisors to believe that this is part of a plan to undermine their authority or even eliminate their jobs. Committee members may believe that employee involvement will undermine the grievance procedure. Misperceptions on the part of other employees may lead them to believe that this is part of a plan to speed up production and reduce personnel. To dispel these misperceptions at Ford, plans included letters from the joint steering committee, informational meetings, articles in the facility newspaper, informational brochures, bulletin boards, and special visits by members of the NJCEI, if believed necessary. It was also the responsibility of the steering committee to determine what kind of education and training was needed, when it was needed, and who would receive it.

Step 6. *Initiation of the pilot project.* Steering committees were responsible for selecting the framework for the pilot project, providing project guidelines, overseeing the orientation and training of participants, providing a place to meet, ensuring access to resources, providing direction to the consultant and the employee involvement coordinator, and monitoring progress. In keeping with the narrow definition of employee involvement used in its early stages at Ford, selecting the framework for the pilot project meant selecting either problem-solving groups or quality circles and then defining the scope of their task. In general, the particular framework used was a function of the orientation of the consultant whom the committee had selected to assist them. The major differences between the frameworks recommended by the consultants were the scope of the problems addressed and the type of training provided. Some problem-solving groups addressed a broad array of problems, ranging from those that affected quality of worklife to those that affected quality of the product, whereas some quality circles focused more exclusively on quality of the product. Problem-solving groups received training in team building, generic problem solving, and presentation skills; quality circle groups received training in cause-effect diagrams, graphs, Pareto diagrams, basic statistics, and presentation skills.

At a minimum, the pilot project guidelines provided to the groups by the local steering committee included the following elements. Participation in the groups would be strictly voluntary. Group meetings would take place on company time, usually an hour a week. If meetings occurred after regular working hours, participants would be paid overtime. The groups could not deal with any issues covered by the contract. The groups would decide which problems they would work on, provided that they were concerned with work or the work environment and were not covered by the contract. There would be no formal measurement of the groups' performance.

Using the guidelines established by the NJCEI and the local steering committee, the consultant played a lead role in designing the project, conducting the training, facilitating the first few meetings, and providing feedback on problems and progress to the steering committee and the groups. In carrying out these functions, the consultant was assisted by the local employee involvement coordinator, who was expected eventually to take over the responsibilities of the consultant.

The most significant event in the history of the pilot project was the first presentation to the steering committee. It was typically a very emotionally charged event, characterized by a tremendous amount of pride in accomplishment. If there was any skepticism on the part of any member of the steering committee about the importance of participation to employees and the value of employee involvement, it was usually dispelled during this meeting.

Step 7. *Evaluation and fine tuning.* Successful employee involvement projects require pausing periodically to ask several questions: Is our process working? Is it achieving our mutual goals?

What should we be doing differently? Four criteria were used to determine whether the involvement process at Ford was working and achieving its goals. They were the presentation of recommendations to the steering committee by the problem-solving groups, the opinions of the groups, the quality of the education and training, and the expansion of the process to other work groups.

Probably one of the most remarkable aspects of the employee involvement process was the agreement on the part of management that there would be no formal, quantitative measurement of the groups' performance. Given the culture of the company, this was no easy concession. It was expected that the local steering committees would learn from their mistakes and that they would use their day-to-day experiences to adjust and refine the process. Also, from their contacts with other facilities, steering committees would be able to share information that would lead to further refinements in the process. Generally, these refinements came in the form of changes in education and training, the availability of resources, the composition of the groups, and even the location of the meeting place for problem-solving groups. Three of the most significant refinements in the process were the appointment of a full-time hourly facilitator to work with the employee involvement coordinator; the establishment of Employee Involvement Centers within each facility—areas that were set aside for education and training; and the development of a diagnostic tool, the Employee Involvement Questionnaire, to assist steering committees in planning, implementing, and evaluating employee involvement.

Step 8. *Expansion.* As each pilot project proceeded, the steering committee worked with the consultant, facilitator, and coordinator to develop a plan for expanding the process to other work groups. The plan included the identification of additional work groups receptive to employee involvement, the incorporation of changes in the process learned as a result of the pilot project, the specification of any additional resources required, a timetable for expansion, and the communication of the plan to employees. As it turned out, the pilot projects led not only to an increase in the number of problem-solving groups but also to the implementation of other forms of expansion, such as the following:

- *Interface groups.* In the course of identifying or solving problems, the groups discovered that some of their problems cut across other work groups. This led to the formation of interface groups—that is, intergroup problem-solving teams.
- *Opportunity teams.* Formed on an ad hoc basis as needs and

opportunities were identified, opportunity teams were usually initiated because of upcoming work-related changes (for example, new technology, line rebalancing, product changes, facility modifications). Composition of these teams varied widely.

- *Special project teams.* Formed around an event (for example, open house, auto show, NJCEI visit), these groups were larger than a typical problem-solving group. They disbanded when the specific project was completed.
- *Linking teams.* Usually made up of representatives from several teams to deal with certain process or systems issues, linking teams could be interdepartmental or intershift.
- *Sunset teams.* Usually, these teams, formed to deal with spinoff projects from problem-solving teams, were comprised of employees who were not formal members but who had an interest in a specific project identified by a team. They disbanded when the specific project was completed.
- *Launch teams.* Formed to participate in the final stages of product and process development, launch teams provided coordination across various groups vital to a successful launch (for example, process and design).
- *Vendor quality teams.* Teams were formed to meet with vendor representatives or counterpart employee groups between plants, either within or outside the company. They discussed issues and developed mutually acceptable solutions, often establishing ongoing channels for communication and problem prevention.

As the positive reactions of the hourly employees to employee involvement became common knowledge within the facility, it was not long before salaried problem-solving groups were being formed. The positive reaction of hourly employees also stimulated more facilities to form steering committees and launch employee involvement.

The above steps are not necessarily sequential. For example, preparation of the organization can be occurring at the same time that the steering committee is conducting its diagnosis and selecting its pilot site. In addition, the eight-step process is seen as being cyclical, repeating itself as employee involvement expands throughout the facility.

Supportive Actions

As employee involvement took root and spread throughout company facilities, the union and management were actively involved in various supportive actions to reinforce the process. Attention was focused on reinforcement through dissemination of communications, expansion of education and training, and addition of resources.

Communications. Between 1979 and 1986, the NJCEI disseminated twenty-six newsletters. These letters covered a wide range of topics, such as the membership, structure, and role of the NJCEI; guidelines for implementing employee involvement; instructional information on the decision-making role of the local joint steering committees; information on joint union-management attendance improvement efforts; funding of attendance at "outside" employee involvement–related courses, seminars, and workshops; and guidelines for the use of hourly employees as employee involvement facilitators. These letters were sometimes accompanied by informational pamphlets, booklets, handbooks, and, on one occasion, a reference guide. (See the Appendix that concludes this chapter for a selective listing of these and other documents describing Ford's employee involvement effort.)

Many facilities held state-of-the-plant meetings with all employees, or with groups of several at a time, to share information on facility issues and to highlight employee accomplishments. Local management and local union newspapers and magazines featured individual groups and their projects. During this period, nearly every issue of *Ford World,* the company's newspaper, contained articles on the achievements of local facilities. Many national publications also featured articles on the UAW-Ford employee involvement process. In addition, numerous speeches were made by union and management representatives at conferences, workshops, and national conventions.

Education and Training. As the process expanded and the participants became more sophisticated, a need developed for additional training to supplement the local training. As a result, a number of centrally administered joint workshops are now offered to participants. One of the first and most successful of these was the Joint UAW-Ford Employee Involvement Process Workshop, which was developed specifically for the employee involvement coordinators (salaried) and facilitators (hourly). It was designed to provide participants with a brief history of employee involvement; an understanding of the eight-step guidelines and guidelines for the use of consultants; specific instruction in organizational diagnosis, management styles, group dynamics, and communications; and an opportunity for information sharing. In its six years of operations, over 1,200 people have attended this ongoing workshop. Some of the other workshops are:

- *Employee Involvement Creative Problem-Solving Workshop,* designed to develop skills, behaviors, and attitudes for creating, gaining acceptance for, and implementing new ideas.
- *Instructional Skills Workshop,* designed to enable coordinators, facilitators, and problem-solving-group leaders to upgrade their instructional skills and prepare them to conduct employee involvement training at their locations.
- *Consulting Skills Workshop,* designed to prepare trainers, coordinators, and facilitators in the techniques of consulting.
- *Participative Management–Employee Involvement Workshop,* designed to prepare managers and supervisors to execute their responsibilities more effectively in the implementation of employee involvement by focusing on the relationship between participative management and employee involvement, organizational norms, leadership styles, conflict resolution, decision making, and positive reinforcement.

Conferences proved to be another effective way for facilities to share their learning experiences and to supplement their formal training. Typically, they include keynote speeches by union leaders and company executives, talks by outside subject experts, experiential exercises, information-sharing sessions, and action planning. These conferences are conducted on a division-wide basis (a division is a unit of the company that has multiple facilities).

Resources. As the process expanded and the need for assistance increased, additional resources became available to the facilities. The most significant of these are the following:

- *Consultant Certification Committee,* which is responsible for evaluating the consultants' competency and ensuring that their approaches are consistent with the spirit and principles of employee involvement.
- *Hourly Employee Involvement Facilitators,* who assist the steering committees by conducting training for employee involvement participants, scheduling meeting rooms, preparing status reports, arranging for supplies, and facilitating communication between local parties involved in employee involvement.
- *Division Employee Involvement Committees,* which include UAW national representatives servicing a division and selected representatives of division and plant management and which have as their major purposes providing support to the local facilities and reinforcing local ownership of employee involvement.

- *Division Training Activities,* which function to provide consulting and training services to the facilities upon request.

Significant Developments

1982 Negotiations. Both the 1982 negotiating process between the UAW and Ford and the resultant agreement were hailed by the news media as a major breakthrough in labor relations. Both union and company representatives expressed the belief that their participation in employee involvement had laid the foundation for this historic process and agreement. Working together, under the guidance of the NJCEI and within the framework of the local joint steering committees, the negotiators had learned firsthand how to build trust and open communications, and how to relate to each other more effectively. As a result, when they came to the bargaining table, they came in a problem-resolution mode based on a history of successful local experiences. Ford and the UAW reached a new agreement after only thirteen days of actual bargaining.

The new agreement included important provisions specifically designed to promote communications, fact finding, problem solving, joint training—and, in general, to provide a high level of reasoned cooperation. Two unique aspects of the agreement related to employee involvement.

First, the Mutual Growth Forum was a new structure designed to function at both the national and local levels. Such forums were an adjunct to the existing collective bargaining process. They provided a new framework intended to promote sound union-management relations through better communications and systematic fact finding, and to advance discussion of certain business developments that are of mutual interest to the union, the employees, and the company. They built on the lessons learned through participation in employee involvement but were considered to have different origins and purposes.

Second, there was provision for the UAW-Ford Employee Development and Training Program, which had two goals: (1) to provide training, retraining, and development opportunities for active employees and (2) to arrange for training, retraining, and developmental assistance for employees displaced or laid off because of changes in the business environment. In addition, funds were provided to assist in sponsoring the attendance of local steering committee members, local coordinators and facilitators, and similar local personnel at employee involvement–related courses, seminars, and workshops offered outside the company.

First National UAW-Ford Employee Involvement Conference.
Key responsibilities of the NJCEI include reinforcement of the steering
committees, recognition of their accomplishments, and stimulation of
further expansion of employee involvement. Toward these ends, in
1982 the NJCEI sponsored a joint UAW-Ford Employee Involvement
Conference. Over 500 people, including union leadership, Ford
executives, joint steering committee members, coordinators, and
facilitators gathered in Dearborn to listen to words of encouragement,
share their experiences, attend workshops, and discuss future plans.
The reactions of the participants were overwhelmingly positive. The
workshops, which provided for maximum interaction between
participants, were the core of the program. They dealt with the
following topics:

- Making employee involvement a way of life.
- Improving the work environment and employee attitudes.
- Joint steering committee effectiveness.
- Effective utilization of salaried coordinators and hourly
  facilitators.
- Strengthening management and union commitment to employee
  involvement.

In a way, this conference represented the revitalization of the
Ford Motor Company. The spirit of employee involvement was
evident in the workshop discussions and reflected in the speeches made
by union leadership and executive management. For example, Donald
E. Petersen, then president of Ford Motor Company, said, "It took
employee involvement to bring us together tonight. It took employee
involvement to foster a new spirit and attitude that flourished at the
bargaining table only seven months ago. And it took employee
involvement to chart a new standard for labor and management
relations. . . . I believe that we are just beginning to grasp the potential
that lies ahead. . . . I want Ford to be recognized as a 'people'
Company—and I want our performance to be measured by our human
enterprise as well as our economic enterprise. . . . We are here because
we believe in employee involvement and in mutual commitment to
common goals."

Just prior to the national conference, the NJCEI sponsored a
special survey to obtain employees' opinions regarding the impact of
employee involvement on various aspects of their work and work
environment and to determine employee perceptions about how well
the process was functioning. Over 2,000 hourly employees, both
participants and nonparticipants in employee involvement from seven

facilities in which employee involvement had been under way for at least twelve months, took part in the survey. The results, which were disseminated at the conference, confirmed what local steering committees had known for some time: employees believe that employee involvement has a beneficial effect on them, their jobs, and their work environment, and it works especially well where there is a high level of local union and management commitment.

The findings (see Table 14.1 for selected results) reveal that there were significant improvements in the way nonparticipants viewed their work and their work environment. This is believed to be attributable, in part, to the "spillover" effect employee involvement has when efforts are visibly supported, recognized, and publicized; when attitudes of nonparticipants are enhanced because participants solicit nonparticipants' views, give feedback, and talk favorably about their participation; and when participants produce results that positively affect their fellow employees.

Mission, Values, and Guiding Principles. For several years, pressure had been building within the company to develop a company operating philosophy and a set of guiding principles. After much discussion, and the direct involvement of many top executives, a statement of Mission, Values, and Guiding Principles (see Figure 14.1) was submitted to and approved by the Board of Directors in November

Table 14.1. Selected Items from Employee Involvement Survey (N > 2000).

Statement	Percentage of Participants Favorable		Percentage of Nonparticipants Favorable	
	Before	*Now*	*Before*	*Now*
The people who report to my supervisor work as a team.	44	74	45	58
I am satisfied with the chance I have to accomplish something worthwhile.	27	82	35	59
All in all, I am satisfied with my job.	58	82	67	75
The union and management are working together to accomplish employee involvement objectives.	—	77	—	60
The union was right to get involved with employee involvement.	—	91	—	80

Figure 14.1. Mission, Values, and Guiding Principles.

MISSION

Ford Motor Company is a worldwide leader in automotive and automotive-related products and services as well as in newer industries such as aerospace, communications, and financial services. Our mission is to improve continually our products and services to meet our customers' needs, allowing us to prosper as a business and to provide a reasonable return for our stockholders, the owners of our business.

VALUES

How we accomplish our mission is as important as the mission itself. Fundamental to success for the Company are these basic values:

People — Our people are the source of our strength. They provide our corporate intelligence and determine our reputation and vitality. Involvement and teamwork are our core human values.

Products — Our products are the end result of our efforts, and they should be the best in serving customers worldwide. As our products are viewed, so are we viewed.

Profits — Profits are the ultimate measure of how efficiently we provide customers with the best products for their needs. Profits are required to survive and grow.

GUIDING PRINCIPLES

Quality comes first — To achieve customer satisfaction, the quality of our products and services must be our number one priority.

Customers are the focus of everything we do — Our work must be done with our customers in mind, providing better products and services than our competition.

Continuous improvement is essential to our success — We must strive for excellence in everything we do: in our products, in their safety and value — and in our services, our human relations, our competitiveness, and our profitability.

Employee involvement is our way of life — We are a team. We must treat each other with trust and respect.

Dealers and suppliers are our partners — The Company must maintain mutually beneficial relationships with dealers, suppliers, and our other business associates.

Integrity is never compromised — The conduct of our Company worldwide must be pursued in a manner that is socially responsible and commands respect for its integrity and for its positive contributions to society. Our doors are open to men and women alike without discrimination and without regard to ethnic origin or personal beliefs.

of 1984. In that same month, at a worldwide management meeting, Henry Ford II also endorsed the above statement. In April 1985, Don Petersen and Red Poling (chairman and president, respectively), at a quarterly meeting of senior executives, spent several hours discussing the implications of the Mission, Values, and Guiding Principles. Mr. Petersen concluded the meeting by saying that "many components have already developed local sets of values and principles, many of them related to participative management and employee involvement, and should be commended for their efforts. It is expected that the Company Mission, Values, and Guiding Principles will reinforce these and other efforts that have been underway for some time."

Lessons Learned and Shared

Many Ford affiliates, other companies, and public agencies have come to Ford seeking information about the lessons that have been learned about employee involvement and the pitfalls to be avoided, and many Ford representatives and union leaders have talked about their experience throughout the United States and in many other parts of the world. Listed below are some of the lessons that have been shared.

Participative Management Defined

In the early stages of employee involvement, Ford's focus was on the formation of problem-solving groups—that is, groups of individuals who got together with their supervisor in a structured setting to identify and solve problems related to the work or work environment. However, as the groups became more experienced and expanded their activities, it became clear that the concept of employee involvement needed to be redefined in keeping with the emerging forms of the groups.

It also became evident that in the desire to introduce employee involvement on the factory floor, most of the efforts had been devoted to educating and training hourly employees. Many managers and supervisors who obviously were crucial to the long-term success of the process had been ignored. Although the managers and supervisors received orientation on employee involvement and were encouraged to practice participative management, it was not clear to many of them what was meant by *participative management* and what its relationship was to employee involvement. As a result of these factors, an operational definition of participative management was developed, employee involvement was redefined, and a model to explain their interrelationship was generated.

Participative management is defined as the techniques and skills that managers use to provide employees with opportunities to participate actively in key managerial processes (planning, goal setting, problem solving, and decision making) affecting job-related matters. It is concerned with participation as viewed from the *manager's perspective* and is likely to be present when an employee agrees with such indicators as, "I participate in the decision-making process," "Sufficient effort is made to get my opinions," and "I participate in group problem solving." These are indications that employees believe they have opportunities to participate. It should be noted that managers can receive as well as provide opportunities for participation. *As employees,* they have opportunities provided by their supervisors to participate—employee involvement. *As managers,* they provide opportunities for their subordinates to participate—participative management. Therefore, employee involvement is a process that applies throughout all levels of an organization.

Participative management and employee involvement are really two sides of the same coin. You cannot have one without the other (see Figure 14.2). These new definitions were used in the design of a Participative Management-Employee Involvement Workshop for

Figure 14.2. Participative Management-Employee Involvement Model.

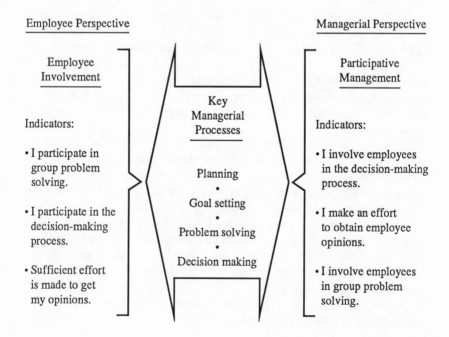

Employee Perspective   Managerial Perspective

| Employee Involvement | Key Managerial Processes | Participative Management |

Indicators:

• I participate in group problem solving.

• I participate in the decision-making process.

• Sufficient effort is made to get my opinions.

Key Managerial Processes

Planning
•
Goal setting
•
Problem solving
•
Decision making

Indicators:

• I involve employees in the decision-making process.

• I make an effort to obtain employee opinions.

• I involve employees in group problem solving.

managers and supervisors and the development of a publication that explains the concepts and provides guidance on how to implement participative management and employee involvement.

Several of the factors that Ford has found crucial to the successful implementation of participative management–employee involvement are listed below.

Leadership Acceptance. Probably the most frequently asked question is, How do I get top management or union leadership, or both, to accept employee participation? Experience indicates that the greatest success in gaining acceptance comes from encouraging skeptics to visit facilities that have successfully implemented some form of employee involvement. The opportunity to talk with peers seems to have the greatest impact. For example, when Ford of Australia's management approached the union, the Vehicle Builders Employees' Federation of Australia (VBEFA), to discuss joint implementation of employee involvement, there were some union leaders (and possibly some Ford managers) who were strongly resistant to the concept. In an attempt to overcome this resistance, Ford of Australia sent a contingent of union leaders and managers to the United States to learn firsthand what it was all about. They received an orientation from representatives of the NJCEI and, most important, they visited a couple of Ford facilities and had an opportunity to talk with local union leaders, local management, and employees on the floor. As a result of this visit (as reported by the Australians), Ford of Australia and the VBEFA proceeded with the launch of employee involvement.

Common Understanding. The knowledge required to gain initial acceptance to agree to launch a pilot project is not the same as the knowledge and understanding needed to implement, expand, and sustain employee involvement. Developing this level of understanding is one of the most difficult issues to deal with, because most union leaders and managers are trained to be action-oriented. They want results. As they prepare to take action, however, they often find that they have different understandings of employee involvement, its goals, and its methods. That is why it is important to provide a conceptual framework, operational definitions, and guidelines for implementation. It is also at this stage that a consultant can be very valuable. This common understanding can be further enhanced if the consultant encourages leaders to be directly involved in the implementation process itself.

Crisis/Champions. The opportunity to implement employee involvement requires a crisis, a champion, or both. If a crisis develops and employee involvement is perceived as a potential remedy, the champions will surface. On the other hand, if there is no crisis, and the only champions are human resource people, they can take steps to develop champions. The project at the Indianapolis plant, noted earlier, is a good example of the latter. Stan Surma, the Transmission and Chassis Division labor relations manager, met with Jack O'Connor, the industrial relations manager of the Indianapolis plant, and me to discuss a strategy for initiating employee involvement. The strategy we settled on turned out to be very simple, but effective. The three of us met with Marv Craig, the plant manager, to discuss the project, its objectives, the funding, and the use of consultants. The situation was perfect for him to balk at this proposal—and he did—because at this time his plant was the best-performing plant in the division and at the leading edge in organizational development innovations. For several years, Marv Craig had been an advocate of participative management in his plant. Why did it need employee involvement? Why not select a poorly performing plant? We made the point that if employee involvement could produce improvements at the best-performing plant, then it certainly would have application in all the other plants. Furthermore, it would support his other improvement efforts. The plant manager agreed, and the project went forward. Professor Edward Lawler (see Chapter Ten) was selected as the prime consultant for this project. The rest is history.

Policy/Contract Wording. There is no doubt that actions speak more loudly than words and that actions are really the basis on which the commitment of the union and management to the employee involvement process is judged. However, the existence of a company policy statement and an agreement of joint support as a part of the contract can be crucial in the orientation of the local union leadership and the local management. For example, in the early stages of employee involvement at Ford, representatives of the NJCEI used the 1979 Policy Letter and the contract as leverage to encourage the local parties to initiate employee involvement. The policy statement and contract can clearly communicate that successful implementation of employee involvement is the responsibility of line management and the union leadership.

From Participative Management to Employee Involvement

Many employee involvement, quality of worklife, and quality circle efforts seem to be conceived as something that top management tells lower management to do. These kinds of efforts are never able to sustain themselves (see Chapters Ten, Eleven, and Twelve). One critical aspect of implementing employee involvement is that top management must ensure that managers, at *all* levels, have the same opportunity to participate as their subordinates. At Ford, employee involvement is a process that applies to all employees, regardless of their position in the company.

"Process," Not "Program." Employee involvement should be defined as a process, not a program. A *process* is a series of activities or actions that leads to a particular set of outcomes and has no time boundaries. A *program* is a plan or schedule that has a beginning and end. Treating employee involvement as a program is one of the principal factors contributing to the failure of employee involvement efforts. Union leaders, lower-level managers, and employees are reluctant to invest their energy in another top management quick-fix "program." For example, on a visit to the company's Dearborn engine plant, members of a problem-solving group made a presentation to representatives of the NJCEI. One of the members of the problem-solving group, in response to a question, made an important observation related to the issue of program versus process. He said, "I have been involved in many programs over the last twenty years to make improvements in the workplace, and none of them have ever lasted. Again, you raised my expectations with employee involvement. It has made me feel good about coming to work. If this turns out to be just another 'program,' I'll never trust you again." It goes without saying that under no circumstances should employee involvement be labeled a *human resource program*. If it is to sustain itself, it must be perceived as an ongoing process. However, it does require the support of the human resource function, especially in the area of education and training. In the long term, it also requires a change in the role of the human resource manager, who must function as a change agent as well as an administrator.

Resource Investment. The old adage "You don't get something for nothing" applies to employee involvement, a process that requires an investment of money, time, facilities, and people. It requires extensive education and training, access to business information, and consulting assistance. Providing these resources is the responsibility of line management. However, it helps if employee involvement is part of the contract. It is no secret that the auto industry, in general, and the Ford Motor Company, in particular, were drowning in red ink in the early eighties. As a result, Ford initiated an extensive cost-cutting program. However, the financial and human resources required to sustain employee involvement were not affected. These funds and people were considered "sacred."

Participative Structure. The long-term goal of employee

involvement is an organizational transformation. In most organizations, this means changing from an organization that is authoritarian, impersonal, and management-oriented to one that is participative, personal, and employee-oriented. This change cannot occur if the organization attempts to use the existing organizational structure. A parallel organization must be established to plan, implement, guide, and support the process.

Local Ownership. An apparent key to success is local ownership. This translates into local control over objectives, methods, resources, communications, consultants, and evaluation within the guidelines promulgated jointly by the top management and union leadership. The parties must have the right to determine whether or not they are ready to implement employee involvement and to call a recess in activities if they have reasonable cause.

The NJCEI has stuck to its guns on this issue, and there is no doubt that it has been a key factor in the success of the process. For example, when it came to measuring the effects of employee involvement, the NJCEI set no specific criteria. This was the responsibility of the local parties. No systematic attempts were made to determine the extent to which employee involvement was contributing to increased efficiency or effectiveness. The emphasis of the NJCEI was on the quality of the process. Except for surveys used to collect data on the opinions of employees about the value of the process to them and to the quality of the effort, anecdotes are the only source of direct evidence of the impact of employee involvement at Ford.

Revitalization. Employee involvement efforts must have the means to counteract the pressures in almost all organizations to return to the status quo. Access to adequate resources, encouragement from the joint steering committee, local education and training, and local recognition of accomplishments are all potential means of support. For example, funds have been made available through the UAW-Ford Employee Development and Training Program to cover financing of networking conferences and attendance at outside training courses. An advanced training workshop is under development for facilitators and coordinators. Corporate Education and Training has made available courses in conflict resolution, instructional skills, team building, listening skills, and time management. The NJCEI has published a UAW-Ford Employee Involvement Reference Guide. All of these activities reinforce the importance of people to the success of the process.

Demise of the Four P's. During the course of the implementation of this process, four major obstacles to success have surfaced at various times. They are referred to as the four P's: politics, personality, platitudes, and perseveration.

- *Politics.* There have been several instances in which local management or union politics delayed implementation of employee involvement or resulted in a recess of activities. For example, there have been union elections during which one of the candidates for bargaining chair, as part of the campaign, professed opposition to employee involvement and won the election. This resulted in either a recess of activities or a temporary setback in expansion of employee involvement at that facility. In such cases, the NJCEI makes an assessment of the situation to determine what action, if any, they should take to get the process back on track.
- *Personality.* There have been several cases in which the personalities of a manager or union leader were in conflict with the philosophy or the goals of employee involvement. For example, a few plant managers opposed employee involvement because it challenged an autocratic style of management that had been their key to success for many years. In these cases, the manager is reminded that employee involvement is a policy of the company and that managers are expected to act accordingly. Such actions are included as part of the performance appraisal discussion.
- *Platitudes.* There have been several cases in which managers or union leaders have given only lip service to employee involvement. They were politically astute enough not to overtly resist employee involvement, because it was part of the contract and the policy of the company. However, their actions spoke more loudly than their words. For example, a division training manager was conducting a joint training session for the management and union leadership at a plant. The plant manager opened the training session by extolling the virtues of employee involvement and its importance to the plant. However, instead of joining in the training session, he explained to the group that he had more important things to do back in his office. He wished them success with their training and left. His platitudes did not fool anyone. As soon as he left, both management and the union leadership began to question his commitment to the process. In these cases, the managers are reminded of their responsibilities, and their behavior is discussed as part of the performance review.
- *Perseveration.* For many managers and union leaders, employee involvement requires a significant change in their day-to-day behavior. It requires a great deal of discipline on the part of both parties not to slip back into the old ways of doing business. The

tendency is to continue doing those things that are comfortable, even though they may have lost their usefulness. In one plant, this tendency toward perseveration was handled in the following way: there was an agreement made among managers in this plant that whenever a manager was exhibiting signs of perseveration, another manager could alert him by using the code words "reverting to the familiar."

Status Report

Virtually all Ford locations now have active joint steering committees. There are more than 175 coordinators and facilitators, of whom about half are hourly employees. More than 1,200 employees have attended the jointly conducted Employee Involvement Process Workshop for coordinators and facilitators. All management has been exposed to employee involvement and participative management through communications, and more than 10,000 managers and supervisors have received training in participative management and employee involvement concepts, techniques, and skills. More than half of the company's hourly employees have had some type of employee involvement–related orientation or training.

Employee involvement has also evolved into many "second-generation" applications. In addition to voluntary problem-solving groups, there are widespread communication and information-sharing efforts between management and employees; team visits and team sharing between facilities; team sharing with outside vendors, dealers, and suppliers; and an expanding emphasis on involving midlevel management and union leadership and promoting natural work teams as the basic unit.

The recognizable and agreed-upon effects of employee involvement are widespread. Face-to-face communication between employees and supervisors has improved: there are more and better facility-wide messages, newsletters, open houses, and the like. Communication among departments, between facilities, and with staffs has improved. Teams have tackled numerous efficiency problems, making improvements that have saved money and made jobs easier to perform. Employees have participated in advance reviews of products and have made suggestions to improve design and manufacturing processes; they have participated in rearranging lines and machines; they have taken action to eliminate scrap and rework; they have visited suppliers to seek improved quality; and they have proposed ways to prevent problems from happening. Ford's "Quality Is Job One" television and print commercials have featured team members demonstrating the contributions of employee involvement to product quality, thereby providing recognition for the employees, the union, and the company. Teams have also made contributions to community relations: they have made displays for local auto shows, assisted with community projects (such as park improvements), raised money and collected food for the needy, and conducted tours of Ford facilities for the handicapped. According to company indices, product quality has improved more than 50 percent for cars and 47 percent for trucks. It is generally agreed that Ford has the best quality of the three principal U.S. automobile manufacturers.

Epilogue

What you have just read is one person's recollection of the people and events that shaped the history of the UAW-Ford employee involvement process. It draws on the work of many individual contributors, who deserve recognition for the time and energy they devoted to making employee involvement successful. Obviously, only a very few of them have been recognized as part of this chapter.

This account of employee involvement may leave the reader with the impression that it was like a river flowing swiftly, in a straight path, without any bends, backtracks, or obstacles. This is far from the truth. The process *has* had its bends, backtracks, and obstacles. What started as a small trickle became a stream, and this has since developed into a full-sized river as each small tributary added its resources and power. It has developed such a strong network of tributaries that it will continue to flow for the foreseeable future. Its energy has been harnessed to create a new relationship between labor and management, a better quality of worklife, and a better quality of products and services.

As I reflect on my own participation, I think of the unique opportunity it has provided for me to apply my knowledge, skills, and abilities as an industrial-organizational psychologist; to meet many conscientious and dedicated people throughout the Ford world; and to be part of an organizational change effort that has had a positive effect on so many people.

As one of the representatives of the NJCEI, I visited most of the Ford facilities to assist in explaining employee involvement. On many of these trips, I accompanied Al Hendricks, who was a member of the NJCEI and UAW special projects director. In the early stages of the process, he was responsible for clarifying the role of union leadership in employee involvement. He, as much as anyone, deserves special recognition for his contribution to the success of employee involvement.

He and I became very good friends, especially after we discovered that we both were Minnesotans. I had graduated from the University of Minnesota and he had chaired the bargaining unit at Ford's Twin Cities assembly plant. He made an observation that I think reflects the real power of employee involvement. He said that for as many years as he could remember, he had been attending the UAW national conventions. At the early conventions, there were signs on the walls bearing the words "Dignity and Respect in the Workplace." He believed that despite all the progress made by the UAW, it was only when we negotiated employee involvement as a joint union-management educational process that he saw real, meaningful progress toward dignity and respect in the workplace.

As I said previously, my participation in the implementation of employee involvement took me all over the Ford world. On a visit to the Ford Lio Ho plant, Taiwan, the manager of the engine plant, Davey Lui, put employee involvement in perspective for me. When talking about employees, he said, "We have done a good job in capturing their arms, legs, and minds, but the real secret is in capturing their hearts. Isn't that what employee involvement is all about?"

Appendix

Banas, P. A. "Employee Involvement Guidelines—The Eight Steps." Paper presented at the Society of Automotive Engineers International Conference, Detroit, Feb. 1981.

Banas, P. A. *The Relationship Between Participative Management and Employee Involvement.* Dearborn, Mich.: Ford Motor Company, 1983.

Banas, P. A. "Cultural Change—Lessons Learned." Remarks at the Division of Business, Industry, and Labor, National University Continuing Education Association Conference, Washington, D.C., Jan. 1986.

Botkin, J., Dimancescu, D., and Stata, R. *The Innovators: Rediscovering America's Creative Energy.* New York: Harper & Row, 1984.

Burck, C. G. "Working Smarter: What's in It for the Unions." *Fortune,* Aug. 1981, pp. 6-8.

"Driving to Rebuild Ford for the Future." *Business Week,* Aug. 4, 1980, pp. 70-71.

Education and Personnel Research Department. *Continuous Improvement Through Participation: A Guide for Managers and Supervi-*

sors on Participative Management and Salaried Employee Involvement. Dearborn, Mich.: Ford Motor Company, 1984.

Ephlin, D. F. "The UAW-Ford Agreement—Joint Problem Solving." *Sloan Management Review,* 1983, *24* (2), 61–65.

Ford, H., II. "Our Corporate Culture: The Way I See It." Remarks at the Ford Worldwide Management Meeting, Dearborn, Mich., Nov. 1984.

Guest, R. H. "The Sharonville Story: Worker Involvement at a Ford Motor Company Plant." In R. Zager and M. P. Rosow (eds.), *The Innovative Organization: Productivity Programs in Action.* Elmsford, N.Y.: Pergamon Press, 1982.

Pestillo, P. J. "Employee Involvement Enables Ford to Lead Change, Not Be Led by It." *Financier,* Sept. 1983a, pp. 34–38.

Pestillo, P. J. "Labor Relations and Employee Involvement." *Business–Higher Education Forum,* June 1983b, pp. 24–28.

Petersen, D. E. "The Second Bottom Line: A Discussion of the Historic Ford-UAW Contract." Remarks at the Alfred P. Sloan School of Management Distinguished Speakers Series, MIT, Cambridge, Mass., Apr. 1982.

Savoie, E. J. "The New Ford-UAW Agreement: Its Worklife Aspects." *The Worklife Review,* 1982a, *1* (1), 1–10.

Savoie, E. J. "The Power of Employee Involvement." Remarks at the Institute of Newspaper Controllers and Finance Officers, Washington, D.C., Oct. 1982b.

Savoie, E. J. "Current Developments and Future Agenda in Union-Management Cooperation in Training and Retraining of Workers." Remarks at the annual spring meeting of the Industrial Relations Research Association, June 1985.

Savoie, E. J. "Creating the Workforce of the Future." Statement submitted to the President's Advisory Committee on Mediation and Conciliation, Sept. 1986.

Smith, M. "Employee Involvement Fuels Dramatic Turnaround at Ford's Louisville Assembly Plant." Labor-Management Cooperation Brief 9, U.S. Dept. of Labor, Bureau of Labor-Management Relations and Cooperative Programs, 1986.

UAW-Ford National Joint Committee. *Employee Involvement: What's It All About?* Dearborn, Mich.: Ford Motor Company, 1980.

UAW-Ford National Joint Committee. *Employee Involvement . . . It Works!* Dearborn, Mich.: Ford Motor Company, 1981.

UAW-Ford National Joint Committee. *EI . . . It Makes a Difference.* Dearborn, Mich.: Ford Motor Company, 1982a.

UAW-Ford National Joint Committee. *To Compete: We Need Each Other.* Dearborn, Mich.: Ford Motor Company, 1982b.

UAW-Ford National Joint Committee. *UAW-Ford Employee Involvement: A Special Survey Report.* Dearborn, Mich.: Ford Motor Company, 1982c.

UAW-Ford National Joint Committee. *Employee Involvement: Handbook II—Concepts and Ideas for Continuing Progress.* Dearborn, Mich.: Ford Motor Company, 1983.

UAW-Ford National Joint Committee. *UAW-Ford Employee Involvement: The UAW-Ford EI Process for Local Unions and Management.* (Rev. ed.) Dearborn, Mich.: Ford Motor Company, 1986.

Yates, P. "What's Creating an 'Industrial Miracle' at Ford?" *Business Week,* July 30, 1984, pp. 80–81.

15

ᒧᒤᒧᒤᒧᒤᒧᒤᒧᒤᒧᒤᒧᒤᒧᒧ

Productivity: Conclusions and Forecasts from Industrial- Organizational Psychology

John P. Campbell
Richard J. Campbell

The prospect of bountiful discoveries in unknown or poorly charted territories is perhaps the most alluring aspect of the Frontiers metaphor. The search involves uncertainty and high expectations and the nagging temptation to revert to old ways of viewing and doing things. Our contributors have aimed for a balance between the known and the to-be-discovered, and we seek a similar balance here in this concluding chapter. We make no attempt to summarize all that has gone before; rather, our focus is on promising new directions and how our current knowledge and theory can help us pursue them.

There is ample evidence throughout this volume that it is safe for Inspector Clouseau to significantly reduce his uncertainty. Industrial and organizational psychology has virtually everything to do with productivity; however, this confident assertion must be qualified in two ways. One is obvious: the contributions are limited to those involving people. What is not obvious is why labor productivity has received so little attention in productivity analyses and policy formulation at the national level in the United States (see Chapter Five). We suspect that it has much to do with our second qualification: that is, practically all of the contributions of industrial and organizational psychology affect productivity *indirectly*. Our psychological interventions typically focus on enhancing performance and under certain conditions will influence major components of the efficiency ratio (productivity) by increasing output, lowering costs, and so on. It still appears to us that a critical frontier is the need for conceptual clarity regarding the constructs of productivity and performance. This is more than a definitional problem and a need for differentiation among constructs. Rather, it is a need for a renewed effort toward a more complete conceptual understanding and measurement of the performance domain.

The Performance Domain

It clearly seems useful for policy makers to define productivity as an efficiency concept and to acknowledge that there can be no single, ultimate measure of productivity. The specific composition of a productivity index should reflect the goals of the system in a valid way. Also, total productivity can be disaggregated in various ways—for example, by level and sector. Most important, productivity measurement depends fundamentally on purpose. A clear illustration of this is Taira's description of the Japanese emphasis on sector productivity and the use of the sector measure as a spur to productivity improvement in manufacturing (Chapter Three). Guzzo's review (Chapter Four) shows that the dependent variables in psychology are not productivity measures and that we do not view measuring productivity ratios at the individual level as very useful. Rather, our emphasis should be placed on measuring performance and developing better ways to ensure that the performance sought by the organization is supportive of the organization's goals. It is the latter that will determine the effectiveness of performance, along with the myriad of other factors that can limit the contribution of performance to the productivity ratio.

Mahoney (Chapter Two) suggests that it is appropriate that industrial and organizational psychology continue to focus on the dependent variables of performance and costs or inputs rather than on the efficiency ratio. He discusses the variable of effectiveness in the context of aggregate units and argues that effectiveness measures may indeed be more critical than physical efficiency or productivity for a particular purpose for a particular enterprise. However, he also argues that productivity measures are important tools for goal setting, planning, monitoring, and feedback at the enterprise level. His discussion is congruent with our belief that a major frontier for psychology is improved understanding of the linkage between performance and effectiveness. Many of the contributing authors help make the case by citing numerous examples of psychological interventions that influence performance, the outcomes of which are not realized because of a lack of congruence with organizational goals or mitigating factors in the situation. The recurring descriptions of how difficult it is to maintain a treatment-induced change over a long period of time are good indicators or symptoms of this underlying problem.

It is perplexing and inexplicable that industrial and organizational psychology has devoted so little effort to the systematic explication of the performance domain. In the case of most independent variables, such as abilities and motivation, we have reasonably well developed theories to guide research and practice. The absence of models and theories of performance is a gap that needs to be closed. In our view, this is a very critical frontier and an important place to concentrate future development effort. Project A (Campbell, 1986) provides an example of this type of effort. A model has been developed for the performance domain that recognizes the multidimensional nature of performance and provides multiple measures of each major factor. The loop to effectiveness is completed by incorporating management judgment into the process of determining what performance factors are critical for achieving organizational goals. While Project A is far from complete, the early results are illustrative of how a serious attempt to "model" performance can benefit both science and practice. For example, variance on the different performance components is accounted for by different ability and personality factors, and they play a different role in selection versus classification.

The years of neglect of the performance domain suggest to us not that performance is an intractable problem but that it is a frontier to be aggressively pursued. We have spent far too much of our history in hand-wringing about the "criterion problem" and in believing that the answer lies in being able to identify the appropriate objective measures that must surely be lurking somewhere in the organization's archives.

A Look at Individual Chapters

Parts Two, Three, and Four of this book provide strong documentation that industrial and organizational psychology has much to contribute to productivity, through either the numerator or denominator of the efficiency ratio, and it can do so in a variety of ways. It also seems clear that there has been an acceleration in research and development on the knowledge base relative to productivity concerns, as in the developments in training over the last fifteen years. The issue is where we go from here. We address this issue by first looking at the substantive areas themselves and conclude with a critical look at what the preceding chapters suggest about the tools of the trade of industrial and organizational psychology—our theory, research, and practice, and their interplay.

We have tried hard to make the point that articulating organizational goals and translating them into specifications for performance that will support or produce outcomes that the organization values is the key linkage between performance and effectiveness. An entire chapter (Chapter Thirteen, by McLagan) is devoted to one approach to this process. Other aspects we will try to highlight in the remaining pages are timeliness, effective treatments or interventions, and the summative or interaction effects of multiple interventions. *Timeliness* refers to the need for a future orientation in rapidly changing organizations. Guzzo (Chapter Four) underscores the need to anticipate changes in management practices and captures the idea that our research and theory must somehow get in front of or at least catch up to the practical innovators. McLagan (Chapter Thirteen) gives future conditions and goals a core position in her approach to the design of jobs. One of the most promising levers we have for linking organizational goals and performance is the design of jobs. This, combined with the other outcomes of manipulating job characteristics described in Chapter Nine, makes job design a particularly promising frontier, if only we can shift the research paradigm from computing correlations between perceived job characteristics and expressed job satisfaction back to the actual redesign of jobs. Finally, we look for clues to a better understanding and exploitation of multiple interventions. For example, better selection can help improve the outcomes of training. In contrast, there is the potential conflict between a self-managing team that selects its members and the team's failure to use what we know about skills and abilities in selection. Studying both potential benefits and potential conflicts can be useful.

As we progress through the chapters, two interesting changes take place. On the independent variable side, we move from the "least interventionist" approach of personnel selection toward multiple interventions, culminating in self-managing teams. This is a concomitant trend toward greater complexity in the dependent measures in terms of both the variety of outcome measures examined and the level of aggregation. A selection-classification strategy is less interventionist, in the sense that once a higher-ability person is selected for an organization, there are, relatively speaking, few costs associated with preventing the decay of those abilities. Traits are traits. They may not be fully exploited, but they cannot be taken away. Similarly, while training is an intervention, its objective is to make relatively stable changes in individual knowledge or skill. Such changes belong in the "trait" and not "state" category and thus incur lower maintenance costs, relatively speaking. However, when motivation becomes the basis for change, the intervention becomes very "state"-oriented, and it requires considerable effort to support the changes in performance produced by motivationally based interventions. This makes all such interventions fundamentally different than selection or training. What individuals or groups decide to do one day, they may decide not to do the next day. As the chapters move to more and more complex motivationally based interventions, the need to account for situational interactions becomes stronger and stronger.

The second trend in the chapters is the increasing prominence of participation as an ingredient of the intervention strategy. Participation has a dominant place in the history of behavioral science interventions into the management of organizations. What began as the participation of work groups in making decisions about methods and procedures with which they were directly concerned has progressed to quality circles, the self-directed work group, and the extensiveness of the Ford employee involvement process. In a sense, we (the United States) are moving toward a higher order of participation—an order that is similar to that practiced in certain European countries (Dachler and Wilpert, 1978).

Given participation's dominance in intervention strategies, it is surprising (even unbelievable) that the basic meaning and nature of participation has received so little conceptual and research attention. There are certainly many studies that attempt to relate a participation intervention to one or more outcomes (that is, evaluation studies). However, there is very little research directed at what participation actually is. What is an appropriate description of its major design parameters? What mechanisms explain why it affects certain dependent variables the way it does? What cognitive processes does it set in motion? Here, ladies and gentlemen, is a frontier that is so fundamental that the small amount of basic research directed at understanding it boggles the mind.

Having mentioned these two general issues, we would like now to recount some specific points from the different chapters that we think are especially deserving of attention.

The relatively sophisticated state of theory and research in personnel selection does not prevent Burke and Pearlman (Chapter Six) from finding important directions for new research that have the status of frontiers. The key one is the need for developing better linkages between the well-developed taxonomies of abilities and jobs. That is, we are now in a position to begin estimating real population parameters as regards the relationship between major aspects of individual differences and the major components of job performance in major job populations. If the appropriate meta-analytical techniques are combined with good taxonomic models of individual attributes and job performance components, we can accumulate a data base of far-reaching importance. The bottom-line question is, How big a matrix will be required to account for the variance in attribute-performance relationships? If, as Burke and Pearlman argue, the required number of job families does not exceed ten and a relatively small number of ability domains will describe the attribute space, systematic validation data aggregation becomes even more useful as a practical tool. A demonstration that selection systems can validly use virtually all the information provided by current measurement technology would be a most valuable outcome. Also, Burke and Pearlman highlight the need to go beyond ability measures in selection when they suggest that for jobs where performance can have unusually serious consequences (for example, some high-level management positions), noncognitive predictors or situational context variables could be highly relevant. Finally, their suggestions that there are other metrics than dollars for utility measurement and that utility estimation procedures derived for selection could be applied to other interventions are important observations. Our old friend, personnel selection, has not yet run out of frontiers.

Not surprisingly, Chapter Eight, on training, provides an illustration of the approach to performance and effectiveness emphasized in this volume. A basic theme is that we simply must be more explicit about what we mean by *competent* or *expert* performance. The training design model presented is a set of key steps for implementing the approach. Two design frontiers center around the reemergence of the aptitude treatment interaction and trainee motivation as significant sources of variance in training effects that can be captured to some degree in virtually any training program. We must pay at least as much attention to design as to method. We would also argue that the training design itself is on the verge of a genuine paradigm shift. It will be the result of increasingly complete "theories of knowledge," coming both from industrial and organizational psychology (as in leadership theory) and from cognitive psychology (the prime example being problem solving and decision making), and a shift from evaluating methods to finding out how particular domains of knowledge or skill can best be taught. If such a paradigm shift indeed takes place, future reviews of the literature will center around the dependent variable rather than the independent variable.

Ilgen and Klein's three examples of applications of choice theory in Chapter Seven bring home the difficulty of translating relatively abstract theory into the specifics of an application. More critically, they show the tendency for applications based on a particular theory to draw on other theories. Two forces seem to be at work: one is the lack of comprehensiveness of any one theory; the other is the overlap between theories. These, plus the observation that commonalities among constructs can result in manipulations of variables within one theory that are viewed as confounding variables in another, provide a logical stepping stone to the development of a set of integrating concepts. We obviously don't need unnecessary problems in an already complicated field. The resulting "constructs for understanding behavior" do yield a more parsimonious set. If they provide better cues for guiding interventions, as the authors suggest, they will represent a clear step forward. One of the most interesting outcomes of this collapsing of constructs is the focus on beliefs as the variables most open to change. It suggests some interesting ideas—for example, that abilities, through their influence on performance, affect the individual's expectations for future performance. Similar motivational effects are postulated in the training area. Another suggestion that appears useful and straightforward to implement is the use of attitude surveys to assess employee beliefs about contingencies and about the values they attach to outcomes.

As discussed by Ilgen and Klein, the research by Pritchard and his colleagues uses a very interesting approach to the development and scaling of effectiveness measures. What Pritchard calls *product indices* are *effectiveness indicators* in our terminology. That is, the correlation between differences in what individuals or groups actually do (performance) to produce a product and differences in quantity or quality of what actually results (effectiveness) is not necessarily 1.00. For example, even the "best" (in terms of performance) of repair shops may not have a good "return rate" because of an unseen defect in several batches of spare parts supplied by a vendor. When Pritchard's product indices are scaled against effectiveness, as he uses the term, he is really asking for judgments about the utility of different levels of an outcome for the goals of the organization. An interesting ingredient is the participation by individual work-group members in the scaling of effectiveness. To the extent that participation has beneficial effects and the effectiveness judgments truly mirror the organization's goals, this is a very useful procedure. The fact that these functions are not necessarily linear and may not be the same for all outcomes makes a great deal of sense and leads to a number of fascinating research questions. For example, would different types of judges produce different utility functions? If so, why? Why are these functions not linear? Surely one reason must be that the perceived cost-benefit ratio is not the same for all levels of an outcome. This makes the utility scale (or *effectiveness scale,* in Pritchard's terms) more like a productivity metric, as it was defined in Chapter Two. If we inquired about what costs were being taken into consideration by the judges, and found some reasonable answers, the clarity with which we could relate economic indicators of productivity to measures of performance and effectiveness (as in Chapter Five) would be increased significantly.

Chapter Nine, dealing with the job characteristics–job performance link, illustrates the myriad problems involved in obtaining clear effects in large field interventions. While it would be much more convincing to have field studies under various combinations of moderators, as the authors concede, the meta-analysis results do provide a very informative look at factors that have been postulated or interpreted as influencing the results of the job characteristics–job performance link. The substantial amount of variance in this relationship explained by the model is important in assessing the potential impact of job characteristics on job performance, but the impact of range restriction and the model's specifications for maintaining the distinction between independently observed job characteristics and incumbent perceptions of job characteristics make interpretation both more complex and more intriguing. It would be very useful now to see some confirmative experimental studies. Meanwhile, the results do add importance to the role played by job design in achieving effectiveness.

After reading Chapter Ten on quality circles, we find it difficult to avoid the conclusion that, despite the paucity of research and lack of a clear trend for performance effects, the analysis and models presented by Ledford, Lawler, and Mohrman are quite convincing in arguing that the prevailing design of quality circles severely limits the likelihood of their enhancing productivity. The dim outlook for the more general model, the parallel organization, is even more disconcerting. While the authors offer suggestions for improved designs of quality circles that alter their parallel organization design features, it is still the case that the history of the quality circle intervention, *in the United States,* illustrates some of the worst features of how we try to improve performance and labor productivity with new "programs." In Japan, the quality circle became very much an integral part of operational management. In the United States, it too often has been just another program that is expected to do good things without incurring too many costs and without becoming a fully integrated management responsibility. The QC cycle so clearly described in Chapter Ten is the result. It is an all-too-familiar story. There is no doubt that even the most garden-variety work group possesses expertise that would be of great value if it could be captured and applied. The optimum procedure by which recovery of available expertise can be integrated into the ongoing management of the enterprise is still a frontier.

The discussion of self-managing teams by Goodman, Devadas, and Hughson is set in the context of participation but goes considerably beyond the quality circle in the complexity of its multiple interventions and the interactions with the organizational environment in which they are embedded. The restrictions of the parallel organization are gone. However, the complexity of the interventions (in which teams control both their production tasks and team design) and their interactions with the setting make evaluative studies difficult, so we do not have very good answers concerning their impact on performance. The finding that the more rigorous designs showed more modest effects suggests even further caution. While Goodman and his colleagues do see modest performance effects, their insistence that the establishment of self-managing teams without alteration of the environment will have little effect has a familiar ring. Their description of the capability of the technological system to constrain and even eliminate any effect of the intervention illustrates Mahoney's admonition regarding attribution problems and our worries about the factors that reduce the correlation between performance and effectiveness. Their position on the changing of pay systems corresponds with Hammer's view, and their collectively perceived need to provide supportive training and a compatible value system in the surrounding organization is virtually identical to Banas's position on what is required to keep the Ford program going. Although Goodman and his colleagues range far beyond psychological interventions in their analysis, they provide a useful and comprehensive view of the issues psychologists must face in making attributions about the effects of their interventions on productivity or organizational effectiveness.

Hammer (Chapter Twelve) provides a very different perspective on productivity improvement efforts with her review and analysis of pay and other financial rewards. Her conclusion that participation is a necessary feature but that psychologists overemphasize its role relative to the wage-effort bargain in programs such as the Scanlon Plan could well provide an insight into the problem of sustaining psychological interventions. While noting the lack of theory regarding gainsharing in particular, she offers several testable hypotheses that invite research. Because gainsharing is closely related to employee performance and has produced positive results, it is a good candidate for research resources. The case made for organizational commitment as the causal variable is appealing. Furthermore, Schuster's suggestion that the Scanlon Plan success is a function of the organization's commitment to high worker involvement and Lawler's position that gainsharing increases worker commitment to the organization identify a timely avenue of research, given the buffeting of organizational commitment in this period of rapid organizational change.

The two chapters on application (Thirteen and Fourteen) illustrate the intensive effort required to implement psychologically based interventions. Two key features of the flexible job modeling approach are the linking of performance requirements to organizational goals and the emphasis on forecasting future products and competencies. The framework is geared toward enabling an organization to restructure jobs and roles quickly—an important capability in a period of rapid organizational change. It is an expert system employing Delphi-type consensus processes, and its efficacy depends to a considerable extent on the competence of the expert analysts themselves.

Ford Motor Company's experience with employee involvement makes extensive use of multiple support mechanisms designed to maintain the process. The tactical approach used by Ford adopts many of the suggestions offered in earlier chapters. Ford began with problem-solving groups and then moved to more advanced or intensive forms of participation. This particular case suggests that maintaining an employee involvement program requires much more effort than starting one. The major concern of the Ford project appears to be motivational; that is, the assumption is that this change in day-to-day behavior is something foreign to the organization, difficult to tolerate, and that people tend to revert back to earlier behaviors. Banas believes that if there is not a continuing force or effort to support employee involvement, it will probably not survive. Ford's effort is now over five years old, and still viable. Is there a time or stage at which the support effort can be reduced and at least the motivation for employee involvement can be self-sustaining? It is a question worth some empirical testing. The support described in the Ford case is multifaceted. It includes development of a "champion," extensive training, visible top management support, union support and involvement, codification of approval in policy letters and the union contract, and, perhaps most important, bringing in middle and lower management groups as "recipients" as well as "givers" in employee involvement. A support staff that assists the employee involvement participants is also an important element. It would be useful to know which of these are critical in various settings.

Another crucial aspect of the intervention, in Banas's view, is the need for local control over objectives, resources, and evaluation. If the local organizations have the authority to take action they view as significant, they certainly differ from the parallel organization described by Ledford and colleagues (Chapter Ten). Yet Banas's description of the maintenance problem still connotes a new body struggling with a foreign host. Banas estimates that 25 percent of the Ford facilities initiated some form of employee involvement. Is there some point or critical mass at which the newcomer overcomes the host; and if so, what are the implications for the support required? How might the "spillover" suggested by Banas occur and influence the guest-host relationship?

In the Ford experience, local control over evaluation is reported as sacrosanct, with the only national measures being some items in the employee survey. The survey items reported by Banas deal with quality of the employee involvement process, job satisfaction, and opportunities for accomplishment. Will such data be sufficient to sustain management support, which Banas considers essential, as top managements change? The contrast between Ford and the Japanese situation is dramatic. Taira describes top management's role as one of serving the organization, unlike the approving role described here. Also, Taira describes Japan's effort as a "good-times program" and questions what will happen to union-management relations in bad times. The Ford effort began in tough times and grew as Ford's fortunes in the auto industry blossomed. In fact, Banas indicates that the employee involvement effort is one of the things responsible for Ford's 50 percent improvement in quality. What factors will determine the status of employee involvement if times turn bad and a less supportive top management team appears? Will local performance and productivity measures become an issue? The term *productivity* does not appear in the description of Ford's activities, although *quality* does. This may be a function of the considerable effort expended on ensuring good union-management cooperation and involvement.

The Essence

The editors began this exercise with expectations that were, quite frankly, mixed. We already knew that a variety of means were available with which to change performance. We also knew that individual performance had some relationship to the productivity of the organization. But would there be anything new in all of this? Would there be anything deserving the label *frontier?* Wishful thinking aside, we think the answer is yes. When taken together, the collective contributions of our authors point to some very exciting developments in theory and research.

As described by Mahoney and Taira, the parallels between explicating productivity as a construct and individual performance as a construct are striking. These contributors point to the critical need to *fully* model these two domains, to confront questions of value where they in fact reside, and to render empirical that which is truly empirical. We hope that more and more people will join the argument within this framework (or make a substantive case for why an alternative is better).

Research and theory in selection and classification have at last rid themselves of the blind empiricism that almost smothered them. We are finally on the road to modeling the domain of individual differences as it pertains to selection-classification decisions and thereby building up a general fund of information about what is possible. The modeling of the performance domain is still lagging far behind, and we still curse the criterion problem as if it were a monolithic devil; but the door is now open to begin building a general understanding of performance. To be sure, there are strong disagreements between those who see the latent structures of these two domains as relatively simple and those who postulate a more complex view, but the arguments are beginning to incorporate more useful elements.

A parallel development in training is the realization that modeling the transition from novice to expert and designing training to best facilitate this transition are what is critical. Piling up more and more summative evaluation studies independent of any theoretical framework will not do it for us. Building theories, doing research, and developing design principles around the content of what is to be learned form a much more useful conceptual structure.

The study of motivation has a rich history in our field, and progress here seems to be proceeding at a somewhat more even pace. Nevertheless, the days of the artificial compartmentalization of "theories" seems to be coming to an end. A more general understanding of goals, expectancy judgments, and reinforcers should not be too long in coming.

The work on group- or system-based interventions is finally beginning to deal explicitly with the system parameters that will govern its effects. If nothing else, these chapters point to the death of such interventions as programs. They can't be conceptualized and researched as programs that are tacked on to an organization like a new lighting or air-conditioning system. A major research agenda arises from the need to investigate the optimal way to build and then integrate these treatments into the ongoing management of the organization.

But what of our practice? Many of the implications for practice have already been described. Several bear repeating. One is the important role of unions and the labor contract in many of the multifaceted interventions. While both Japan and Ford take care to develop jointly supported work-force efforts, the cultural differences are striking. Taira's account suggests that Japanese firms have done a very good job of shaping their personnel systems to support organizational goals. American organizations do not appear to have reached a similar level of congruence. Guzzo, in his review of the research, notes that career management has been virtually ignored. Hammer's comments on organizational commitment as an explanatory variable for gainsharing results also suggest that this area needs more attention in organizations.

The concern about maintaining change over long time periods surfaces again and again throughout the chapters. Perhaps the quality circle as a parallel organization is the best illustration of the short life span that results when programs are not an integral part of management responsibility or congruent with organizational goals. If Ford had not brought its lower-level management into employee involvement as employee participants, the effort might not have survived. Goodman and colleagues offer us five ways to enhance the life cycle of interventions; Ledford and colleagues suggest design improvements to help quality circles survive; Hammer warns that satisfaction is not a replacement for financial rewards; and so on. We have a host of useful suggestions for maintaining change that can be used to try to counter the sometimes pervasive effects of the organizational environment described by Banas. Unfortunately, these approaches indicate that we need to change many things if an intervention is to survive.

Finally, we must comment on the role of practice in research and theory. Guzzo claims that research should be neither atheoretical nor apractical. We agree and add that practice should be neither atheoretical nor nonempirical. One way to enhance practice is to keep it embedded in research and theory. Research is more likely to anticipate changes in management practices if researchers are actively involved in practical applications of research findings and of those theories that even the researchers feel are a bit abstract. The best thing industrial and organizational psychology has going for it in its efforts to enhance productivity is its scientist-practitioner model. May it flourish.

References

Campbell, J. P. "When the Textbook Goes Operational." Paper presented at the 94th annual meeting of the American Psychological Association, Washington, D.C., Aug. 1986.

Dachler, H. P., and Wilpert, B. "Conceptual Dimensions and Boundaries of Participation in Organizations: A Critical Evaluation." *Administrative Science Quarterly,* 1978, *23,* 1-39.

Name Index

431

Subject Index